Additional Praise for *Sin Boldly!*

"*Sin Boldly!* This book honors the propensity of our time to understand the human condition in terms of psychology. But, it does so without sacrificing theology. In fact, it brings out the indispensability of theological thought for handling life, giving distinctive perspectives on social and political issues."

Antje Jackelén
Archbishop of Sweden

"Ted Peters brings the theological jewel of the Reformation out of hiding in academic and ecumenical enclaves into the bright light of a new arena . . . the purpose and promise of justifying faith for a new era of believers and searchers. This book will inform and inspire your preaching, teaching, and believing in the crucified and risen Christ who justifies our faith, and in so doing, justifies the faith of the whole Church."

Claire S. Burkat, Bishop
Southeastern Pennsylvania Synod, ELCA

"The mysteries of justifying and liberating faith receive scintillating treatment from Ted Peters, with conversation partners throughout the centuries and across disciplines. Concerned with the fragility of the human soul, in search of its grounding and place in the moral universe, Peters diagnoses theologically the dimensions of the soul's brokenness, weaving in contemporary and autobiographical illustrations. He locates in the dwelling of Christ in faith the critical re-centering and transformation for the spiritually healthy soul with a renewed conscience for justice. Drawing from recent Luther research (including the Finnish Mannermaa school), and with critical perspectives from science and ethics, Peters kneads the Lutheran doctrine of justification by faith with some new yeast to propose a spiritually and ethically promising approach for living with a liberating faith and ability to love. A thought-provoking book, with original mapping and written with authenticity, from the heart."

Kirsi Stjerna

Lutheran Theological Seminary at Gettysburg

"The history of ecumenical discourse since 1517 has been an exercise not just in interconfessional, but also in intraconfessional relationality. The obvious disputes between Catholics and Protestants, up to and including the *Joint Declaration on the Doctrine of Justification* (JDDJ) in 1999, were shaped in ways less obvious but no less powerful by disputes within each of these communities, notably between heirs to Gnesio and Philippist forms of Lutheranism and to Thomist and Molinist forms of Roman Catholicism. This remarkable and timely work by Ted Peters does not claim to resolve the interconfessional disputes, nor does it address the internal Roman ones. But, by provoking a renewed Lutheran and ecumenic discussion of the superior merits of indwelling over forensic justification for proclaiming the gospel not just to the fragile, but to the broken souls of today's conflictual (and still Girardian) world, Peters has not only written a new chapter of the Osiandristic controversy, but has offered Roman Catholics facing a new wave of polarization within their own ranks the relecture of a gospel interpretation that does not reckon with a temporal completion of the healing process."

Richard Schenk, OP
Catholic University of Eichstätt-Ingolstadt, Germany

"Ted Peters approaches the doctrine of justification by grace through faith as a treasured gift awaiting discovery and appropriation by fragile and broken humanity. With the tools of a careful scholar and the language of a creative writer, he sensitively unwraps the gift and makes it accessible to those who long for healing, reconciliation, and wholeness. Without sidestepping the substantive issues and tensions among interpreters of justification, Peters prompts and guides the reader into deeper comprehension and experience of divine grace."

Kenneth L. Carder
Emeritus, Duke Divinity School

"In the beginning of the century, Bishop K. H. Ting (1915–2012), the most influential church leader of China, suggested that because of the misinterpretation by the Protestant missionaries to China, for the sake of reconstructing Chinese theology, the Chinese Church has to temper 'justification by faith' and to teach 'justification by love' instead. *Sin Boldly!* by Ted Peters is not merely a scholarly work that gives a clear Lutheran understanding of justification by faith; it has successfully connected faith and love. This work gives the key to the churches in China, so that living a life of faith can be in good harmony with living a life of love for the reconstruction of theology in China."

Pilgrim Lo
Lutheran Theological Seminary, Hong Kong

"Ted Peters's new book is an accessible theological treatise from an ecumenical perspective offering a thorough and vigorous analysis of ailments of the soul reaching to world politics and culture. It is at the same time a judicious diagnosis of the relationship between faith and quality of life—fragile and broken. His perspicacious treatment of the human condition is an affirmation of his reputation as one of the most lucid and compelling voices in contemporary theology. This book is a must-read for both theologians and pastors."

Vitor Westhelle
Lutheran School of Theology at Chicago

"Many are able to teach and write about theology, but few can tell a theological story as Ted Peters does in this book. With a Lutheran emphasis and ecumenical spirit, these pages let us into a conversation where voices from the north and the south, male and female, Christian and non-Christian, chime into a story that Peters magnificently interlaces. It is the story about a God that can only be told from the perspective of broken and fragile souls. This story is what the Reformation codified as justification by grace through faith, and Peters masterfully inflects this treasure of the church in view of the overlapping horizons that constitute our postmodern public square. Peters incisively illuminates the existential, social, psychological, and political corners of our world from the disruptive yet affirming perspective of the gospel. This is a read that is both traumatic and hopeful. *Sin Boldly!* is beautifully written, persuasively argued, thoughtfully composed, and theologically stirring."

Guillermo Hansen
Luther Seminary

"In the bold and prophetic spirit of Martin Luther, Ted Peters's provocative *Sin Boldly!* elaborates justifying faith and the indwelling of Christ by articulating the theology of grace for fragile and broken souls. This book is a crowning achievement for Peters to expand and apply the horizon of grace of justification and justice in an ecumenical and global context, while sharply analyzing the political rhetoric of self-justification and unraveling the mechanism of scapegoating through a dynamic interpretation of the law-gospel dialectic. Embedded within the life of beatitude, Peters envisions proleptic ethics from God's future—a promise characterized by restorative justice imbued with divine love and symbolized by new creation in the kingdom of God."

Paul S. Chung
Luther Seminary

"In this long-expected sequel to *Sin: Radical Evil in Soul and Society* (1994), Ted Peters investigates into the Christian reflection of sin as forgiven in Christ and experienced as justified in faith from a critical, philosophical, and spiritually inquiring perspective. Consequently, this book is not only a contemporary interpretation of the Christian concept of justification of faith, but much more, namely an example of how justification works, since as Peters shows the Christian concept of justification reflects the experience of transformation of the pure critical and the pure open, uncritical approach to life. These two approaches can be seen as two different human experiences of sin, namely the purely critical, reflective approach to oneself, in which nothing is ever good enough, and the fully uncritical, inquiring, spiritually open approach, in which everything is always good. Peters shows how the concept of justification reflectively contains and transforms these problematic experiences and how it moves beyond itself as a concept and makes room for new reflections on oneself. Exceptionally clear thought and equally communicated, this book is more than a worthy sequel and real Peters!"

Johanne Stubbe Teglbjærg Kristensen
University of Copenhagen

"Read this remarkable book! Peters has charted with amazing accessibility a long-needed contemporary account of the meaning and connections between justification, faith, robust moral life, and daily spirituality in a Lutheran vein. Moreover, he does so by engaging the hard questions, the questions and conundrums that permeate contemporary culture. Peters brings to bear years of 'ecumenical engagement,' that is, dialogue and creative mutual interaction with human experience and 'knowing' both inside and outside the Christian church. The conversation list ranges from religion and science, to theories of justice, to 'spiritual but not religious,' fundamentalists, UFOs, progressives, new atheists, ethicists, ecumenical relationships, to theologians of every stripe, and more. Read this book! The lines of a deeply confessional response are evident to those who know what to look for but the whole is presented with a stunning simplicity that at turns engages, provokes, delights, challenges, and inevitably leads to 'ahas.' He has something to challenge everyone—a something that will yet leave you utterly grateful you journeyed with this deceptively profound engagement."

Roger A. Willer, Director for Theological Ethics
Office of the Presiding Bishop, ELCA

"Ted Peters invites us into an exploration of how self-justification, in all of its forms, simply wraps duct tape around our fragile souls, protecting us from reality and the gospel itself. There were moments when I thought that he was simply intent on irritating or angering each of the academic disciplines and the full range of the political spectrum. Then it became clear. This is a book about the pastoral care of fragile and broken souls and their distinctive journeys. Ted Peters explores the depth of the human condition and power of the gospel to heal and save."

Steven L. Ullestad, Bishop
Northeastern Iowa Synod, ELCA

Sin Boldly!

Sin Boldly!

Justifying Faith for Fragile and Broken Souls

Ted Peters

Fortress Press
Minneapolis

SIN BOLDLY!

Justifying Faith for Fragile and Broken Souls

Cover design: Alisha Lofgren

Library of Congress Cataloging-in-Publication Data

Print ISBN: 978-1-4514-8768-8

eBook ISBN: 978-1-4514-9673-4

The paper used in this publication meets the minimum requirements of American National Standard for Information Sciences — Permanence of Paper for Printed Library Materials, ANSI Z329.48-1984.

Manufactured in the U.S.A.

This book was produced using PressBooks.com, and PDF rendering was done by PrinceXML.

Contents

Foreword

Martin E. Marty

While this book is not only for those who are Christian or those who are not and may never be Lutheran, it would be a waste of your time and it would blur the theme if I did not introduce Martin Luther in this first paragraph.

Just as sunlight brightens the path through an otherwise dark forest, the thoughts of Martin Luther illuminate *Sin Boldly!* Luther informs every page, and with Ted Peters's deft guidance, he will jostle his way into much of the argument.

Introducing Martin Luther in a book on justification, as in the biblical context of "justification by grace through faith," is a natural move. After all, in the history of theology, Luther has a patent (but by no means a monopoly) on prime ways of speaking about justification. Perhaps we can even picture him waiting in the wings, readying himself to preach justification, here in print, to a new generation. Past, present, and future churches who bear his name, against his will, noisily announce that the teaching of justification by faith is the doctrine by which the church stands or falls. Back in

Mao's China, where and when the churches were oppressed and their teaching repressed, the government had to yield enough to allow, grudgingly and guardedly to be sure, a slot for pushed-together Christian churches. The Lutheran contingent among them was called "The Justification-by-Faith Church of Christ." This suggests that even totalitarian labelers do not get everything totally wrong.

Ironically, the idea of the self is prominently and critically portrayed both in this book and in the situation of the Lutheran Church in China, which was forced by the government to adhere to the Three-Self Patriotic Movement after 1951. While the Red Chinese versions of the self were designed to imprison the soul, Peters helps us see, in a rich variety of ways, that the soul need not be imprisoned and that, under the gospel of Jesus Christ, it is made free. The freedom results from a particular activity of God that some Christians, influenced by the apostle Paul and, closer to our time, by Martin Luther, call "justification."

Uh-oh! End a long word with -ation and you risk losing some members of the audience. Luther himself, the champion of the concept, thought so. He once said that he did not like to preach on justification because it put some people to sleep or led others to be restless and talkative. So what did he do? He said that he told stories about God's actions toward humans. People were hungry for what these stories effected in them, but they were lost whenever abstract doctrines, which are more at home in the classroom than in the pulpit, were preached at them, or past them. Ted Peters must have been paying attention and must have observed the same, because he, too, makes his point by telling stories or pointing to concrete things and vivid events. Think of the cross or of water (as in baptism) and the like.

Many Lutheran theologians have debated justification to the point that sometimes their nuances have nuances and their footnotes need footnotes. In 1999, high-level Lutherans and highest-level Catholics announced an agreement on justification by faith, *The Joint Declaration on the Doctrine of Justification.* They did not come to perfect agreement, and no doubt every Lutheran who cares about these things regards the concord as an unfinished product, though its contents bury many old hatchets. But in the context of lived faith, we can read the declaration and find it liberating. I like to tell the story told by Winston Churchill about a man who risked his life to save eleven-year-old Johnny, who was thrashing around in deep water, drowning. After the desperate rescue, while both the rescuer and the rescued were still gasping for air, Johnny's mother came up and growled a question to the lifesaver: "Where's Johnny's cap?"

Peters cares about Johnny and all others overwhelmed by figurative deep waters who, concerned for their own selves, set out to justify themselves. In my reading, this book marvelously shows why that strategy is futile, even deadly. In an unforgettable coinage, the author speaks about the "fragile soul" that is at stake in the drama of life and death, good and evil. The fragile soul has no effective instruments to bring about rescue and lead that soul to wholeness, health, and—let me risk a word ending in -ation—salvation.

The justified person, daily made free of the limits of the old self, now experiences newness of life. Happily, the author concerns himself with the follow-up, which allows for new possibilities. Here, as elsewhere in his writings, Peters is eager to link the love of God, which one experiences through justification by God and not by the self, with the justice of God. In that context, he reminds us that the concern for justice must be urgent. Creatively, he points to the typical small child who, untutored in dogma or law, is likely to protest "That isn't fair!" when he or she experiences injustice. Building on such observations, Peters provokes thought about how the daily-justified believer lives a life open to justice.

Late in the book, the author ventures into what is still semi-explored territory in the contemporary church as he complements talk of "forensic" justification with the reality of Christ "indwelling" in the justified person. There is biblical warrant for both concepts. The image for the "forensic" is taken from the court of law in which the person under indictment or found guilty discovers the case against himself has been wiped away. The image of the "indwelling" Christ points to an intimate bond between God in the flesh of Jesus Christ and the repentant human. After having written about the "fragile soul" and the "broken soul," Peters writes that now "Christ's real presence in the human soul makes all the difference. This divine indwelling rewrites the meaning of justification by faith. Jesus died as a just person. He is himself just; so he needs no self-justification. When the Holy Spirit places the just Jesus within our faith, Jesus' justice becomes our justice. He has justified us, so to speak."

Essayist Joseph Epstein, critiquing self-obsessed writers who write self-indulgent memoirs, advises that confessional writing "ought to be the same as that for confession in religion: be brief, be blunt, be gone." Ted Peters is sufficiently brief and blunt about the self, but instead of being "gone," he shows how the Christly justified person—one in whom the "indwelling Christ" is active—is daily given the opportunity to embody and express love and justice in the world.

Martin E. Marty
Professor Emeritus
The University of Chicago

Acknowledgments

Although I had been planning to write *Sin Boldly!* as a sequel to my 1994 publication, *Sin: Radical Evil in Soul and Society*, it took two decades to finish the manuscript's first draft. I felt awkward. It was with some trepidation that I elected to follow an unconventional entrée into the subject matter. Rather than entering through the front door of the dogmatic debate, I decided to climb in through a rear window. In writing this new book, I furtively crept up on justification by divine grace from the perspective of its opposite, namely, self-justification by sinners. I was a timid prowler, so I thought I might need some extra flashlights to see my way forward.

I would like to express my gratitude to those who read portions of the *Sin Boldly!* manuscript and provided me with those flashlights, in the form of critical suggestions: Chris Antal, Kenneth L. Carder, James Childs, Sharon Guy, Kristen Johnston Largen, Derek Nelson, Karen Ann Peters, Risto Saarinen, Richard Schenk, and Kirsi Stjerna. Also helpful were the pastors and friends who read the manuscript and offered helpful comments during the 2014 Week of Renewal at Pacific Lutheran Theological Seminary: Kathryn Beck, Tom Beck, Sherri Frederikson, Greg Fritzberg, Joel Langholz, Paul Leslie, Bill Strehlow, Garrett Struessel, Sharon Swanson, Sara Wilson, and Brach Jennings. I offer a special "thank you" to Martin E. Marty for the foreword, for our collegiality, and for the decades in which Professor Marty has provided such insightful leadership in the world of theological scholarship.

Abbreviations

BC — *The Book of Concord: The Confessions of the Evangelical Lutheran Church.* Edited by Robert Kolb and Timothy J. Wengert. Minneapolis: Fortress Press, 2000.

CD — Karl Barth. *Church Dogmatics.* Edited by G. W. Bromiley and T. F. Torrance. 4 Vols. Edinburgh: T&T Clark, 1936–62.

DP — Plato. *The Dialogues of Plato.* Translated by B. Jowett. 2 Vols. New York: Random House, 1892.

GG — *The Gift of Grace: The Future of Lutheran Theology.* Edited by Niels Henrik Gregersen, Bo Holm, Ted Peters, and Peter Widmann. Minneapolis: Fortress Press, 2005.

Inst. — John Calvin. *Institutes of the Christian Religion* (1559). Edited by John T. McNeill. 2 vols. Louisville: Westminster John Knox, 1960.

JDDJ — Lutheran World Federation and the Catholic Church. *Joint Document on the Doctrine of Justification.* 1999. See web version: http://www.vatican.va/roman_curia/pontifical_councils/chrstuni/documents/rc_pc_chrstuni_doc_31101999_cath-luth-joint-declaration_en.html.

LW — *Luther's Works.* American ed. Vols. 1–30, edited by Jaroslav Pelikan. St. Louis: Concordia, 1955–67. Vols. 31–55, edited by Helmut T. Lehmann. Minneapolis: Fortress Press, 1955–86. Translated from *Luthers Werke, Kritische Gesamtausgabe.* Edited by J. F. K. Knaake, et al., 57 vols. Weimar: Bohlau, 1883.

Phil. — *The Philokalia.* Compiled by St. Nikodimos of the Holy Mountain and St. Makarios of Corinth. Translated and edited by G. E. H. Palmer, Philip Sherrard, and Kallistos Ware. 4 vols. London: Faber & Faber, 1979–95.

RPP — *Religion Past and Present.* Edited by Hans Dieter Betz, Don S. Browning, Bernd Janowski, and Eberhard Jüngel. 14 vols. Leiden, Neth.: Brill, 2007–14).

SysT   Paul Tillich. *Systematic Theology*. 3 vols. Chicago: University of Chicago Press, 1951–63.

ST   Wolfhart Pannenberg. *Systematic Theology*. Translated by Geoffrey W. Bromiley. 3 vols. Grand Rapids, MI: Eerdmans, 1991–98.

TI   Karl Rahner. *Theological Investigations*. 22 vols. London: Darton, Longman, and Todd, 1961–76; New York: Seabury, 1974–76; New York: Crossroad, 1976–88.

VRE   William James. *The Varieties of Religious Experience*. Gifford Lectures Series 1901–2. London: Longmans, Green, 1928.

Preface

Sin boldly! That's what Martin Luther advises. Of all the aphorisms and slogans generated by this revolutionary thinker five centuries ago, this is the one I like best. It's enigmatic, puzzling, stalwart, liberating. The maxim "Sin boldly!" most dramatically expresses the exhilarating freedom that erupts from a robust soul filled to the brim with faith and love.

Fragile and broken souls would do well with a large dose of courage, daring, and hardiness. Justifying faith provides that boldness.

Although I'm a theologian who loves arcane and abstract ideas, I have long pondered a rather practical question: Can faith make one's daily life better? More vibrant? More robust? After working thoroughly through the issues, I have arrived at an answer: yes, indeed. How? By relieving our anxiety, which is manifest in the practice of self-justification. When we discover that we don't need to justify ourselves because we have been justified by God, we experience both contentment and vitality. What St. Paul's concept of "justification-by-faith" points to is the transformative presence of the crucified and living Christ in the human soul, placed there by our gracious God. In *Sin Boldly!*, we will see how all this takes place.

I like the ambiguous phrase used in the subtitle of the book—*Justifying Faith*. This phrase could mean two things. First, it could mean that if we are persons of faith we'd darn well have good reasons for it. We need to justify why we would choose to embrace faith in a secular world that seems to get along quite well without it. Twenty percent or more of us are "nones," that is, persons who respond with "none" on questionnaires regarding religious affiliation. The aggressive New Atheists among us dub faith as something foolish, a residual from an outdated religious era that should be replaced with reason, science, and secularism. The spiritual-but-not-religious among us replace old-fashioned faith with post-religious intuition, experience, and meditative practice. Can faith be justified in this situation? In the pages that follow, we will see that there are good reasons for living a life of faith, especially faith understood as trust in God.

There's a second meaning. "Justifying faith" means that in the eyes of God we are just. It's God's will that our daily lives be imbued from dawn until dusk with love, compassion, care, and the pursuit of justice in an unjust world. Sometimes we miss the mark, and other times our active pursuit of justice still results in someone getting hurt. The point here is this: justifying faith maintains our relationship with God despite the injustice afoot. God treats the unjust unjustly—that is, God treats the unjust with grace. Does this mean God contradicts Godself? Well, yes, it looks that way. This apparent divine self-contradiction will be sorted out in the pages that follow.

For five centuries, theologians have fought over the meaning of justification-by-faith. The first shot in this war was fired by Martin Luther on October 31, 1517, when the young Augustinian monk posted his 95 Theses on the front door of the castle church in Wittenberg, Germany. Five centuries later, the theological guns are beginning to quiet. Today, we hear only sporadic firing, and the truce flag between the main combatants is flying. Drafts of the final peace agreement—*The Joint Declaration on the Doctrine of*

Justification—are being considered by the disagreeing parties. Soon, we can only hope, the issue of justification-by-faith will no longer be a matter of dispute between the Roman Catholics, Lutherans, Reformed (Presbyterians, United Church of Christ, Evangelicals, and others), or Methodists.

In this book, I will examine what the dispute is all about. However, the details of the dispute will take second place to the primary agenda: the power and value of the concept of justifying faith for illuminating our daily life. Like a magnifying glass that makes invisible things visible, the very call to embrace a justifying faith reveals new dimensions to our self-understanding.

Not long ago, my physicist friend, Rollie Otto, took me on a brief tour of STXM on the campus of the University of California at Berkeley. STXM stands for "Scanning Transmission X-Ray Microscopy." Basically, it's a big microscope. Through the timed use of magnets, the centrifuge sends electrons to speeds up to 99.99 percent the speed of light. The light produced by this process is brighter than the sun. At various points, some of these high-speed electrons are siphoned off, channeled through individual electron microscopes, and used to look at living cells and even the internal makeup of cells. This allows lab researchers to see down to objects only twenty-five nanometers in size. One nanometer is the length of ten hydrogen atoms side by side. The STXM microscope can look at the physics of cells at levels more primary than the biology of the cells. This is the power of light to expand and deepen human understanding.

Theological light offers an analogous power to expand and deepen our self-understanding. A self-examination through the lens of justifying faith uncovers depths and dimensions invisible on the surface level. We human beings are complex. Below the conscious surface lies a complex web of genetic, biological, neural, and psychological circuitry. Just as we can examine our cells through STXM, perhaps the lens of justifying faith can show us what might be going on at the spiritual nano-level within us.

Our thoughts and behavior from moment to moment mark a synthesis of internal self-initiation plus interaction with our physical, social, and spiritual environment. We might ask from time to time: Who am I? The answer must be: I am all of these processes. We might then ask: Am I more than the sum of all of these processes? Yes.

What will the lens of justifying faith uncover? What will it reveal? It will reveal that we lie. One of the blocks to clear self-understanding is that we lie. We lie to others, and we lie to ourselves. This deception does not come in the form of a series of stories we tell others that we secretly know to be untrue. The stories we tell are largely true, at least at the level of consciousness at which the stories are told. What I am talking about is a pattern of misdirected self-understanding that operates at the hinge of the pre-conscious and the conscious. This deception turns on the articulation of what we believe to be true in light of who we think we are. Or, perhaps, in light of who think we ought to be.

I will refer to this pattern of self-deceit as self-justification. To say it more precisely, self-justification refers to justification apart from faith in the God who graciously justifies us. By employing the term *justifying faith*, I will describe the fulfilling and flowering life that results in trusting the God of grace to take care of our justification for us. If we can avoid the temptation to justify ourselves, a cleanliness in our thinking takes over. This cleaner thinking, so to speak, liberates the inner self for an un-self-protective, open, and vulnerable disposition toward loving oneself and others. Suddenly, the world looks more lovable. The psychic work it takes for us to love the unlovable is drastically reduced, and compassion and self-giving become as automatic as the refrigerator door light.

In this book, I will stress the real presence of Christ in the person of faith. The theology of Christ's real presence can be summarized. Jesus died as a just person at the hands of unjust authorities. He is, in himself, just; he needs no verbal self-justification. When the Holy Spirit places the just Jesus within our faith, Jesus' justice becomes our justice. He has justified us, so to speak. If in our faith we are justified by Christ, we have no need to self-justify and, hence, no need to scapegoat others. Our justification is a divine gift, not the product of our self-deception.

In addition, I will stress that the Christ present in our faith is both crucified and resurrected. The suffering of the crucified one is present to us, even in our suffering. The eternity of the resurrected one is present within us—an eternity that transcends even our most sublime vision of the moral universe.

Two kinds of persons could especially benefit from this doctrinal disclosure: those with fragile souls and those with broken souls. Each of us knows what it means to live with a fragile soul, although some suffer more than others. One's soul can become fragile if one is unable to handle the anxiety that wells up from the empty center within the self. Although we think of the soul as the essential self, we protect the self's existence by conforming it to the moral universe. Our moral universe provides the world of meaning within which we live, and to keep it from breaking, we codify it and legalize it and rigidify it and absolutize it. Most devastatingly, we engage in self-justification. That is, we tell ourselves the lie that the soul and the moral universe are at one.

For the fragile soul, justification-by-faith comes as both bad news and good news. The bad news is this: before God, our lies won't work—only truth will. The good news is what we call the gospel: namely, by grace God offers the free gifts of forgiveness and relationship. Because God justifies us, we don't have to justify ourselves. Our salvation is like a Christmas present: all we need do is open it up and make it our own. Then, of course, we can enjoy playing with it.

For the broken soul, the situation is quite different. The soul breaks when the moral universe breaks. Because the centered self is so dependent upon the moral universe that forms its identity, the shattering of the latter leads to the loss of the former. The moral universe evaporates in times of overwhelming trauma, that is, in times of moral injury. Violence and death accompanied by atrocity and betrayal can so overrun one's moral universe that it collapses like a fence in a stampede; the soul gets run over and buried. No amount of forensic justification can lift the fence and fix it firmly in the ground again.

The only healing for the broken soul is relational presence. Accepting presence allows the broken soul to mend, to re-form, to heal. The accepting presence must be gracious, understanding, loving, and transcendent to the now shattered moral universe. It must be the presence of ultimate reality. In this case, justification-by-faith suggests that the presence of the suffering and risen Christ in faith provides a spiritual accompaniment that coaxes a new sense of soul to assert itself.

Beyond justification-by-faith lies the life of beatitude. God's promised future—symbolized by new creation (or the kingdom of God)—becomes present in faith, and faith expresses itself in beatitudinal living. Matthew 5:6: Blessed are those who hunger and thirst for justice, says Jesus, for they will be filled. Or, to say it another way, God's future justice is already present in our thirst for it now. What is curious, if not puzzling, is that our pursuit of justice is, in fact, a form of sinning. To pursue what is already provided by grace is sin. Yet, the life of beatitude motivates us to sin boldly. If you find this knot hard to untie, read on!

Five centuries after the Wittenberg door incident, the statute of limitations has expired on Reformation theology. It's time to bring the treasure out into the public square where it can be enjoyed by all. The insight into the justifying dimension of faith is more edifying and healing to the human psyche than any Freudian psychoanalysis, retrieval of archetypes, meditative technique, behavioral modification, or spiritual retreat. The presence of the resurrected and living Christ within the soul—the actual consolidation, if not new creation, of the soul—reorients our life around a single and eternal center. This spiritual insight is a gift to be shared, not hoarded by a small club of churchgoers.

In the pages ahead, it will be my task to unwrap this invaluable gift out in the open, in public view where all spiritually sensitive and morally responsible people can come to appreciate it.

Ted Peters
Berkeley, California
Easter, April 5, 2015

1

The Fragile Soul and Spiritual Duct Tape

Any breach of the rules I would not tolerate.

—Augustine[1]

I was terrorized by the thoughts of sin and punishment. I couldn't go to church for seventeen years.

—Samuel G. Alexander[2]

While studying in Heidelberg, Germany, some years ago, I rented an attic room. The landlord had many rules, and almost daily I could hear him mutter, "Alles muß in Ordnung sein," which translates, "everything must be in order." Indeed, my landlord felt much better when everyone followed the rules.

1. Augustine, *Confessions,* trans. Henry Chadwick (Oxford: Oxford University Press, 1991) 1.9.19, p. 22.
2. Private conversation with Samuel G. Alexander, Pastor, First Presbyterian Church of San Rafael, San Rafael, CA.

Why, you may ask, is the author of this book talking about a Heidelberg landlord? I thought this was a book about justification-by-faith and bold sinning! Well, it is. One of the traditional problems with the doctrine of justification-by-faith is that is has been tucked away for centuries in a theological museum gathering dust. The only time it's drawn out for viewing is when the curators of ancient ideas want to display quaint historical artifacts. Justification-by-faith might have been important to our religious ancestors, but in our modern and emerging postmodern society, it's long been forgotten, even for churchgoers. Right?

Rather than a forgotten artifact in a theological museum, I believe justification-by-faith is the single most important and life-giving truth. In my judgment, it is the key that unlocks the prison door, the hand that rips off the blindfold, the aloe that cools the burning gash, and the elixir that tastes of Eden. Nothing anchors the temporal soul more securely in eternal reality. Justification-by-faith is not an esoteric text that only licensed theologians can check out of the rare book room. Rather, it's a radiant idea that brightens our daily life, interior thoughts, and deepest murmurings. In the pages ahead, I want to direct this pearlescent glow so that the confusing crisscross of forces at work within the soul become visible.

In this chapter, I want to begin with the fragile soul, the soul that sticks to the rules, the soul of the sheepish sinner. Every one of us has experienced those moments of rigidity shot through with anxiety. Why do we *need* to stick to the rules? Justification-by-faith is like a flashlight that helps us see what's going on in the dark corners.

Fragility in Chicago

I know what it's like to live with a fragile soul. After leaving Heidelberg, I traveled to Chicago to finish my doctorate. My new best friend at the time was Marc Kolden, one year ahead of me in our program at the University of Chicago Divinity School. Like most students at that stage of study, I needed a part-time job.

"I'm leaving my job at Thillens," Marc said. "Want me to recommend you? If I give your name to Mr. Thillens it's a sure thing."

"Sure thing, then, Marc."

First, let me offer a short explanation. Thillens is an armored car company that offers mobile check-cashing services throughout Chicago. Check cashers drive around the city in armored vehicles that stop at factories on payday. Line workers and other blue collars walk with their checks to the parked trucks, where their checks are cashed. The company charges a small fee, to be sure, but the worker goes home with cash rather than a piece of paper. When the checks are deposited at the end of the day, the company collects a profit.

Before Mr. Thillens would hire me, I needed clearance from a detective agency. Today we would refer to this as a background check. The agency was located in the Chicago Loop. After filling out some forms at the detective agency, I was given a polygraph. I signed an innocuous looking contract, which included my agreement to subject myself to another lie detector test in the event of any investigation. Once I'd signed and all details were satisfactorily completed, I purchased my uniform and security sundries.

When I showed up for work the first morning, the office manager asked me if I carried my own gun.

"No," I answered. "I don't own a gun."

"Well, let's see what we've got here for you," he said, looking through some drawers. "Oh, here's one you can use." He pulled out a monster-sized revolver and handed it to me. "And here's a holster to fit it. Just attach it to your belt." He then directed me to the men who would become my crew buddies.

I dutifully armed myself. Later in the day, during a pause in a factory parking lot, I turned to one of my crew buddies who was a moonlighting policeman.

"I don't know anything about carrying a gun," I told him. "Could you help me?"

"Sure. Let me see it." The policeman sized up my weapon. "Well," he went on, "here is the safety. See how it works? On. Off." I was getting an education.

"Now, this is a Colt .45, a six-shooter. You have five bullets in the chamber. I don't know why only five. Notice that the empty chamber is the next one. If you try to fire it, nothing will happen. I recommend you always keep a bullet ready for your next shot."

All of this gave me a sense of security—or was it insecurity? Regardless, I began to imagine getting into a shootout with my Colt .45 and dying for Mr. Thillens' money. I began to scratch my head, figuratively speaking. I wondered if I would need to calm my nerves as I came to work each day because of, what? Danger?

As it turned out, I enjoyed my job. The geography of the "City of the Big Shoulders" became second nature as we drove to factories all around the area. The off duty police officers with whom I worked were interesting company. Carrying a quarter million dollars in cash in a bushel basket became a curious daily routine, and exciting adventures were my lot. I will tell you one story, but only one.

On a Thursday evening, I received a telephone call. It was Mr. Thillens. Instead of going to work the next day, he asked me to report to the detective agency.

I showed up at the Loop office at the appointed time. Would I take a polygraph test? Of course. I sat in the proper chair and allowed myself to be hooked up to the electronic sensors.

The first questions were routine. What is my age? Who is my favorite baseball team? No problems. Each answer registered truthful.

The tester began to interpolate questions regarding missing funds, money apparently stolen from one of Thillens' armored trucks.

"A week ago Wednesday, Mr. Peters, did you steal seventeen hundred dollars from your armored vehicle?"

"No!" I answered.

The polygraph began to dance like a Dallas Cowboys cheerleader.

Later he asked, "A week ago Tuesday did you steal nine hundred dollars from your armored vehicle?"

Again I answered negatively. Again the polygraph needle went wild. A third question regarding an even larger theft precipitated the same electronic acrobatics. The polygraph was saying that I had stolen large sums of money on three separate occasions.

Just to make sure of the readings, the tester ran the test twice more. On each run, it was electronically clear that I was guilty. At first, I was shocked. Then, I became anxious. "Oh, no! What will happen now?"

I was left in the room to worry while the detectives held a meeting. During the meeting, one called Mr. Thillens on the phone to explain the evidence they had collected. What action should they take?

After their conference, I was told that Mr. Thillens would like to have me retested. Could I come in on Monday? Yes, of course I could.

I headed for home, my head hung low. My eyes could only view the pavement in front of my shoes as I walked to the Illinois Central train station. I can't remember a weekend more filled with anxiety, fear, worry, and even despair. Sound sleep was out of the question. It appeared my future would no longer remain in my hands. What would happen? Prison?

On Monday, I showed up promptly at the detective agency and was escorted into the polygraph room. A new person had been appointed to test me. He hooked me up to all the electronic sensors, and the test began. Just as it had the previous Friday, the needle went into a break dance when I answered the key questions regarding the three thefts. The polygraph was convinced that it had caught me telling falsehoods.

"Let me try an experiment," said the tester. "This time, listen to my questions, but don't answer. Say nothing. Can you do that?"

"Yes, certainly."

As usual, we made it through the routine questions, which set a baseline. Then came the big one: "Did you steal seventeen hundred dollars from a Thillens truck?"

I said nothing and sat silent. Still, the polygraph needle danced an Irish jig. The same thing happened with each of the other two indicting questions. We repeated the test. It became evident that even though I said nothing, the polygraph was reporting that I was telling a falsehood.

"How do you feel when I ask you questions regarding the theft of money?" the tester asked me.

"Well, I feel kind of nervous," I responded. "I get uptight."

"I thought so," he said. "I have a theory. I believe you are an ultra-scrupulous person. An ultra-scrupulous person has a difficult time with the polygraph. The polygraph measures nervous reactions; and we deduce that these nervous reactions are due to feelings of guilt over lying. Now, Mr. Peters, you feel guilty even though you're not lying."

I nodded in agreement.

He went on. "The polygraph is ineffective for about ten percent of the people we test. It doesn't work on a sociopath because a sociopath feels no guilt when lying. And, curiously, it does not function very well with an ultra-scrupulous person either. You've just seen why. Let me mention that I used to be a Roman Catholic priest before becoming a detective. I'm ultra-scrupulous too. That's why the detective agency appointed me to test you this morning."

When I walked from the testing room to the office, Mr. Thillens was waiting for me. "I see you've passed the test," he said. "I know who the thief is, based on other evidence. It's not you. But I still needed to have you tested because it's in our work agreement."

We chatted for a little while. Then he said, "Mr. Peters, I look forward to seeing you at work tomorrow morning."

It took only a nanosecond for me to make a decision. "No, Mr. Thillen, I don't think you'll see me at work tomorrow. I quit. I quit as of this very minute. I don't think I could ever spend another weekend like this one." We chatted for a few minutes, and he graciously accepted my resignation with apologies for the ordeal. I walked to the train station with a cheerful skip. More than the weight of a Colt .45 had been lifted.

My soul was fragile. It had been constructed with a set of emotional LEGO® bricks, rules for scrupulous moral behavior. I could not conceive of a time or a place in which I would behave with something less than complete integrity; and the very thought of stealing money precipitated an emotional reaction.

This means I had internalized a moral universe. Perhaps this moral universe originated with my family, my community, my church tradition, or even came from God on Mount Sinai. Whatever the source, the values I inherited were no longer external. They were—and are—internal. My inner self and my external worldview were isomorphic. A crack in one caused a fissure in the other. Even the mere thought of stealing precipitated a minor earthquake in my psyche. I relied upon my moral universe to ward off chaos and maintain integrity.

By no means am I alone with my fragile soul. Countless religious and non-religious persons live with an underlying anxiety that influences the relationship between their souls and the world. We don't like to see cracks in either one. When a crack appears, we race to patch it up with spiritual duct tape. That duct tape usually takes the form of rigidity, absolutism, perfectionism, dogmatism, and such.

Now, I am not bragging about being scrupulous. Quite the contrary. Scrupulosity is a symptom. The disease is an unnecessary fragility that robs us of robust living. I wouldn't be writing this book if I were hopelessly imprisoned in shamefaced fragility and dogmatic duct tape. However, my own experience contributes to my perception and to my conviction that this is an important part of human experience for us to understand. When the living Christ is present in the human soul—which is what justification-by-faith alerts us to—then daily life becomes robust, not fragile.[3]

Sticking to the Rules

Sticking to rules protects us from anxiety. Rules, we mistakenly think, provide a secure bulwark against the threatening forces of chaos in our psyche. And, if we believe the rules we obey are eternal, then we feel eternally secure against temporal temptations that rob us of our hard-won eternity. Eternal and universal reality are constructed according to the principles of justice; and we want our temporal soul to be formed in consonance with this eternal justice.

3. The *fragile soul*, as I employ the term here, does not necessarily refer to the unhappy or melancholy soul described by William James. The melancholy soul, according to James, is divided; whereas the fragile soul, I believe, may rest in a modicum of confidence that its conformity to the moral universe is intact. Here is James on the melancholy soul: "Unhappiness is apt to characterize the period of order-making and struggle. If the individual be of tender conscience and religiously quickened, the unhappiness will take the form of moral remorse and compunction, of feeling inwardly vile and wrong, and of standing in false relations to the author of one's being and appointer of one's spiritual fate. This is the religious melancholy and conviction of sin that have played so large a part in the history of Protestant Christianity." James, *VRE* 170–71. The concept of the fragile soul may include the melancholy soul as a subcategory, but fragile souls may enjoy a satisfactory daily life with only occasional moments of anxiety or shame.

To be able to say, "Sorry, but you know the rules as well as I do," provides one's soul with the comfort that eternal order brings.

Why stick to the rules? Because a little voice whispers inside our psyche: *You're not good enough,* or *Somebody's looking; they'll see you're not good enough.* If we stick to the rules and admonish others to stick to the rules, we are telling that damnable inner voice to shut up. Shutting up that voice provides comfort for our soul, to be sure; but it is an uneasy comfort that is easily disturbed.

I think of the human soul as something like the eye at the center of a vortex. Liquid swirls around a center, almost vacating the center. Imagine an electric beater preparing whipping cream in a round mixing bowl. In cyclone fashion, the ingredients swirl, and the center empties. Yet the center still marks the invisible axis around which everything else spins.

Let me press this analogy further. That empty vortex around which everything swirls is your soul, my soul. The swirling cream is your or my daily life: our metabolism, our thinking, our activity, our identity. The perimeter of the mixing bowl provides the limit. If it were not for the limit imposed by the mixing bowl, we would fly off into chaos. Everything would lose its form, and the center would disappear. The limit provided by the mixing bowl is our worldview, our moral universe.

At the center is a vacuum—well, actually, a low-pressure zone, a relative vacuum. At the center of all this hullabaloo is a virtual absence, a hollowness, an emptiness. As long as you and I give our attention to the external swirling, we don't notice the emptiness at the center. In those fragmentary moments when one does notice, one becomes aware of the fragile existence of his or her own soul. A tropical depression begins to look like a personal depression.

Chaos is avoided by the moral universe that keeps all this activity within limits. But what if that mixing bowl begins to show cracks?

What if we feel the threat of chaos? We may race to patch up the cracks with duct tape, establishing new limits with spiritual duct tape. The fragile soul is always on watch, ready to protect the empty center.

The fragile soul fears the nothingness at the center. The threat of that nothingness is experienced as anxiety: the fear of non-being. It is the fear that death will put all our swirling to an end. We fear plummeting into the abyss of black emptiness. "Tiefe Ewigkeit" (deep eternity), said Friedrich Nietzsche—deep, endless, incomprehensible eternity.

In its panic to protect the empty center with an external perimeter of controlled chaos, the fragile soul shelters itself within a world of its own imaginary self-construction. In later chapters, I will show how this patched up perimeter we call our *world* becomes a moral universe that supports our own delusions, our own self-justifications, our own intolerance. The spiritual duct tape with which we hold the fragile soul together is called *perfectionism* in common parlance; theologians refer to it as *legalism*, or *works of the law*, or *self-righteousness*.

Scaring the Hell Out of Us

You or I might want to live a life of scrupulous adherence to religious dogmas or moral codes if we believe that God demands such absolutism. We might shake in our boots if we're told that our eternal salvation or damnation depends on our ability to observe every detail of the divine law.

Our fragile souls might require extra support if we are told that the deity is an almighty god, a righteous god, a just god, a vengeful god, or worse, an arbitrary and predestining god. If our only hope for pleasing this deity is scrupulous obedience to the rules and regulations, then we would make the requisite commitment. We would tremble in fear whenever we found ourselves in violation or think of ourselves as sinners. Each sin would release a gusher of anxiety, overwhelming us with the fear of losing eternal life.

America's most influential theologian is the eighteenth century divine, Jonathan Edwards. Edwards is largely responsible for the Great Awakening of the 1740s and is remembered for his erudite interpretations of the Calvinist tradition. Edwards assumed that in our natural condition we human creatures are condemned to everlasting hell but that divine grace acts to elect some of us for salvation—some, but not all. Our rigorous obedience to the divine law testifies that we belong among the elect rather than the damned. Am I saved? Am I damned?

One of Edwards's sermons is particularly notable, "Sinners in the Hands of an Angry God." Note how God is described: angry. Imagine yourself, a sinner, slung in mid-air between heaven above and hell below. What holds you? What keeps you from falling? Only one thing: God's inscrutable will.

> Natural men are held in the hand of God over the pit of hell; they have deserved the fiery pit, and are already sentenced to it; and God is dreadfully provoked, his anger is great towards them as to those that are actually suffering the executions of the fierceness of his wrath in hell, and they have done nothing in the least to appease or abate that anger. . . . all that preserves them every moment is the mere arbitrary will, and uncovenanted, unobliged forbearance, of an incensed God.

> Your wickedness makes you as it were heavy as lead and to tend downwards with great weight and pressure towards hell; and if God should let you go, you would immediately sink and swiftly descend and plunge into the bottomless gulf. Unless we are born again and made new creatures . . . being dead to sin . . . [we could remain] in the hands of an angry God.[4]

4. Jonathan Edwards, "Sinners in the Hands of an Angry God," in *The Works of Jonathan Edwards*, ed. Henry Rogers and Edward Hickman (London: Ball, Arnold, and Col, 1840), 2:9.

If I had sat as a child in Pastor Edwards's congregation and heard only such sermons, the hell would be scared right out of me. I don't want to be dropped into the bottomless gulf, the pit of hell! My motivation for living a holy and virtuous life would be sky-high, and living with a fragile soul would be quite understandable. I would work diligently to cover up my sins so that none of my friends could see them, so that I could hide my sins from God and even from myself. I would be tempted to live the life of a lie, a lie that would persuade this angry God to lift me out of hell into heaven.

Many who identify themselves as "spiritual but not religious" (SBNR) report having left their childhood church experiences behind. "As a kid, I was a terrorized Baptist," one host for the Waking Times radio show told me. Grown-up souls seek liberation from religious terrorism.

Mainline Christian churches long ago gave up fire-and-brimstone sermons. Worship today is sedate and tasteful, exuding the values of a middle-class moral universe. Yet, in their own quiet way, worship services communicate that we worshippers are worms, wriggling obsequiously in the dirt. The medium is generic guilt or what Wolfhart Pannenberg calls "indeterminate and generalized feelings of guilt."[5] Morning Prayer in the *Book of Common Prayer* opens with these familiar words: "Almighty and most merciful Father, We have erred, and strayed from thy ways like lost sheep. . . . We have offended against thy holy laws. We have left undone those things which we ought to have done. . . . And there is no health in us."[6] Like lowering a great gray pall, the liturgy places us all into a pit of indeterminate or generalized guilt. No account is taken of your or

5. Wolfhart Pannenberg, *Anthropology in Theological Perspective,* trans. Matthew J. O'Connell (Louisville: Westminster John Knox, 1985), 287.
6. *The Book of Common Prayer* (Oxford UK: Oxford University Press, 1929) 6.

my actual life; rather, this sentence to the guilt pit is generic. It's a liturgical class action, so to speak.

I am by no means recommending we eliminate confession from communal worship. However, we need to look for and recognize those factors that might contribute to the fragility of the soul. We need to ask honestly: What do we do to frighten fragile souls into buying more spiritual duct tape?

Atheists leap upon this particular dimension of religion by arguing that religion is a disease caused by anxiety and fear; science is the right cure. As Bertrand Russell puts it, "Religion is based primarily and mainly upon fear. It is partly the terror of the unknown and partly . . . the wish to feel that you have a kind of big brother who will stand by you in all your troubles and disputes. Fear is the basis of the whole thing—fear of the mysterious, fear of defeat, fear of death. . . . Science can help us to get over this craven fear in which mankind has lived for so many generations."[7] The fears on Russell's list are existential fears such as the terror of the unknown. Preachers such as Edwards add an angry God to the list of things to fear. In our own era, we can add an additional fear: the fear that our belief system and our moral universe might be false. No wonder so many of our souls exist in a state of fragility.

The fragility of our souls might also be something we generate from within. Likewise, fragility might be something created in us by an image of an angry, demanding, and lawful God who keeps track of our sins and exacts retributive justice toward sinners. In either case, we build a dike to keep back the flood of anxiety. As the French established the Maginot Lie to protect their country from German invasion, we resort to our own Maginot Line: legalism. We obey the divine law, and we demand that others do so as well.

---

7. Bertrand Russell, *Why I Am Not a Christian* (New York: Simon & Schuster, 1957), 22.

Anxiety and the Terror of Religion

What makes the sheepish soul fragile is anxiety. "An incessant anxiety stalks us," observes former Methodist bishop and theologian, Kenneth Carder.[8] Anxiety is the gasoline that drives the fragile soul toward rigidity.

Our primary defense is to retreat into absolutism. Absolutism takes many forms in today's public square. Watch how some people and institutions contend that "the sanctity of (human life) is *infinite*; at the core of great art lies divine and inexplicable *genius*; consciousness is a problem too hard for us mere mortals to understand; and—one of my favorite targets—what I call *hysterical realism*: there are always deeper facts that *settle* the puzzle cases of meaning. These facts are real, *really* real, even if we are systematically unable to discover them."[9] Daniel Dennett tells us that concepts such as infinity, genius, consciousness, and realism function as unassailable absolutes, protected from erosion by the hurricane force of the Darwinian revolution. Religious absolutism is only one kind of absolutism; but Darwinian evolution dissolves them all in the rushing rapids of relativity. Dennett contends that Darwin relativizes everything, which would probably come as a surprise to Darwin. Be that as it may, we often do retreat into absolutes to protect ourselves from anxiety. And we do so just as Dennett describes it.

The self-justifying attempt by the fragile soul to construct a worldview secure against the external attacks from hostile forces relies upon fixities and essences. It relies upon definitions of reality that are unassailable, or at least appear unassailable within the worldview of the fragile soul. The fragile philosopher will appeal to essence; the fragile scientist will appeal to the exclusivity of empirical knowledge;

8. Kenneth L. Carder, *Living Our Beliefs*, rev. ed. (Nashville: Discipleship Resources, 2009), 70.
9. Daniel C. Dennett, *Intuition Pumps and Other Tools for Thinking* (New York: W. W. Norton, 2013), 204, Dennett's italics.

the fragile politician will appeal to divine blessing for the nation; while the fragile religious devotee will appeal to orthodoxy. All such appeals function as spiritual duct tape to prevent breakage.

A better antidote to the anxiety experienced by the fragile soul is to recall what St. Paul tells us in Rom. 8:33b (NASB): "God is the one who justifies" (*theos ho dikaiosune*). If God justifies us, then we don't have to. The gospel of justifying grace eliminates the need for spiritual duct tape because it plugs up our nuclear void with a theonomous or God-grounded center, giving our moral universe both the strength of steel and the flexibility of a rubber balloon. Yet, I ask: Why is this good news not being heard?

Spiritual Bullies

Proclaiming the Christian message can come as bad news to the fragile soul, as we saw in Jonathan Edwards's sermon. An exalted vision of Christian perfection may reinforce other intimidations that the fragile soul must deal with on a daily basis. The fear of missing the mark, falling short of someone's expectations, disappointing the boss, looking too fat in the mirror, or violating God's law can ruin the day for a fragile soul. The fragile soul already feels diminished.

To make matters worse, spiritual bullies in the pulpit or on television take sledgehammers to our protective bowls. We fear we may run out of spiritual duct tape before we can patch up the cracks. Imagine a pulpiteer preaching like Martin Luther on the law of God: "Therefore the proper use and aim of the Law is to make guilty those who are smug and at peace, so that they may see that they are in danger of sin, wrath, and death, so that they may be terrified and despairing, blanching and quaking at the rustling of a leaf (Lev. 26:26)."[10] Such a declaration of one's guilt would turn a tiger into a sheep, a muscle into flab, a dynamic self into pliable putty. If I would hear this message from a spokesperson for God, my daily life would be filled with timidity, if not trembling.

However, this terrifying use of the law is only the left hand of God, at best. God's right hand is raised in grace, in blessing, in gospel, in comfort. "The Gospel, however, is a proclamation about Christ: that He forgives sins, grants grace, justifies, and saves sinners," Luther announces.[11] Without this gospel, we'll have to mortgage our house to buy enough spiritual duct tape to protect us from damnation.

For reasons difficult to fathom, the very religion that purports to follow Jesus has pressed the mute button on the life-giving power of this gospel. We hear the law that condemns, not the gospel that gives life. Instead of living a secure and robust life of muscular faith, both our teachers and disciples snivel and whine, blubbering on in sheepish fragility. We grovel before the standards of perfection, and we cower in fear that our inadequacies might become exposed. Measurements, milestones, merits, awards, and orthodoxies rule our psyches like Caligula ruled Rome. Like sycophants in the emperor's royal court, we create a fictional public image by bowing and fawning before the ambient opinions of what is acceptable, respectable, admirable, good, just, and true. And in our rare moments of self-bolstering, we assure ourselves that we stand for eternal justice, the unassailable good, and what is absolutely right—what Luther refers to as "the Law." In doing so, the fragile soul becomes

10. Luther, *Commentary on Galatians* (1535), in *LW* 26:148.

11. Ibid., 26:126. "The Gospel in its essence is the oral proclamation of forgiveness," says Heidelberg's Edmund Schlink, *Theology of the Lutheran Confessions,* trans. Paul F. Koehneke and Herbert J.A. Bouman (Minneapolis: Fortress Press, 1961), 198. In contrast, Schlink's student, Wolfhart Pannenberg, believes the gospel should refer to more than merely the forgiveness of sins. The gospel should include the inbreaking of God's kingdom in Jesus as well as the promise of salvation, understood as full reconciliation. It should also include the mission of the Church to spread the gospel, which is more than merely a dialectical counterpart to the law. On this point, Pannenberg sides against what he thinks Luther says and supports what Barth says. "Barth rightly opposed the restriction of the gospel to the proclamation of the forgiveness of sins (*CD*, IV/3, 370)." Pannenberg, *ST*, 2:460–61.

temporarily hidden beneath self-justifying bravado. Nevertheless, fragility is ever present, sapping our soul of honesty, integrity, and authentic caring. To make matters worse, Christian sermonizers—preachers whom Cathleen Falsani calls "spiritual bullies"[12]—man their pulpits like a captain on the bridge; they manipulate our already innate anxieties and turn timidity into terror. The perpetual fear of eternal damnation turns a fragile soul into a petrified self. We fragile ones go through the motions of life, but we don't really live it.

Romans 8:33b, "God is the one who justifies," should be heard by us as good news, as grace, as gospel. The gospel is aimed at liberating our selves from fragility and our souls from the endless unrolling of duct tape. The result of such liberation is bold sinning. "Sin boldly!" might become a motto for the graced soul. Falsani reminds us that this was said by "Martin Luther, that great theological hoodlum and father of Protestantism."[13] Falsani adds, "In other words, if you're going to screw up, at least do it with feeling." She continues:

> Sin boldly.
> Believe in grace even more boldly.
> Love without limits.
> Live this life.[14]

The Self, the Soul, and the World in Relation to God

As the reader may notice, I frequently use the terms *self* and *soul* interchangeably. In addition, sometimes I'll mix up *soul* with *spirit*. Even so, such terms deserve precise definition.[15] Well, at least this is

---

12. Cathleen Falsani, *Sin Boldly: A Field Guide for Grace* (Grand Rapids, MI: Zondervan, 2008), 100.
13. Ibid., 104–5.
14. Ibid., 107.

what most theologians think. Nevertheless, I would like some overlap between terms just to show that what the self experiences affects the shape of the soul. Destructive experiences can distort the soul, whereas experiences with God's grace shape and sanctify the soul.

Let me attempt a few precise definitions. When working a few years ago on a co-authored book with two treasured colleagues, Karen Lebacqz and Gaymon Bennett, we gave considerable thought to defining key terms. We concluded that

> the term *soul* refers to our inmost essence as an individual self, while the term *spirit,* which overlaps with *soul* to be sure, refers to our capacity to relate with one another and with God. While the word *soul* connotes who each of us is as an individual, the word *spirit* connotes that dimension of our personal reality that unites us with others. . . . The soul is not a ghost-like entity that simply inhabits a body. Rather, to speak of soul reminds us that as embodied creatures we have a center of identity, a centered self. . . . *Souls and centered selves are formed by and develop in spiritual relationships!*[16]

That vacuum at the center of our whirling self is where we will deal with the question of the soul—with or without an essence—and its relationship to the uncontrollable winds that blow around it.

---

15. One of the most illuminating attempts at terminological precision is Michael Welker's exposition of key terms in the writings of St. Paul, with special focus on the trichotomous self as body (*soma*), soul (*psyche*), and spirit (*pneuma*). Welker first distinguishes between flesh (*sarx*) and the body (*soma*); the flesh is at war with the spirit but the body makes a home for spiritual influence. It is through the heart, not the soul, that God's spirit prompts our transformation. "The activity of God's Spirit does not penetrate directly into the psyche. Rather its effects flow via the heart into the human body and then indirectly upon the soul." Welker, "Flesh–Body–Heart–Soul–Spirit: Paul's Anthropology as an Inderdisciplinary Bridge-Theory," in *The Depth of the Human Person: A Multidisciplinary Approach,* ed. Michael Welker (Grand Rapids, MI: Eerdmans, 2014), 55. More relevant to our treatment here is Welker's observation that, for St. Paul, "*psyche* encompasses an individual, earthly life—an earthly, bodily, and spiritual individuality that, while created by God, has not (yet) been filled by God's Spirit" (ibid., 54). In my treatment of justifying faith, terms such as *soul* and *self* allow the heart and the divine Spirit to influence and even shape the meaning.

16. Ted Peters, Karen Lebacqz, and Gaymon Bennett, *Sacred Cells? Why Christians Should Support Stem Cell Research* (New York: Roman & Littlefield, 2010), 207, italics in original.

What we have avoided here is making a traditional metaphysical commitment regarding the soul. Is it by nature immortal? No. "Our soul only becomes immortal because of our spiritual relationship with the eternal God. To think of a human person in the fullest sense is to include body, soul, and spirit in relationship to community and to God."[17] If we become blessed with subjective immortality, it will be a gift from God's spirit; it will not be due to the endurance of the empty center of our human activity.[18]

Our concern in writing the book, from which I quote, was human dignity. We asked: How do we ground human dignity? We ground dignity in the "infinite value of the human soul." These are the words of Adolf von Harnack, writing a century ago. The teachings of Jesus, said Harnack, may be grouped under three heads: "firstly, the kingdom of God and its coming; secondly, God the Father and the infinite value of the human soul; and thirdly, the higher righteousness and the commandment of love."[19] Harnack's tradition lives on in our century. Without using the word *soul,* Dwight Hopkins contends that "the progressive liberal theologian believes the authentic person is committed to the ultimate significance of human lives in this world."[20] At work here is a moral understanding of the soul, not a metaphysical one. Along with Harnack and Hopkins, I contend that each human person has infinite and ultimate value. To put it another way, we treat one another as a moral end, never merely as a means. The heavy word *soul* seems to bear this moral weight.

17. Ibid.
18. By "subjective immortality," I refer to eternal life, which you or I enjoy as a conscious subject. This contrasts with "objective immortality," which refers to someone else remembering us after we are dead. A tombstone inscription or scholarship fund set up in our name might give us objective immortality—other people remember us as an object—for a few generations or so.
19. Adolf Harnack, *What Is Christianity?*, trans. Thomas Bailey Saunders (New York: Harper, 1957), 51.
20. Dwight N. Hopkins, *Being Human: Race, Culture, and Religion* (Minneapolis: Fortress Press, 2005), 162.

Here's another definition I like. "The soul represents a hypothetical point in the individual's subjectivity: the point from which it is possible to become aware of the existence of an essential self or of its possible loss and corruption."[21] That hypothetical point is the vortex at the center of the swirl of daily activity. I'm concerned about the soul's role in centering us, and I'm concerned about its possible corruption or even loss when the bowl's perimeter cracks and falls apart.

Just as the center and the perimeter are correlates, so also the soul and the cosmos are correlates. Or, to be a bit more precise, the soul and the perceived moral universe are correlates. If we lose one, we lose the other. Stanford bioethicist William Hurlbut asserts that "the moral sense provides the very infrastructure of personal identity and unifies reason, emotion, and intuition."[22] He adds, "moral norms must be believed; and to be believed they must be understood to be true as well as useful."[23] Our moral sense is grounded in reality, in truth, in a world of meaning, or what I call here the *moral universe*. If the moral universe breaks, so do we. If we're fragile, we try to prop up our moral universe with spiritual duct tape so that we can keep our soul intact.

---

21. Richard K. Fenn, "Introduction: Why the Soul?," in *On Losing the Soul: Essays in the Social Psychology of Religion,* ed. Richard K. Fenn and Donald Capps (Albany, NY: SUNY, 1995), 2. In the present book, I would like to pursue a phenomenology of the soul without being drawn into the voluminous discussions of the metaphysics of the soul. William James followed a similar method: "When I say 'Soul,' you need not take me in the ontological sense unless you prefer to; for although ontological language is instinctive in such matters, yet Buddhists or Humians can perfectly well describe the facts in the phenomenal terms which are their favorites. For them the soul is only a succession of fields of consciousness . . . [For me, 'Soul' refers to] the hot place in man's consciousness, the group of ideas to which he devotes himself, and from which he works, call it *the habitual centre of his personal energy.*" *VRE*, 195–96. I find "*the habitual centre of his personal energy*" to be less than adequate, even though it points to the phenomenal direction I plan to follow. Italics in original.

22. William B. Hurlbut, "Science, Ethics, and the Human Spirit," in *The Oxford Handbook of Religion and Science,* ed. Philip Clayton and Zachary Simpson (New York: Oxford University Press, 2006), 883.

23. Ibid., 885.

If we turn directly inward in search of our soul or our self, we will come up empty-handed. What we will see is an empty vortex around which our sensory interaction with the physical world swirls. In this swirl is also our moral universe. At the center is emptiness. We would like to see a rock-solid self or an immortal soul, but that's not what we see. A center, yes. A substance, no. The inextricable relation our empty center has with our surrounding environment is something we understand intuitively even if we cannot find a discreet "I" there to do the seeing. What we as an ego or an "I" hope to see in the surrounding swirl is a moral universe—an eternal universe of justice—that will guarantee our eternity. If we can ground the center in the periphery, and if the periphery is eternal, then we too will enjoy that eternity. But what if this belief in an eternal rule by justice turns out to be false? What if life on planet Earth has no meaning beyond what we ourselves imagine belongs to that external swirl? What if the atheists and materialists are right? Will we have hoped in vain? Does the eternal God come to us at the center or at the periphery?

In contrast to us, God's perimeter is nowhere, and God's center is everywhere. It was Nicholas of Cusa (1401–64) who gave us the phrase to describe God, whose "center is everywhere and circumference is nowhere."[24] A robust soul is centered in the divine center, but this shared centering comes to us as a gift of God's grace.

With descriptions such as these in mind, my concern in this book has to do with the formation of the soul, the structure of the intra-centered self. In addition, I am concerned with our spiritual relationship to God, our exo-centered self. A healthy centering of the self structures a soul for a healthy relationship with God. Or, perhaps it works in reverse: a healthy relationship with God provides the self

---

24. Nicholas of Cusa, *Of Learned Ignorance,* trans. Germain Heron (New Haven: Yale University Press, 1954), 111.

with a center and, accordingly, structures the soul. Our temptation is to attempt to center the soul on the self without regard to God, which can only lead to permanent death.

The Self as the Soul's Fire

Although I occasionally use *soul* and *self* interchangeably, I believe we can distinguish them even if we cannot separate them. Perhaps another analogy might illuminate the relationship. Imagine a fireplace. Imagine an old-fashioned fireplace before tree logs were replaced by gas jets. What you see is a burning log, and what you feel is heat. The soul's relationship to the self is akin to the relationship of the log to the flame. There is but one fire, yet the log remains stable while the flame dances and leaps and flickers. The essence of one's soul remains stable because God maintains its continuity and identity over time. The self dances and leaps and flickers; it constantly redefines itself, modifies itself, grows, shrinks, and heats up the environment.

Upon arriving at the site of a burning building, a firefighter chooses one or more of the following three strategies: (1) deny the fire fuel, (2) deny the fire oxygen, or (3) reduce the temperature. To take a hose and squirt water on what is burning denies the fire oxygen and lowers the temperature. This helps put the fire out.

Fragility in the soul tends to put out the fire of the self. This is due to the wetness of *heteronomy*. Paul Tillich employs this term to refer to the subordination of the self to an alien law.[25] When the self finds itself enslaved to perfectionism or legalism or always-be-rightism, it's like throwing a wet blanket over the fire. The wetness of the blanket denies the fire oxygen to breathe and lowers the fire's temperature.

25. Tillich, *SysT*, 1:147–50.

What happens then? Smoke squeezes out of the sides and creases of the blanket and fills the room. The self suffocates as the fire itself gradually becomes extinguished. The log turns charcoal black while the fire cools and drops out of existence.

The robust soul, in contrast, fuels a self like a log fuels a roaring flame. The robust soul, in contrast to the fragile soul, lives out of *theonomy* (*theos* [God] and *nomos* [law]). Theonomy looks like autonomy (being a law unto oneself, *auto*), but the center of the autonomous self in this case is rooted in the center of ultimate reality, God. The log is God's log, an everlasting source of spiritual, psychic, and even physical fuel for life. As I said above: a robust soul is centered in the divine center, and this shared centering comes to us as a gift of God's grace.

The self that realizes its center is located in the center of ultimate reality—in God—is a robust soul.[26] This is a self that burns brightly and flames exuberantly. The self that seeks to smother itself with a wet blanket risks leaving a wet, charcoaled log that is too cool to heat anyone up. The smoke is suffocating.

The Dilemma of the Soul

The human soul faces a dilemma, a tug of war between individuation and participation.[27] If, on the one hand, we individuate the self to the exclusion of relations with others, we become alone, isolated. If, on

26. For the most part, my treatment of the soul and self in this book is phenomenological, not ontological. However, when I turn to the ontological dimension, I find myself in sympathy with the scheme offered by Wolfhart Pannenberg, according to which our creaturely essence and our creaturely eternity are determined by God's bestowal of fulfillment in the eschatological consummation. "The eschatological future is the basis for the lasting essence of each creature that finds manifestation already in the allotted duration of its life and yet will achieve its full manifestation only in the eschatological future." *ST*, 3:603.

27. Tillich provides a most illuminating description of this polar tension between individualization and participation in *SysT*, 1:174–78.

the other hand, we so surrender the self in participation with others, we become absorbed and lose our individual identity. To affirm our individual selfhood is to deny our spiritual bond with others; while to deny our self on behalf of a spiritual bond with others risks losing the self entirely.

Do we risk sacrificing our self in order to share a spiritual bond with God? Do we sacrifice our autonomy to become enslaved to a divine heteronomy? Friedrich Schleiermacher considered this dilemma. "The human soul," he writes, "has its existence chiefly in two opposing impulses. Following the one impulse, it strives to establish itself as an individual. . . . The other impulse . . . is the dread fear to stand alone over against the Whole, the longing to surrender oneself and be absorbed in a greater, to be taken hold of and determined."[28] What is the poor soul to do? If we surrender the self's individual identity, we can enjoy a spiritual bond with God. But, if we surrender to God, then we cease to be a self, cease to be who we are. Ugh!

Well, maybe this is not the reality we actually face. A spiritual relationship with God does not erase the self's identity. In fact, just the opposite is the case. It is God who affirms us as an individual person-in-relationship. Our relationship to God is not one of absorption but rather one of love. If we drop a cup full of ginger ale into the ocean, it dissipates and becomes so totally absorbed that it is no longer ginger ale. However, this oceanic dilemma is not the reality of our relationship with God; God does not dissolve us but rather saves us. It is better to think of the individual self as a burning flame, dependent on the fuel God provides yet still dancing and reaching toward the stars. With God, we touch those stars, and it is the self who enjoys the touching.

---

28. Friedrich Schleiermacher, *On Religion: Speeches to Its Cultured Despisers*, trans. John Oman (New York: Harper, 1958), 4.

No one can speak more eloquently to the resulting consciousness of spiritual oneness than Schleiermacher:

> The contemplation of the pious is the immediate consciousness of the universal existence of all finite things, in and through the Infinite, and of all temporal things in and through the Eternal. Religion is to seek this and find it in all that lives and moves, in all growth and change, in all doing and suffering. It is to have life and to know life in immediate feeling. . . . Without being knowledge, it recognizes knowledge and science. In itself it is an affection, a revelation of the Infinite in the finite, God being seen in it and it in God.[29]

More on the Self, the Soul, and the World in Relation to God

While I'm at it, let me work on definitions of additional terms I will use later in this book: *self, world,* and *moral universe.*

What is the self? We need to get beyond the fire metaphor for a moment. You are a self. I am a self. We remain our selves over time, despite all the changes we take into our selves. The self's "grandeur or dignity is . . . derived from its ability to transcend the temporal flux and to touch the fringes of the eternal," writes Reinhold Niebuhr.[30]

In part, the self is a gift to us from our neurocircuitry. Before we can identify the self with language or with a name, our brains organize our thoughts around a core self. In addition, our brains prepare us to understand other human persons as selves with their own self-understanding. We call this *empathy.* Via empathy, we can feel another person's pain. Feeling someone else's pain is made possible by a brain structure—allegedly the structure of mirror neurons in the frontal cortex—that permits analogical thinking. In

---

29. Ibid., 36.
30. Reinhold Niebuhr, *The Self and the Dramas of History* (New York: Charles Scribner's Sons, 1955), 217–18.

other words, because a centered self knows her own pain, she or he can, by analogy, know the pain of another centered self. "Neurobiology argues that our understanding of others is based on an analogical self-other relationship: by nature, we are capable of understanding others because our brain consists of neural systems that give access to others' minds by simulating their state of being as self-state and subsequently projecting them towards the other," writes Rebekka Klein in Heidelberg. "Thus, neurobiology confirms the hypothesis that an analogical relationship between the self and other forms the basis of 'how we know others.'"[31] If such a hypothesis regarding the neurological basis for empathizing with the pain of others is confirmed, then this would help explain the rise in nearly every culture of a Golden Rule ethic: we treat others as we ourselves wish to be treated.

This element in neuroscience may provide a biological explanation for why we love stories or, more importantly, why stories of others and stories about ourselves merge and unite to form a single world of meaning. The brain does not "distinguish much between reading about an experience, or listening to a description, and actually encountering it," writes Jennifer Ouellette, reporting on advances in neuroscience.[32] This "may offer a clue as to why human beings love stories so much. . . . The more brain regions are involved, the more vivid our experience will be."[33]

---

31. Rebekka A. Klein, "How Do We Know about the Self: Theoretical, Experimental, and Neural?," in *How Do We Know? Understanding in Science and Theology*, ed. Dirk Evers, Antje Jackelén, and Taede A. Smedes (London: T&T Clark, 2010), 63.

32. Jennifer Ouellette, *Me, Myself, and Why? Searching for the Science of Self* (New York: Penguin, 2014), 264.

33. Ibid., 265. My review of the options for modeling the self or ego or first person perspective comes up with five discrete models:

　　1. *Ego continuity*, according to which a persistent self-awareness or even an immortal soul inhabits an ever changing physical body and physical environment.

　　2. *Self as confused expression of a higher self*, according to which one's individual soul is but a manifestation of the over-soul, the spiritual reality that unites all things.

If this is the case, we can understand how a story told about God's grace at work in the life of a person two millennia ago, Jesus of Nazareth, can become my story or your story. Our self-understanding can become informed by—actually experienced as—this story, actually this history. The story of God's grace experienced by someone else can help to structure one's own soul, so to speak, due to the effectiveness of history.[34] If we define the *gospel* as "telling the story of Jesus with its significance," our neurocircuitry will facilitate Jesus' story becoming our own story. Similarly, other stories will have the same potential for distorting the soul as the Jesus story has for wholesome self-formation.

Knowledge gained from the neurosciences is new and exciting but minimal in its explanatory power. It is premature to assert with confidence that we have sufficient knowledge to explain the relationship between the brain, the mind, consciousness, and the self. That these are related is too obvious to deny; how they are related remains a question to be investigated.

In the meantime, I will work with a phenomenological understanding of the human self. Theologian Paul Tillich does about as well as anybody in his description of the self—a self that obtains its definition from the dynamic of a center in relationship. "A self is not a

3. *Self as delusion*, the position taken by many philosophers who claim to base their cognitive theory on neuroscience. This is the reductionist model according to which no substantial ego exists. The self is a fiction.

4. *Self as story or narrative*, according to which the self is an evolving social construction whose identity is defined by our history, our story. Jennifer Ouellette belongs in the self-as-narrative model.

5. *Self as experiential dimension*. Here, "the self is claimed to possess experiential reality, is taken to be closely linked to the first-person perspective, and is, in fact, identified with the very first-person *givenness* of the experiential phenomena," according to Dan Zahavi, who directs the Center for Subjectivity Research at the University of Copenhagen. Dan Zahavi, *Subjectivity and Selfhood: Investigating the First-Person Perspective* (Cambridge, MA: MIT Press, 2008), 106. My own position comes closest to the experiential dimension model, though I do have some sympathies toward the story or narrative model.

34. Later, in a brief discussion of hermeneutical philosophy, I will show how effective history (*Wirkungsgeschichte*) structures human consciousness and becomes constituent to faith.

thing that may or may not exist; it is an original phenomenon which logically precedes all questions of existence. . . . [a human person] is a fully developed and completely centered self . . . an ego-self."[35] When we first wake up in life, we begin with a self and develop self-consciousness. From within the self's consciousness, we begin to ask existential questions such as: Who am I? Why am I here? What is the meaning of my life? At this level, the self is a given. Even so, the self also changes, develops, and grows. When a self loses its center, it can disintegrate and dissolve. Only the swirl is left, or the mixing bowl fails to provide limits so that temporary chaos is followed by loss of form and identity.

A determining point for later discussions in this book is Tillich's recognition that the self and its world are mutually dependent. "Because man has an ego-self, he transcends every possible environment. Man has a world. . . . 'World' is not the sum total of all beings. . . . The world is the structural whole. . . . There is no self-consciousness without world-consciousness."[36] To say it another way, the self and the world are two poles of a single prior relationship. The self sits in the center, while the world surrounds it in meaningful relationship. While entities in our environment—what we perceive through our five senses—with which we do not have a meaningful relationship certainly exist, they do not belong to our world of meaning, our life-world, or our worldview (*Weltanschauung*), including what we will call our *moral universe*.

The perimeter of the mixing bowl houses our worldview, our world of meaning. It marks the limits of our moral universe and prevents the chaos that would result from the eggbeaters losing their containment. If the bowl cracks, we hasten to patch it up with spiritual duct tape. If we fear the emptiness of the center, we may

35. Tillich, *SysT*, 1:169–70.
36. Ibid., 170–71.

delude ourselves into thinking that more duct tape will calm our fears.

With this in mind, one would expect me to use the term *world* consistently as the correlate to the self because this term connotes world-of-meaning. However, I occasionally use the term *universe* here, as admittedly incoherent that may be. Obviously, the term *universe* should indicate our *environment,* the surrounding reality that includes both what is meaningful and what is not meaningful. My theologian friends with the raised eyebrows would likely demand such precision. Nevertheless, where I should say *world* I frequently use the term *moral universe.* Why? Because the term *moral universe* is used in contemporary literature that deals with broken souls. A broken soul is a self that disintegrates because the moral universe—a person's actual world of meaning—disintegrates. The bowl breaks. The whipping cream stops swirling, and the interior vacuum evaporates. The soul becomes lost or broken, so to speak.

In order to attune my study with others that deal with the role of the moral universe in the self-world relationship, please note that *moral universe* refers to the world of meaning in the life of the human self. Without an intact moral universe, the soul evaporates.

Creating Our Souls

Contemporary reductionists argue that no soul exists. Willing to repudiate centuries of belief in body-soul dualism, today's materialists aver that what we think of as the mind's activity is in fact the brain's activity. Neurophilosopher Patricia Churchland provides an example: "Mental states are in fact states of the physical brain itself, not states of a metaphyhsical soul."[37] When we examine human neurocircuitry, we don't see any soul lodging in our heads or anywhere else in our bodies, for that matter. Churchland adds, "Soul theory is floundering because there is no soul."[38] If we reduce all mental activities to physical activities, then to our perception, the soul disappears. So does the spirit. "Man no longer has need for Spirit: it is enough for him to be Neuronal Man,"[39] contends Jean-Pierre Changeux.

Theologian Keith Ward is not bullied by brain researchers or neurophilosophers who want to collapse the soul into the brain. "A careful and accurate view of scientific theories and discoveries will show that, though dramatic, they do not at all undermine belief in the human soul, its distinctiveness and unique value."[40] Solid science sides with Ward. "Despite claims trumpeted in popular media," writes neurobiologist Mario Beauregard and science journalist Denyse O'Leary, "the new discoveries have *not* explained away basic concepts such as consciousness, the mind, the self, and free will. Hypotheses that reduce the mind to the functions of the brain or deny that the mind exists have remained just that—hypotheses. They are based not on convincing demonstrations of evidence."[41] Solid science has not trashed the soul or scrapped the spirit. The human soul exhibits

37. Patricia S. Churchland, *Touching a Nerve: The Self as Brain* (New York: W. W. Norton, 2013), 49. Let's face it, any materialist investigation into the functions of the human brain will not locate or isolate the self, the soul, or the person. Physicist Michio Kaku weighs in by identifying the sense of selfhood with the actions of the left hemisphere of the brain. "This is where our sense of a unified self comes from. Although consciousness is a patchwork of competing and often contradictory tendencies, the left brain ignores inconsistencies and papers over obvious gaps in order to give us a smooth sense of a single 'I.'" *The Future of the Mind* (New York: Doubleday, 2014), 59. One might conclude from this that the self or first person perspective is a delusion, a trick played on us by the left hemisphere of the brain. Theologically, this is beside the point. The corollary of the theological concept of justifying faith is that God, who creates something out of nothing, can create an eternal life out of the temporal psychic experience of selfhood. This is the case regardless of the relationship between the brain and the mind.

38. Churchland, *Touching a Nerve*, 53. "The death of the brain, the facts suggest, entails the death of the mind. . . . What could a soul be, since memory, skill, knowledge, temperament, and feeling all seem to depend on activities of neurons in the brain?" (ibid., 264).

39. Jean-Pierre Changeux, *Neuronal Man: The Biology of Mind*, trans. Laurence Gary (Oxford: Oxford University Press, 1985), 169.

40. Keith Ward, *Defending the Soul* (Oxford: Oxford University Press, 1992), 9.

41. Mario Beauregard and Denyse O'Leary, *The Spiritual Brain: A Neuroscientist's Case for the Existence of the Soul* (New York: Harper, 2007), 104 (italics in the original).

emergent properties that are not exhaustively entailed in our physical substrate. The soul exists; and it is more than brain functioning. "God is the true end of the soul, and in this sense, its goal, its proper purpose and true nature, lies beyond the physical universe," rightly contends theologian Ward.[42]

Although sympathetic to such a defense of the soul's independence, I do not want to defend traditional body-soul metaphysics.[43] What I believe is pertinent to our discussion of justification-by-faith is the assertion that the continuity and redemption of our personhood—our resurrection as body, soul, and spirit—is the result of divine activity. It is not a built-in product of physical or even metaphysical processes. This leads me to stress a long-overlooked dimension to justification-by-faith—namely, soul-formation or person-formation by God's gracious activity. God creates a soul in each of us that does not need duct tape maintenance.

Faith makes the person (*fides facit personam*), contends Martin Luther. What might this mean? We will explore the role of faith in person-making or soul-making in the pages that follow.

In his Heidelberg Disputation (April 1518), Luther spoke of two loves, one human and the other divine: "The love of God does not find, but creates, that which is pleasing to it. The love of man comes into being through that which is pleasing to it" (*Amor Dei non inuenit, sed creat sum diligible, Amor hominis fit a suo diligibili*).[44] We human beings love what already exists. The objects of our love already please

---

42. Ward, *Defending the Soul*, 151.

43. My own position emphasizes the person holistically, using the term *soul* to deal with the person's essence or center. Neuroscientist Malcolm Jeeves, similarly, denies a metaphysical dualism on behalf of a holistic view of the human person. "There is thus a duality, but not a dualism: the ontological reality of person is primary, and is neither mental nor physical." Malcolm Jeeves, "Brains, Minds, Souls, and People: A Scientific Perspective on Complex Human Personhood," in *The Depth of the Human Person*, 103.

44. Martin Luther, *Heidelberg Disputation* (1518), in *LW*, 57:57; See also Tuomo Mannermaa, "Two Kinds of Love: Martin Luther's Religious World," trans. Kirsi I. Stjerna (Minneapolis: Fortress Press, 2010), chap. 1.

us. Even our ideas of what should exist fit into this category: they already exist in the mind and already please us.

God, in contrast, creates what God loves. Right now, God is creating your soul and my soul, the result of which will be something most pleasing to God. Hence, if you look into the center of the whirlwind of your life and find it empty, don't dismay. God is creating a you, a real you, which will be eternally pleasing both to yourself and to God. We experience this creation dynamic within our faith. What this process feels like is liberation. God creates us by liberating us from bondage to fragility, from enchainment to something that is less than our true self.

God's grace creates the self.[45] Said differently, God's grace liberates the self from the non-self. Furthermore, for today's women, the liberating effect of grace takes a particular form. Women in countless societies find themselves oppressed by the weight of feminine images that do not fit them. The inherited language of a woman's self-understanding saddles her with essences, expectations, demands, and subordinations. Such alien images are as incarcerating as original sin. Something from within calls out for liberation. Liberation of the self is the way grace creates the self. As Serene Jones writes,

> In the doctrine of justification, one encounters a theological logic in which the self is radically undone or deconstructed by a judgment set upon her, not by merit or nature, but by divine decree, a decree that calls into question all the identifying descriptions we are wont to put upon ourselves and others. When interpreted from a feminist perspective, this doctrine allows one to critique the hold traditional gender conceptions have upon the self. Grace undoes it.[46]

---

45. Pannenberg has his own way of sorting out the vocabulary. "We are all persons in our psychosomatic totality . . . Totality and personhood are linked . . . Selfhood, however, means identity in all individual life . . . over a stretch of time . . . personhood transcends all the singularities and changes of circumstances because it finally draws upon the relation to God as the source of its integrity." *ST*, 2:200.

46. Serene Jones, "Companionable Wisdoms: What Insights Might Feminist Theorists Gather from

By grace, a fragile soul can become a robust soul and live daily out of a God-given identity.[47]

Becoming a healthy or robust soul is one of the aims of those among us who are spiritual but not religious. Whereas Christians in the past sought to diminish the self to make room for God, in our own era, it is the already diminished self we implore God to strengthen. "Salvation is not being saved from ourselves, escaping some dreadful state of judgment, damnation, and hellfire at the hands of a wrathful God," writes Diana Butler Bass. "Rather, it is being saved to ourselves, finding what was lost and the joy of discovery in the hands of a loving Creator."[48]

And Her Soul Felt Its Worth

If God can create the universe out of nothing by simply saying, "Let there be . . . ," then certainly God can create one's soul with a few gracious words. This is the point Nadia makes. Nadia is the founding pastor of House for All Sinners and Saints in Denver, Colorado, and author of the blog, "Sarcastic Lutheran: The Cranky, Beautiful Faith of a Sinner and a Saint." Nadia provides us with a Rocky Mountain answer to the *Prairie Home Companion*.

Nadia reports how, when she was a teenager, she had difficulty listening to a youth minister's sermon, which was filled with do's and don'ts. "I just couldn't say *yes* to what seemed like God's *conditional maybe* to me," she says. Nadia then proceeds to retell the story of the

Feminist Theologians?," in *The Blackwell Companion to Postmodern Theology,* ed. Graham Ward (Oxford: Blackwell, 2001), 299.
47. "The doctrine of justification locates our identity in God's actions for us through Jesus' death on the cross . . . Our identity is something we receive, not something we achieve." Ann Fritschel, "The Quest for Identity: Evolutionary Roots of Consumerism and Stewardship," *Currents in Theology and Mission* 41, no. 2 (April 2014): 97.
48. Diane Butler Bass, *Christianity after Religion* (New York: Harper, 2013), 182.

Annunciation, in which Mary is declared to be a "favored" person. "I think God looked upon her [Mary] with favor because it's God's nature to look upon young peasant girls—and prostitutes and tax collectors and adulterous kings and lawyers and fishermen—with favor; because God's just like that. Read the book!"[49]

Read the book. The book Nadia refers to here is the Bible, of course. The Bible tells a story—the story of ancient Israel. This story is a history of God's grace in action. God looked upon all of Israel as God looked upon Mary: with favor. The story of Israel and the story of Mary are stories laced with grace. The stories of Israel and Mary are also your story and my story. When we see ourselves as characters in the great story of grace, we see ourselves as graced. In fact, we become graced souls. Graced souls sin boldly, not sheepishly.

The Robust Soul and Bold Living

Researcher William James studied the robust soul extensively. He knew what it looked like. The experience of being graced by God leads to a transformation, an extra-moral or supra-moral transformation.

> The transition from tenseness, self-responsibility, and worry, to equanimity, receptivity, and peace is the most wonderful of all those shiftings of inner equilibrium, those changes of the personal centre of energy, which I have analyzed so often; and the chief wonder of it is that it so often comes about, not by doing, but by simply relaxing and throwing the burden down. The abandonment of self-responsibility seems to be the fundamental act in specifically religious, as distinguished from moral practice.[50]

49. Nadia Bolz-Weber, "And a Soul Felt Its Worth: A Sermon on an Overlooked Miracle," *Sarcastic Lutheran* (blog), December 10, 2013, http://www.patheos.com/blogs/nadiabolzweber/2013/12/and-a-soul-felt-its-worth-a-sermon-on-an-overlooked-miracle/, italics in original.
50. James, *VRE*, 289.

As James puts it, the transition of the soul happens not "by doing" but by relaxing. Not through "moral practice," but through relaxing. The robust soul is the fragile soul on a very good day. Or better yet, the fragile soul energized by divine grace enjoys a good day every day.

The fragile soul longs to follow the path of the robust soul. But, enticing detours divert it from this destiny. One detour is simple self-justification. By applying self-justifying duct tape, the soul attempts to defend its inner fragility through simply declaring itself to be just, good, and right. We simply tell ourselves how good we are. And we will tell others usually by dropping hints but on occasion by bragging. Unfortunately, this is a fake form of robustness which leaves a black hole of anxious trepidation within our inner self. Could we overcome this fake justification with genuine justification? Could we climb a spiritual ladder and then, when on top, declare ourselves to be actually justified?

This ambitious path of self-justification might lead up hill; it might lead to spiritual mountain climbing. This is the detour taken by the heroic soul, by the spiritual athlete. This path is better described as a spiritual ladder. At the top of the ladder resides the moral universe. The spiritual champion intends to confidently ascend the ladder through valiant self-sacrifice and rigorous soul conformity. The yoga of the Hindu sanyasin or the discipline of the Buddhist monk or the vision quest of the New Ager or even the suicide in terrorist martyrdom provide road signs directing us toward eternal spiritual victory. If after only one more step on the ladder I can plant my victory flag, I can genuinely delcare that I have justified myself.

What these detours divert us from is the gospel path. According to the gospel, it is a waste of time for the fragile soul to seek its own justification; because justification is offered by God as a free gift. Through imbibing the gospel, our anxious fragility is transformed into a life characterized by the fruits of the Spirit: love, joy, peace, patience, kindness, generosity, faithfulness, gentleness, and self-control (Gal. 5:22-23).

Just as the fragile soul is universally human, climbing souls can be found in virtually every civil society. "Whether the hero be ridiculous or sublime, Greek or barbarian, gentile or Jew, his journey varies little in essential plan," writes Joseph Campbell. "Popular tales represent the heroic action as physical; the higher religions show the deed to be moral."[51] The heroic soul is the fragile soul climbing to the top of the spiritual ladder. What the climbing soul hopes to find at the top of the ladder is a moral universe, an intact moral universe that unambiguously defines ultimate reality and rewards the soul with eternal justice. Eternal goodness or rightness is the prize to be won through the spiritual athleticism of the heroic soul.

The alternative—the way of the robust soul—differs from self-deceit or spiritual athleticism. The robust soul includes gratitude for God's grace and, out of this gratitude, feels the fire of passion burning with compassion for a world in need of grace. Rather than absorb the moral universe into his or her soul, the robust person of faith makes the neighbor's agenda into his or her own agenda. In faith, the robust soul relies on the objectivity of God's atoning work and enjoys subjectively the presence of the living Christ. The presence of Christ within the robust soul bursts forth like a spring rose in color and beauty.

The robust soul practices daily an attitude of gratitude. The faith of the robust soul explodes in love toward the neighbor. The incarnate presence of the crucified and risen Christ in our daily, almost subconscious, demeanor displays God's grace in, with, and under what would otherwise appear ordinary. But there are times when the ordinary can become extraordinary. Through guided meditation,

---

51. Joseph Campbell, *The Hero with a Thousand Faces,* 3rd ed., Bollinger Series (Novato, CA: Joseph Campbell Foundation, 2008), 30.

accompanied by worship and prayer, the fragile soul experiences the full reality of the cosmic Christ in the galaxies and the atoms, in the universe and the heart. For others, the experience takes the form of a special enlivening by the Holy Spirit in the bestowal of charism. This is a life-transforming moment.

Conclusion

As the fragile soul directs itself on the path toward the robust soul, detours threaten to divert it. The easiest detour is simple self-justificaiton–that is, to simply declare that I am good, right, or just. This simple self-justifiction usually includes an element of self-deception, a lie we tell ourselves. What this self-declaration of justness provides is spiritual duct tape over the cracks in the fragile soul; and this duct tape temporarily prevents full breakage.

Some among us are more energetic, more ambitious. We decide to actually become good, right, or just. We follow the detour that leads us up the moral mountain or, better, up the spiritual ladder. We pursue the life of virtue or the discipline of conformity to the moral order of the universe. We expect that our spiritual athleticism will win us the ultimate trophy.

The gospel message provides a sign that points in a different direction. The path to the robust soul is one the God walks. In fact, it is a path that God walks toward us. When God arrives, so to speak, God offers to give us what we seek apart from our self-deceit and our ladder climbing. Goodness and rightness and justness become a gift to us, a gift of divine grace which we accept in faith. At his point, the robust soul explodes on its own. All the fragile soul needs to do is enjoy it and, of course, say "thank you."

Doctrinally, what I am talking about here is justification-by-faith. No matter how fastidiously Reformation Protestants treasure this doctrine, surrounding it with theological halos, its real value is much broader and much deeper. Like the electron microscope, the concept of justifying faith shines a bright light into the dark recesses of the human soul and reveals to us who we are. It illuminates the human condition. It illuminates the dynamics of divine presence within our innermost self, within the emptiness that we fear lurks in our core. It illuminates the actions of God's grace within the human soul.

Justifying faith comes to us as gospel, as news about the graciousness of God. In order to hear this news about God, however, we must also hear news about ourselves. What we learn about ourselves is that we have been hiding something. We have been hiding the self behind a facade of self-justification. This facade of self-justification must be shattered before we can enjoy the inner peace brought to us by the news that God justifies us. Because God justifies us, we do not have to. We no longer need to defend ourselves, make ourselves look good, or fool ourselves into believing that we are, in fact, what we want others to think of us.

Our daily inclination is to draw a line between good and evil and then to place ourselves on the good side of the line. We do this unconsciously when we follow the rules. We do this somewhat consciously when someone accuses us of incompetence or malfeasance. We do this consciously when meeting someone new, when we try to look good for others. We do this nervously when we try to keep guilt from rising up into awareness and disturbing us with depressing thoughts. Most viciously, we do this when we exact harm on someone through gossip, violence, war, or genocide.

What the gospel reveals is surprising. It's counterintuitive. When we draw the line between good and evil and then place ourselves on the good side of the line, the gospel reports that God is on the evil side of the line. Really!? Yes, truly. When we pursue what we deem to be the good, God sides with those who become victimized by our pursuit. When we pursue justice, God sides with those who suffer from our pursuit of justice. When we stomp on the accelerator of our own virtuous achievements, a poisonous gas comes out of our exhaust pipe that suffocates those we are leaving behind. What we are blind to is that our own pursuit of self-justification victimizes others, and our gracious God sides with the victims. To say it another way, our virtues are just as deadly as our vices, and God, among others, suffers from our virtues.[52]

This is bad news. Here we thought that identifying ourselves with what is good or just or true would define us as good or just or true. Unfortunately, this is not how reality works. Reality is much more complex, nuanced, and ambiguous. We need a light to shine on our situation so that we can see what needs sorting out. Unfortunately, when what is hidden comes to light, it's bad news for us.

The gospel is not *only* bad news. To be sure, the gospel reveals our inclination to self-justify and even lie to ourselves, but there is more to it than that. The gospel also reveals that God is gracious. God justifies us by placing the crucified and risen Christ into our soul. The result is a justifying faith. Once we realize that we can get out of the business of justifying ourselves, the world suddenly looks different. No longer do we need to defend ourselves from a hostile world by identifying ourselves with what is good or just or true. We can live in the world—we can love the world—as if it is our world, with or without the lines we draw between good and evil. When appropriate, we can sin boldly.

---

52. "The totality of our depravity consists in the blindness: We do not even see that *our virtues are as sinful as our vices.*" Gerhard Forde, "Christian Life," in *Christian Dogmatics,* ed. Carl E. Braaten and Robert W. Jenson (Minneapolis: Fortress Press, 1984), 2:453 (italics in the original).

2

The Legalist within Us

The world stubbornly insists upon being right.

–Martin Luther[1]

Out beyond ideas of wrongdoing and rightdoing,
there is a field. I will meet you there.
When the soul lies down in that grass,
the world is too full to talk about
language, ideas, even the phrase *each other*
doesn't make any sense.

–Rumi[2]

The outer shell of a Kosta Boda bowl is thick glass. Since 1742, glassmaker Kosta Boda in Småland just south of Stockholm has been

---

1. Luther, *The Sermon on the Mount*, in *LW* 26:16.
2. Rumi, "Out beyond Ideas," in *The Essential Rumi*, trans. Coleman Barks (San Francisco: HarperSanFrancisco, 1995), http://peacefulrivers.homestead.com/Rumipoetry1.html, (italics in the original).

making artistic glassware that decorates many home interiors in Europe and North America. Kosta Boda glassware may look delicate, but it is sturdy. Normally, it does not need reinforcement. Duct tape would add nothing to its strength and would only detract from its beauty. Yet, a fragile soul might want to reinforce the exterior with spiritual duct tape, just in case. One brand of such duct tape is legalism, the most popular form of self-justification. We protect the inner swirl and the vacuous center with an external shell of "rights" and "shoulds" and "oughts" and "no-no's" and rules or laws, in addition to an unflinching commitment to justice.

But there's another way. Daily life could be tastier, more enjoyable, and overflowing with compassion. When the divine spirit of Christ is lodged at the center of our otherwise vacuous vortex, we become filled rather than empty. Rather than being shaped by the surrounding swirl, the soul is formed by the inner effervescence of God's grace and love. It becomes bold.

For those of us who are fragile souls (sometimes without knowing it), those legalistic patches can become "no trespassing" signs that tell God's Spirit to stay away. We need to take down the signs. Authentic faith welcomes the Holy Spirit; it rejoices in the divine presence. What's more, authentic faith welcomes the neighbor; it rejoices in sharing love beyond the bowl's outer edge.

The Spiritual Fragileometer

Now, if the reader can tolerate a touch of humor, I would like to introduce *The Spiritual Fragileometer.* In the middle of the fragileometer, we find the fragile soul—a person whose anxiety over the emptiness at the self's center leads to spiritual panic, which leads to the application of spiritual duct tape to prevent the glass shell from breaking. The fragile soul can easily become legalist. At the far right is the broken soul, the soul whose shell has broken and is beginning to sink in anomie and despair. We find broken souls among those overwhelmed by moral injury. At the left is the healthy soul, the robust soul, the joyful person living out of trusting gratitude for divine grace.

The Spiritual Fragilometer

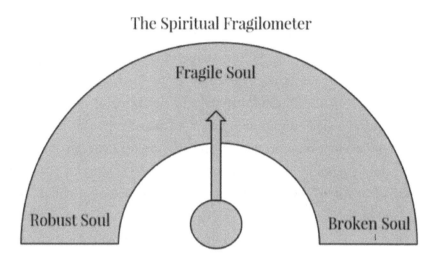

Fragile Soul

Robust Soul

Broken Soul

Fundamentalist Fragility

The media and many scholars tend to think of fundamentalists as relying on dogmatic absolutes and legalistic morality. The fundamentalist view of the Bible (verbally inspired by the Holy Spirit in its original autographs and infallible in content) seems absolutist—so absolutist that it can lead to bibliolatry, that is, worshipping the Bible more than the God who is revealed in the Bible. Fundamentalist congregational life seems riddled with legalism, with strict divine laws, and with moral do's and don'ts that are certainly confusing if not also frightening. While fear of burning forever in hell is enough to motivate a clean, righteous, and just life, it makes for a fragile motivation.

Growing up in a fundamentalist family with the daily terror of everlasting damnation leads many among us to flee rigid religion for either atheism or a spirituality free of such fear. Virtually every atheist or SBNR (spiritual but not religious) person who is also a recovering fundamentalist tells the same story. Having grown up in a morally rigid and religiously frightening atmosphere, many fundamentalist children seek out membership in more progressive churches when they enter adulthood. In addition, many recovering fundamentalists include the story of how, when they went to the university and studied Darwinian evolution, they felt the need to give up Christian belief entirely. The rejection of their Christian upbringing often includes the adoption of secularism and agnosticism, or even atheism. Their fragile religion fractured, then broke.

These grown-ups in flight remember their childhood fundamentalism as not enough fun, too much damn, and insufficient "mentalism." This, however, is a most unsympathetic dismissal of fundamentalism, and I would like to avoid being dismissive. However, the temptation is too much. The historian Mark Noll certainly sounds dismissive (and I must confess I think he's funny as well) when he writes, "The scandal of the evangelical mind is that there is not much of an evangelical mind. . . . American evangelicals are not exemplary for their thinking, and they have not been so for several generations."[3]

In their academic treatment of fundamentalisms (in the plural) at work in many religious traditions, Martin Marty and Scott Appleby describe fundamentalist movements as both conservative and creative:

> Beleaguered believers attempt to preserve their distinctive identity as a people or group. Feeling this identity to be at risk in the contemporary era, these believers fortify it by a selective retrieval of doctrines, beliefs,

3. Mark A. Noll, *The Scandal of the Evangelical Mind* (Grand Rapids, MI: Eerdmans, 1994), 3.

and practices from a sacred past. These retrieved "fundamentals" are refined, modified, and sanctioned in a spirit of pragmatism: they are to serve as a bulwark against the encroachment of outsiders who threaten to draw the believers into a syncretistic, areligious, or irreligious cultural milieu. . . . fundamentalism is at once both derivative and vitally original.[4]

It appears to me that all vital traditions—whether fundamentalist or non-fundamentalist—combine conservative retrieval with creative adaptation. Still, the description by Marty and Appleby helps us see the fragile soul at work in fundamentalism, creatively patching up what it fears is a crumbling perimeter.

Fundamentalism appears to be a fragile form of faith. Like the sturdy oak tree that breaks and falls in a strong wind, fundamentalism falls hard when its scriptural authority and rigid morality lose their rootedness. The other extreme, a rootless form of faith, is like a tumbleweed; it gets carried this way and that depending on the direction the spiritual wind is blowing. What we need is to be rooted firmly in a justifying faith so that we can climb like a bougainvillea toward the sky.

My concern in this chapter is the rigidity, absolutism, and legalism of the sheepish sinner. Such rigidity can come in a religious or non-religious form. Even though "fundamentalism is almost always associated with religion," writes Martin Marty, it may come in the form of "an outlook on life that can characterize the non-religious as well."[5] The fragile soul patches up the cracks with spiritual duct tape, which is the case within any worldview—Christian or non-

---

4. Martin E. Marty and R. Scott Appleby, "Introduction: A Sacred Cosmos, Scandalous Code, Defiant Society," in *Fundamentalisms and Society*, ed. Martin E. Marty and R. Scott Appleby (Chicago: University of Chicago Press, 1993), 3.

5. Martin E. Marty, "Fundamentalism," *Encyclopedia of Science and Religion*, ed. J. Wentzel Vrede van Huyssteen, 2 vols (New York: Macmillan, Thomson, Gale, 2003), 1:346. Cathleen Falsani describes Martin Marty as "perhaps the greatest living historian of American religion." *Sin Boldly: A Field Guide for Grace* (Grand Rapids, MI: Zondervan, 2008), 106.

Christian, religious or non-religious. Self-justification is a virtually universal human propensity.

Islamic Zeal and Atheist Jihad

Today's zealous atheists attack Christians, Jews, and Muslims because of alleged absolutism and rigidity, and their complaint is virulent, aggressive, and missionary. The New Atheists are out to convert religious believers to non-belief. Why? Because, as the New Atheists believe, science can supply all that religion has previously offered, but without the narrow-minded dogmatism, negativism, and fanaticism that (they believe) so often plagues religion.[6]

What we have been referring to as the fragile soul is responsible for the dogmatism and even fanaticism the atheists oppose. Curiously, it is equally responsible for the form taken by its atheist opposition.

As we try to understand this atheist complaint, two things beg our attention. First, today's aggressive atheists paint all religion with the same brush; that is, all religion is painted the color of violent fanaticism. Second, the atheist complaint turns into an absolutism of its own making. Atheism becomes a fanaticism that threatens counter-violence against religion. In short, there's no place where the human psyche can hide to escape the tragedy wrought by the fragile soul.

Belligerent atheist Sam Harris provides an example of the fragile soul at work within evangelical atheism. Harris complains that "religious faith remains a perpetual source of human conflict."[7]

---

6. An advertisement for the Freedom from Religion Foundation in *Scientific American* headlines, "In Reason We Trust," and cites Harvard's Steven Pinker saying, "the biology of consciousness offers a sounder basis for morality than the unprovable dogma of an immortal soul." *Scientific American* 311:1 (July 2014): 27. By drawing a line between good and evil and placing the "sounder basis for morality" on the good side of the line and the "immortal soul" on the evil side, atheism that claims science as its basis works hard to attract converts. Hence, today's atheism is evangelistic.

According to Harris, we need to stamp out religion in order to bring peace on Earth. The religions Harris particularly wants to eliminate are Islam, Christianity, and Judaism. These irrational and violent religious traditions are holdovers from a premodern era, and they must be vanquished. "All reasonable men and women have a common enemy. . . . Our enemy is nothing other than faith itself."[8]

At the top of Harris's hit list is Islam. Don't think it is only the "extremists" who are a danger to society, warns Harris. Islam at its core is violent. "The idea that Islam is a 'peaceful religion hijacked by extremists' is a fantasy . . . because most Muslims are *utterly deranged by their religious faith*."[9] Harris objects here to liberal and tolerant Muslims because this very liberalism and tolerance permits and even encourages extremism. In this way, even the non-extremist Muslims are excoriated, though the extremists are said to be the problem.

Liberal or tolerant Muslims fail to gain Harris's approval because the problem with Islam lies at its core. Harris complains that the the Qur'an, thought to be literally the word of God, teaches devout Muslims to commit themselves to holy war against all non-Muslims. Harris cites one dangerous passage after another, such as, "The only true faith in God's sight is Islam. . . . He that denies God's revelations should know that swift is God's reckoning" (Qur'an 3:19). The Qur'an and its concept of *jihad*, or holy war, are essential not just for suicide bombers but for all devout Muslims. "On almost every page," writes Harris, "the Koran instructs observant Muslims to despise nonbelievers. On almost every page, it prepares the ground for religious conflict. . . . Islam, more than any other religion human beings have devised, has all the makings of a thoroughgoing cult of death."[10]

---

7. Sam Harris, *The End of Faith: Religion, Terror, and the Future of Reason* (New York: W. W. Norton, 2004), 236.

8. Ibid., 131.

9. Sam Harris, *Letter to a Christian Nation* (New York: Alfred A. Knopf, 2006), 85 (italics in the original).

According to Harris, this cult of death gets additional energy from teaching young men that if they become suicide bombers they will go straight to paradise, avoid the judgment, and receive a reward of seventy virgins for their pleasure. What can we expect from a religious teaching such as this? Harris's response: "The only future devout Muslims can envisage—*as Muslims*—is one in which all infidels have been converted to Islam, subjugated, or killed."[11]

A few years ago, I lectured at Gadjah Mada University in Yogyakarta, Indonesia. The audience numbered about sixty, thirty of whom were Muslim professors and doctoral students. It appeared to me that the Muslims present would likely belong in the moderate or liberal camp of Islam. When I cited Harris and described Muslims as "utterly deranged by their religious faith," they laughed out loud. I asked why they were laughing. "Well, we know that's what many Westerners think of us," a couple remarked. Rather than feel insulted, the Muslims simply resigned themselves to this misunderstanding. They accepted this false image as something they might have to live with but didn't seem to take it too seriously.

Let's get back to what Sam Harris says. As a cult of death, Islam is a threat to us. Islam is our enemy. What should we do? Harris prescribes a two-fold defense. First, we should teach rationality. We should teach our children to think critically and to evaluate religious claims on the basis of evidence. Once we have examined religious beliefs, we will discover that they are unfounded. We will emerge from our outmoded religious beliefs into the freedom of a truly liberal society. If teaching reason is less than successful, however, then we should move toward a second form of self-defense, nuclear war.

Did I just say nuclear war? Yes, I did. According to Harris, the threat posed by Islam might call for a nuclear strike. "The only

10. Harris, *End of Faith*, 123.
11. Ibid., 110, italics in original.

thing likely to ensure our survival may be a nuclear first strike of our own. Needless to say, this would be an unthinkable crime—as it would kill tens of millions of innocent civilians in a single day—but it may be the only course of action available to us, given what Islamists believe."[12] Let me summarize the logic of Harris's call to arms: because of "what Islamists believe," we are justified in dropping a nuclear bomb on them.

Harris is giving expression to Western anxiety and fear. This anxiety leads him to propose his own form of atheist jihad against Islam. "The West must either win the argument or win the war. All else will be bondage."[13] His logic is flabbergasting. Because religion is violent, it should be vanquished, and we the non-religious may need to vanquish the religious population with anti-religious warfare. This is the road to peace on Earth. Really!?

When I cited Harris on launching a preemptive nuclear strike, my Gadjah Mada audience did not laugh. I inquired again about how they felt after hearing this public call to arms. "That's going too far," they murmured. Harris's verbal terrorism has a way of striking fear into the hearts of those who might find themselves on the receiving end of a nuclear bomb.

Harris's road to peace includes the threat of maximum violence. Might there exist a peaceful road to peace? Might we be able to enlist religious moderates or religious liberals—perhaps even those with whom I was conversing at Gadjah Mada University—to seek out a peaceful path to peace with religious extremists? No, argue the atheists. Moderate or liberal religious persons are not to be trusted, because they're still religious. Harris indicts "religious moderates" as part of the problem. By respecting Islam's literalism, religious moderates tacitly approve of Muslim belligerency.

12. Ibid., 129.
13. Ibid., 131.

The Oxford University field marshal leading the atheist armies is Richard Dawkins. He agrees with Harris. "I do everything in my power to warn people against faith itself, not just against so-called 'extremist' faith. The teachings of 'moderate' religion, though not extremist in themselves, are an open invitation to extremism."[14] Dawkins continues: "Suicide bombers do what they do because they really believe what they were taught in their religious schools; that duty to God exceeds all other priorities, and that martyrdom in his service will be rewarded in the gardens of Paradise."[15] The very tolerance shown by moderates or liberals imputes respect to religious fundamentalists and extremists who do not deserve that respect.

In short, atheist extremism has issued a call to arms against religious extremism. And, because moderate or liberal strains within religion give quarter to the enemy, they too must be wiped out. What is so important to acknowledge here is that the fragile soul is busy commanding allegiance among both religious and anti-religious forces. Anti-fanaticism can become just as fanatical as fanaticism. Evangelical atheism has drawn a line between good and evil, with atheism on the good side and religion on the evil side. This justifies wiping out religious believers either through scientific reason or, if this fails, nuclear warfare.

Absolutism at Home and Abroad

At this juncture, let's attend to what John Benson contributes to this discussion. "Islam today has its fanatics, devoted believers who will give their lives for their cause. But in the past (and still today?) we Christians have had our fanatics too." These are a veteran theologian's reflections at the tenth anniversary of September 11, 2001. The fragile

14. Richard Dawkins, *The God Delusion* (New York: Houghton Mifflin, 2006), 306.
15. Ibid., 308.

soul is vulnerable to fanaticism, to absolutism, and even to violence if necessary to keep the duct tape sealed. This leads Benson to write, "We in religion need to do our best to warn people (even indoctrinate them?) against absolutist ways of thinking and living . . . we need to teach a kind of common sense pragmatism that never expects absolutes of any kind this side of the grave."[16] We need to indoctrinate our side against the absolutism of both the other side *and* our side, he says.

It is not Islam, per se, that leads devotees to violence; rather, it's the absolutism within Islam. It is not Christianity, per se, that leads devotees to violence; rather, it's the absolutism within Christianity. So goes the logic. Although this makes sense in part, I worry a bit. Might we be tempted to embrace an anti-absolutist absolutism? Might liberal or relativistic religious believers distance themselves from their fellow devotees? Might we put those other absolutists into our scholarly zoo and stare at them without asking about our own fragility of soul?

What is healthy about this discussion of absolutism and fanaticism is that a theologian such as Benson can see the problem within his own Christian tradition. We Christians can confess our sins, or at least we can publicly confess the sins of those absolutists or extremists among us. And by confessing our own absolutist or extremist proclivities, we can feel justified in our anti-fanaticism.

Pure Doctrine

What is the best weapon to be used in the war against the absolutists and fanatics in both the religious and anti-religious armies? Avoidance? Empathy? Unconditional positive regard? Perhaps we

16. John Benson, "Some Reflections on Sunday, September 11, 2011," *Dialog* 51:1 (Spring 2012): 1.

should use a counter-absolutism or doctrinal fanaticism? Suppose we fight back with pure doctrine?

Historically, Lutherans have been merciless in their denunciation of their opponents: the legalists who justify themselves through works of the law. They [monks] "torture themselves in vain with their self-devised works," complains Luther in the Large Catechism.[17] "It is vain and ungodly to trust that these works satisfy God's law," writes Philip Melanchthon in his *Apology of the Augsburg Confession*.[18] The *Smalcald Articles* lift the rhetoric to a level of vituperative elegance: "We topple the pope and everything that is built upon our good works, because it is all built upon a rotten, flimsy foundation: good works or law. . . . Therefore the whole edifice is nothing but deceitful lies and hypocrisy."[19]

To combat the devilish reliance upon good works, the lethal arrow in the Lutheran quiver has become pure doctrine (*reine Lehre*). Against their "devilish doctrine," says Luther when rallying the evangelical troops for ecclesiastical battle, "we ought constantly to shout and cry out against all who preach and believe falsely and against those who want to attack, persecute, and suppress our gospel and pure doctrine, as the bishops, tyrants, fanatics, and others do."[20] It takes pure doctrine to defeat the profane teachings of those who wrongly believe we can justify ourselves through the good works produced by our moral conscience.

Lutheran Orthodoxy selected this reliance on pure doctrine from the cafeteria of Reformation offerings. Because the enemy of pure doctrine is change, conservatives protect purity from the adulteration that comes with change. Nickolaus Selnecker (1530–92) has bequeathed to us a poem, remembered by Robert D. Preus:

17. *BC*, 403.
18. Ibid., 211.
19. Ibid., 318.
20. Ibid., 446.

And ever is there something new
Devised to change Thy doctrines true;
Lord Jesus! as Thou still doest reign,
These vain, presumptuous minds restrain.[21]

What the Reformers of the sixteenth century were fighting against was a school of thought, an institutionally supported doctrine regarding how salvation is accomplished. The battle between the established Roman Catholic Church and the upstart Reformers could be described as ideological, as a struggle between competing and apparently irreconcilable theologies. Each side sought to purify its own doctrine, thereby to sharpen the points on its arrows for theological conflict. The Reformers who felt they had won the doctrinal battle engraved their pure doctrine on a theological rock, and in the centuries since, they have tried to protect this rock from erosion. If we stand on this solid, doctrinal rock, will we be protected from the fragile soul?

The Reformation victory took place in the sixteenth century. Five centuries later, how should we assess what is going on today? Beneath the ideology of *works righteousness,* or *legalism,* or whatever we might wish to call it, we find the fragile soul. Medieval Roman Catholic theology is but one doctrinal codification of a common structure at work in the human mind. The fragile soul belongs to the human race as such. It is universal. Though some individuals seem to get along without it, by and large, each of us exhibits traits of the fragile soul (though some more than others). And human beings in groups find no escape from the damage the fragile soul can inflict, as we will see in the chapters to come. The fragile soul is pre-religious, so to speak; it affects our disposition whether we belong to a formal religious institution or not.

21. Robert D. Preus, *The Theology of Post-Reformation Lutheranism*, 2 vols. (St. Louis: Concordia, 1970–72), 1:28.

So I ask: Will pure doctrine protect us from the vicissitudes of the fragile soul? No. A striving for purity in doctrine has its value, to be sure; but the fragile soul can effect damage within pure doctrine just as well as within any heterodox doctrine. In fact, a passionate and rigid adherence to pure doctrine can distort the soul as much as outright belief in the ideology of good works. Here is my point: what is at stake is not the content of pure doctrine but rather the purity in our attitude toward it. Such purity in attitude can be a form of spiritual duct tape, a "no trespassing" sign to keep the divine spirit and human compassion away.

This may at first seem confusing. Reformation theology is dedicated to stamping out legalism, works righteousness, and authoritarianism. Yet, who is calling the kettle black? Can the reformers exhibit the same fragility and legalism as those they are trying to reform? Perhaps we are talking less about the content of a healthy theology and more about the mood or tone or demeanor of the theologians. After all, we are talking about your and my faith and what contributes to a robust or authentic faith.

The takeaway is this: our conscience can panic as it pursues religious teaching in its maximum purity. Do we have the right faith? Do we have enough faith? We panic, says Nadia: "When the hard stuff in life happens, not only do we feel crappy, but then we have to add to it also feeling totally inadequate about our faith, which just makes it all worse."[22] This panic is stirred up by an underlying anxiety, the same anxiety that drives the fragile soul to seek security in legalism. If we believe our eternal survival depends on getting the doctrine just right—on believing just the right thing—then we will stop at nothing to purify our central beliefs to the utmost degree.

22. Nadia Bolz-Weber, "Sermon on Faith, Doubt, and Mustard Seed Necklaces," *Sarcastic Lutheran* (blog), October 7, 2013, http://www.patheos.com/blogs/nadiabolzweber/2013/10/complaining-to-god-a-sermon-on-faith-doubt-and-mustard-seed-necklaces/.

The net result is the same rigidity, absolutism, and intolerance that accompanied the very legalism pure doctrine sought to combat. Such is the paradoxical yet ubiquitous influence of the fragile soul engaged in sheepish sinning.

The Unhappy Consciousness, Yesterday

Sheepish sinning should elicit a response of confession within us. We need to confess our absolutism, repent, and then . . . do what?

Paradoxically, this public confession of one's sin (meaning the sin of absolutism) can testify to devotion, holiness, or an admirable spirituality. Again, watch out! Confession itself can lead to a disguised form of self-justification because the fragile soul plays tricks on itself, almost deliberately, to keep itself fragile. Despite God's offer of comforting grace, we prefer living with anxiety, and we justify this choice to accentuate our anxiety by calling it godly. How is this trick performed?

Let me introduce the term *unhappy consciousness.* The nineteenth-century philosopher G. W. F. Hegel introduced the concept of the unhappy consciousness (*das unglückliche Bewußtsein*) to describe a self that is divided within itself. One's consciousness "feels itself in the bitterness of soul-diremption. It is the movement of an infinite yearning . . . a yearning [for what] is the unattainable 'beyond' which, in being seized, escapes or rather has already escaped."[23] Our feeble and finite attempt to grasp the unattainable infinite twists and mangles our inner life, resulting in a distortion of the soul.

Imagine yourself as a monk or a nun in a monastery. You are practicing asceticism—that is, you are abstaining from worldly pleasures to pursue spiritual goals. You have made vows of obedience,

---

23. Georg Wilhelm Friedrich Hegel, *The Phenomenology of Mind: The Unhappy Consciousness,* http://www.stjohns-chs.org/general_studies/philosophy/Romantic/hegel.html.

poverty, and chastity. Your sexual abstinence is accompanied by a scrupulous interior vacuum cleaning that rids you of sins such as dirty thoughts, pride, or judgment of others. You cultivate virtuous habits such as prayer, hospitality, compassion, and almsgiving. You extinguish your self (your ego) and replace it with devotion to God and love for neighbor.

Such ascetic discipline can be spiritually healthy, to be sure. Yet, you risk the chance of an unhappy and inverted logic taking over: *the unhappier I am the happier I am.* The more you suffer, the better you feel. The degree of your happiness becomes correlated to the degree of your spiritual agony. You decide to mortify the flesh to liberate the spirit.

Among the ascetic texts collected by Maximus the Confessor (580–662) in Constantinople, we find this piece of counsel: "Afflict your flesh with hunger and vigils and apply yourself tirelessly to psalmody and prayer; then the sanctifying gift of self-restraint will descend upon you and bring you love."[24] St. Theodoros, a seventh-century monk of the monastery of St. Sabas near Jerusalem, also demonstrates this reverse logic: "This path [of self-denial] is harsh and steep, but those who pursue it wholeheartedly and with good hope, and who aspire after holiness, find it attractive and full of delight, for it brings them pleasure, not affliction." [25] Theodoros turns to the question of whether or not to enjoy fine wine. He first cites Scripture, but then he offers quite a divergent piece of advice. "'Wine makes glad the heart of man' (Ps. 104:15). But you who have professed sorrow and grief should turn away from such gladness and rejoice in spiritual gifts."[26] By denying the pleasure of tasting a fine wine, the monk experiences gladness and rejoices for it. This seems so

24. Maximus the Confessor, "First Century," in *Phil.* 2:57.
25. Theodoros, "A Century of Spiritual Texts," in *Phil.,* 2:33–34.
26. Ibid., 2:20.

counterintuitive, yet this is the unhappy consciousness at work in the fragile soul.

In the West, the paradoxical logic of the unhappy consciousness is discernible in St. John of the Cross, who recommends "the mortification of the four great natural passions: joy, hope, fear, and grief." The ascetic saint should be passionless, aroused by neither joy nor grief, neither hope nor fear. "Let your soul therefore turn always . . . not to what tastes best, but to what is most distasteful. . . . not to what pleases, but to what disgusts." What is the result of such self-discipline? "In this spoliation, the soul finds its tranquility and rest."[27] Self-emptying yields divine fulfilling. To be unhappy is to be happy.

In Europe, the unhappy consciousness occasionally took advantage of physical self-flagellation. Imagine yourself not only denying yourself the taste of Napa Valley wine but also whipping yourself. You select your weapon: a rod, a switch, or a cat-o'-nine-tails. Self-inflicted pain is a "matter for suffering for God," reports Madeleine Sophie Barat, founder of the Sacred Heart order in 1800. "Nothing but pain makes my life supportable."[28] The more your flesh hurts, the better your soul feels. This is the curious logic of the unhappy consciousness.

As a young Augustinian monk, Martin Luther knew well this unhappy consciousness. It drove him to hate God.

> But I, blameless monk that I was, felt that before God I was a sinner with an extremely troubled conscience. I couldn't be sure that God was appeased by my satisfaction. I did not love, no rather I hated the just God who punishes sinners. In silence, if I did not blaspheme, then certainly I grumbled vehemently and got angry at God. I said, "Isn't it enough that we miserable sinners, lost for all eternity because of original sin, are oppressed by every kind of calamity through the Ten Commandments?

27. Cited by James, VRE, 305–6. James describes the "undiluted ascetic spirit" as "the passion of self-contempt wreaking itself on the poor flesh" (ibid., 304).
28. Cited by James, ibid., 310.

Why does God heap sorrow upon sorrow through the Gospel and through the Gospel threatens us with his justice and his wrath?" This was how I was raging with wild and disturbed conscience.[29]

Luther's fragile soul seemed to be created by the angry God Edwards later describes. Luther sought in vain to satisfy that angry God through works of the law, that is, monastic law. By making himself physically unhappy, Luther was supposed to experience spiritual happiness. However, it did not work. Eventually, the unhappy consciousness necessarily fails in its vain attempt to make the fragile soul genuinely happy.

The Unhappy Consciousness, Today

The unhappy consciousness is alive and well in Berkeley, California, where I teach theology. Rarely does one find a progressive Christian engaging in mortification of the flesh, repudiation of pride, or self-renunciation. Certainly not in Berkeley! Even so, progressive Christians retain the unhappy consciousness. Today, self-flagellation takes on the disguised form of self-denunciation in racial, class, and gender categories. The white professional male is morally denounced because of his social location, and those complicit, such as white middle class women, share in the verbal self-flagellation. Faculty and students at the Graduate Theological Union recently went through a cultural phase in which meetings began with the ritual of identifying our perspective: all those in attendance introduced themselves by literally "confessing" their social location. We reported the vested class or racial interests that condition, if not pervert, our intellectual judgments. Allegedly, the equivalent of original sin is lodged in our social location, which destines us to prejudice against persons of

---

29. Luther, *Preface to the Complete Edition of Luther's Latin Writings*, 1545, *LW*, 34:336–37.

color, women, and gay people. Confession cleanses. Once everyone's confession had been received, the meeting could begin. From this experience, I concluded that the more condemned liberal white people feel, the more holy or righteous they feel. Verbal self-flagellation has replaced the cat-o'-nine-tails.

Why the Christian Church Is in Deep Trouble Today

The Christian church in the twenty-first century is in deep trouble. The enemies of the Christian faith are better armed, shoot straighter, and are passionate about their commitment to bring down the Christian religion. It is an objective fact that the church has enemies, and these enemies are publically aggressive. The best defense the Christian church can muster, in my judgment, is not a counterattack against its enemies. Rather, the best defense is to cease and desist sponsoring fragile souls and to bolster, strengthen, and embolden robust souls. Contrived fundamentalist shaming, commitment to pure doctrine, and white liberal anti-white self-flagellation—all of which perpetuate the idiocy of the unhappy consciousness—are a public embarrassment that is hidden from our own sanctimonious eyes due to the self-inflicted blindness of ecclesiastical self-justification. Today's church is weak, vulnerable, and culturally detestable, yet our church leaders continue to pronounce spiritual inanities and pious piffle as if the church's medieval walls were impenetrable. Without a retrieval of the gospel of grace, those walls will crumble within two generations of this writing. Only the gospel empowered by the living God will provide *ein feste Berg* (the mighty fortress).

The Christian worldview is slipping away from the iPhones and computer screens watched by the rising generation. In a recent survey, university undergraduates in North America described themselves in the following ways: thirty-two percent as religious, thirty-two percent as SBNR (spiritual but not religious), and twenty-eight percent as secular (meaning non-religious). Eight percent of those asked offered no response. "Probably the most unexpected finding was that college-age Americans are divided among not two but three distinctive worldviews: religious, secular, and spiritual."[30] Even though this survey did not investigate the makeup of these worldviews in the detail that I plan to here, I believe it is illuminating to see a survey asking about competing worldviews. A worldview includes a moral universe, and the relationship of the soul to a chosen moral universe is both decisive and subtle. Those of us who affirm faith in the God of grace must work out with fear and trembling what this will mean in the cultural crossfire between competing worldviews.

I spend considerable time outside church circles because of my commitment to pursue *theology of culture*.[31] I want to situate myself in the crossfire. This places me within a number of communities in which the God of Christian faith is at minimum ignored and in some cases laughingly ridiculed. In particular, you can find me these days among research scientists (especially physicists, cosmologists, geneticists, stem cell researchers, and my favorite, astrobiologists); New Agers and those who claim to be SBNRs; Big Historians who tell the story of creation without a creator; UFO investigators and even UFO believers, who are expecting salvation to drop from our skies as the gift of an advanced extraterrestrial technology; Transhumanists or cyber-techies planning actively to evolve the next

---

30. Barry A. Kosmin, "The Secular Are Skeptics: The Worldviews of Today's University Students," *The Skeptical Inquirer* 38:4 (July/August 2014): 38.

31. My approach to the *theology of culture* follows the path blazed indirectly by Paul Tillich and, more directly, by one of my professors at the University of Chicago, Langdon Gilkey. Called the *Hermeneutic of Secular Experience,* this method attempts "to see what religious dimensions there may be . . . in ordinary life . . . which will uncover what is normally hidden and forgotten." Langdon Gilkey, (Indianapolis: Bobbs-Merrill, 1969), 234.

intelligent species, which will supplant and replace the current human race; and homeless women who have dropped out of the middle class and into poverty because of the twin whammies of divorce and the downturn in the economy. In all but the last group, the God of Christian belief is disregarded, impugned, and on occasion even blasphemed. It hurts me to witness this blasphemy; but I remain present with open ears.

At a recent international UFO congress, George Noorey, popular radio host of *Coast to Coast*, asked the audience of eight hundred, "How many of you believe in UFOs?" About six hundred hands went up. Without taking much of a breath, he followed this with a second question: "How many of you believe in God?" I watched. Perhaps two hundred hands went up. The ratio was 3:1 in favor of UFOs over God as the object of belief. What is going on here? Hostility toward old-fashioned religious commitments?

New Age proponents with whom I associate deride what they perceive as the negativity in traditional Christian piety. "Dead from the neck down, with no humor, no sex, no aesthetic sensibility whatsoever, wasting away, spending one's days and nights ignoring the world and lost in prayer . . . what a strange God, that," writes Ken Wilber. "Well, no more. Dead to life, dead to the body, dead to nature, dead to sex, dead to beauty, dead to excellence: that never was a real God anyway, but merely a desiccated distillation of the things that men and women always had the most difficulty handling, and things from which God became the Great Escape."[32] Just as Lutherans were merciless in their denunciation of medieval spiritual practices, so also the post-Christian crowd can be merciless in its denunciation of the faith they reject.

32. Ken Wilber, *Integral Spirituality* (Boston: Integral Books, 2006), 206.

At a recent Transhumanism conference, one comedian-like speaker, David Fitzgerald, ridiculed the Christian religion for its contradictions, for approving genocide in the Old Testament, and for the utter confusion in the New Testament concerning the sacrificial death of Jesus for the forgiveness of sins. The Bible is crazy, he said, because it approves stoning people to death, polygamy, and God's bloodthirsty demand for human sacrifice. The Christian religion is immoral, he said, because it hides child abuse (priests abusing altar boys). The speaker laughed. The audience laughed and hooted and applauded. "Our one hope for the future of humanity," he trumpeted, "is that among our college students the number of atheists is growing."[33] The hope for humanity, according to aggressive atheists, is that disbelief in God is on the increase. Missionaries for disbelief are making conversions.

What might this mean for those among us who still love Jesus? Has the time come for publicly defending our faith in the God of grace? If so, then the life of faith must deliver. It must deliver a faith that is bold, strong, coherent, ennobling, and morally admirable. Yes, a faith that sins boldly must be morally admirable. But how? Will the fragile soul that protects itself from breaking by using duct tape in the form of self-righteousness and pure doctrine do the trick? By no means. Our persistence to prop up fragile faith in this way is the leak that will sink the church's boat.

The Indwelling Christ

I would like to be nice and say "thank you" to the theologians for their attempt to conserve pure doctrine; I would like to thank the legalists among us for holding up worthy moral ideals; and I would

---

33. David Fitzgerald, "Sex and Violence in the Bible," *YouTube* video, 42:19, November 28, 2013, https://www.youtube.com/watch?v=SY0cniU30zk.

like to thank my white anti-white liberal friends for championing racial equality. But frankly, I can't be nice. None of these external fixes can comfort us in our anxiety or secure our spiritual bowl from cracking or breaking. Nor can they provide the spiritual strength we need for the challenges of the coming century. Only a firm faith—sans spiritual-duct-tape patches—can deliver us. Firm faith is provided by Jesus Christ dwelling within our yet-to-be-formed souls.

According to the gospel of grace, faith is rooted firmly because Christ is present. Christ is "the One who is present in the faith itself," says Luther. "Therefore the Christ who is grasped by faith and who lives in the heart is the true Christian righteousness . . . Here, there is no work of the Law."[34] Such divine presence in the human soul cannot help but form and transform the soul. It is not the patches on the perimeter but rather Christ in the center that provides soul formation and transformation. "Ultimately this view is quite mystical," observes Kirsi Stjerna, "for it recognizes Christ as being personally present in the believer, rather than merely his benefits. Faith in this view also is more than an abstract virtue. It is a reality-changing instrument that unites the divine and the human, ontologically."[35] In sum, patching the fragile soul with legalism or pure doctrine (both examples of heteronomy) is a useless exercise that only enhances our anxiety and overlooks a wondrous gift already present—namely, the indwelling Christ.

---

34. Luther, *Lectures on Galatians*, in *LW*, 26:129–30.
35. Kirsi Stjerna, "Luther, Lutherans, and Spirituality," *Spirituality: Toward a 21st Century Lutheran Understanding*, ed. Kirsi Stjerna and Brooks Schramm (Minneapolis: Lutheran University Press, 2004), 40–41.

Conclusion

Some souls are more spiritually robust than others. One symptom of a soul in pain is moral fragility covered over by legalism, as we have observed. The fragile soul prompts the legalist to play by the book and to demand only what is right. It pains the fragile soul when falling short. As a result, falling short is soothed over by pure doctrine and absolutist beliefs, right along with lies, self-justification, scapegoating, and violence. In even more spiritual pain, the broken soul is the morally injured person engulfed in despair and considering suicide. The person with a broken soul has lost the moral universe. His or her self is collapsing from within. Healing for the fragile soul requires maintenance of the moral universe, while healing for the broken soul requires a relationship that transcends the now-shattered moral universe. God's presence in faith offers healing power for both. God's presence in faith fuels a leaping flame and fires up the robust self.

Christ's real presence in the human soul makes all the difference. This divine indwelling rewrites the meaning of justification-by-faith. Jesus died as a just person. He is, in himself, just; therefore, he needs no self-justification. When the Holy Spirit places the just Jesus within our faith, Jesus' justice becomes our justice. By this means, God has justified us, so to speak. Romans 8:33b: "God is the one who justifies" (*theos ho dikaiosune*).

If in our faith we are justified by God in Christ, we have no need to self-justify and, hence, no need to scapegoat others. Our justification is a divine gift, not the product of our self-deception. Let me add: the Christ present in our faith is the resurrected one. The eternity of the resurrected one is present within us, an eternity that transcends even our most sublime vision of the moral universe. The tortured logic of the unhappy consciousness gets laughed away as the person of faith elects to sin boldly.

For five centuries theologians have debated how to get clear on the way in which God's grace accomplishes this. This book will delineate with precision both what is at stake theologically and the value of justification-by-faith for an integrated human spirituality.

Having made this promise, it will be worth our time to pause and examine our inner desire to make ourselves at one with the justness of the universe. To our love for justice we now turn.

3

Our Love of Justice

Law is the king of all, of mortals as well as of immortals.

–Plato, quoting Pindar[1]

If God exists, we need to ask: Is God just? If we affirm that God is just, then we must ask why. Is justice just because God has established justice, or is God just because God adheres to the laws of justice? Which comes first, God or justice?

What is important about these questions, I think, is that we intuitively believe that justice is eternal, universal, and everywhere valid. To say that justice is local or relative or merely one's private opinion seems inadequate.

Justification-by-faith is important because it pours the moral beverage that allays our deep inner thirst for justice. We love justice. We may not think about it every day, but that doesn't make it any less true. We love justice. We want justice. We want justice for ourselves. We want to think of ourselves as just; and we want the laws of

---

1. Plato, *Gorgias* 484, in *DP*, 1:544.

justice to reign in our lives, the lives of others, and in the universe. The curious message of the Christian gospel is that God places this universal justice within each soul, even while we are living in an unjust world. When we live out of justifying faith, we experience a foretaste of this universal and even eternal justice, even though it's only a foretaste and not yet a full thirst-quencher.

At the very least, this taste will get us started. In addition, however, we need to describe something that may at first seem disconcerting. In our haste to slake our thirst for justice, we may drink haphazardly from too many wells. Instead of pure justice, we may prematurely assuage our thirst with a sickening self-justification. Self-justification is the shadow side of justice that pollutes our psyche with deceit and condemns our world to violence.

This subject gets still more disconcerting. The moral universe upon which we rely to prop up the structures of justice might be less than ultimate. Our moral universe might turn out to be less reliable than we had thought. The solid ground of justice upon which we try to construct our self and our self-understanding may turn out to be sand, sand blown away by the winds of relativity and heartbreak. When the winds of vicissitude blow away the house that justice built, we may find ourselves leaning on God, and only God.

That's Not Fair!

Is justice hardwired into our brains?[2] Shortly after young children begin to speak, it's not long before we hear them exclaim: "That's not fair!" (often accompanied by a stomp of the foot and an angry face). Is a sense of fairness built into our genetic code or cerebral wiring?

We all know the debates over nature and nurture. The nativists or naturists will argue that our moral sense is built-in; it is an a priori intuition that we are born with. The empiricists or nurturists, in contrast, will argue that moral codes come from social convention; they are a posteriori, that is, learned from our social context. With advances in brain research moving rapidly and the cults of neuroscience and neuropsychology continuing to develop, the expectation is that we'll soon be able to explain everything (including our love for justice) in terms of neuronal firings. As far as I'm concerned, it doesn't really matter whether the naturists or the nurturists win the explanation contest. What is important is what we observe every day—and what we observe is that we can scream "That's unfair!" at quite an early age. It appears that human beings work with a preformed sense of justice, which is later developed by some, into an educated or sophisticated ethic of justice.

2. Naturalists assert that justice is hardwired into our brains. Experiments involving babies and young children seem to confirm an innate desire to aid others in need and to render justice in the form of retribution or revenge. Michael Shermer contends that "two neural networks in the . . . brain are engaged to act: to help a fellow human in trouble or punish the perpetrator. . . . Rescue is sweet, but so is revenge." Shermer, "The Genesis of Justice," *Scientific American* 310:5 (May 2014): 78. The naturalism to which Shermer appeals is the kind we find in sociobiology with its doctrine of the selfish gene, which is modified by group selection and reciprocal altruism. Our hardwired moral sense "evolved to solve several problems at once in our ancestral environment: be nice to those who help us and our kin and kind and punish those who hurt us and our kin and kind. . . . This is why constitutions of our nations should be grounded in the constitution of our nature" (ibid.). My own observation is that children exhibit the "That's not fair!" reaction at a very young age, which suggests some primitive level of justice. Historically speaking, Shermer's evolutionary theory of justice applies solely to tribal morality. It does not apply to modern notions of justice, which have universal application. It takes the insight of a philosopher such as Plato or a prophet such as Jesus to see beyond what is hardwired into our brains.

We feel the tension between justice and injustice at a gut level, just below what makes us rational. At the rational level, we try to align the conscious self with that gut-level love for justice. This attempt to align our rational level with our gut level is sometimes called *rationalization.* Here, I call it *self-justification.*

The gut-level commitment to fairness is actually only one of at least five ways in which our intuitions ground our moral commitments on justice. According to moral psychologist Jonathan Haidt, we also make additional gut-level commitments concerning care, loyalty, authority, and sanctity.[3] Intuitively, we know that care is right and that inflicting harm is wrong. Intuitively, we also know that loyalty to our family, our team, our economic class, our race, and our nation are right and that betrayal and treachery are wrong. Intuitively, we know that respect for authority is right and disrespect is wrong. Finally, we intuitively respect the body as the temple of the sacred; this is right, and "thingification" or debauchery is wrong.

Well, almost. Something distinguishes the first two (fairness and care) from the other three (loyalty, authority, and sanctity). Fairness and care are universal. The other three intuitive forms of justice belong to the in-group versus out-group differentiation. Because we human beings are so strongly inclined to draw a line between who is in and who is out—a line between we and they or between us and them—what we think is just may be only tribal and not universal. We owe our tribe or in-group loyalty, authority and sanctity, to be sure; but to whom do we owe fairness and care? Genuine fairness and care go well beyond our tribe or in-group; they apply universally to all people of all times and all places, even to animals or life-forms that are nonhuman. Under no circumstances are unfairness and harm to be justified. Universal fairness and care are founded on a

3. Jonathan Haidt, *The Righteous Mind* (New York: Vintage, 2012).

transcendent or metaphysical foundation of justice. In some instances, loyalty, authority, and sanctity might conflict with the requirements of universal justice.

In-group justice is less than universal. When it comes to loyalty, for example, we justify ourselves when we can say we are "a company man," or "a real fan," or "supportive of the administration's policies," or, most dramatically, a "patriot." No one can approve of disloyalty or betrayal. The traitor is unjust, and punishment is justified. One implication of loyalty, however, is that it is divisive. Loyalty allies one side against the other side. While loyalty appeals to justice, in its concrete form, it pits one team or one nation against another team or another nation. Loyalty is preferential and as preferential unjust, which is why we ask our judges in court to suspend their loyalties when rendering a verdict.

When it comes to authority, a soldier's salute is fitting, proper, and respectful. The salute affirms and extends the authoritarian moral universe within which the soldier lives. However, civilians in modern democracies lean toward anti-authorianism. The other side of the authority coin is an egalitarianism that elicits a sense of rebellion against authority. Whether submitting to authority or rebelling against it, authority provides a quadrant within our moral universe. In the minds of egalitarians, authority becomes tyranny when the equality of everyone is sacrificed to the bully in charge. To be considered just, one must identify with the movement for liberation *from* authority. Conservatives tend to justify themselves according to the hierarchical calculus while liberals tend to justify themselves according to the egalitarian calculus. Both live in the same moral universe and justify themselves accordingly.

When it comes to the sanctity of the human body, we divide the world into the clean and the unclean, the pure and the polluted, the sacred and the profane. Our intuition tells us that we need to protect the body from intrusion, infection, and injury. Rites of purification as well as hygienic practices make intuitive sense and provide moral grounding for taboos, aversions, and our reactions of disgust regarding excrement. We justify ourselves by identifying with what is clean.

At some gut level, our intuition tells us that these five—fairness, care, loyalty, authority, and sanctity—are grounded in a transcendent reality: justice. The first two may be more universal than the second three, yet it is important to acknowledge that justice belongs first to the bowl's perimeter rather than the center of the soul's cyclone. Before we think about it and before we try to explain it, we already love justice. We seldom think directly about justice, though it is ever present on the rim of our consciousness.

Now, what is justice? And furthermore, is God just?

Bully Justice?

We certainly know what justice is not. We know immediately that bullying is unjust. Bullies victimize. Their victims get treated unfairly and uncaringly. The bully must be held accountable to some higher standard of justice, a standard that judges the bully. In addition, when somebody gets hurt, we know that someone has acted immorally. The bully is immoral because the victim gets hurt.

Thrasymachus tried on the bully theory of justice, just to see if it fit. In Plato's *Republic,* Thrasymachus says: "I proclaim that justice is nothing else than the interest of the stronger."[4] When Thrasymachus looks around the room, no one nods in agreement. Another character in the *Republic,* Glaucon, contends that it is better to appear to others to be just than to actually be just. The Thrasymachus Principle is that

---

4. Plato, *Republic* 1.338s, in *DP*, 1:603.

justice is defined by the interests of the bully. The Glaucon Principle is that looking good is better than being good. I will ignore the Glaucon Principle for the time being and examine in more detail the Thraysmachus Principle.

The bully view of justice justifies the strong when they pick on the weak. It justifies powerful nations invading and conquering weak nations. It justifies the thievery of armed robbers who steal from unarmed storekeepers. It justifies tax structures that favor the rich while making the working class pay.

In Plato's writings, Socrates objects to the bully view. He replaces it with an anti-bully justice. Justice is "absolute and eternal and immutable," making both the weak and the strong equal in relation to absolute justice, he argues.[5] However, we may have to concede that Thrasymachus's bully view better describes the kind of justice operative in today's practical affairs.

Charles Darwin gave us our theory of biological evolution, a theory that would fill Thrasymachus with glee. According to this theory, variations in inheritance are acted upon by natural selection. The species that survive this selection are called *fit*, which means reproductively fit. The common phrase, "survival of the fittest," has become synonymous with natural selection. Translated into social ethics, "survival of the fittest" justifies—according to Social Darwinists—allowing the poor to die by the wayside while favoring the rich, the healthy, and the powerful. If one were to deny the eternal and universal principles of justice, then ethics could be grounded in nature. What does nature do? Nature, in the form of evolution, favors the strong over the weak. Nature teaches what Thrasymachus teaches, namely, justice is "nothing else than the interest of the stronger."

5. Plato, *Republic* 5.479s, in *DP*, 1:743.

"But, that's not fair!" screams a little voice from within us. What happens in nature is not good enough. Whatever justice is, it is not exemplified in the killing of the wildebeest by the lion or the gobbling up of small businesses by large corporations. The concept of justice gives us leverage to judge what happens in nature, society, and even in our own souls. Justice must be transcendent. Justice must be more than merely the interest of the stronger!

Deep down, I think, we all love justice. By imagining a moral universe in which justice is ultimate, the fragile soul can feel safe from the bully. What happens to the fragile soul when the moral universe is trumped either by fracturing or by divine grace, or by both?

Justice in the Soul and in the Cosmos

We require a moral universe—a meaningful world structured justly—if we are to enjoy an integrated self. The self or the soul orients itself around the ultimate good. "Symmetrically," begins philosopher Charles Taylor, "the assurance that I am turned towards this good gives me a sense of wholeness, of fullness of being, as a person or self, that nothing else can."[6] Our subjectivity requires organization around an objective ground of value, a good, a reliable moral universe. Without the good, the self loses its center and disintegrates. In order for the self to be a self, we rely upon a universe ordered toward what is good, just, and true.

This means we innately love justice. We want to identify ourselves with what is just; and some of us pursue justice with passion. What is

6. Charles Taylor, *Sources of the Self: The Making of the Modern Identity* (Cambridge, MA: Harvard University Press, 1989), 63. A theological anthropology must acknowledge that one characteristic of the human self is that it is open to what is beyond the self. As human persons, we are fundamentally inclined to seek what is transcendent, including a moral universe. "Therefore we say: human beings are bodily creatures who have a fundamentally unlimited transcendentality and unlimited openness to being as such in knowledge and freedom." Karl Rahner, *TI*, 21:42.

there about justice that deserves our love and our devotion? Answer: justice makes available what is ultimately good.

Each of us desires to be identified with what is just, even in our most private and quiet moments. Yet, we know that justice cannot be produced from within us. We do not manufacture justice. Rather, justice is something we reach out for. We seek it. We attune ourselves to justice. We align ourselves with a justice that transcends us. We invoke transcendent justice when trying to define ourselves, when trying to establish our identity. We would like our souls to be formed according to the pattern of justice, and we would like our world to be conformed to this just pattern as well.

Why? Because justice is not only good; it is also eternal. Well, at least we think justice is eternal. If one's deepest inner self—the soul—can be grafted onto the eternal trunk of justice, then we can share in its eternal flowering. Is it true?

The idea of an eternal moral universe first surfaced in ancient Athens. In his play, *Antigone,* Sophocles (495–406 B.C.E.) writes: "Nor deemed I that thy decrees were of such force, that a mortal could override the unwritten and unfailing statutes of heaven. For their life is not of to-day or yesterday, but from all time, and no man knows when they were first put forth."[7] The laws of justice transcend this life. They were here before we were born and remain in effect beyond our death. Beyond death, justice will have the last word, even if the bullies get away with injustice in this life. To pass from this life into the next requires passing through the door of judgment.

This means our daily moral actions have eternal meaning and consequence. Evangelical Dinesh D'Souza describes the connection between our moral universe and eternal life in this way: "So when we believe in life after death, we affirm cosmic justice, and this gives us

7. Sophocles, *Antigone,* http://classics.mit.edu/Sophocles/antigone.html.

hope that good will be finally rewarded and evil punished. Morality becomes both easier and more worthwhile in this framework."[8] You and I intuitively believe that cosmic justice is universal and eternal, thus making it worth our while to conform our souls to its moral standards.

But, I ask, is it actually the case that justice is eternal? Perhaps it is only immortal. We could imagine that justice might be immortal, that it could survive death; but that doesn't necessarily mean that justice is eternal. To be immortal, it would only need to survive death. To be eternal, it would need to be ultimate. Is justice ultimate? What is important here is that we intuitively believe that justice holds sway both in this life and beyond death. But how far should we take this notion?

Immortality vs. Eternity

Some philosophical and religious traditions treat justice as immortal but less than eternal. In ancient India, belief in the law of karma is one such way. Cause and effect are metaphysical principles, say Hindus and Buddhists, so unjust actions become causes for negative karmic reactions, either in this life or in the next. No one can escape what karma exacts. If we do not suffer punishment for our injustices in this life, we will find ourselves in a social bondage that is a fitting recompense when we are reborn. The wheel of rebirth spins with one incarnation after another. It spins until we climb the ladder of karmic moral achievement and reach the point of liberation. When we reach this point, we jump off the wheel into a blissful state of cosmic union, a state that is free from any future incarnations. The law of karma transcends human death and is, therefore, immortal; but

---

8. Dinesh D'Souza, *Life after Death: The Evidence* (Washington DC: Regnery, 2009), 215.

in itself, it is less than eternal, less than ultimate. Somewhere between immortality and eternity, justice gets off the spinning wheel, and eternity expresses a post-justice unity of all things in Brahman.

How is karmic justice administered? Is it automatic, or is it personal? Hindus in the Vedanta tradition believe karma is personally administered by a divine figure named Ishvara. Buddhists and Jains, in contrast, tend to see the law of karma as fixed, mechanistic, and automatic. For Jains, karma consists of a subtle layer of legal dirt that gathers around the human soul, blocking the self's self-transcendence. For a Jain, the pure soul becomes polluted with negative karmas (note the plural). Thoughts as well as actions accumulate multiple karmas that contaminate and imprison the self. Each soul can strive for right thinking and right action, reducing its incarceration and leading eventually to liberation. In this case, karma operates as a self-sustaining mechanism without any need of an external god or goddess to manage it. Whether personally or impersonally administered, the laws of karma are immortal laws that affect us in this life and the next. Justice is immortal, according to Hindus, Buddhists, and Jains. Is justice eternal? Apparently not.

I find the ancient Athenian philosopher Plato to be most helpful in clarifying just how the human psyche works. In *Gorgias,* the philosopher affirms that "communion and friendship and orderliness and temperance and justice bind together heaven and earth and gods and men, and that this universe is therefore called Cosmos or order."[9] The cosmic order is home to ideal justice, to the eternal justice of which our temporal attempts at just living are but short-lived shadows. The just universe provides the blueprint for ordering the soul. All the soul need do is rationally appropriate justice in its own self-formation. Let me emphasize the focal point here: justice

9. Plato, *Gorgias* 508, in *DP*, 1:569.

structures the objective universe. This objective justice can become internalized and can structure the soul through moral reasoning. In other words, the bowl's perimeter forms the center's shape. Now, we are ready for the next step.

Which Is Better: Perpetrating Injustice or Suffering Injustice?

Within the setting of Plato's voice speaking through Socrates, we are asked: Which is better, to perpetrate injustice or to suffer injustice? If you perpetrate injustice, you may become wealthy, powerful, dominant, revered, or glorified. If you suffer injustice, you may become unhealthy, marginalized, despised, imprisoned, or even dead before your time. Which is better? Which is worse? Socrates answers that it is better to be a victim of injustice than to perpetrate it. Of "these two evils, the doing injustice and the suffering injustice . . . we affirm that to do injustice is a greater [evil], and to suffer injustice a lesser evil."[10]

How can he say this? It is obvious that the inflictor of injustice is the one who profits, who wins the spoils of war. It is the thief who takes home the merchandise. It is the conqueror whose name goes down in history. On what grounds does Socrates contend that being the victim is better than victory?

The answer has to do with the formation of the soul. The perpetration of injustice deforms the soul. As a Jain might say, the soul of the unjust person gathers karmic dirt. As Socrates might say, perpetrating injustice estranges or alienates the soul from cosmic order. It is better to face death with one's soul in order than in disorder. The soul deformed by injustice will be unable to find attunement with cosmic order beyond death. It is imperative that one

---

10. Plato, *Gorgias* 509, in *DP*, 1:570.

become justified within this life in order to find unity with what is eternal in the next life.

To suffer injustice is not, by itself, a good thing. Rather, I am speaking of an individual who pursues justice in this life. In the pursuit of justice, his or her soul is formed by this pursuit. He or she becomes a just person. If the just person suffers injustice and dies, a reward—a just reward—awaits him or her on the other side of death. Death provides a moment of judgment, and the just soul passes through the judgment to immortal bliss.

Through the mouth of Socrates, Plato puts it this way: "He who has lived all his life in justice and holiness shall go, when he is dead, to the Islands of the Blessed (to the island of Makarios), and dwell there in perfect happiness out of the reach of evil; but . . . he who has lived unjustly and impiously shall go to the house of vengeance and punishment, which is called Tartarus."[11]

Note that two contrasting principles have been identified. The first is the Thraysymachus Principle: justice is found in the will of the stronger—or, to put it more succinctly, might makes right. In vivid contrast, the second is the Socrates Principle, which holds that justice is the excellence of the soul. In a later chapter, I will engage a third, the Glaucon Principle: it is better to appear just than to actually be just. At this point, I will focus on the Socrates Principle: the excellent or just soul finds eternal life.

Does the Socrates Principle appear in the New Testament? Take a look at 1 Pet. 3:17[12]: "For it is better to suffer for doing good, if suffering should be God's will, than to suffer for doing evil." There are some similarities, but the two ideas are not quite identical. According to the Socrates Principle, the soul is made just by living a just life. According to the New Testament, the soul receives its justice

11. Plato, *Gorgias* 522, in *DP*, 1:583.
12. Unless otherwise noted, all Scripture quotations are from the *New Revised Standard Version*.

as a gift of God's grace, wrought by the work of Jesus Christ. First Peter 3:18: "For Christ also suffered for sins once for all, the righteous for the unrighteous [the just on behalf of the unjust], in order to bring you to God." The justness of Christ becomes a gift of God's grace to the unjust human soul.

In addition, I find it significant that Socrates's name for the paradise beyond the grave, *Makarios*, is the same word Jesus employs in the Sermon on the Mount, which we translate, "blessed." Of course, Jesus spoke Aramaic and the text here is in Greek; nonetheless, it's noteworthy that the writer of the Gospel of Matthew selected this word. Matthew 5:6-9: "Blessed are those who hunger and thirst for righteousness, for they will be filled. Blessed are the merciful, for they will receive mercy. Blessed are the pure in heart, for they will see God. Blessed are the peacemakers, for they will be called children of God." To Greek language readers of Matthew, Jesus' Beatitudes connote life on Plato's island of paradise. That's what it means to be blessed.

Even more fascinating, I think, is the word for "righteousness" in Matt. 5:6—*dikaiosune*. It comes from the root, *diké*, meaning justice, integrity, rule by law, and civic responsibility. It can also be translated as "justification." Those who hunger or thirst for *dikaiosune* are pursuing justice; they are pursuing justification or an exacting of justice in our society. This pursuit is not in vain, says Jesus, and it could apply to one who suffers injustice and dies a victim.

Much more could be said here about Plato and Jesus. However, I will stick to the central point: namely, we live with the intuition that justice is immortal, that justice transcends this life. To die with a just soul means we will enjoy life-beyond-death in a state of blessedness. Our spiritual task in this life, then, becomes the formation of the soul according to the laws of the cosmic order, of the moral universe. The inner temporal self becomes a mirror reflecting the immortal order of the universe.

Such is the picture of reality painted by the fragile soul. The healthy component of this picture is that it includes the soul's love for justice. Still, we must ask: Is this the way reality actually works?

The Soul as a Work of Art

Plato says that the life worth living begins with self-knowledge. Know yourself first (*gnostheauton*). But we need to ask: Is there a self to know? Or do we create the self (or the soul) by constructing it out of justice?

The modern so-called "California Cult of the Self," as outsiders or non-Californians like to call it, ran into this question. The doctrine of self-actualization or self-realization in therapy and New Age spirituality attempted to liberate the authentic self from its imprisonment by the super-ego, from its incarceration by moral rules and regulations. Like a peach, by peeling away the fuzzy skin of social convention and the soft flesh of internalized moral maxims, the authentic self would emerge like the peach's stone. This was the original assumption made during the rise of New Age spirituality in the 1960s and 1970s. However, upon internal examination, the human personality turned out to look more like an onion than a peach. Once the onion's scales (or leaves) are peeled away, nothing remains. An onion is only a configuration of its scales, nothing more. There is no stone-solid self beneath the surface, only layers.

With nothing at the center, what are we to do? Live soulless? Or, could we construct a soul? French philosopher Michel Foucault tried to retrieve Plato's spirituality by developing a plan to "care" for the soul. Caring for the soul creates the soul like an artist creates a work of art. "The principal work of art which one must take care of, the main area to which one must apply aesthetic values, is oneself, one's life, one's existence."[13] Foucault believes that healthy self-care leads to a peaceful disposition, an avoidance of doing harm to others. "If you take proper care of yourself . . . you cannot abuse your power over others."[14] Foucault may be French, but he exhibits the spirit of California.

In contrast to the California mindset, which tries in vain to liberate a nonexistent soul from the external world, I have suggested that what makes us who we are as a self is the tensile interaction of the inner with the outer. The moral universe provides the blueprint for any self-construction or self-formation. According to both Plato and Foucault, the pursuit of self-construction is motivated in large part by our internal love of justice. If we are to build a soul, it should be a just soul. Yet, the critical question must be asked again: Is this the way reality actually works?[15]

Loving Justice

Virtually all people love justice, or at least we say we do. It is difficult to imagine someone admitting privately, let alone publicly, "I love injustice."

In September 2000, an interdenominational group of Jewish scholars composed a brief yet significant document, "*Dabru Emet: A Jewish Statement on Christians and Christianity.*" These scholars attested to a large swath of unity, affirming that Jews and Christians believe in the same God; that both seek authority from the same book; that Christians respect the claim of the Jewish people upon the

---

13. Michel Foucault, "On the Genealogy of Ethics," in *Ethics: Subjectivity and Truth*, vol. 1 of *Essential Works of Foucault 1954–1984*, ed. Paul Rabinow (New York: New Press, 1997), 271.
14. Ibid., 288.
15. No, this is not the way reality really works, at least not reality blessed by divine grace. In the chapters to come, I will examine what this means.

land of Israel; that both revere the moral principles of Torah; that Jews acknowledge Nazism was not a Christian phenomenon; that the irreconcilable difference between Jews and Christians will not be settled until God redeems the entire world as promised in Scripture; that relations with Christians will not weaken Jewish practice; and that Jews and Christians must work together for justice and peace.[16] They invoked justice, along with peace, as transcendent values that facilitate unity between Jews and Christians.

Justice is not something that provides an advantage only for individuals; justice transcends the individual. It belongs to the community and to the universe. For Roman Catholic ethicists, justice also belongs to the common good. Besides the good of the individual, there is the good that is linked to living in society: the *common good*. It is the good of "all of us"—individuals, families, and intermediate groups who together constitute society. According to former Pope Benedict XVI, justice is a good that is sought not for its own sake but for the sake of the people who belong to the social community, for only they can effectively pursue their good within it. To desire the *common good* and strive towards it "*is a requirement of justice and charity.*"[17] Within the framework of the common good, Benedict XVI's successor at the Holy See, Pope Francis, gives priority to the poor among us. "Each individual Christian and every community is called to be an instrument of God for the liberation and promotion of the poor, and for enabling them to be fully a part of society. This demands that we be docile and attentive to the cry of the poor and to come to their aid."[18] Attending to the needs of the poor constitutes the pursuit of justice, of the common good.

---

16. On *Dabru Emet*, see www.westviewpress.com/christianity/injewishterms.
17. Pope Benedict XVI, *Caritas in veritate* [Encyclical on Integral Human Development in Charity and Truth], Vatican Website, June 29, 2009, sec. 7, italics in original; http://www.vatican.va/holy_father/benedict_xvi/encyclicals/documents/hf_ben-xvi_enc_20090629_caritas-in-veritate_en.html.

The common good transcends what we deem to be good for ourselves individually. In the work of Dwight Hopkins, the common good is the priority of the human community over the individual. "Due to Christian beliefs, nature, reason, and justice concerns, we prioritize the selves before the self. The selves, in turn, include the community, communal values, and the common good. . . . So community is a given."[19] Whether the common good is prior or in mutual dialectic with the individual, one can conceive of justice only as communal, only as transcendent to the individual self, yet also formative for the individual self.

The present global situation is a desert to the person who thirsts for justice. Unjust economic structures that oppress the poor or unjust cultural patterns that inflict racial discrimination enrage a passion for revolution. Public discourse that implicitly ridicules certain sexual orientations or dismisses the elderly fuels the fires of discontent and calls for a righting of what is wrong. "Because humans are created in the image of God and have equal dignity, justice requires equal treatment," says Karen Lebacqz.[20] The common good requires a shared commitment to dislodge the bullies and establish a universal justice.

The common good is not limited to only the human sphere. Justice applies to all of creation. On Earth, it includes the animals and the health of the entire biosphere. By coining illuminating vocabulary, environmental ethicists try to draw us into an understanding of the scope of justice. The term *environmental injustice* describes the

18. "Selected Quotes of Pope Francis by Subject," in "Development," United States Conference of Catholic Bishops Website, November 24, 2013, no. 187, http://usccb.org/search.cfm?q=Francis IN 11/24/13.

19. Dwight N. Hopkins, *Being Human: Race, Culture, and Religion* (Minneapolis: Fortress Press, 2005), 116.

20. Karen Lebacqz, "Justice and Biotechnology: Protestant Views," in *The Routledge Companion to Religion and Science,* ed. James W. Haag, Gregory R. Peterson, and Michael L. Spezio (London: Routledge, 2012), 452.

present situation, namely, the unfair distribution of environmental harm and good, especially regarding health. The term *sustainable economics* challenges the market system as such "by making production decisions not on the basis of market or consumer demand, but on the basis of the rate at which resources could be replenished," says Roman Catholic ethicist Celia Deane-Drummond.[21] By putting on our justice-tinted glasses, we are able to see injustice more clearly.

Here, the term *justice* refers to an agenda and a task, which is to overcome the present situation of injustice with an envisioned state of justice. The present state of environmental injustice can be described as a humanly produced state of evil. The term *anthropogenic evil* refers to "evil that arises indirectly through the growth in human populations, industrialization and the economy, leading to the production of pollutant wastes which then have devastating impacts on other species and on human populations through processes such as climate change and habitat destruction."[22] Our ethical task is to overcome anthropogenic evil and to establish a new level of justice: environmental justice. The soul hungry for justice cannot establish justice except in relationship; and in this life, the soul is inextricably related to the neighborhood, the city, the nation, the world, the ecosphere, and even to the cosmic environment.

In addition to spatial relationships, hungering and thirsting after justice includes a temporal dimension that envisions future generations. The common good includes persons yet unborn, to whom we are morally responsible. Projects for integral human development cannot ignore coming generations, contends Benedict XVI, "but need to be *marked by solidarity and inter-generational justice*, while taking into account a variety of contexts: ecological, juridical,

---

21. Celia Deane-Drummond, *Eco-Theology* (London: Darton, Longman, and Todd, 2008), 21.
22. Ibid., 116.

economic, political and cultural."[23] Justice is as immortal as it is universal, the former pope presupposes.

This inherent love of justice can be shared by both religious and post-religious people. Justice speaks up even within the psyche of the atheist. The notorious Oxford pariah, Richard Dawkins, sees himself as a person committed to justice.

> In practice no civilized person uses scripture as ultimate authority for moral reasoning. Instead, we pick and choose the nice bits of scripture (like the Sermon on the Mount) and blithely ignore the nasty bits (like the obligation to stone adulteresses, execute apostates, and punish the grandchildren of offenders). . . . Evidently, we have some alternative source of ultimate moral conviction which overrides scripture when it suits us. That alternative source seems to be some kind of liberal consensus of decency and natural justice . . . And, wherever that liberal consensus comes from, it is available to all of us, whether we are religious or not.[24]

Dawkins can verbally assassinate religion, yet he preserves the life of our shared commitment to justice.

The light I am trying to shed here reveals a decisive point: we live in a world saturated with injustice. We critique existing injustice according to the criterion of justice, which appears to us as an ideal, a dream, a vision, or a goal. In order to walk through the door to God's promised kingdom, we must pass through the judgment in which injustice is replaced by justice. God cannot live in an unjust world; nor can we. The fulfillment God has promised us must necessarily include the purging of injustice. According to black liberation theologian James Cone, "No eschatological perspective is sufficient which does not challenge the present order. If contemplation about the future distorts the present reality of injustice

---

23. *Caritas in veritate*, sec. 48, italics in original.
24. Richard Dawkins, "You Can't Have It Both Ways: Irreconcilable Differences?," *Skeptical Inquirer* 23:4 (July/August 1999): 63.

and reconciles the oppressed to unjust treatment committed against them, then it is unchristian and thus has nothing whatsoever to do with him who came to liberate us."[25] Justice liberates us from injustice.

The phrase I've used here, "loving justice," can mean two things. On the one hand, it refers to our inherent capacity to appreciate what is moral, to our spontaneous grasping of what it means to be fair, and to our desire to exact fairness. On the other hand, "loving justice" can refer to a trait or characteristic of justice. Can justice be loving?

Conclusion

Self-justification is not pure narcissism. The self-justifying soul seeks to conform itself to something that transcends itself, namely, the moral universe. Our love of justice is an authentic love. We love what transcends us. It is the case that we love justice whether we genuinely pursue a just social order or whether we disingenuously pursue our own self-justification. Here is my thesis: the fragile soul attempts to form itself—to justify itself—according to the structure of eternal justice and, thereby, inherit eternal life.

The problem, however, is that to pursue eternal life by following the path of justice is folly. Pursuing justice is a divine vocation, to be sure, but it is not the boat that ferries us to the Isle of the Blessed.

According to this book's theme verse, Rom. 8:33b, "God is the one who justifies" (*theos ho dikaiosune*). God's justification is an action on God's part, an action that results in us receiving justice as a gift. The person of faith is justified by God's grace, which transcends even what we believe is the eternal structure of justice. This justifying work of our gracious God is what provides us with eternal life.

25. James H. Cone, *A Black Theology of Liberation* (Philadelphia: J. B. Lippincott, 1970), 241.

Your or my pursuit of justice in our world is an end in itself, a good in itself. It is not a means to something further. It is not a means to get from temporal living to eternal life.

4

Justice and Our Moral Universe

The soul by nature transcends;
it is oriented away from itself, to what is beyond itself.

–Keith Ward[1]

Like the outer shell of a Kosta Boda bowl, the outer shell of the soul's world is the moral universe. The moral universe is structured according to the principles of justice. We invoke these principles of justice—such as goodness, rightness, fairness, caring, loyalty, authority, and sanctity, when engaging in self-justification. However, we rarely stop to analyze our worldview, which includes our moral universe. We take it for granted, even though without it our very souls would disintegrate into emptiness.

In this chapter, let's continue to savor our love of justice. First, I will cut the justice pie into three large slices: distributive justice, retributive justice, and restorative justice. If we hunger for justice, we need to ask: Which slice will satiate us?

---

1. Keith Ward, *Defending the Soul* (Oxford: Oxford University Press, 1992), 143.

Distributive Justice

Distributive justice is what is assumed when the child exclaims, "That's not fair!" The child wants the same amount of chocolate milk and cookies as a brother or sister gets. An even distribution of goods or opportunities constitutes justice in this sense.

The problem for the mother and father is that they must determine the principle by which the even distribution is to take place. Should the milk and cookies be distributed in equal portion to each child simply because each is an individual? Or should some sort of merit status be invoked, such as giving a larger glass of milk to the taller or older child on the grounds that he or she is the bigger kid? How can a parent avoid the accusation of being unfair? More classically, ethicists ask: How can we treat similar cases similarly? How can we give each person his or her due? Understandably, distributive justice can be puzzling to parents.

Distributive justice is not puzzling to ethicists, however. Harvard philosopher John Rawls constructed his entire theory of justice on the foundation of fairness. Justice *is* fairness. Rawls went on to argue that rational persons willing to take a disinterested position will support or even create institutional life according to the principles that insure fairness. The aim of justice as fairness, Rawls argues, is "the symmetry of everyone's relations to each other."[2]

Fair distribution becomes a bit more complicated, however, when we introduce the exchange of goods. Communative justice—equality and peace in the community—will require fairness in exchange as well as in ownership. We become acutely aware of fairness when we confront injustice sponsored by institutions and systems that are

---

2. John Rawls, *A Theory of Justice* (Cambridge, MA: Belknap Press of Harvard University Press, 1971), 3.

responsible for unfair distribution; in such cases, lopsided wealth is usually gained from unfair exchanges.

Liberation theologians made this conceptual jump from injustice to justice in the 1960s and 1970s when they announced that God has a preferential option for the poor. For his part, the controversial ethicist Charles Curran looks for practical applications of Christian virtues, including the mandate to redistribute the world's resources for the benefit of the poor. "Christian virtues (e.g., mercy, compassion, justice) and Christian values or principles (e.g., preferential option for the poor, the sanctity and dignity of human life) affect quandary ethics."[3]

Attention to economic justice for the poor depends upon a prior vision of God's gift of creation and equal and participatory access to this gift. Uneven distribution of wealth is a sign of injustice, say ethicists. The 1985 *Pastoral Letter on Catholic Social Teaching and the U.S. Economy*, which was drawn up by the National Conference of Catholic Bishops, relies upon three fundamental commitments: (1) fulfilling the basic needs of the poor is the highest priority; (2) increasing participation for the marginalized is a high priority; and (3) investment policies should be directed to benefitting those who are poor or economically insecure. While these are not policies in themselves, they are norms by which policies can be judged.[4] The three commitments function as middle axioms between the ideal of distributive justice and policies to effect communative justice (or social justice). As Karen Lebacqz's interprets it: "Discrepancies of wealth indicate a situation in which some fail to remember that the goods of the earth are given for use by all; such a situation is unjust

---

3. Charles E. Curran, "How Does Christian Ethics Use Its Unique and Distinctive Christian Aspects?," *Journal of the Society of Christian Ethics* 31:2 (Fall/Winter 2011): 27.
4. National Conference of Catholic Bishops, *Pastoral Letter on Catholic Social Teaching and the U.S. Economy*, second draft (October 7, 1985), cited by Karen Lebacqz, *Six Theories of Justice* (Minneapolis: Augsburg, 1986), 73.

because it violates both the social nature of human beings and the purposes for which God gives the riches of the earth."[5] Her thinking begins with the present situation of injustice, invokes the ideal of distributive justice, and then works toward reformative or restorative justice.

Proposed reforms in distribution are not limited to the economic sphere, even though one dare not leave economics out of the equation. Cultural wealth and inclusivity are goods begging for distributive justice. Lutheran ethicist Cynthia Moe-Lobeda tries to uncover and expose the cultural lies that we tell ourselves, such as the self-justifying lies that maintain unfair racial and gender privilege in Western society. She is particularly concerned about the just place of women in society. "Structural violence," which remains invisible under the blanket of cultural lies, "brutalize[s] women," she writes. Structural violence takes the form of "white racism and economic exploitation." Moe-Lobeda advocates truth-telling to expose the misdistribution, followed by steps to right what is wrong. "Therefore, a primary task of Christian faith is truth-telling, seeing clearly what is going on. I refer to this as moral vision. . . . For the church to serve the well-being of women, it must seek to dismantle the white racism and economic exploitation that damage the lives of women the world over."[6] The failure of our society to embody distributive justice sets the stage for the ethical drama played out in the lives of those who love justice.

Loving justice is one thing. Loving those persons who are victims of injustice is another. To love justice per se is to love an ideal, an abstraction. To love persons, some of whom may be victims, is to love the neighbor for the sake of the neighbor. The fragile soul risks

5. Lebacqz, *Six Theories of Justice*, 75.
6. Cynthia Moe-Lobeda, "Being Church as, in, and against White Privilege," in *Transformative Lutheran Theologies*, ed. Mary J. Streufert (Minneapolis: Fortress Press, 2010), 198–99.

loving abstract justice, whereas the robust soul loves the neighbor by pursuing distributive justice. *For the robust soul, justice is the means; the neighbor is the end.*

Retributive Justice

Justice is a serial killer. Yes, you heard me right. The pursuit of justice perpetuates violence.

This will be made clear as we turn to the next slice of the justice pie. *Retributive justice,* commonly known as revenge, is a means for getting even, for balancing crime and punishment. Historically speaking, revenge precedes the more modern principles of retributive justice, which is executed by the state rather than the clan or tribe. Whether we call it revenge or retributive justice, the key principle is to get even. Retribution is the "angry face" of justice as fairness.

To even the scales of justice through revenge is a delusion, but it is a powerful delusion. Recall in Homer's *Iliad* how Achilles becomes enraged at the death of his cousin and friend, Patroclus. Achilles is overcome with "a great frenzy to kill." His killing is justified because he would right the wrong done to Patroclus. "Before Patroclus had met his fate, I was better disposed to spare the life of a Trojan," says Achilles. "But now no Trojan, not one, shall ever escape death when a god delivers him into my hands."[7] The cycle of mutual killing is perpetual. One might achieve retribution, but it is a form of justice without peace. "If our primitive urge to exact revenge overcomes our civilized feelings of restraint," warns Edward Tick, "we descend into the savage."[8] The savage rage for justice leaves death and debris in its spiraling path.

7. Homer, *The Iliad,* trans. by Stephen Mitchell (New York: Free Press, 2011), 21.100–106, p. 338.
8. Edward Tick, *War and the Soul: Healing Our* Nation's *Veterans from Post-traumatic Stress Disorder* (Wheaton: Quest Books, 2005), 90.

Elliot Rodger blazed such a path near the University of California Santa Barbara campus on a Friday evening, May 23, 2014. Nearing the age of twenty-two, Rodger felt ignored and underappreciated by women he wanted to date. Potential girlfriends were failing to appreciate his inner qualities. This frustrated and angered him, and he interpreted his frustration as the fault of the human race. Rodger saw himself as a victim of injustice; and he wanted justice. Consequently, he sought justice by going on a shooting rampage. He began by shooting his roommates at close range, and then he drove through the streets shooting women wherever he saw them. A dozen were wounded, half of whom died from their injuries. The terror ended when Rodger put a bullet in his own brain. In a manifesto he published online announcing his plan to kill, he describes his life as "a story of a war against cruel injustice."[9] Seven people died so that revenge—retributive justice—could be enacted. We love justice, but our deluded visions of justice can be deadly.

Sometimes revenge has rules, and following the rules marks the turn from revenge to retributive justice. The inherited revenge culture of the Pashtun in Pakistan and Afghanistan make this vivid. *Nang* means honor; *badal* refers to the personal code that requires retaliation for an offense against that honor. Bloodshed requires retaliatory bloodshed. Reciprocal revenge establishes the balance of justice. The law of *meerata* requires that some offenses to tribal honor mandate the annihilation of all members of an offending family. Once the death sentence has been carried out and retribution has been completed, the cycle of violence can be concluded with a purification rite. Ideally, at this moment, the victor can establish peace through *melmastia*, a generous spirit of forgiveness. Forgiveness

---

9. Elliot Rodger, "My Twisted World: The Story of Elliot Rodger," *Scribd*, published by Matthew Keys, May 24, 2014; http://www.scribd.com/doc/225960813/Elliot-Rodger-Santa-Barbara-mass-shooting-suspect-My-Twisted-World-manifesto.

becomes available only after retributive justice has been exacted—only after the entire family of the guilty party has been murdered—and only one rival stands victorious.[10] This is how retributive justice is understood in a tribal context or in a Mafia context. In practice, the state of justice is never attained. One more act of revenge seems to be required to end the justification process. And so, the cycle continues unabated. Justice will be achieved only after the next murder...and the next...and the next.

This form of retributive justice is alluded to in Jesus' Sermon on the Mount: an eye for an eye or a tooth for a tooth. The law of the *talio* in the Old Testament is the tribal notion that revenge must be taken for each assault. If you kill my brother, I'll kill yours. Then, in retaliation, you, will kill my cousin. I'll then kill yours. On and on it goes in most cases, retribution without end. Stanford philosopher René Girard describes our incessant drive for retributive justice as a never-ending sequence of crucifixions. "The most humiliated persons, the most crushed, behave in the same fashion as the princes of this world. They howl with the wolves. The more one is crucified, the more one burns to participate in the crucifixion of someone more crucified than oneself."[11] In the name of justice we hunger and thirst after revenge.

In the Hebrew Scriptures, we find a mixed picture of God. On the one hand, God is quite like a tribal leader, taking revenge and recompense on enemies. In Deut. 32:41, God says,

I will take vengeance on my adversaries,

and will repay those who hate me.

---

10. See David Ignatius, *Bloodmoney,* (New York: W. W. Norton & Company, 2012), chap. 21.
11. René Girard, *I See Satan Fall Like Lightening* (Maryknoll, NY: Orbis Books, 2001), 21.

Nahum 1:2 describes the God of Israel this way:

> A jealous and avenging God is the Lord,
>
> > the Lord is avenging and wrathful;
>
> > the Lord takes vengeance on his adversaries
>
> > > and rages against his enemies.

On the other hand, by asking God to take up the task of revenge, retributive justice is removed from the tribe's responsibilities. In the Torah, Lev. 19:18, we find: "You shall not take vengeance or bear a grudge against any of your people, but you shall love your neighbor as yourself: I am the Lord." By assuming the task of retributive justice, God removes the responsibility from his people's shoulders. "Vengeance is mine," says the voice of God in Deut. 32:35. God will assume the responsibility of exacting retributive justice. It appears that God has cut himself a large slice of retributive justice.

At this point, one might object: "Vengeance isn't the same thing as justice, is it? Justice is, er, uh, a principle according to which each person receives what is his or her due. Right?" Right. The principle of revenge expresses a primitive sense of injustice—"That's not fair!" To make things seem fair, each unjust deed is met by a fitting punishment that allegedly renders an unjust situation just. Exacting revenge is the principal means for self-justification. Once I exact punishment, then I will be just, and the unjust situation will be righted. Vengeance is what retributive justice looks like in a tribal setting. A jail sentence is what retributive justice looks like in civil society. The threat of retaliation by America's "might" is what retributive justice looks like in geopolitics.

Historically, revenge belongs to tribal society while justice belongs to civil society. In feuds between families or clans or tribes, retribution is passionate, personal, and never-ending. In civil society—especially in the modern West—the job of retributive justice is taken over by the state, the police force, the courts, and the prison system. Civil justice is rational and impersonal. Once the perpetrator is behind bars, the cycle of revenge is broken. At least, we hope it is. What underlies both tribal revenge and civil processes is the idea that justice is achieved through retribution. No doubt the criminal justice system of the modern state is an improvement over tribal revenge, but the latter has never completely disappeared.

One of the lessons that the human race never seems to learn is that violence, even in the name of retributive justice, reaps only more violence. "Violence never saves, for it only has the power to destroy or prevent something worse. It cannot create life or restore broken relationships," writes Rita Nakashima Brock.[12] Take another bite of the justice pie.

Restorative Justice

Restorative justice, sometimes called *reparative justice,* is the third slice of the justice pie. Its goal is reconciliation, harmony, freedom, and peace. Restorative justice requires distributive justice, to be sure, yet it also seeks to end the spiral of vengeance and violence. Because every act of retribution is an act of violence, even if it is done in the name of what is just, restorative justice seeks to end all violence (including just violence) so that the common good can embrace both freedom and peace.

Once the verdict has been rendered in a criminal case, the needs of the victims and the responsibilities of the offender are brought together. The offender offers an apology, restores stolen property,

12. Rita Nakashima Brock, "The Cross of Resurrection and Communal Redemption," in *Cross Examinations: Readings on the Meaning of the Cross Today,* ed. Marit Trelstad (Minneapolis: Augsburg, 2006), 242.

or performs community service. By recognizing that the victim of a crime is an individual or a community rather than the state, restorative justice requests that the offender take action to repair what had been broken.

When apartheid fell in South Africa in the mid-1990s, the new president, Nelson Mandela, sought restorative justice. Even though the black races and underclasses had suffered injustice for decades under the ruling Afrikaans population, to let loose a spirit of retribution would have led only to chaos and a new chapter in the story of that nation's racial violence. Mandela carefully shepherded a process of reconciliation in which former oppressors and victims could meet in mutual respect and shared responsibility for a cooperative future. The victims took on an active role, and in some cases, they offered forgiveness to the offenders—a forgiveness that replaced retribution. The criteria for retributive justice were trumped by the criteria for restorative justice.

The process of restoration was facilitated by the Promotion of National Unity and Reconciliation Act of 1995, passed by the South African parliament. This led to the Truth and Reconciliation Commission. The challenge was formidable. If you are a Zulu or a Venda, how do you face an Afrikaaner who may have tortured your relatives or murdered your child? Yet, for the sake of national unity, something greater than retributive justice was needed. In many cases, forgiveness trumped revenge. Without public confession and forgiveness, no reconciliation or restoration would have been possible.

Restorative justice makes sense if and only if it is accompanied by a new and more just social order. "A new social order has to be created," writes Ambrose Moyo of Zimbabwe. "There can be no reconciliation without a visible effort to bridge the gap between the impoverished majority and the rich."[13]

New Testament scholar David Brondos comes close to substituting restorative justice for retributive justice. "True justice is not about punishing wrongdoing, as if that in itself set things right and corrected injustice, but about establishing conditions in which all have what they need and can be well and whole," he writes. "We see those who have committed crimes as people who have adopted ways of being and behaving that are destructive and unhealthy and therefore need to be transformed and healed through various forms of attention, support, caring, and guidance."[14] Retributive justice is a serial killer; restorative justice attempts to end the killing sequence.

What this suggests, I think, is that restorative justice must aim at distributive justice while bracketing retributive justice. Retributive justice alone restores nothing. To be sure, we ought not eliminate retributive justice completely, yet restorative justice requires something more. More important than retribution is putting an end to the cycle of violence, an end to what all parties deem to be justified violence. The new social arrangement must be rescued and redeemed from the cycle of revenge, retaliation, punishment, and division. Martin Luther King envisioned a post-racist and harmonious society and asked previous victims to set aside their legitimate yearnings for retribution. "May all who suffer oppression in this world reject the self-defeating method of retaliatory violence and choose the method that seeks to redeem."[15] Restorative justice takes us beyond defeating previous injustice by constructing a new justice; it invites both the oppressed and their oppressors to join the single community of justice. King says that nonviolence "does not seek to defeat or

---

13. Ambrose Moyo, "Reconciliation and Forgiveness in a Unjust Society," in *GG*, 151.

14. David Brondos, "Rethinking Justice and the Gospel of Grace," *Dialog* 52:4 (December 2013): 288.

15. Martin Luther King, "Nonviolence and Racial Justice," in *A Testament of Hope: The Essential Writings of Martin Luther King, Jr.*, ed. James Melvin Washington (New York: Harper & Row, 1986), 9.

humiliate the opponent, but to win his friendship and understanding. . . . The end is redemption and reconciliation. The aftermath of nonviolence is the creation of the beloved community, while the aftermath of violence is tragic bitterness."[16]

Impersonal Justice

The Greeks and Romans personified justice as a goddess: Greece has Dike, and Rome has Justitia. However, when one looks at this goddess in sculpture, two features are immediately striking. First, she is holding a balance. The balance is what Lady Justice uses to calculate justice. On one side is the wrong, and on the other side is the just act that makes the wrong right. To keep both sides equal is the task of justice, especially distributive and retributive justice.

What is also striking is that Lady Justice is wearing a blindfold. She cannot see whether you or I sit on one or the other side of the balance. She is impersonal. By being impersonal, Lady Justice is fair. She does not favor the insider over the outsider, the rich over the poor, a relative over a stranger. We trust Lady Justice more because she's impersonal.

As important as fairness is in distributive and retributive justice, the impersonality of fairness falls short of human fulfillment. Something is missing. Even when justice is best served, it is as cold as steel, as crushing as a steamroller. That is because justice lacks the personal dimension. Our innermost soul wants to be treated personally, caringly, and lovingly. Do we need more than justice?

16. Ibid., 18.

From Justice to Mercy

Yes, we need more than justice. We need mercy. To be treated personally, we need mercy; and we need mercy if restorative justice is going to redeem us from an unjust past.

"Mercy trumps justice. To fully heal the wounds of injustice and to nurture habits of justice, mercy is required," writes ethicist James Gilman.[17] Mercy is an expression of gracious love; and only mercy can render justice personal or restorative. "Mercy constitutes the subjective disposition of which benevolence is the objective, behavioral manifestation."[18] Mercy offers forgiveness, benevolence, and rewards that go well beyond what justice-as-fairness requires. "It is not that justice is a vice; it is indeed a virtue. But just as in poker a Queen—a very good card—is trumped by an Ace, the Ace does not diminish the power of the Queen, it only supersedes it. The benevolence of mercy does not diminish justice, but supersedes it in order to establish and sustain it."[19]

Even if justice is our goal, mercy as benevolence might be needed to attain that goal. Injustice cannot be healed by justice alone. Only mercy can heal. "Liberal justice often cannot of itself overcome injustice and establish the substantive, egalitarian economic outcomes that human dignity and social civility require. A politics of mercy is necessary in order to displace structures and habits of injustice and establish and sustain a dignified, sustainable livelihood [of] all citizens."[20]

Brondos would say it somewhat differently. Rather than mercy trumping justice, he would contend that justice itself is an expression of mercy—that is, a product of grace. "Until we understand and

17. James E. Gilman, *Christian Faith, Justice and a Politics of Mercy: The Benevolent Community* (Lanham, MD: Lexington Books, 2014), 21.
18. Ibid., 136.
19. Ibid., 36.
20. Ibid., 18.

affirm that God's justice is not *opposed* to God's love and grace but is an *expression* of that love and grace, we cannot grasp the gospel."[21] Even granting this, justice as an expression of love and grace is best described as an Ace, not a Queen.

The Liturgy of the Soul

Our moral universe in its immortal form is transcendent to every empirical form we know. The justice of Dike or Justitia transcends what we see balanced on her scale. Our everyday experience is ambiguous—a confusing mixture of the just and the unjust. Only in our minds do we distinguish them. Only in our minds does the simulacrum of transcendent justice shimmer and dance with insubstantial lure. But it can lure our soul only if it is there, only if it is real.

Catherine Pickstock of Cambridge University offers a shocking yet suggestive interpretation of Plato's *Republic* (Plato's ideal city, polis, or state). As I have already noted, the justness of the inner soul and the justness of the state are both measured by a transcendent standard, namely, immortal justice. Yet we must ask: How does either the city or the soul have access to this justice by which both are judged? Pickstock's answer: liturgy. According to the criterion of the cosmic moral order, the embedded liturgy in public festivals orders the individual soul as well as the body politic. "Through the articulations of liturgical enactment the city becomes unified in the manner of a collective higher soul," she writes.[22] Among other things, this implies that to pursue justice we must go beyond philosophy and enter the domain of theology, of doxology, of ritual, of liturgy.

---

21. Brondos, "Rethinking Justice and the Gospel of Grace," 287.
22. Catherine Pickstock, "Justice and Prudence: Principles of Order in the Platonic City," in *The Blackwell Companion to Postmodern Theology,* ed. Graham Ward (Oxford: Blackwell, 2001), 172.

"Liturgy is the secret middle term which binds soul, city, cosmos, and [eternal] Forms."[23]

Those of us who worship in Christian churches are well aware of how the liturgy paints a visual and audible picture of the cosmos by ordering all things in creation toward the God of redeeming grace. The Christian image of the just city is not Plato's Athens; rather, it is the new Jerusalem. Revelation 21:2-4:

> And I saw the holy city, the new Jerusalem, coming down out of heaven from God, prepared as a bride adorned for her husband. And I heard a loud voice from the throne saying,

> "See, the home of God is among mortals.
> He will dwell with them;
> they will be his peoples,
> and God himself will be with them;
> he will wipe every tear from their eyes.
> Death will be no more;
> mourning and crying and pain will be no more,
> for the first things have passed away."

The new Jerusalem—what Jesus calls the "kingdom of God"—stands in judgment against the injustices of every empirical city, state, kingdom, or empire and even of every soul. The prophetic challenge posed by God's transcending justice is iterated dramatically by John Caputo: "The poetics of the kingdom is prophetic—a diction of contradiction and interdiction—that 'calls for' (*prophetein*) the rule of God, calls for things to happen in God's way, not the world's. . . . The whole idea is to speak out in the name of justice, in the name of God, and to call for the coming of the kingdom, to pray and weep for the coming of justice."[24] Within our worship service, our liturgy places

---

23. Ibid., 173.
24. John D. Caputo, "The Poetics of the Impossible and the Kingdom of God," in *Blackwell Companion to Postmodern Theology*, 472.

us momentarily in eternity, in God's kingdom, in the new Jerusalem that has not yet fully descended to Earth from heaven.

To live in the cosmic home of this liturgy is to sense the unity of all things in one moral universe. But it is more than that. We sense that our moral universe is embedded in an even more ultimate and more exalted divine reality. We open our minds in prayer and ask that this sublime reality form our inner soul, that it ready our soul for eternal life.

When we exit the church and walk out into the surrounding world, competing liturgies await us. They ambush us and seduce us with alternative ultimates, alternative moral universes. The ideal liturgies of Plato's republic are replaced in our day by liturgies composed by Thrasymachus—national festivals that trick us into applauding the interest of the stronger or the mere semblance of justice rather than genuine justice. The soul becomes subject to deformation through nationalism, patriotism, jingoism, and militarism, which I will discuss in a later chapter.

Is Justice Immortal?

It is a puzzle of dramatic consequence to ask the question: Does a transcendent order of justice exist by which the human community and the individual soul are judged? Or is this order of justice merely a projection of certain human imaginations and traditions? Should you and I bet our life's meaning on it? Or, by denying it, would we be smarter to surrender to selfish desires and the spirit of our tribal community? For the fragile soul, immortal justice is more real than this temporal life.

During World War II, the Dutch told of a German soldier who was willing to suffer injustice rather than perpetrate injustice. As part of an execution squad, the German soldier was ordered to kill innocent Dutch civilians who had been captured. Before firing commenced, he stepped out of rank and refused to shoot his weapon. He was immediately charged with treason and ordered to stand with the condemned prisoners. He did so and was executed that day along with the other prisoners.[25] He invoked a standard of justice that transcended the spirit of his German military community. This German soldier's faith in a metaphysical standard of justice is worthy of immortal validation. I suspect that Socrates would expect to meet him on the Isle of Makarios.

Transition, Not Yet a Conclusion

Now, you may be asking: Why this discussion of justice? Where is it leading? What's next? Here is my thesis: the fragile soul attempts to form itself—to justify itself—according to the structure of eternal justice and, thereby, inherit eternal life. But where will this thesis take us?

As you can see, I have considerable sympathy for Plato on the matter of eternal justice and the cosmic order. I believe Plato's teachings about justice are wholesome. However, he is absolutely wrong. Forming one's soul according to the model of eternal justice will not justify us, nor will it provide a ticket to eternal life.[26]

---

25. See Lt. Col. Dave Grossman, *On Killing* (New York: Little, Brown, 2009), 227–28.
26. My critical addendum to Plato differs from that of other critics for whom Plato's dualistic metaphysics is unsatisfactory. Most recently, French philosopher Alain Badiou applauds Plato for pursuing transcendent justice but replaces Plato's metaphysics with his own materialistic dialectic. Plato "launched the idea that conducting our lives in the world assumes that some access to the absolute is available to us, not because a veridical God is looming over us (Descartes), nor because we ourselves are the historical figures of the becoming subject of such an Absolute (both Hegel and Heidegger), but because the materiality of which we are composed participates—above and beyond individual corporeality and collective rhetoric—in the construction of eternal truths." *Plato's Republic: A Dialogue in 16 Chapters*, trans. Susan Spitzer (New York: Columbia University Press, 2012), xxxi.

While the moral universe constituted by immortal justice (as pointed to by Plato) is certainly important, our relationship to God is a step or more higher on the ladder of being. At least, it is according to John Wesley and Charles Wesley:

Scarce can our daring thought arise
To thy pavilion in the skies;
Nor can Plato's self declare
The bliss, the joy, the rapture there.[27]

To employ spatial imagery, our relation to the God of Jesus Christ stands above Plato's justified soul.

Plato's view has a second problem. Even though what Plato describes appears wholesome in principle, in daily practice it fails due to the fragility of the soul. It fails because of what happens when we lie to ourselves in the fruitless attempt to patch up the soul's cracks. We lie to ourselves about eternal justice by identifying what should be universal justice with what is particular or tribal; we conflate absolute justice with that which furthers our own interest or that of our community, race, class, or nation. We engage in perpetual self-justification, and in practice, this justification looks more like Thrasymachus or Glaucon than Socrates.

Recall this book's thesis verse: Rom. 8:33b, "God is the one who justifies" (*theos ho dikaiosune*). This verse leads to a correlate thesis: the person of faith is justified by God's grace, which transcends even what we believe is the eternal structure of justice; and this justification by grace in faith is what provides us with eternal life with God. It is God who forms our souls by making the crucified and risen Christ present to our souls. It is Christ's justice that justifies us, not

---

27. John and Charles Wesley, "Eupolis' Hymn to the Creator," in *Hymns and Sacred Poems* (London: Straham, 1739), 1. http://divinity.duke.edu/sites/default/files/documents/cswt/04_Hymns_and_Sacred_Poems_(1739)_mod.pdf.

our conformity to Plato's eternal standard or our successful self-deceptions.

This is my thesis and my correlate thesis. Shall we say antithesis? Or how about a synthesis of the two? Such a synthesis might look like this: the person of faith already justified by Christ's justice pursues justice. The purpose of pursuing justice is not to form one's own soul; rather, it is to establish and protect justice in the world. *Our motive for pursuing justice in our world is not soul-formation; it is love of neighbor.* The pursuit of justice is motivated by love of neighbor. This places the pursuit of justice in the service of love. To love, we now turn.

5

From Justice to Love

Come Lord, stir us up and call us back,
kindle and seize us, our fire and our sweetness.

–Augustine[1]

Charity goes beyond justice, because to love is to give, to offer
what is "mine" to the other; but it never lacks justice, which
prompts us to give the other what is "his," what is due to him by
reason of his being or his acting.

–Pope Benedict XVI[2]

For justice to become personal, it must be loving. Love transcends
and reshapes justice. The mistake made by the fragile soul is the
assumption that justice is ultimate, that justice is eternal. Certainly,

1. Augustine, *Confessions,* trans. Henry Chadwick (Oxford: Oxford University Press, 1991), 8.4.9,
p. 138.
2. Pope Benedict XVI, *Caritate in Veritate* [Encyclical on Integral Human Development in Charity
and Truth], Vatican Website, June 29, 2009, sec. 6, http://www.vatican.va/holy_father/
benedict_xvi/encyclicals/documents/hf_ben-xvi_enc_20090629_caritas-in-veritate_en.html,
(italics in the original)

justice transcends our cultural filters, and it may even be immortal; but ultimate it is not. What is ultimate is God's grace. We know this grace when we experience love.

One of my tasks as a theologian is to pause, reflect, and think through what I am experiencing. The experience of God's love, which is manifested in gifts of grace that we appreciate through faith, is well worth such a pause. "I am reflecting on, and feeling grateful for, the love God has for us," writes Kristin Johnston Largen, editor of *Dialog: A Journal of Theology*. This divine love "inspires and inspires not only the love humans return to God, but also all genuine acts of love in the human community."[3] God's love is what it's all about. Theologically, I will reflect on this divine love at work in the soul and in our relationship to our neighbor.

I have just said that the theologian reflects upon life's experience for the purpose of understanding and even justifying what we believe about our gracious and loving God. Yet our theological and even doctrinal beliefs do more than that. They shape us, just as all beliefs influence us. Believing rightly contributes to living rightly. "Beliefs matter!" trumpets Kenneth Carder. "They shape us."[4] Can we be shaped by our belief that God loves us in a personal way? Might this belief shape our interpretation of justice?

From Justice to Love

When it comes to God's love of the world, more than justice is at stake. We must rely upon God's mercy, love, and grace. The justice for which we hunger and thirst cannot be accomplished through effecting bare justice or naked fairness. It requires justice dressed in forgiveness and grace.

---

3. Kristin Johnston Largen, "The Erotic Passion of God," *Dialog* 49:1 (March 2010): 7.
4. Kenneth Carder, *Living Our Beliefs*, rev. ed. (Nashville: Discipleship Resources, 2009), 35.

In previous chapters, we have seen how the psyche of the fragile soul seeks justice usually through self-justification. In relationship to the soul, justice can look like a chain-link fence. Our justice fences others off; it creates outsiders. Justice may completely surround us, and it may be transparent; but impersonal justice is made of steel, and the gates can be locked shut. Justice by itself is cold and foreboding. This led Reinhold Niebuhr to coin one of his aphorisms: "Any justice which is only justice soon degenerates into something less than justice. It must be saved by something which is more than justice."[5] That "more than" is gracious loving.

Love is *justice plus*, according to Paul Tillich. "Justice as proportional justice cannot fulfill the quest implied in a concrete situation, but love can. . . . For love shows what is just in the concrete situation."[6] Love fulfills justice while softening and applying justice in a relationship of grace.

The question of distributive justice and its relationship to grace is addressed vividly in Jesus' parable of the workers in the vineyard. It is worth our time to recall how this story goes.

In Matt. 20:1-16, we read the following:

> For the kingdom of heaven is like a landowner who went out early in the morning to hire laborers for his vineyard. After agreeing with the laborers for the usual daily wage, he sent them into his vineyard. When he went out about nine o'clock, he saw others standing idle in the marketplace; and he said to them, "You also go into the vineyard, and I will pay you whatever is right." So they went. When he went out again about noon and about three o'clock, he did the same. And about five o'clock he went out and found others standing around; and he said to them, "Why are you standing here idle all day?" They said to him, "Because no one has hired us." He said to them, "You also go into the vineyard." When evening came, the owner of the vineyard said

5. Reinhold Niebuhr, *Moral Man and Immoral Society* (New York: Charles Scribner's Sons, 1931), 258.
6. Paul Tillich, *Love, Power, and Justice* (Oxford: Oxford University Press, 1960), 82.

to his manager, "Call the laborers and give them their pay, beginning with the last and then going to the first." When those hired about five o'clock came, each of them received the usual daily wage. Now when the first came, they thought they would receive more; but each of them also received the usual daily wage. And when they received it, they grumbled against the landowner, saying, "These last worked only one hour, and you have made them equal to us who have borne the burden of the day and the scorching heat." But he replied to one of them, "Friend, I am doing you no wrong; did you not agree with me for the usual daily wage? Take what belongs to you and go; I choose to give to this last the same as I give to you. Am I not allowed to do what I choose with what belongs to me? Or are you envious because I am generous?" So the last will be first, and the first will be last.

What's going on here? Jesus is describing the boss as generous. No one received less than he or she was due. Some received more. No law can fittingly determine whether more is just or not. We might even conclude that more is unjust. Perhaps more accurately, generous giving goes beyond what justice can discern. The grace of the boss exceeds the calculus of the principles of justice.

The globally known musician, Bono, offered some thoughts about justice at the annual presidential prayer breakfast in Washington, DC, in 2006:

Look, whatever thoughts you have about God, who He is or if He exists, most will agree that if there is a God, He has a special place for the poor. In fact, the poor are where God lives . . . But the one thing we can all agree [on], all faiths and ideologies, is that God is with the vulnerable and poor. God is in the slums, in the cardboard boxes where the poor play house . . . God is in the silence of a mother who has infected her child with virus that will end both their lives . . . God is in the cries heard under the rubble of war . . . God is in the debris of wasted opportunity and lives, and God is with us if we are with them . . . And finally, it's not about charity after all, is it? It's about justice.[7]

7. Bono, remarks at the National Prayer Breakfast, February 2, 2006, transcript, *USA Today*, http://usatoday30.usatoday.com/news/washington/2006-02-02-bono-transcript_x.htm.

Bono underlines the presence of God in the lives of the poor and the vulnerable, in the slums, and in the cardboard boxes where homeless people seek shelter. God is present to the silent mother and her infected child. God hears the cries of war victims rising up from beneath the rubble. God's compassionate presence is what Bono thinks about when he uses the word *justice*. Bono's intuition is that care is good and harm is not. This idea of justice entails much more than the image of the blindfolded Dike or Justitia.

Christians often employ concepts such as grace or love or charity at this juncture. Love can deliver more than justice can, according to Niebuhr. "Love is thus the end term of any system of morals. . . . the obligation of life to life is more fully met in love than is possible in any scheme of equity and justice. They are negated because love makes an end of the nicely calculated less and more of structures of justice."[8] Justice has love as its end. Love employs justice for its own end.

Perhaps Bono trumps the term *charity* with *justice*, but Benedict XVI reverses the trump. "*Charity goes beyond justice*, because to love is to give, to offer what is mine to the other; but it never lacks justice, which prompts us to give the other what is his, what is due to him by reason of his being or his acting. I cannot give what is mine to the other, without first giving him what pertains to him in justice. If we love others with charity, then first of all we are just towards them."[9] Which term trumps which matters little. The main point is that the impersonal principles of fairness require a personal and powerful loving presence.

Here, the former pontiff attempts to imbue or enrich impersonal justice with personal concern, with love or charity, and with a

8. Reinhold Niebuhr, *The Nature and Destiny of Man*, Gifford Lectures Series, 2 vols. (New York: Charles Scribner's Sons, 1941), 1:295.
9. *Caritas in veritate*, sec. 6 (italics in the original).

striving for the common good. Applying justice to our global economic situation, he calls for trust. The Holy Father is asking that we embrace trust in our economic dealings, which will raise our society to a new level of justice, to commutative justice.

> In a climate of mutual trust, the *market* is the economic institution that permits encounter between persons, inasmuch as they are economic subjects who make use of contracts to regulate their relations as they exchange goods and services of equivalent value between them, in order to satisfy their needs and desires. The market is subject to the principles of so-called *commutative justice*, which regulates the relations of giving and receiving between parties to a transaction. But the social doctrine of the Church has unceasingly highlighted the importance of *distributive justice* and *social justice* for the market economy, not only because it belongs within a broader social and political context, but also because of the wider network of relations within which it operates. In fact, if the market is governed solely by the principle of the equivalence in value of exchanged goods, it cannot produce the social cohesion that it requires in order to function well. *Without internal forms of solidarity and mutual trust, the market cannot completely fulfill its proper economic function.*[10]

The function of the market is to fulfill justice says the former pope. He is referring to a higher form of justice—reformative justice—that anticipates a society imbued with charity and support for the common good. Structural injustice must be met by social reformation on behalf of a vision of restorative justice.

Similarly, Moe-Lobeda argues that the pursuit of justice is the way love loves, especially in the face of structural evil. "The challenge includes *seeing* systemic evil for what it is and acknowledging it, *resisting* it, and creating more just alternatives," she writes. "Thus, where the neighbor suffers because of injustice, love will not simply bind up the wounds of the suffering. Love will seek to undo the injustice. The response of neighbor-love to slavery was not just to

---

10. Ibid., sec. 35 (italics in the original).

bring relief to individual enslaved people; it was to abolish slavery. In short, *the norm of neighbor-love includes the norm of justice.*"[11] On the one hand, love supersedes justice. On the other hand, justice paves the road love follows.

I would like to conclude this section with an already answered question: Can justice love? Can the pursuit of justice itself become a form of loving? Can the striving for justice effect love in a restorative fashion that transcends justice in its distributive and retributive forms? Yes. This is the goal of what theologians refer to as the political use of the law.

The Political Use of the Law

Distributive and retributive justice are the tools employed by the body politic to express God's love in society and to protect us from damage done by those who are not loving toward their neighbors. Political leaders in a secular society may not acknowledge that they are responsible to God for carrying out their duties, but the truth is, they are.

Martin Luther referred to this responsibility on the part of our leaders and citizens as the political use (*usus politicus*) or civil use (*usus civilis*) of the law. "By means of the political use," writes Bernard Lohse, commenting on Luther's view, "external order on earth is to be maintained, and peace and the securing of justice preserved."[12] Even if formulated in the words of human legislators, this law for our social order comes from God. Justice transcends those who are responsible for establishing and protecting justice. Whether called

---

11. Cynthia D. Moe-Lobeda, *Resisting Structural Evil: Love as Ecological-Economic Vocation* (Minneapolis: Fortress Press, 2013), 176 (italics in the original).
12. Bernard Lohse, *Martin Luther's Theology: Its Historical and Systematic Development,* trans. Roy A. Harrisville (Minneapolis: Fortress Press, 1999), 271.

the first use of the law (by Christians) or *Torah* (by Jews), the task of the law is to create and sustain community under the conditions of peace and justice. Intuitively, we know this, even if our current set of political power mongers are corrupt and unjust.[13]

The laws we live by, whether the Ten Commandments of Moses or the legislation of our government, are positive expressions of a more fundamental natural law. At least, this is what Luther thought. "It is natural to honor God, not steal, not commit adultery, nor bear false witness, not murder; and what Moses commands is nothing new. . . . they [just moral codes] have been implanted in me by nature, and Moses agrees with nature."[14]

Although it may be dimly burning, God has buried the light of natural law within the human conscience. Taking an admittedly minimalist approach, Philip Melanchthon identifies four components to the law of God inborn in us. First, we intuitively hear from within us a voice commanding us to "Worship God!" Second, "since we are born into a life that is social, a shared life," we are prompted to "harm no one but help everyone in kindness." Third, "if it is impossible that absolutely no one be harmed," then we set up a government with police and courts to keep "the number of harmed . . . to a minimum." Fourth, "property shall be divided for the sake of public peace . . . to alleviate the wants of others through contracts."[15] This law is natural, built-in, innate, and universal, according to Melanchthon.

The light of natural law shines dimly, however, leaving much of our civil life in the shadows. Some civic leaders strive for genuine justice, and we should be grateful to them. Yet not all social arrangements conform to what is natural. Consider slavery, for

---

13. See Ted Peters, *God—The World's Future for a Postmodern Era*, 2nd ed. (Minneapolis: Fortress Press, 2000), 282–83.

14. Luther, *How Christians Should Regard Moses*, in *LW* 35:168.

15. Philip Melanchthon, *Loci Communes*, Library of Christian Classics 19 (Louisville: Westminster John Knox, 1969), 52–53.

instance. "What is more foreign to nature than slavery?" asks Melanchthon rhetorically.[16] Although natural law may enlighten the civic mind, any society can elect to live in the shadows rather than the light.

This brings up the issue of relativism. Are the criteria of justice or the standards of right and wrong relative to each particular social context? Yes, this is obviously the case. However, we need to probe further: To what degree do laws differ from cultural context to cultural context? In a radical or moderate way? Most Roman Catholic and Protestant theologians would label the cultural differences as modest, not radical, because each culturally specific moral universe is a variant of a single universal moral universe.

It is widely thought that such relative standards appeal to a more universal and sometimes unformulated intuition regarding moral order. Theologians frequently appeal to the concept of natural law (which is not to be confused with the laws of nature touted by Social Darwinists) to explain this: "I know that some people say the idea of a Law of Nature or decent behavior known to all men is unsound, because different civilizations and different ages have had quite different moralities," says C. S. Lewis pensively. "But this is not true. There have been differences between their moralities, but these have never amounted to anything like a total difference. . . . Men have differed as regards what people you ought to be unselfish to—whether it was only your own family, or your fellow countrymen, or everyone. But they have always agreed that you ought not to put yourself first. Selfishness has never been admired."[17] While each social context will formulate its respective codes for exacting justice or for discriminating right from wrong, beneath

16. Ibid., 53.
17. C. S. Lewis, *Mere Christianity* (New York: Macmillan, 1943), 19.

these particular formulations lies a more fundamental intuition that a trustworthy moral universe exists.

This trustworthy moral universe transcends our world situation today as the future transcends the present. We live in a situation of injustice. Justice requires that we transform present injustice—that we establish a just society for all who live in it. For Dwight Hopkins, it is the pursuit of this justice that makes us human. "I claim that one becomes a human being by gearing all ultimate issues toward compassion for and empowerment of people in structural poverty, working-class folk, and the marginalized."[18] The prow of Hopkins's ship of justice is compassion.

When we move to institutionalize our vision of transcendent justice in any given social context, we must apply the universal to the particular. Legislated laws or policies must be tailor-made for the specific social location in which they govern. They apply to all members of a community, believers and non-believers alike. "Because the civil use [of the law] concerns the relation to the neighbor in ever-changing circumstances," it applies to "all creatures . . . These laws apply to all, but not all phrase it in the same way," writes Vitor Westhelle.[19] The first use of the law maintains a specific community according to a shared moral universe, according to the principles of universal justice specifically applied. We might refer to the process of applying universal justice to the specific community as *communicative reason.* "This communicative reason is what can be exercised across human communities regardless of religious allegiances. And the end of reason is to prevent chaos, produce equity (*Billigkeit*), and bring about civil justice and peace."[20] According to

18. Dwight N. Hopkins, *Being Human: Race, Culture, and Religion* (Minneapolis: Fortress Press, 2005), 7.
19. Vitor Westhelle, *The Church Event* (Minneapolis: Fortress Press, 2010), 70–71.
20. Ibid., 71.

the first use of the law, justice establishes and maintains peaceful community in all of its forms—distributive, retributive, and restorative.

Who belongs to this just and peaceful community? Our families? Our towns? Our nation? The entire human race? The whole biosphere on planet Earth? "There is good warrant for extending the notion of neighbor beyond the human species to all other fellow creatures in the community of creation," writes Elizabeth Johnson.[21] She's right, in my judgment. Our neighbor includes all living things on our planet, even the planet itself. Someday, our neighbor might even include creatures who live beyond the Earth's pull.

In 2013, Marilyn Matevia finished a doctoral dissertation at the Graduate Theological Union in which she proffered a biocentric theory of justice. Her self-assigned task was to include fish in the community of justice. "My primary purpose in this project is to identify an approach to justice that gives meaningful consideration to the needs and interests of other animals when they come into conflict with those of human beings."[22] Because so much of existing justice theory is based on a hypothetical social contract—even Rawls's justice-as-fairness theory is based on a social contract—Matevia observes that we humans have not been able to include non-human life in our community of justice; animals are unable to become parties to a contract. Yet Matevia argues that justice does apply to the non-human sphere—even to fish. What I find admirable here is that Matevia works out of a vision of restorative justice that is motivated by a love for all of God's creatures. Thus, she sets about the creative task of including all animals within our moral universe. Justice here is pressed into the service of loving animals. I suspect that if we

21. Elizabeth A. Johnson, *Ask the Beasts: Darwin and the God of Love* (London: Bloomsbury, 2014), 281.
22. Marilyn Matevia, "Casting a Net: Prospects for a Theory of Justice for All" (unpublished PhD diss., Gradutate Theological Union, Berkeley, CA, 2013).

were to randomly interview fish in the ocean, most would have no knowledge that Marilyn Matevia loves them. Still, this is the first use of God's law at work.

Law provides a handle with which we can get a grip on justice. "Law is concerned with the question of the nature of our humanity," writes Pannenberg, "the fulfillment of which is sought in human life together, whether it is in the framework of an existing society or, in dissatisfaction with that society, in the revolutionary drive toward a new formulation of life in community."[23] Whether preserving the just order of an existing community or envisioning a future community more just, this is the first use of the law at work.

The Beauty of Justice

There is something inherently beautiful about the political use of the law, especially as it pertains to the vision lifted up by restorative justice. Isaiah 9:6-7 offers us a prophetic vision:

> For a child has been born for us,
>
> > a son given to us;
>
> authority rests upon his shoulders;
>
> > and he is named
>
> Wonderful Counselor, Mighty God,
>
> > Everlasting Father, Prince of Peace.
>
> His authority shall grow continually,
>
> > and there shall be endless peace
>
> for the throne of David and his kingdom.

23. Wolfhart Pannenberg, *Ethics,* trans. Keith Crim (Louisville: Westminster, 1981), 39.

He will establish and uphold it

with justice and with righteousness

from this time onward and forevermore.

The zeal of the Lord of hosts will do this.

Isaiah's vision is biocentric in that it includes the animals. As Isa. 11:6 says,

The wolf shall live with the lamb,

the leopard shall lie down with the kid,

the calf and the lion and the fatling together,

and a little child shall lead them.

Although this peaceful and just society will be the gift of a zealous God, it provides the model for all administrators of justice to emulate.

Such a vision exudes aesthetic power. It evokes a dimension of awe, respect, hope, and even reverence. In short, the vision of a just and peaceful world is itself a work of art. It is no accident that Plato considered beauty—along with justice, truth, and goodness—to be eternal. A former friend and Berkeley colleague, the late Alex Garcia-Rivera, believed art by itself can elicit a hope for a transcendental innocence, an eschatological redemption. "Art's true beauty is not simply the pleasure it gives but, insofar as it gives witness to the spiritual struggle to truly see, it also affirms the goodness of our humanity nourishing the hope that someday human evil shall be transcended and 'all tears will be wiped away.'"[24] The overcoming of evil with goodness is a beautiful thing.

---

24. Alijandro Garcia-Rivera, *A Wounded Innocence: Sketches for a Theology of Art* (Collegeville, MN: Liturgical Press, 2003), 53.

The ethicists among us are responsible for drawing middle axioms that connect this beautiful vision of the ideal state of justice with practical policies that can guide us in transforming our present unjust situation. The philosophers among us find this to be a difficult task. In our concrete social locations, we prioritize what counts as fair or just differently. There exists a competing collection of vested interests, and each claims justification by the same or a similar ideal. Nobel Prize-winning economist, Amartya Sen, takes up the ethical and philosophical task by trying to construct a theory of justice that deals with the practical. "Justice-enhancing changes or reforms demand comparative assessments, not simply an immediate identification of '*the*' just society (or 'the just institutions')."[25] Our attempts to transform present unjust social structures so that they better reflect the ideal state of justice requires middle axioms that connect our abstract vision to our practical situation.

However, this is not the point I wish to stress here. Rather, I wish to acknowledge that deep within us a quiet voice lies ready to speak up. That quiet voice is ready to shout, "That's not fair!" When we hear ourselves speaking up in this manner, pause to reflect. Does it arise from an inherent trust we place in our moral universe? Are we answering a call from the transcendent, who asks us to embrace, enhance, and establish justice throughout God's creation?

However, the voice that trumpets, "That's not fair!," is not the only voice that rises up from within. Another can be heard—a sigh too deep for words.

---

25. Amartya Sen, *The Idea of Justice* (Cambridge, MA: Harvard University Press, 2009), 401, italics in original.

Which Comes First: God or Justice?

Let's re-ask Plato's question in the Euthyphro: Which is more ultimate, justice or God? At one level, it hardly makes a difference which one takes priority within our moral universe. On a daily basis, we revere justice when we do God's will. For Mexican liberation theologian Jose Miranda, "to do justice" is interchangeable with "to know God."[26]

Are the two interchangeable? Not for Minjung theologian Kwon Jin-Kwan. "Justice refers to an overarching agreed-upon rule which regulates the relations among social groups and individuals and, according to which a society and country is to be structured," he writes.[27] He then turns to an ontology of justice. "Justice is a temporal but transcendent reality. It must actualize itself here and now, but still it transcends its temporal actualizations expressed in laws, actions, or systems."[28] This makes justice immortal. But is it ultimate? No. God is ultimate. "Finally, justice in ontological conception has its root in the divinity. Justice, peace, and life are in unity because they are rooted in the divine being. The purpose of justice is life and peace."[29] Justice is immortal, to be sure, but justice is the means through which God grants life and peace. When Euthyphro returns from his coffee break, Kwon will tell him that only God is ultimate, not justice.

And I agree; God is prior to justice. Why do I hold this position? Not because God invents justice as an arbitrary product of the divine will. Justice, we trust, is internally coherent and not arbitrary, not reducible to the will of the stronger or even the will of a divine bully. Nor do I prioritize God because this is what we see in the ancient

---

26. Jose Porfirio Miranda, *Marx and the Bible: A Critique of the Philosophy of Oppression* (Maryknoll, NY: Orbis Books, 1974), 45.
27. Kwon Jin-Kwan, "Justice and Subject in Christianity and Buddhism: An Ontological Study," *International Journal of Contextual Theology in East Asia* 19 (June 2013): 44.
28. Ibid., 50.
29. Ibid., 59.

Near East—in Egypt, Mesopotamia, and Israel—where the sun-god or Yahweh dispense justice to maintain tribal or communal loyalty.[30] Nor do I prioritize God because of the divine role in liberating justice in which, according to Yong-Bock Kim, "God is the mediator of justice in favor of the victims. This means that he is the sole cause of justice. His promise represents the victim's hope for justice."[31] These are *not* the reasons I give for subordinating justice to God.

Rather, I give priority to God over justice because of grace. There are moments when God elects to be unjust, when God acts graciously or generously in ways that transcend the requirements of either distributive or retributive justice. God is not bound by the strict requirements of justice. Rather, God's generous grace can trump justice, at least on occasion. Just how grace trumps justice will taken up later.

Right now, I'd like to make a different point. I'd like to draw attention to the fact that we Christians, though heavily influenced by Plato, have taken a step beyond Plato in terms of the relationship between justice and God. The reality of God transcends the reality of justice, even immortal justice.

Recall that, for Plato, the order of justice is external to the individual soul and that the soul incorporates the order of justice through internal reasoning. The reasoning soul copies the moral universe, so to speak, and the just soul is formed by copying external justice. Now, consider this: God is closer to you than you are to yourself. Rather than copying the objective blueprint of the moral universe to form your soul, you turn to the reality beneath and undergirding your soul from within—namely, God.

---

30. Eckart Otto, "Justice and Righteousness: Bible," in *Religion Past and Present*, ed. Hans Dieter Betz, Don S. Browning, Bernd Janowski, and Eberhard Jüngel, 14 vols. (Leiden, Neth.: Brill, 2007–14), 7:106–107.
31. Yong-Bock Kim, "Justice and Righteousness: Missiology," in *RPP*, 7:115.

God as Intimate to the Soul

What do I mean here? Let's begin with St. Paul describing the role of the Holy Spirit in prayer. Romans 8:26: "Likewise the Spirit helps us in our weakness; for we do not know how to pray as we ought, but that very Spirit intercedes with sighs too deep for words." Sighs too deep for words! Paul is not describing a rational appropriation of an external or objective structure of justice. Rather, the Spirit of God speaks from within the soul in sighs too deep for words.

This led St. Augustine to aver that God is closer to us than we are to ourselves. "But you [God] were more inward than my most inward part and higher than the highest element within me" (*interior intimo meo et superior summo meo*).[32] Thomas Aquinas generalizes that God is present "in all things innermostly,"[33] and St. Ignatius Loyola, founder of the Society of Jesus, reflects on God's inner presence. "I will consider how God dwells in creatures; in the elements, giving them existence; in the plants giving them life; in the animals, giving them sensation; in human beings, giving them intelligence; and finally, how in this way he dwells also in myself, giving me existence, life, sensation, and intelligence; and even further, making me his temple, since I am created as a likeness and image of the Divine Majesty. Then . . . I will reflect on myself."[34]

God's spiritual presence resides within us at a level deeper than the soul, let alone the soul's just—or even unjust—form. At this level, divine presence is dressed in love rather than justice. "When it comes to God," writes Taylor commenting on Augustine, "the right measure is to love without measure. So both for better and for worse,

---

32. Augustine, *Confessions* 3.6.11, p. 43.
33. Thomas Aquinas, in *ST,* 1.8.1. Thomas Aquinas, *Summa Theologica* in Christian Classics Ethereal Library, http://www.ccel.org/ccel/aquinas/summa.toc.html
34. Ignatius, *The Spiritual Exercises of Saint Ignatius: A Translation and Commentary*, trans. George E. Ganss, SJ (St. Louis: Loyola Press, 1992), 95.

the will leaps beyond the desire to appropriate to a cosmos ordered for the Good."[35] The loving soul carries and bears and transmits divine love. Copying an external or objective moral universe is superseded, though not obviated, by the living love of the living God in the human soul.

What about transformation? What is the Christian variant of Plato's just soul? Our transformation is due to the work of the Holy Spirit within us. If we return to St. Paul, we'll find a clue. As 1 Thess. 5:23 reads, "May the God of peace himself sanctify you entirely; and may your spirit and soul and body be kept sound and blameless at the coming of our Lord Jesus Christ." Note the threesome: spirit, body, and soul. All three become sanctified by the work of God's Spirit. If we understand a person as body plus soul, then the spirit becomes the transformatory influence.

"For Paul there is no idea of a separation of the soul from the body," comments Troels Engberg-Pedersen. "Instead, Paul prays that the pneuma and soul (*psyche*) and body (*soma*) of each individual believer may be kept blameless in its entirety at the return of Christ."[36] In the person who has not yet received the spirit (*pneuma*), the soul is indissolubly tied to the body, to the flesh (*sarx*). The arrival and influence of the spirit lifts the person—both body and soul—into the image of God, which is the image of the resurrected Christ who is the Son of God. Engberg-Pedersen concludes that "Paul's anthropology is both inherently cosmological and quite simple: body (*soma*) and soul (including [*psyche* or] the *nous*) belong in the earthly sphere and are therefore intrinsically 'sarkic'. . . In believers, body and soul have received an infusion of divine, heavenly pneuma, which has then

35. Charles Taylor, *Sources of the Self: The Making of the Modern Identity* (Cambridge, MA: Harvard University Press, 1989), 139.
36. Troels Engberg-Pedersen, *Cosmology and Self in the Apostle Paul* (Oxford: Oxford University Press, 2010), 103.

begun its transformative work; eventually, this may render both body and soul pneumatic through and through, thereby removing them completely from the earthly spheres of sarx."[37] In sum, the presence of God's Spirit in our personhood transforms us from what is earthly to what is heavenly, from the bonds of death in the flesh to liberation from death's chain, from the temporal to the eternal. That empty vortex at the center of our whirling sarkic life is filled by the presence of the living Christ, placed there by the Holy Spirit.

Allow me to note what is not said here. What is not said is that the soul of believers will be transformed from injustice to justice. What is not touted by Paul is that a just soul on earth receives a ticket for a trip through the doors of judgment to a just heaven. Our thirst for more justice is not quenched by more justice.

What then does our unquenchable thirst for justice tell us about ourselves? What can we learn from our hope that justice will transform our unjust world? This desire from within to become at one with an eternal justice is a divine voice speaking within us. It is the voice of the prophet placed within each conscience by the Holy Spirit. Like a cell phone sounding, it is a divine call to transform not ourselves but our world. Curiously enough, we may have to sin boldly to get the job done.

Conclusion

What I see these days among my Christian friends and colleagues is a passion for justice, a zeal for restorative justice that is frequently called "liberation." Faith is active in love, and I sense that our generation is blessed because of it. This fervor for justice is borne out of compassion for the victims of injustice and an ardor to see things

37. Ibid., 105.

turned rightwise. A prudent strategy requires an analysis of the situation, an identification of the repressive structures, and a practical plan for revolution accompanied by the establishment of enduring just institutions. A key point I wish to stress in this book is that the zeal for restorative justice is healthy when its goal is to make a better life for the victims of injustice; but it is not healthy if we want to identify ourselves with what is just. *The pursuit of justice should serve the benefit of the victims rather than one's own self-constitution as a just person or, worse, the build up the reputation of a liberal instiution.*

Once we look at human behavior through the theologian's lens, we can see through the smokescreen that blinds us to our own behavior. Justice is a serial killer. That's a fact, and it's a fact we try to deny. We would rather declare ourselves just than put an end to killing, whether figuratively (in economic competition) or literally (in warfare). The Christian theologian would like us to see that if we are justified-by-faith, we need not justify ourselves. Therefore, we can put an immediate end to our own participation in the never-ending cycle of human violence.

However, this is a tricky proposition. For my next quest, I will try to unravel the trickiness.

If reality is actually the way Plato describes it, then this is good news. Our internal disposition is to attune ourselves to a moral universe that is organized according to the metaphysical principles of justice—which, we must assume, is true for all persons. In this platonic view, we find the foundations for a liberal doctrine of the human person. According to liberal anthropology, each of us innately loves justice. If we simply liberate our inner love for justice, we will actualize justice and produce both a just soul and a just society. It all seems so easy.

Unless, of course, we lie to ourselves. Unless, of course, the soul is formed by lies instead of truth.

Enter the conscience. The conscience provides the standards of justice and judgment within the psyche. It exerts a powerful influence on the self and the soul. But can we trust our conscience?

6

Consciousness and Conscience

Every day my conscience makes confession,
relying on the hope of your mercy as more
to be trusted than its own innocence.

–Augustine[1]

I enjoy being someone else and then it isn't enjoyable anymore
and I need to be known and that's when I come home.
So my mind can be renewed by what is so familiar,
the old hymns, God watching the sparrows,
the gates of thanksgiving.

–Garrison Keillor[2]

Many of the fragile souls among us who have fled conservative
Christian homes for post-religious spirituality have a similar
complaint: "I didn't like feeling like a worm in church. All this talk

---

1. Augustine, *Confessions,* trans. Henry Chadwick (Oxford: Oxford University Press, 1991), 10.3.3, p. 180.
2. Garrison Keillor, *The Keillor Reader* (New York: Viking, 2014), 90.

about sin and grace made me feel worthless. I need to escape from sin and grace." While getting rid of sin might appeal to many of us, I doubt that we want to eliminate grace.

Spirituality: Can We Scrap Sin and Grace?

Should we scrap all this traditional stuff about sin and grace? Does the inner psyche require it, or can we dispense with it? Might we be spiritually healthier without the dialectic between sin and grace? In the next few paragraphs, I will ask: Who would like to jettison and who would like to keep sin and grace, and why?

If we posed this question to someone who claims membership in the SBNR club ("spiritual but not religious," sometimes called the "seeker" or "spiritually independent" or "post-religious"), the answer would be yes, let's scrap it. To be sure, not every SBNR is a genuine seeker. However, by declaring loudly, "I am spiritual but not religious," a message is sent to those who do not hide their evangelical zeal: "Bug off and leave me alone." Even so, there are genuine seeker SBNRs who object to the traditional concept of sin and proffer a much more affirming anthropology.

For seeker SBNRs, "personal spirituality has to do with cultivating a mystical feel for God's presence in the natural world. What makes a religious idea 'true' is whether it helps individuals become inwardly receptive to what Emerson described as the 'divinity that flows through all things,'" says Robert Fuller. In the SBNR view, the ubiquitous divinity places potential within each of us, and our spiritual task is to actualize this potential. But false ideas get in the way of actualization, especially negatives such as the idea of sin. If we falsely believe ourselves to be born into sin, then this will block, if not repress, one's self-actualization. Therefore, the seeker seeks liberation from this repressive doctrine. "Seekers have new understandings of the self and the self's inner connection with God. In sharp contrast to the belief that humans are born into the condition of sin, they affirm the self's infinite potentials."[3]

Key to the seeker SBNR view is that the divine potential lies within. We seek the transcendent from within and do not search for it beyond ourselves. To subject ourselves to an external authority such as scripture or creed or priesthood would be heteronomous, that is, subordinating the self to a foreign or inauthentic authority. Rather, we should turn to self-expression as the road to self-actualization. If the theologian suggests that we need to *understand*—that is, *stand under*—the message from Scripture that judges us to be sinful, the SBNR dubs this as an impediment to self-realization. The SBNR seeks liberation from the concepts of sin and judgment against sin.[4]

Well, maybe not completely. Seeker SBNR spirituality is not necessarily narcissism. It might better be described as *flow*. The divine flows through us, and we must subordinate the ego to this transcendent flow. "Prayerful intention and focused surrender are ways to create a will beyond ego and a state of flow in our lives," says Michael Murphy, cofounder of the Esalen Institute in Big Sur, California, along with colleagues James Redfield and Sylvia Timbers. The divine energy that flows through us can be described as grace.

3. Robert C. Fuller, *Spiritual but Not Religious* (Oxford: Oxford University Press, 2001), 76. Karl Rahner would encourage SBNRs in their seeking. "Ally yourself with what is genuine, with the challenging, with what demands everything, with the courage to accept the mystery within you. It simply tells us: go on, wherever you may find yourself at this particular moment, follow the light even though it is as yet dim; guard the fire even though it burns low as yet; call out to the mystery precisely because it is incomprehensible. Go, and you will find—hope, and your hope is already blessed interiorly with the grace of fulfillment." Rahner, TI, 5:21.

4. In the late nineteenth century, William James examined the Mind-Cure movement, a forerunner to the late twentieth century New Age movement and its successor, the SBNR subculture. The needs met by the dialectic between sin and grace could be met, said James, by this new spiritual practice. "The mind-curers . . . have demonstrated that a form of regeneration by relaxing, by letting go, psychologically indistinguishable from the Lutheran justification by faith and the Wesleyan acceptance of free grace, is within the reach of persons who have no conviction of sin and care nothing for the Lutheran theology. It is but giving your little private convulsive self a rest, and finding that a greater Self is there." James, VRE, 111.

"'The winds of grace are always blowing,' said the Indian mystic Sri Ramakrishna, 'but to catch them we have to raise our sails.'"[5] Might SBNR spirituality scrap sin but keep grace?

Sin and Grace in Christian Spirituality

What about specifically Christian spirituality? Some might argue that the Wesleyan tradition exemplifies the larger Western or Latin tradition, according to which the dialectic between sin and grace defines the human relationship to God. "The basic Christian confession," writes Wesley scholar Randy Maddox, "is that God has graciously come to fallen humanity, seeking to restore our right standing, our faculties, and our moral character (likeness of God)."[6] It is difficult to conceive of a Christian narrative in which the drama of sin and grace do not constitute the plot. Yet in contemporary spirituality, the matter becomes much more nuanced.

A colleague of mine, Sandra Schneiders, headed the graduate program in spirituality at the Jesuit School of Theology in Berkeley for decades. She defines spirituality in this way: "Spirituality is . . . the experience of conscious involvement in the project of life-integration through self-transcendence toward the ultimate value one perceives."[7] Note a couple of idea here. First, integration. Spirituality is the pursuit of an integrated self, presumably the overcoming of a

---

5. James Redfield, Michael Murphy, and Sylvia Timbers, *God and the Evolving Universe* (New York: Putnam, 2002), 146–47.

6. Randy L. Maddox, *Responsible Grace: John Wesley's Practical Theology* (Nashville: Abingdon Kingswood, 1994), 83.

7. Sandra Schneiders, "Approaches to the Study of Christian Spirituality," in *The Blackwell Companion to Christian Spirituality*, ed. Arthur Holder (Malden, MA: Blackwell, 2011), 16. Spirituality centers and integrates the person. "An 'integrated' life will tend to have 'integrity.' It is this kind of life that can be called complex. Furthermore, a complexified life is characterized by emergence. A person whose energies are organized, whose powers are focused, tends to solve problems and invent novel solutions in vocational pursuits or personal relationships." Carol Rausch Albright, *Growing in the Image of God* (Ottawa, Can.: Novalis, 2002), 60.

scattered or disintegrated self. This will become important later when I discuss moral injury.

The second idea to note is the conflation of "transcendence" with "the ultimate value one perceives," which is confusing. An essential aspect of the concept of transcendence is that, by definition, it transcends what we perceive. To live with consciousness of transcendence is to live in the *metaxy*, the juncture or tension between what we perceive and what lies beyond. The Nicene Creed alludes to this by including both the visible and the invisible—what we perceive and what stands in judgment over what we perceive.

Would Schneiders want to scrap sin and grace? No. Both our sin and God's grace belong within this new and healthy integrated self. Schneiders is a Roman Catholic religious; she is a nun. Yet we can see some overlap between her goal of an integrated self and that of the SBNR to actualize the potential from within.

Let's look at another view. Ann Carr and I were classmates at the University of Chicago. She stayed on as a professor there for a number of years, until her untimely death. Like Schneiders, Carr is a Roman Catholic nun engaged in developing a spirituality that leads to healthy self-integration. "Spirituality today names not only the interior life of Christians, especially the experience of prayer, but also the ways in which the Christian life is outwardly practiced in everyday life. It includes life-styles, attitudes, ideas, values, habits, and activities, images, stories, beliefs, even emotions and bodily expressions that are chosen as appropriate response to God and to the salvation, the life of love and union, that God continually offers."[8] This might be one of the most comprehensive definitions of spirituality I know.

---

8. Ann E. Carr, *Transforming Grace: Christian Tradition and Women's Experience* (New York: Harper, 1988), 201.

Carr concerns herself also with the woman's movement and attends especially to the emerging consciousness of women. "A feminist spirituality would be distinguished as a spiritual orientation that has integrated into itself the central elements of feminist criticism of the patriarchal tradition. It is the spirituality of those who have experienced feminist consciousness raising and so have critical questions about inherited patterns and assumptions about gender differences and the implications of these for social and ecclesial roles and behavior."[9]

Would Ann Carr scrap sin and grace? Not completely. Rather, she presses for a "theological reconstruction" that "begins with criticism of traditional Christian doctrines of sin and grace as cast exclusively in terms of male experience." Regarding the concept of sin specifically, Carr declares that the traditional understanding of sin creates tension within feminist spirituality.

> Feminists point out that the Christian theology of sin as fundamentally pride, overriding self-esteem, or ambition is the result of a totally male-oriented set of reflections. And while this theology may adequately reflect male experience, the experience of women is precisely the opposite. The 'sin' of women would more likely be characterized as a lack of pride, lack of self-esteem, lack of ambition or personal focus. The women's movement has encouraged women to develop these characteristics to offset the triviality, lack of discipline and serious responsibility that have constituted the stereotypes of the female personality.[10]

From this, one might conclude that Christian feminists should scrap the patriarchal concepts of sin and grace that we have inherited in the tradition. However, such a move by feminists would not entirely eliminate the concept of sin; rather, it would revise it. The

9. Ibid., 206.
10. Ibid., 58.

result would be an understanding of sin and grace that incorporates women's distinctive experience.

In the fall of 1979, I invited the late Joseph Sittler to make a presentation to my students at Pacific Lutheran Theological Seminary in Berkeley. I asked him to address the question: What is distinctive about Lutheran spirituality? He opened by saying he didn't think Lutherans were very spiritual. (Joe was a bit of an iconoclast.) This aroused our attention.

Sittler went on to describe the Lutheran commitment to listening to God's Word, to surrendering to the transcendent voice of God. To understand God's Word is to stand under it, to allow ourselves to be guided by it, and to submit to its judgment. He added, "This is why scientific criticism of the Bible grew up within a primarily Lutheran context. We are committed to the truth; and if a scientific (*wissenschaftlich*) critique of Holy Scripture provides greater insight, then we are willing to submit to that." Two generations later Kirsi Stjerna similarly describes Lutheran spirituality as "essentially Word-centered."[11]

This suggests that Lutheran spirituality does not satisfy itself with an internal pondering of God's nature or even the enjoyment of God-consciousness. Rather, spirituality refers to the transformation of our 'dispositions and habits in order to make us better lovers of our neighbors. The experience of God's presence in faith expresses itself in works of love. To a recognizable extent, the spirituality of our daily life is a recapitulation of the life led by Jesus. "What God does in Christ has a shape; it is an entering into human life, a suffering, a dying, a resurrection from the dead. This lived-out structure of the Christ-deed of grace is identical with the lived-out interior drama

---

11. Stjerna, "Luther, Lutherans, and Spirituality," in *Spirituality: Toward a 21st Century Lutheran Understanding,* ed. Kirsi Stjerna and Brooks Schramm (Minneapolis: Lutheran University Press, 2004), 43.

of the life of the believer. Faith is participation, and participation is reenactment, and the stages of the reenactment are the same as the stages of the Act."[12] Because the death and resurrection of Jesus sets the paradigm for the dialectic between sin and grace, spiritual formation includes its recapitulation in us individually and in the church collectively.

Had renowned world religions scholar Huston Smith been on site, he might have agreed with Sittler and Stjerna. "The goal is not altered states but altered traits."[13]

In sum, we can discern multiple answers to the question posed previously: Should we scrap the dialectic between sin and grace? The seeking spirituality of the SBNR would say yes, get rid of sin but keep the grace. Christian feminist spirituality would keep both sin and grace but would revise our understanding to include what is distinctive about women's experience. Finally, Lutheran spirituality (which could include Christian feminist spirituality) would subordinate the soul to the transcendent message that we receive through Scripture, and it would recapitulate in our lives the paradoxical dialectic between sin and grace experienced by Jesus the Christ.

With this discussion of Christian spirituality in mind, I will now turn to an examination of the human conscience. For centuries, Christians have viewed the conscience as the battlefield where sin and grace struggle, where death and life contend in mortal combat, where eternity and time compete for the soul. What could this mean for us today?

---

12. Joseph Sittler, *Essays on Nature and Grace* (Minneapolis: Fortress Press, 1972), 34–35.
13. Huston Smith, *The Way Things Are: Conversations with Huston Smith on the Spiritual Life,* ed. Phil Cousineau (Berkeley: University of California Press, 2003), 97.

Conscience

I like to think of each of us as a whole person. I tend to think that the self or soul connotes the center or core of unique personhood, leaving our more surface traits to be shared with those around us. This idea of a center or core is inextricable from the context of a holistic view of each of us as a person. As a whole, each of us is greater than the sum of the parts of which we are made. My seventh grade science teacher once asked the class: "If we separate out all the chemicals that make up our body, how much would they be worth at the drug store?" He later answered, "$4.75," and we all laughed. We know intuitively that no division into parts can maintain the properties of the whole. A person is more than a mix of chemicals.

The holistic model also includes our temporality. We are who we are over time. We are our narrative, our biography, our story. At any given point in life, we are not yet who we are. Only at life's completion can one's identity be discerned. It is the end that determines the meaning of the whole. When it comes to the promise of eternal life, it is only at our resurrection into God's everlasting kingdom that one's true self and true identity is firmly established. At that point, one's soul will have been formed. The whole of our personhood includes our temporal whole.

With this holistic model in mind, I would like to look at some of the parts of our consciousness.[14] Specifically, I would like to parse the conscience, the will, and the intellect. Carving up consciousness into these slices is unavoidably abstractive, but this exercise will help illuminate some of the dynamics that take place in our interior life.

What is important about the conscience is that it makes the home for welcoming cosmic justice into the soul. The conscience attempts

14. When Luther wrote his commentary on Galatians in 1535, he used the Latin term *conscientia*. Although it looks like it should be translated as "conscience," sometimes it actually means "consciousness." *LW*, 26:10n4. Conscience structures consciousness, at least in part.

to structure itself according to the model of the moral universe within which we live. The conscience internalizes the external standards provided by our concept of what is just, right, and good.[15]

The Conscience and the Moral Universe

Which came first, the moral universe or the conscience? If we quiz the conscience, it will answer: "Why, the moral universe, of course! I simply try to conform to the standards of universal justice. It's my job to establish a just soul that matches the transcendental and eternal standard of what justice requires." Agnostics or nihilists might suggest the reverse: our conscience merely projects its values onto an otherwise amoral universe. Cosmic justice does not exist, but it comforts the fragile-minded among us to think that it does. So goes the projection theory. In what follows, I will begin by accepting as axiomatic what the conscience itself tells us about itself.

Sometimes the conscience sets up a miniature courtroom within the soul. It passes judgment as to whether contemplated actions of the will are right or wrong, and it praises or condemns us after the fact. If our conscience condemns us, we have a bad day. If our conscience praises us, we feel authentic. Guilt results from self-condemnation; joy results from self-authentication. As such, conscience has become "the *measure* of evil in a completely solitary experience," remarks philosopher Paul Ricoeur.[16]

Because the conscience measures evil, we sometimes underestimate the degree of joy that an active conscience can afford us. Revered

15. Our conscience is not merely a subjective projection. Rather, it is produced by transcendental awareness, by the correspondence of our inner conscience with the outer standard set by the moral universe. "The drive to value rewards success in self-transcencence with a happy conscience and saddens failures with an unhappy conscience." Bernard J. F. Lonergan, SJ, *Method in Theology* (New York: Herder and Herder, 1972), 35.

16. Paul Ricoeur, *The Symbolism of Evil* (Boston: Beacon Press, 1967), 104, italics in original.

Jewish theologian Martin Buber relishes the "self-enjoyment of the moral" person. The moral person enjoys a unity he or she shares with a reality that transcends what we call "moral values." Profound morality is a source of happiness because it is grounded in the depth of transcendent reality. "Both the conduct of a man's life and his happiness in their nature transcend the realm of ethics as well as that of self-consciousness. Both are to be understood only from a man's intercourse with God."[17]

Because the conscience attunes itself to the justice that transcends it, the moral life feels like it is in harmony with the divine. "Rain cannot fall without a cloud, and we cannot please God without a good conscience," writes St. Mark the Ascetic, an early-fifth-century hermit.[18] But before we take it for granted that the conscience expresses what is truly God's will, let's look at the matter more closely.

More needs to be parsed here. Note how Martin Buber distinguishes between the moral values we take for granted and the divine that transcends these moral values. God and God's vision of justice transcend our own moral values, yet our adherence to our moral values opens a door to a relationship with the divine that lies beyond these moral values. Genuine harmony comes from "intercourse" between God and the soul.

Two things are happening here. On the one hand, our conscience believes it is grounded in a transcendent source of justice, a standard of judgment that lies beyond our own private wishes and desires. On the other hand, this transcendence may be a delusion. What transcends the self may be less than ultimate; it may be nothing more than the worldview we have inherited from our families or our communities. The conscience may be nothing more than the

---

17. Martin Buber, *Good and Evil* (New York: Charles Scribner's Sons, 1952), 54–55.
18. St. Mark the Ascetic, "On Those Who Think That They Are Made Righteous by Works," in *Phil*, 1:131.

introjection of a super-ego whose standards are dictated by cultural context. If these two observations about the conscience obtain, then the soul confronts a problem. Can the conscience be trusted? The conscience advertises that it is grounded in the standards of justice that transcend us; but might this be false? Might the conscience simply mirror the relative values of our social location? If so, then the conscience is nothing more than a tool for group narcissism.

Conscience and Will

The conscience judges what the will wills. Moral judgment can be rendered prior to a willful act, or it can evaluate an act in retrospect. Within one's consciousness, the conscience evaluates action in dialogue with the will. Following this train of logic, it may feel like we're talking on both ends of the telephone. We are.

The task of our conscience, says Martin Luther, is judgment. For Luther, acts of the will are called "works," and the conscience judges these works. He writes, "Conscience is not the power to do works, but to judge them. The proper work of conscience . . . is to accuse or excuse, to make guilty or guiltless, uncertain or certain. Its purpose is not to do, but to pass judgment on what has been done or should be done, and this judgment makes us stand accused or saved in God's sight."[19] The will, according to Luther, provides the power to act (*virtus operandi*), while the conscience provides the power to judge (*virtus iudicandi*).

Although the power to judge comes from inside us, the criteria for judging comes from beyond us; it comes from what we believe to be cosmic justice or God's will—or the two together. We live in a moral universe. The self or the soul is structured according to the moral

19. Martin Luther, *The Judgment of Martin Luther on Monastic Vows*, in *LW*, 44:298.

universe that, in turn, structures our worldview. The conscience strives to attune the will to a transcendent measure of what is just or right or good.

We sometimes experience this transcendental judgment as a conflict of wills. It's almost as if we have two wills, not one. Augustine attests to this apparent conflict in his *Confessions*. One will is bound, chained, imprisoned; the other will strives for liberation but falls short. The result is a divided self, which means a self in turmoil. "The consequence of a distorted will is passion. By servitude to passion, habit is formed, and habit to which there is no resistance becomes necessity. By these links, as it were, connected one to another (hence my term a chain), a harsh bondage held me under restraint." On the one hand, Augustine felt like his will was in bondage to passion, which was accompanied by a chain of habits that fed this passion. On the other hand, Augustine felt like he had a second will, a will to break the chain and free his self from his habit. "So my two wills, one old, the other new, one carnal, the other spiritual, were in conflict with one another, and their discord robbed my soul of all concentration."[20] This final word, "concentration," suggests an unfulfilled desire for unity of self and singularity of mind—what Kierkegaard calls "purity of heart." I will take this up again when I analyze Jesus' Beatitudes.

Evidently, Augustine's conscience played a filtering role. His conscience judged one will to be imprisoned in sin and the other will to be holy and good in its desire and inclination. The question arises: Does it make sense to speak of two wills? Would it be better to speak of a single bound will struggling to be free? Or might it better to say it is the self or the soul who is striving for liberation from the chained

---

20. Augustine, *Confessions* 8.5.10, p. 140.

will? Do we need the term "will" at all if it is the self-determination of the soul that concerns us here?

Regardless of how we employ our terms, Augustine was experiencing what William James calls the *divided self*. The self (or one's personhood) strives for integration into oneness; thus, the persistence of a divided self creates tension and dis-ease. James describes this experience as "melancholy in the form of self-condemnation and sense of sin."[21] When someone is confident that his or her conscience is grounded in God—in the true good that transcends even justice—then obeying one's conscience provides inner peace and serenity. Few there are among us, however, who find themselves able to obey their conscience and live daily in peace and serenity. Most of us live with fragile souls that we busily patch up with duct tape.

Conscience and Intellect

Now that we can distinguish between the conscience and the will, we must distinguish the conscience from the intellect. The intellect invests itself in constructing ideas regarding the truth of things. The intellect wants to know, and it wants to know only what is true. Like the intellect, the conscience also pursues truth. However, the conscience cannot guarantee the truth deduced by the intellect. Although the conscience can judge between right and wrong, it cannot judge between truth and falsehood. If the intellect commits a person to believing something that is false, the conscience will be subject to corruption and may even mislead the will. If "thinking, mind, and opinion are corrupt, [then] an impure conscience also follows; because as the mind judges, so the conscience dictates."[22]

21. James, *VRE*, 171.
22. Luther, *Lectures on Titus*, in *LW*, 29:47.

Intellectual truth is required for a healthy conscience. If we can take responsibility for forming the conscience, we can ask the intellect to form the conscience according to divine truth, combined with our own sound judgment.

Let me repeat: we can ask the intellect to find the truth. Once we are confident that we have found the truth, we may ask the conscience to bind the will to this truth. We want to form the conscience according to what is both true and good and then will what is both true and good. You may be wondering: Just who is it that is asking this of the intellect, conscience, and will? My answer: the soul. The empty vortex in the middle of life's swirl asking to be filled with what is true, good, and eternal.

Forming the Conscience the Cultural Way

Shin Dong-hyuk is, as of this writing, the only prisoner ever to escape from *Camp 14,* the Kaechon "total control" internment camp in North Korea. This slave labor camp houses prisoners from three generations: grandparents, parents, and their children. All die in camp, usually by age 45, from starvation, illness, torture, or overwork. No prisoner leaves, ever.

Shin was born in the camp in 1982. Camp 14 became his world, his only world. The moral universe of the camp became his moral universe. He had no idea that there might exist alternatives. He believed the world consisted of two classes of persons, slaves and guards. He was a slave. It was his destiny.

When at age fourteen he overheard his mother and older brother plotting an escape, he informed the guards. His mother and brother were taken to the execution lot and shot to death. He felt no remorse. He felt he'd done the moral thing, a justified act according to the moral universe he had come to rely upon growing up in the only world he had ever known. In a "Sixty Minutes" interview for television with Anderson Cooper, Shen provided two reasons for this action: he would be rewarded with a square meal and he would be upholding the moral code of the camp. By acting according to the camp conscience, he became responsible for the death of his own family members.[23]

This took place when he was fourteen. Nine years later, at age twenty-three, he and a friend planned an escape. This older friend had been imprisoned after living in the outside world. He had told Shin about the world outside. Shin began to yearn for this world, a better world. So, he conspired with his new friend to escape.

Tragically, during the escape attempt, his friend was killed, electrocuted by a hot fence. Shin climbed over his friend's dead body, using it as insulation from the electrical charge. Shin alone made it, despite a harrowing ordeal.

After Shin adapted to a new life in South Korea, his values began to change. He heard laughter in a way he'd never heard it before. He saw happy families sharing this laughter. Shin began to revere and respect and appreciate family life. When he reflected on his action back in the camp–the deed that led to the death of his mother and brother–guilt began to grow. According to his new standard, his conscience told him he had done something wrong. His reformed conscience made him aware he'd done something for which he is now sorry. The new worldview of South Korean family life replaced his previous internment camp worldview; and his conscience changed its judgment regarding Shin's action.

This heartbreaking story causes me to think about my own growing up. My home town is Dearborn, Michigan. As a young child I inherited the moral universe shared by my parents, the Ten Commandments, and the culture of Dearborn. This shared moral

23. Sixty Minutes. http://www.cbsnews.com/video/watch/?id=50136263n, accessed 5/20/2013.

universe provided the criteria by which my conscience judged me and others. Once I had left my home town for university life, my worldview changed. So did the direction of my moral compass. The change was not radical, to be sure; but I did sense that I was adopting higher standards of justice that would trump those with which I had grown up. There is nothing unusual about this, of course. Still, it suggests how finite and perspectival our moral universe is likely to be, even if we are hoping that our standards of justice transcend all perspectives.

The conscience exerts a powerful presence within our consciousness. It may seem ultimate. But, the moral universe of the conscience is itself a social construction, a worldview we share in large part with the community that surrounds us. The conscience can become distorted, and if this happens then our soul becomes distorted as well. Deep down we yearn for the confidence that our conscience is aligned with what is eternally just, everlastingly true. Even the most fragile of souls wants to be grounded in truth, ultimate truth. Yet, how can we be sure we can trust the conscience we have?

Forming the Conscience the Roman Catholic Way

Pope Benedict XVI, formerly Joseph Ratzinger, offers a contemporary reading of the conscience quite similar to Luther's. It is important, says the retired pontiff, that the conscience be rooted in the truth, especially divine truth that transcends our consciousness. If the conscience is subservient to our consciousness, then it can be manipulated. If the values and demands of the conscience are the result of subjective projection, then it can only mislead us by providing justification for sinful behavior. The conscience of Nazi functionaries was bound to the standards set by the Fuhrer, Adolf Hitler, thereby providing justification for murder and genocide. The intellect must be grounded in truth so that the conscience can order the soul around the truth. Ratzinger wants us to shun "the justifying power of the erroneous conscience . . . in other words . . . firm, subjective conviction and the lack of doubts and scruples that follow from [the conscience] do not justify man."[24] In short, the conscience depends upon the intellect to ground it in what is true. Otherwise, the conscience will supply a false justification for our willful actions.

What is the transcendent truth on which the conscience should be grounded? The pontiff's answer: the gospel. "This is the real innovation of Christianity: the Logos, the truth in person, is also the atonement, the transforming forgiveness that is above and beyond our capability and incapability."[25] With the gospel as the foundation upon which the truth of the conscience is built, let us ask the Holy Father: Who will do the building? Who will connect the gospel foundation with the need of the intellect to translate transcendent truth into criteria for guiding and judging our daily spiritual practices? His answer: the magisterial office of the Roman Catholic Church. "This means that the Church's magisterium bears the responsibility for correct formation."[26] Obedience to the magisterium

---

24. Joseph Cardinal Ratzinger, *On Conscience* (San Francisco: Ignatius, 1984), 17.

25. Ibid., 40.

26. Ibid., 63. The United States Conference of Catholic Bishops acknowledges two dynamics in the life of the conscience. First, the conscience can be formed, and second, it is the responsibility of church leadership to teach the morality by which our conscience should be formed. In a recent document, "Forming Consciences for Faithful Citizenship: A Call to Political Responsibility from the Catholic Bishops of the United States," we can see how church leaders assume responsibility for the formation of the conscience yet defer from direct intervention in American elections. "We are to teach fundamental moral principles that help Catholics form their consciences correctly, to provide guidance on the moral dimensions of public decisions, and to encourage the faithful to carry out their responsibilities in political life. In fulfilling these responsibilities, the Church's leaders are to avoid endorsing or opposing candidates or telling people how to vote." United States Conference of Catholic Bishops Website, 2007, http://usccb.org/issues-and-action/faithful-citizenship/forming-consciences-for-faithful-citizenship-document.cfm. Most Roman Catholic moral theologians believe that the conscience is the voice of God at work within the human soul; therefore, it is the responsibility of the *magisterium* to form each individual conscience according to the divine will, which is all well and good. However, what is overlooked, in my judgment, is that a well-

(*obsequium religiosum*) produces a conscience guided and judged by the truth that transcends our subjectivity. Apotheosisizing the magisterium may attract the Holy Father, but the very idea strikes fear into the hearts of many of us, Catholics included. Can we trust the moral judgments of the magisterium? No. The magisterium is no more reliable than the generals in charge of Camp 14 or the Sunday school teachers of my Dearborn upbringing.

The problem here is twofold. First, the conscience can be misleading. The conscience can be malformed, erroneous, even dangerous. It may be necessary at times to appeal to a higher standard of morality than the conscience exacts. It may be necessary at times to judge one's conscience by appealing to . . . what? A still higher conscience? Things are getting a bit confusing.

The second problem is that the conscience can crush. For those of us with fragile souls, who try to live according to the dictates of the conscience, we inevitably fall short. We miss the mark. We feel guilty—and dirty and polluted and alienated and estranged. If we believe that the conscience within the soul is the voice of God, then we believe that God is condemning us, damning us in our sin. If the conscience is the sole voice of God, then we are unable to hear the message that God is gracious. *In addition to listening to the voice of the conscience, we need to hear the voice of the gospel.* According to the gospel, God loves us even while our consciences condemn us: "God proves his love for us in that while we still were sinners Christ died for us" (Rom. 5:8). The gospel contravenes the tyranny of the conscience with the announcement of forgiveness, comfort, liberty, and empowerment. Any church teaching that deals with conscience formation without any mention of the gospel risks

---

formed conscience can crush the fragile soul with the burden of guilt. God needs separate access to the human soul, distinguishable from conscience. God needs a way to speak a word of grace, of forgiveness, of comfort. To say it another way, the gospel communicates divine grace in a way that should be distinguished from the conscience.

espousing a judgmental God, a God without grace. This only worsens the tyranny the conscience wreaks.

Let me make the matter plain: never conflate the conscience with the gospel! To make this mistake leaves the fragile soul with no way to experience God's grace.

Forming the Conscience the Methodist Way

For centuries, theologians have felt smugly confident about the precision of their map of the human soul. However, this triple factor interaction—conscience, intellect, and will—is not as neat as it sounds. Ask someone who is engulfed in a spiritual battle. Sometimes spiritual wrestling is like tangling with a tiger. The battle may take place internally, yet the struggle feels brutal and bloody all the same. For his part, John Wesley underwent spiritual bloodletting. He found attending to his soul a return to the battlefield over truth and conscience. "I think, verily, if the Gospel be true, I am safe: for I not only have given, and do give, all my goods to feed the poor; I not only give my body to be burned, drowned, or whatever God shall appoint for me; but I follow after charity . . . I show my faith by my works, by staking my all upon it . . . But in a storm I think, 'What if the Gospel be not true?' Then thou art of all men most foolish. For what hast thou given thy goods, thy ease, thy friends, thy reputation, thy country, thy life?"[27] Is Wesley foolish for having sacrificed so much on account of his belief that the gospel message is true?

For Wesley, the conscience and the will take their lead from the intellect. Only the intellect is responsible for determining whether the gospel message is true or false. When the intellect waffles between truth and untruth, the conscience and the will wait for orders. Wesley

27. John Wesley, "First Methodist 'Class Meeting' Called by That Name," *The Heart of Wesley's Journal,* ed. Robert E. Coleman (New Canaan, CT: Keats, 1979), 29.

instructed his conscience and will to behave as if the gospel message were true. This resulted in the willful performance of good works, which were approved by his conscience. Whatever doubts plagued Wesley's struggling soul were taken up into his faith; as a result, his conscience and his will directed him toward a life of charity and neighbor love.

On a daily basis, faith needs to take doubt up into itself, absorb it, and mold it into something productive. The conscience can condemn us for being foolish or stupid for believing impossible things, for maintaining a religious practice that our secular neighbors have given up because it is allegedly out-of-date, simplistic, or even oppressive. In the twenty-first century, being religious is no longer cool. Expressing faith in God is no longer respected. If we allow our consciences to be formed by faith's critics or secular skeptics, we might condemn ourselves from within. Wesley's example provides a practical way through the conflict: to trust God *as if* the gospel message is true. This leads to a life of compassion, care, and neighbor love. My wager is this: the Holy Spirit will reinforce the joy of such a life, and an internal sense of fulfillment will take over. When in doubt, doubt your doubt and trust the Holy Spirit to take care of the rest.

The God the Conscience Manipulates

Obeying one's conscience tends to produce a feeling of well-being. "The drive to value rewards success in self-transcendence with a happy conscience and saddens failures with an unhappy conscience," writes Bernhard Lonergan.[28] By fulfilling the standards of transcendent justice which the conscience values and prescribes, we

28. Bernard J. F. Lonergan, S.J., *Method in Theology* (New York: Herder and Herder, 1972), 35.

are more likely to have a good day. After all, most of us would rather avoid feelings of guilt and rejoice in the self-satisfaction of living with a clean conscience. But what happens when the standards of justice prescribed by the conscience are too high? What if we can't attain them? One solution might be to ask the intellect to simply lower the standards to a level we can reach. If the god of justice seems too exalted, we could simply redraw our picture of this deity to fit the more modest demands of our revised conscience.

From the point of view of the conscience, cosmic justice and the deity of cosmic justice are the same thing. Whether God obeys the laws of justice or whether God has decreed the laws of justice is immaterial to the conscience. Conformity to the requirements of justice satisfies the conscience, giving it the sense that all is well between the soul and God. This is the good life, the life of joy. A lower level of moral standards combined with a deity who's on our side means that daily life can be guilt free. Or so it seems.

With this in mind, let's ask the theological question: Does the conscience faithfully represent God in the soul? Or does the conscience betray God in the soul? Can we trust the conscience to connect us with the divine? Or should we withhold trust because the conscience constructs an idol to replace the true God?

John Calvin and Martin Luther disagree on the answer. According to Calvin, we can trust that God has placed his revelation within the soul through the conscience. "Conscience refers to God. A good conscience, then, is nothing but inward integrity of heart."[29] In contrast, according to Luther, the conscience manufactures its own divine image, an idol that requires shattering by a revelation from the true God of grace. Who is right, Calvin or Luther? Does the

---

29. John Calvin, *Institutes of the Christian Religion* (1559), ed. John T. McNeill, 2 vols. (Louisville: Westminster John Knox, 1960), 3.19.16; 1:849.

conscience speak for God? Or can the conscience be manipulated to speak for our own designs?

Must we choose, or can we acknowledge both views? I would like to propose a synthesis. While we should certainly thank the conscience for making us aware of the possibility of a transcendent grounding of ultimate reality in divine justice, we must remain suspicious that the conscience may project a misleading image of God that hides the liberating grace of God. We may, on occasion, need to stand up and say: I'm not going to let my conscience bully me! I'm going to sin boldly! But before we continue further down this path, I would like to take a little more time to analyze this question: Can we trust the conscience?

Let's allow the projectionists (or social-constructivists) to influence the discussion. Might we actually project an image of God that conforms to the laws of justice that we want to envision? If cosmic justice is apprehended by the conscience in a subjective or perspectival manner, just as every other scrap of human knowledge, might our working simulacrum of the deity of justice be molded to fit our preferred image? Does the imagination mold and manipulate our mental picture of justice right along with our mental picture of God, and if so, according to what standards? To put it another way, can we trust the conscience?

Buber rightly distinguishes between our moral values and the God who transcends our moral values. But is the conscience always as careful as Buber when making this distinction? Can we trust the conscience to tell the difference?

Perhaps this seems like a ridiculous question. Can I trust my conscience?! After all, my conscience is me! Or is it? Bear with me while I sort out this matter of sin and grace. We've just gotten started.

If we want to paint a mental picture of the deity of justice, what will that deity look like? Obviously, such a deity will look a lot like the justice that frames the picture painted by the conscience. Such a divine figure will promulgate laws that prescribe just behavior and condemn unjust behavior. To conform to such laws constitutes moral behavior, and to disobey these laws constitutes immoral behavior. The conscience knows the difference, and it will remind us with some frequency. The deity of the conscience is a deity that fits within the gears that make the wheels of conscience spin efficiently. From time to time, the intellect must stop to ask: Is this the true God, or is it an idol the conscience has shaped for its own purposes? The fragile soul does not pause to ask such questions, but I will.

At this juncture, recall that the conscience presumes that a deity exists—a deity responsible for cosmic justice. Theologians call this awareness *natural revelation*, and it can arise for any person in any time and place. It is an awareness prompted by the conscience. To become an atheist in our day requires a twisting or reshaping of this inherent awareness. Be that as it may, the conscience believes it is answering a call that comes from the realm of transcendent justice; therefore, it is a small step to affirm the existence of a deity responsible for the laws of justice. The job of the conscience is to form the soul according to the laws of justice and, thereby, enjoy eternal life.

Let us zero in for a moment on the deity that the conscience imagines. The conscience places this deity in its mini-courtroom as judge. The judge pronounces the whole person guilty or innocent. If guilty, we might forfeit eternal life, and such a judgment could ruin an otherwise perfectly nice day.

Luther subjectivized our image of God. According to him, we project the kind of deity we would like to have, or think we ought to have. Therefore, the question becomes: Do we trust in the true God, or do we trust an idol of our own making?

> A "god" is the term for that to which we are to look for all good and in which we are to find refuge in all need. Therefore, to have a god is

nothing else than to trust and believe in that one with your whole heart. As I have often said, it is the trust and faith of the heart alone that make both God and an idol. If your faith and trust are right, then your God is the true one. Conversely, where your trust is false and wrong, there you do not have the true God. For these belong together, faith and God. Anything on which your heart relies and depends, I say, that is really your God.[30]

Calvin thought the same way. "Man's nature . . . is a perpetual factory of idols."[31] The god of the conscience can easily become an idol of our own manufacture. For the fragile soul to develop a healthy faith, this faith must be grounded in the true God, and the conscience must be formed by this truth.

Acknowledging the reformers' recognition of this mechanism in human consciousness, one might surmise that our propensity for idolatry would lead us to project the image of a deity who fulfills our desires. Certainly, we are tempted to pretend that God is a lot like Santa Claus, filling our wish list like a pharmacist fills a prescription. We may be tempted to pretend that God is a sap, too dumb to object to anything we might propose and justify. However, the conscience is tricky. It projects an image of God as judge, God as enforcer of the moral universe. Our functional image of God becomes the conscience writ large. To be sure, the true God is not fooled by our intra-psychic manipulations. In contrast to our image of God, the true God is self-defining. The true God challenges and even judges our image of God as judge.

At a certain level, we intuitively know this, which indicates that not only is the human psyche a bit complicated but it may also deliver mixed messages. What happens so frequently is that the fragile person gives his or her heart to a divine judge, a divine keeper of the law, so to speak. In order to secure entrance into the eternity

30. Luther, *Large Catechism*, BC, 386.
31. Calvin, *Inst.*, 1.11.8.

of a just universe, we imagine God the judge as the gatekeeper. But according to Luther, this risks idolatry. Because humans "had this natural knowledge about God, they conceived vain and wicked thoughts about God apart from and contrary to the Word; they embraced these as the very truth, and on the basis of these they imagined God otherwise than He is by nature."[32] What we get from the divine Word, says Luther, is the announcement that God is gracious. Without this revelation through the Word, the deity we imagine will look like a dispenser of justice, judgment, and condemnation.

Randall Zachman fastidiously studies both Luther and Calvin. He asks about the kind of deity the conscience tries to imagine:

> Of special interest is the god before whom the conscience thinks it stands, because that god turns out to be a portrayal of the conscience to itself and not the God who reveals himself in God's Word. Knowing that there is a god who is to be worshiped, but not knowing *who* this god is or *how* this god is to be worshiped, the conscience portrays a god to itself and invents its own way of worshiping: namely, it sees God as a righteous judge who hates sin but who delights in works of the law. Thus, at the heart of all false knowledge of God . . . is the conscience's attempt to testify to itself about God and its status before God on the basis of what it sees and feels, that is, works of the law.[33]

In sum, the intellect, will, and conscience regularly engage one another in a convoluted conflict over just who God is and how the soul should be formed in concert with God's moral universe. What too frequently gets missed is that the true God is a gracious God.

It appears that in Zachman's account the conscience actively influences the intellect. Rather than the intellect corrupting the conscience, the reverse takes place. In accordance with a motive as

---

32. Luther, *Lectures on Galatians*, in *LW*, 26:400.
33. Randall C. Zachman, *The Assurance of Faith: Conscience in the Theology of Martin Luther and John Calvin* (Minneapolis: Fortress Press, 1993), 20, italics in original.

yet undiscerned, the conscience coerces the intellect into a distorted belief system. Quite specifically, the intellect becomes coerced into believing God to be the author of justice, the formulator of moral laws, the judge over our failure to live in conformity to these laws, and the judge who sentences us to condemnation. In this way, the fragile soul constructs an image of God always ready to smack our fragile selves with a hammer and break us to pieces. The deity constructed by the conscience is not the God of grace revealed in the gospel.

What is even trickier about the god of the fragile soul is that this god can be manipulated. If this is the imaginary deity the heart attaches to, then we have established a mechanism whereby we are granted eternal life as a reward for the good works we perform in our temporal life. If we engage in works of justice and charity and get everything right, then the moral universe is obligated to grant us what we deserve.

At this point, the discussion gets even trickier. Suppose we miss the mark and feel we deserve judgment and condemnation? Do we end up losing our eternal reward? No. But why? Because we lie about it. That is, we self-justify and declare that we are justified whether it's true or not. I will address this near-unconscious phenomenon of self-justification in detail in a future chapter. For the moment, the takeaway point is this: the conscience wants to construct a moral universe in such a way that the soul establishes its own justice through works of justice. Failing this, it lies about it.

We lie not once but twice. The first lie we tell ourselves is that the deity is conflated with our moral universe—that God and justice are the same thing. The second lie the conscience tells us is that we meet the standards, that our intentions are just, and that fairness requires a reward. From time to time, a little voice may whisper that it's all a sham, but we shout down that little voice with self-justifying boasting.

"The religion of the conscience, therefore, is fundamentally a theology of glory," writes Zachman. "The attitude of God toward us may be known directly through the judgment of the conscience: if the conscience condemns, so does God; if the conscience acquits, so does God. . . . If the conscience does feel sin, then one has an angry God who sentences one to death and to eternal damnation . . . the religion of conscience does not lead toward faith in a gracious God, but rather further and further away from it."[34] The god of the conscience looks like a clone of the conscience itself because the conscience manufactured this god.

Suppose that this manufactured image of God as the rewarder for works of justice is inaccurate. Suppose it's distorted. Suppose the true God is different than this image concocted by the conscience to enforce its view of justice.

Luther contends that this image we have of God is a distortion because the true God is gracious. Yes, indeed, the true God is the sponsor of justice and the formulator of moral laws. But in addition, the true God provided a fulfillment of justice in the incarnate form of Jesus Christ. What happens in faith, says Luther, is that the Christ who fulfills the laws of justice is present in, with, and under the person of faith. The result is our liberation. The product is our joy in the moral life, a moral life fulfilled by God in Christ. Faith reorients the conscience. Instead of judgment rendered against the

34. Ibid., 36–37. "Luther understands all idolatry to be based in the phenomenon of the conscience, whereby the conscience imagines God to be a judge who is only gracious toward those who are aware of their righteousness. Calvin, in contrast, holds that the conscience is the sense of divinity within all people, which leads all to seek the knowledge of God from creation. Idolatry for Calvin is derived both from the sense of divinity in the conscience, and from the taste of divinity that is derived from the awareness of the powers of God in creation and distorted by blindness and ingratitude, leading to the formulation for carnal conceptions of God" (ibid., 244).

will's failures, judgment is rendered on Christ's innocence: Christ's innocence becomes our innocence. "It is in this way that conscience discerns and judges between Christ's works and its own. It embraces the works of Christ and speaks in this way: Through these works shall I be justified, through them saved, through them set free from all sin and evil."[35]

The Logic of the Conscience

At the suggestion of Luther plus Zachman interpreting Luther, let's track the logic of the conscience according to the structure of a syllogism.[36] A moral syllogism begins with a major premise that is generally accepted and that seems undisputable. For example, the cosmos is structured according to the principles of justice for us to obey. In a later chapter that deals with the broken soul, we will see examples of persons suffering from moral injury who would not accept this major premise. Still, this major premise is essential for the fragile soul and perhaps for the rest of us as well.

The major premise is general and universal. It is followed by a minor premise, which is much more specific in scope. This, in turn, is followed by a conclusion regarding one's moral status within a universe grounded in justice. An example follows:

Major premise: Eternal reality is grounded in transcendental justice.

Minor premise: x is a just work.

Conclusion: If I perform x, then I am justified, and I am in harmony with eternal reality.

Here's another:

Major premise: God promulgates just laws.

35. Luther, *The Judgment of Martin Luther on Monastic Vows*, 1521, *LW*, 44:299.
36. Luther, *Commentary on Titus 1-3*, *LW*, 29:47; Zachman, *Assurance of Faith*, 24–25.

Minor premise: x constitutes obedience to God's laws.

Conclusion: If I perform *x*, then I am justified, and I am in harmony with God.

This is quite simple. Even the least-developed conscience can handle such logic. However, a challenge arises at the point in the conclusion where you or I say, "if I perform *x*." Suppose you or I miss the mark and fail to perform? Then what? One of two things will likely happen. First, the fragile soul will simply lie and say that, in fact, "I did perform *x*." Second, the broken soul, who is unable to lie about his or her failure, will deny the major premise.

What Luther and Calvin wish to press upon us is the revelation in Christ that God is gracious. In the case of the conscience's syllogism, it means that we are accepted by God even if we fall short of performing *x*. Because Christ performed *x*, we are justified on his account and not on our own account. That's how grace saves, according to Reformation theologians such as Luther and Calvin. Faith, in this case, consists of trusting the God of grace plus, out of gratitude for the gift of grace, expressing this gratitude in works of justice and love toward our neighbor.

The Catholic Critique of the Lutheran Conscience

Some Roman Catholics do not describe the interior life in these Reformation terms. Consciousness works differently, they say, and the goals of a healthy spirituality must be formulated differently. Their point is this: we don't want to borrow the justice and charity incarnate in Jesus Christ; we want each soul to be so transformed that we embody justice and charity ourselves. Rather than a justification before God that is granted externally by Christ, Roman Catholic spirituality comprises a transformation of the interior life by which we ourselves become just.

"It is all the more important to recall the necessity and the true nature of the interior life, because . . . it is evident that the notion of the interior life is radically corrupted in the Lutheran theory of justification or conversion," argues Reginald Garrigou-Lagrange.

> Luther erred fundamentally, therefore, when he tried to explain justification, not by the infusion of a grace and charity which remit sin, but merely by faith in Christ, without works and without love; making it consist simply in the extrinsic imputation of the merits of Christ, an imputation which covers sins without destroying them, and thus leaves the sinner in his filth and corruption. According to his view there was no regeneration of the will by the supernatural love of God and men....Faith and the extrinsic imputation of the justice of Christ are not sufficient for the justification or conversion of the sinner. He must be willing, in addition, to observe the commandments, above all the two great commandments of the love of God and the love of one's neighbor.[37]

According to Garrigou-Lagrange, the Lutheran view is corrupt. What does an uncorrupted Roman Catholic spirituality look like? It emphasizes interior ownership of the renewed heart, the infusion and possession of divine justice and love.

> We may here emphasize a fundamental truth of the Christian spiritual life, or of Christian mysticism, which has always been taught by the Catholic Church. . . . In the first place it is clear that according to the Scriptures the justification or conversion of the sinner does not merely cover his sins as with a mantle; it blots them out by the infusion of a new life. "Have mercy on me, O God, according to thy great mercy," so the Psalmist implores; "and according to the multitude of thy tender mercies blot out my iniquity. Wash me yet more from my iniquity and cleanse me from my sin. . . . Thou shalt sprinkle me with hyssop and I shall be cleansed; thou shalt wash me and I shall be made whiter than

---

37. Reginald Garrigou-Lagrange, *The Three Ways of the Spiritual Life*, "The Importance of True Conversion," http://www.ourladyswarriors.org/saints/3ways.htm#principle of the interior life.

snow. . . . Blot out all my iniquities. Create a clean heart in me, O God; and renew a right spirit within my bowels. Cast me not away from thy face, and take not thy holy spirit from me. Restore unto me the joy of thy salvation, and strengthen me with a perfect spirit."[38]

Like Plato, this Roman Catholic form of spirituality strives to form the soul according to the pattern of divine justice.

The Lutheran response, as we will see in later chapters, is to distinguish while affirming both passive justification and active sanctification, both faith and love. Passively, justification is a gift of divine grace that is received by the sinner. Actively, the justified sinner spontaneously pursues a life of neighbor love, being transformed from a selfish self into a self-giving self. Despite what critics think, Lutherans believe that they affirm a robust and joy-filled life with God.

Conclusion

Should we scrap the dialectic between sin and grace? By no means. Without this dialectic, we could not follow the path to deeper self-understanding. We would be left to the mercy of our moral universe, to the tyranny of our conscience.

Can we trust the conscience? No. We need to keep a suspicious eye on the conscience for three reasons. First, the moral universe within which the conscience places us might be too small. It might be limited to the worldview of our social location, our tribe, our own self-interest. Our moral universe might appear to be *the* universe, but when subjected to critical analysis, it will be shown to be a mere projection of the interests of those living in our community context.

---

38. Ibid., "The Principle of the Interior Life."

The moral universe sponsored by the conscience may need to be judged by a criterion of justice that transcends it.

Second, when we judge the moral universe (propped up by the conscience) according to a level of justice that transcends it, that standard of justice may also need a similar critique. Searching for justice is like searching for light from within a lacquered set of Russian nesting dolls. We begin inside a small one. After we open it, we find ourselves inside the next larger one. After we open that figure, we find a still larger one. And so on. At what point will the final figure be opened so that the light of eternal justice shines without shadow? One figure transcends another, on and on. We can aspire to the final transcendental level, but few, if any of us, ever open that last figure and live in the shadowless light of pure justice.

Third, the comprehensive way in which the conscience spreads the horizon of our moral universe hides a truth, a truth about God. God is not co-extensive with our moral universe or even co-terminus with metaphysical justice. God is gracious. God is present to us in ways that cannot be accounted for by a justice calculus. If we rely too exhaustively on our justice calculus, our eyes will not be turned to see God when God is present.

While it may seem like we're working with two or three (or more) consciences, we are not. There is only one conscience, and when we need to judge the conscience, it is the intellect we call on and not a second conscience. A telescoping of consciences would only perpetuate the problem of rendering moral judgments at each stage of worldview construction. If we call upon the intellect to put the conscience in perspective, this does not amount to a moral denunciation of the conscience. Rather, it places the conscience in context so that we can understand ourselves more clearly. I am not asking for another moral self-judgment; I'm asking for a deeper self-understanding. A better self-understanding is worth a great deal, I think.

Without this deeper self-understanding, we will be left to the mercies of self-justification. Conscience kills. Conscience threatens to kill us internally with guilt. To avoid death by guilt, we employ the conscience to justify us. As a result, the conscience turns outward and kills others. The conscience will not rest until someone dies.

Self-justification leads to violence against others. In the very act of attempting to come close to final and eternal justice, we wreak havoc and destruction. The cold truth we need to understand is this: our virtues produce as much evil as our vices do. The contrast between self-justification and justification by God's grace becomes invisible when we invest in the former.

As the fragile soul works to patch up threatening cracks, it selects among three alternatives: (1) duct-taping the cracks with self-justification and violence, (2) duct-taping the cracks while climbing a spiritual ladder, or (3) taking the victory lap of the robust soul. In the next chapter, we will look at the most common form of spiritual duct-taping: the dynamics of self-justification in soul and society.

7

Self-Justification

The world stubbornly insists upon being right.
—Martin Luther[1]

Self-justification is more powerful and more dangerous than the explicit lie. It allows people to convince themselves that what they did was the best thing they could have done.
—Carol Tavris and Elliot Aronson[2]

The fragile souls among us want to be right, absolutely right. We want our lives to conform to the eternal criterion of justice, goodness, and rightness because we mistakenly think that we can beat death. God forbid if anyone gets in our way of obtaining eternal life through self-justification! We will decimate and obliterate everyone who obstructs our way. Of course, this is the implicit lie we tell

---

1. Luther, *The Sermon on the Mount*, LW, 26:16.
2. Carol Tavris and Elliot Aronson, *Mistakes Were Made, But Not By Me* (New York: Harcourt, 2007), 4.

ourselves, but it is human nature to live in this lie. Just how do we construct this lie?

Death and Eternal Justice

We are aware that we are going to die. When we die, we will pass from being into nonbeing. Needless to say, our life on this earth is short. There was a time before we were born, and there will be a time after we are gone. We might wish we could be eternal, but we know this is not realistic.

Is the good eternal? To ask it another way, is the moral universe eternal? After all, we were born into a world with moral standards. Our parents told us the difference between right and wrong. Where did they learn this? From their parents? Where did our grandparents learn this? From Moses and the Ten Commandments? The Ten Commandments came from God, correct? And God is eternal, right?

Plato tells us what our intuition tells us: the good, the true, and the beautiful are eternal, and so is justice. Good things we know on earth are partial embodiments of the eternal good. Eternal beauty bleeds through an awe-inspiring sunset or work of fine art. Partial truths can be measured according to an elusive standard of absolute truth, and the injustices in our world are judged according to a transcendental standard of universal justice. Justice will be the measurer of injustice in all times and all places because justice is eternal and injustice is temporal.

Is this line of reasoning valid There are some who doubt it. The SBNRs object to organized religion, as I have mentioned. The popular word *spiritual* now refers to "both a critique of institutional religion and a longing for meaningful connection," observes Diana Butler Bass.[3] Curiously, this judgment against organized religion seems justified by our appeal to a higher and more inclusive standard of justice, a standard allegedly higher than religious people themselves practice. A SBNR would say that because religious dogmatists mistake their own partial truths for the whole truth, they perpetrate injustice. According to critics of institutional religion, traditional dogmatic exclusivity leads religious people to heresy trials, witch hunts, and even war against infidels. Partial truths mistaken for whole truths lead to violence and bloodshed. Secularists, along with SBNRs, feel they need to take a stand against religious dogmatism and bigotry. If the secularist and the SBNR appeal to eternal justice, they believe they are appealing to an eternal criterion that measures the injustice of a temporal religion. What is universally right judges a perspectival wrong. What is inclusive judges what is exclusive. What is big judges what is small. [4] In sum, SBNRs think of themselves as morally superior to the organized religion they have left behind. All of us, regardless of our religious affiliation, want to deem ourselves

---

3. Diana Butler Bass, *Christianity after Religion* (New York: Harper, 2013), 68.

4. Jürgen Habermas relegates religious worldviews to a premodern age of metaphysical thinking, which has been replaced by the postmetaphysical and practical thinking of the modern secular state. Practical reason now grounds universal justice and universal morality, he contends. This implies that even the SBNR perspective would need to be subordinated to that of the secular state on the grounds that SBNRism remains metaphysical and perspectival. Norms are to be set by secular forces, not religious forces, and religious perspectives will be internally better off if they conform. "Instead of grudging accommodation to externally imposed constraints, the content of religion must open itself up to the normatively grounded expectation that it should recognize for reasons of its own the neutrality of the state towards worldviews, the equal freedom of all religious communities, and the independence of the institutionalized sciences." Habermas, "An Awareness of What Is Missing," in *An Awareness of What Is Missing: Faith and Reason in a Post-Secular Age,* by Jürgen Habermas, Michael Reder, Josef Schmidt, Norbert Brieskorn, and Friedo Ricken, trans. Ciaran Cronin (Cambridge, UK: Polity, 2010), 21. If we describe the current situation in terms of a telescoping of inclusivity, traditional religions would be the most exclusive and the smallest; SBNRism would constitute the more inclusive next perspective; and the worldview-neutral postmetaphysical reason of the secular state could claim to be the most inclusive of all. It's time for the secular state to plant the flag of epistemological and moral hegemony! As we will see in later discussions, the secular state is not above making appeals to metaphysical and even religious justifications for perpetrating jingoism, war, and genocide. The secular state, with its allegedly practical reasoning, is quite capable of stealing religious symbols to justify its secular identity and aggression. Despite Habermas's attribution of practical reason to the state, the secular state remains one spiritual force among others. Honest analysis is obligated to point this out.

morally superior. We want to identify with eternal goodness or eternal justice or eternal rightness, whether we say so or not.

Philosophers such as Plato and theologians such as Augustine tell us that the good is, in fact, eternal. And we believe it. That this sense of eternity belongs to human intuition is exemplified in common parlance as well as philosophy. "Diamonds are forever," we are told in jewelry stores. One of the most frequent words that appear on body tattoos is "forever." America, said Abraham Lincoln, should "never perish" from the Earth. Players remembered in the Baseball Hall of Fame are sometimes dubbed "immortal," and one or another will be said to be the "greatest of all time." Theologian Derek Nelson quips that all too often "we crave the steak of eternity, but satisfy our hunger with the SPAM of the temporal."

At this point, I want to dwell less on the eternity of the good and instead emphasize the magnetic draw the good places on the psyche. We daily draw a line between good and evil, and we place ourselves on the good side of the line.[5] When religious people draw a line between good and evil, they place themselves on the good side of the line and place the SBNRs on the evil side. When SBNRs draw a line between good and evil, they place themselves on the good side and place the religious zealots on the evil side. Almost without exception, we all like to place ourselves on the good side of any line that gets drawn.

I dub this *self-justification*. Whether we call it *rationalization* or *justification*, it consists of making a sow's ear look like a silk purse. "The roots of evil thoughts are the obvious vices," says St. Mark the Ascetic in antiquity, "which we keep trying to justify in our words

---

5. I have been developing this description of human nature—drawing the line between good and evil and placing oneself on the good side—since publishing my book, *Sin: Radical Evil in Soul and Society*, in 1994. It helps illuminate theological anthropology. See Derek R. Nelson, *Sin: A Guide for the Perplexed* (London: T&T Clark, 2011), 71–72.

and deeds."[6] Or, according to a contemporary secular rendering, "As fallible human beings, all of us share the impulse to justify ourselves and avoid taking responsibility for any actions that turn out to be harmful, immoral, or stupid. . . . Most people, when directly confronted by evidence that they are wrong, do not change their point of view or course of action but justify it even more tenaciously. Even irrefutable evidence is rarely enough to pierce the mental armor of self-justification."[7] Self-justification belongs to human nature. Now, we ask: how serious are we human beings about self-justification? On the surface, it may appear that we justify ourselves only because we want others to think highly of us. In Plato's *Republic,* Glaucon goes so far as to assert that it is more important to appear to be a just person than to actually be a just person. We "ought to seem only, and not to be, just."[8] As I pointed out in chapter 3, we might call this the Glaucon Principle.

Three Platonic options of understanding justice now stand before us, each of which suggests a different route for our self-justification to take. First, the Thraysymachus Principle: justice is found in the will of the stronger, or in other words, might makes right. Second, the Glaucon Principle: it is better to appear just than to actually be just. Third, the Socrates Principle: justice is the excellence of the soul. Intuitively, we tend to believe that the Socrates Principle will eternalize us, or at least make us immortal.

The Glaucon and Thraysymachus Principles account for some of our behavior, to be sure. Yet I believe the primary motive for self-justification is intuitively rooted in something deeper. The Socrates

6. St. Mark the Ascetic, "On Those Who Think That They Are Made Righteous by Works," in *The Philokalia,* comp. St. Nikodimos of the Holy Mountain and St. Makarios of Corinth, trans. and ed. G. E. H. Palmer, Philip Sherrard, and Kallistos Ware, 4 vols. (London: Faber & Faber, 1979–95), 1:135.

7. Tavris and Aronson, *Mistakes Were Made,* 2.

8. Plato, *Republic* 2.362s, *DP,* 1:625. Jonathan Haidt employs the term "Glaucon Principle" in *The Righteous Mind* (New York: Vintage, 2012).

Principle is concerned with what we deem immortal, perhaps even eternal. As Socrates suggests, within us we feel a strong impulse to pursue authentic justice; but, if we fall short of authentic justice, then a delusion will suffice. With Glaucon's approval, we declare ourselves just by identifying ourselves with eternal justice and letting everyone else know about it. We persuade ourselves right along with others that metaphysical justice already dwells within our soul. It would be intolerable for us to think of ourselves as unjust or immoral, and hence temporal or passing. The good justifies us. The good eternalizes us. Well, at least we think so.

Self-Justification in Common Parlance

If we attune our ears, we can hear self-justifying rhetoric every day. We hear it among our friends, our families, and even when we talk to ourselves. Figuratively speaking, it consists of drawing a line between good and evil and placing ourselves on the good side of the line.

While jogging one day at a local community college track, my attention was drawn to squealing tires on asphalt. I looked up just in time to see the front bumper of a school bus hit a pedestrian, catapulting the woman a dozen feet where she landed in a heap. I raced to the scene of the accident, but before I got there, the bus driver opened the bus door and stepped out onto the street. The driver hollered, "It's not my fault! She stepped right out in front of me!" Along with other onlookers, I ignored the driver and moved toward the injured woman. As it turned out, she had suffered broken legs but nothing life threatening.

When I reconstruct what I heard the bus driver say, I think her logic goes something like this: "There is a line between good and evil. Good people remain on the curb to let traffic pass, whereas bad people step in front of oncoming traffic. The pedestrian walked in front of my bus, and this placed her on the evil side of the line. I am an innocent bus driver; and I did jam on the breaks in an attempt to prevent injury. However, despite this pedestrian's injury, I am right and she is wrong." Not only was the bus driver trying to convince us of her innocence, she was trying to convince herself as well—or so it seems to me. What impels a person to self-justify in this way?

I would like to offer another observation. To the onlookers, it seemed like the bus driver was much more concerned about self-justification than the possible suffering of the woman lying in the street. Self-justification is a form of spiritual duct tape. It prevents the fragile soul from breaking while it hangs out an emotional "No Trespassing" sign.

Hitting a pedestrian with a bus is an accident, even if the driver feels justified. What if we purposefully intend to inflict harm? What if we intend to actually kill another person? Can deliberate killing be justified? Indirectly, everyday gossip provides a verbal and virtual form of murder because gossip frequently includes a kind of cursing that justifies murder.

Self-Justification in Military Parlance

Everyday gossip is a form of self-justification that seems quite innocent. It tickles, says Luther: "Everyone enjoys hearing and telling the worst about his neighbor and it tickles him to see a fault in someone else."[9] But let's look at gossip a bit more closely. Gossip is a form of verbal assassination. On some occasions, it readies us for actual assassination, and in political and military parlance, gossip can become deadly.

---

9. Luther, *Sermon on the Mount*, in *LW*, 21:41.

The average citizen does not want to kill another person. Most days, it is easy to obey the fifth commandment: Thou shalt not kill. It is easy, of course, until one becomes a soldier. How can the organized military overcome our natural inclination to avoid killing other people? Answer: self-justification. But what form does self-justification take? Answer: distancing. The average citizen who becomes a killer feels justified when he or she establishes distance from the victim.

Distancing can be accomplished in a number of ways, each of which treats the victim as a nonperson. The best way to create distance is to dehumanize the enemy, and the dehumanization process begins by ascribing a derogatory name to the potential victim in advance. In the 1960s, American soldiers called persons living in Vietnam "gooks." It's much easier to kill a gook than it is to kill Mr. or Mrs. Nguyen. During the wars in Iraq and Afghanistan, invading troops called the civilians and enemy combatants "towel heads" and "rag heads." I call this kind of language *cursing.*

The naming process or cursing process that incorporates a dehumanizing dimension helps create psychological and moral distance between the killer and the victim. During the Rwandan genocide of the 1990s, the Hutus described the Tutsis as "vermin." The Hutus could justify killing nearly one million Tutsis because the whole world would be better off without vermin.

Distance comes in different forms. *Mechanical distance* begins in boot camp when military recruits are given the opportunity to play video games to get used to killing by killing figures on a screen. By dehumanizing the figures in this way, the step between the video game and combat is made smaller; actual persons are simply substituted for virtual persons. *Physical distance* helps relieve the sense that one is killing actual persons. For example, a drone operator can sip on coffee while targeting a convoy or a house in another country, fire a missile, kill numerous individuals, and then go home to play with his or her kids. Drone killing is a small step beyond virtual killing. *Cultural distance* helps by labeling the enemy in terms of ethnic or racial differences, especially when the enemy is perceived as culturally backward or uncivilized. *Moral distance* is established when the soldier describes the enemy as immoral, dastardly, or dangerous. One gains moral distance by blaming the enemy for starting the conflict, making a counter-invasion an act of retributive justice. *Social distance* is established when the soldiers think of their enemy as beneath them or in a lower class. Distance, according to the analysis of Lt. Col. Dave Grossman, permits "the killer to dehumanize the victim."[10]

With or without a fragile soul, most of us abhor the prospect that we would have to pull the trigger and take responsibility for snuffing out the life of another human person. In order for the conscience to permit it, we need to deny that the victim is another human person. The conscience will permit us to kill other human beings as long as we can successfully justify it. Self-justification takes the form distanciation—distancing ourselves from the humanity we share with the one we are about to put to death.

Self-Justification in Political Parlance

Nowhere is the principle of self-justification more salient than in political rhetoric. "Politicians are the most visible self-justifiers, which is why they provide such juicy examples," observe Carol Tavris and Elliot Aronson.[11]

10. Lt. Col. Dave Grossman, *On Killing* (New York: Little, Brown, 2009), 160.
11. Tavris and Aronson, *Mistakes Were Made*, 3.

My son Paul works in private industry, but as a contractor, he occasionally visits US government weapons test sites. On one occasion, he brought me a gift, something he bought from an alleged "secret" facility. Because of secrecy, he could not divulge the site. He claims it is government issue. In the coat of arms on the tee shirt, we find a hand grenade surrounded by laurel branches—that is, war surrounded by peace. The words on the shirt read: "Admit Nothing. Deny Everything. Make Counter Accusations."

Self-justification through the establishment of moral distance dominates political parlance. "Moral distance involves legitimating oneself and one's cause" in two ways, says Grossman. First, we gain moral distance through the "determination and condemnation of the enemy's guilt, which, of course, must be punished or avenged. The other is an affirmation of the legality and legitimacy of one's own cause."[12] Regardless of the political system, leaders like Glaucon know they need to look good for their constituencies and to the wider world. And nothing looks better than moral superiority.

When advocating socialism to replace capitalism, Adolph Hitler employed moral distance by describing *laissez-faire* capitalism as cruel to the Aryan people, *das Volk*. In order to rid Germany of cruel capitalism, Hitler established National Socialism, what we have come to know as Nazism. Because the Christian religion teaches compassion for the weak, Hitler sought an alternative morality that would support the strong against the weak. He invoked a supra-religious spirit to strengthen his nation. We see how this supra-religious self-justification is invoked in a speech he delivered on September 6, 1938, in Nuremberg.

National Socialism is not a cult-movement—a movement for worship; it is exclusively a *volkic* political doctrine based upon racial principles. In its

---

12. Ibid., 164. "The establishment of the enemy's guilt and the need to punish or avenge is a fundamental and widely accepted justification for violence" (ibid., 165).

purpose there is no mystic cult, only the care and leadership of a people defined by a common blood-relationship. Therefore we have no rooms for worship, but only halls for the people—no open spaces for worship, but spaces for assemblies and parades. We have no religious retreats, but arenas for sports and playing-fields, and the characteristic feature of our places of assembly is not the mystical gloom of a cathedral, but the brightness and light of a room or hall which combines beauty with fitness for its purpose . . . Our worship is exclusively the cultivation of the natural, and for that reason, because natural, therefore God-willed. Our humility is the unconditional submission before the divine laws of existence so far as they are known to us men.[13]

Hitler is post-religious, appealing to a higher spirituality.

Hitler's political policies draw a line between good and evil and then invoke what is good. The sunlight of the open playing-field is good, whereas the mystical gloom of the cathedral is bad. Aryan blood-relationship is good, whereas mystical contemplation is bad. Brightly lit halls and open arenas belong to everybody and are good, while church buildings that attempt to privatize the divine exclusively for their members are bad. Humility in obeying our natural inclinations is good, in contrast to the artificial doctrines of church religion, which are bad. And, most importantly, the divine laws of existence are eternal. National Socialism, in short, is a faithful embodiment of the eternal divine laws of existence.

In his earlier manifesto, *Mein Kampf*, the aspiring Hitler writes: "I believe that I am acting in accordance with the will of the Almighty Creator: by *defending myself against the Jews, I am fighting for the work of the Lord.*"[14] Appeal to the divine is the ultimate appeal in the act of self-justification.

Despite Hitler's own identification with the divine laws of existence and the work of the Lord, most of the rest of the world

---

13. Adolf Hitler, September 6, 1938. http://comicism.tripod.com/380906.html
14. Adolf Hitler, *Mein Kampf* (New York: Houghton Mifflin, 1943), 65 (italics in original).

sees Hitler as an incarnation of evil. The sheer devastation of World War II combined with the attempted genocide of Jews, the mentally challenged, the physically disabled, homosexuals, gypsies, and communists were intolerable and reprehensible. The nature with which Hitler identified his Nazism was, as the poet Alfred Lord Tennyson writes, "Nature, red in tooth and claw" blood red in tooth and claw, the natural world of Social Darwinism and Eugenics. So horrendous was the global destruction he precipitated—the outright murder of six million persons in concentration camps and perhaps sixty million casualties in the war—that the symbols of Satan and Hitler have become conflated in the public imagination.

Subsequent political leaders have learned to draw a line between good and evil, placing themselves on one side and Hitler on the other. In March 2014, US Secretary of State Hillary Rodham Clinton compared Russia's Vladimir Putin with Hitler," and shortly thereafter, the *Washington Post* offered a tally of American leaders engaging in Hitler-cursing.[15]

Just a couple examples will illustrate the principle of scapegoating by invoking the name of Adolf Hitler. "We did not choose to be the guardians at the gate, but there is no one else," President Lyndon B. Johnson said in a speech in 1965 to justify escalating the Vietnam War. "Nor would surrender in Vietnam bring peace, because we learned from Hitler at Munich that success only feeds the appetite of aggression. The battle would be renewed in one country and then another country, bringing with it perhaps even larger and crueler conflict, as we have learned from the lessons of history."[16]

President Bill Clinton could not resist making the same analogy. "What if someone had listened to Winston Churchill and stood up

---

15. Adam Taylor, "Hillary Clinton's Hitler Comparison and the Troublesome Tradition It Fits Into," *Washington Post*, March 5, 2014, http://www.washingtonpost.com/blogs/worldviews/wp/2014/03/05/hillary-clintons-hitler-comparison-and-the-troublesome-tradition-it-fits-into/.

16. Ibid.

to Adolf Hitler earlier?" Clinton said in 1999, justifying NATO bombing during the Kosovo conflict. "How many people's lives might have been saved? And how many American lives might have been saved?" Self-justification in politics consists of drawing a line between good and evil and placing oneself or one's nation on the good side of the line. And it certainly helps if the self-justifier can place Hitler or Satan on the evil side.

As I have said, justice is a serial killer. Geopolitics demonstrates this daily. Hitler thought he was justified in killing the mentally retarded, physically handicapped, communists, Jews, and other less highly evolved individuals right along with all enemies of the German nation. In the decades since, American political leaders have considered themselves to be justified when killing Hitler's equivalents again and again and again. In all of these killings, justice is done. Therefore, justice is a serial killer.

Virtually no one pursues injustice in the name of injustice. We love justice; so if we plan to kill, we paint our killing in the color of that which we love—namely, justice. This makes justice just as deadly as injustice.

In order to prepare for killing in the name of justice, we engage in what I call *cursing* the victim. Cursing consists of ascribing injustice to the victim and justice to ourselves. Cursing is a form of verbal self-justification.

Cursing in Political Liturgy

Catherine Pickstock describes civic liturgy as "the secret middle term which binds soul, city, cosmos, and [eternal] forms."[17] I wish to add that civil liturgy forms the patriotic soul. Geopolitics since the

17. Catherine Pickstock, "Justice and Prudence: Principles of Order in the Platonic City," in *The Blackwell Companion to Postmodern Theology,* ed. Graham Ward (Oxford: Blackwell, 2001), 173.

Second World War rely upon a civic liturgy that includes Hitler-cursing. I contend that our souls should be wary of the threat of deformation posed by the civic liturgy.

As we turn to the civic liturgy in American politics, I will give a bit more attention to the relationship between Hitler-cursing and America's two invasions of Iraq. When the forty-first president of the United States, George H. W. Bush, readied America for war against Iraq in 1991, he identified Iraq's Saddam Hussein with Germany's Adolf Hitler. According to President Bush, Hussein was as evil as Hitler. To take a stand against Saddam Hussein would be tantamount to taking a stand against injustice, despotism, and cruelty. During a news conference on New Year's Day of 1991, the White House resident identified America with the higher values of its calling. "Throughout our history we've been resolute in our support of justice, freedom, and human dignity. The current situation in the Persian Gulf demands no less of us and of the international community. We did not plan for war, nor do we seek war . . . Unfortunately, Iraq has thus far turned a deaf ear to the voices of peace and reason."[18]

America is good. Iraq is bad. Americans are devoted to justice, freedom, and human dignity. Furthermore, Americans are devoted to avoiding war. Iraq, on the other hand, has turned a deaf ear to the voices of peace and reason. In the name of the good, so to speak, America is justified in making its plan for a military strike against Iraq.

A couple of weeks later, the president verbally described Saddam Hussein as evil, thereby establishing moral distance. "While the world waited, Saddam Hussein systematically raped, pillaged, and plundered a tiny nation, no threat to his own. He subjected the people of

18. George H. W. Bush, The President's News Conference, *George Bush Presidential Library and Museum*, January 12, 1991, http://bush41library.tamu.edu/archives/public-papers/2616.

Kuwait to unspeakable atrocities—and among those maimed and murdered, innocent children. While the world waited, Saddam sought to add to the chemical weapons arsenal he now possesses, an infinitely more dangerous weapon of mass destruction—a nuclear weapon."[19] Intuitively, we all know that care is just and harm is unjust, so to take a stand against Iraq's leader is to take a stand against harm in favor of care. If the United States should take action to rid the world of this uncaring evil, then clearly America's war could be justified because it is fought in the name of what is good.

Before I go further, let me remind you of what we are looking at here. We are not measuring the wisdom of President Bush's argument to take the United States into war. Rather, we are trying to illustrate a universal human propensity to offer arguments to initiate or perpetrate violence that depend on self-justification. Whether such an argument passes one's judgment of conscience or not, the fact remains that self-justification either leads to violence or justifies violence already committed.

As history has recorded, the first Gulf War stopped short of removing Saddam Hussein from office in Bagdad. Even though the original justification of this war was to rid the world of a Hitler-like evil, President Bush stopped before conquering Bagdad. Why? Once the US military gained control of the oil fields, then the goals of the war were reformulated. Once America took control of the oil fields, then Saddam Hussein could be allowed to remain in power. The nation's conscience could be satisfied by lowering the standard of moral judgment: controlling the oil became America's new self-justification regardless of the prior goal, namely, ridding the world of Saddam Hussein. This decision eventually warranted a second war,

19. George H. W. Bush, "Address to the Nation Announcing Allied Military Action in the Persian Gulf," *George Bush Presidential Library and Museum*, January 16, 1991, http://bush41library.tamu.edu/archives/public-papers/2625.

which was prosecuted by the forty-third US president (and son of the forty-first president), George W. Bush, after the 9/11 tragedy in 2001. The same justifications were employed after 2001 as were given in 1991. "Tonight we are a country awakened to danger and called to defend freedom. Our grief has turned to anger, and anger to resolution. Whether we bring our enemies to justice, or bring justice to our enemies, justice will be done."[20] The purpose of going to war is for "justice to be done."

Alan Wolfe calls this *counterevil,* or justice in the form of revenge. Wolfe defines *counterevil* as "*the determination to inflict uncalled-for suffering on those presumed or known to have inflicted the same upon you.*" George W. Bush's decision to fight back against the September 11, 2001 terrorists was justified, says Wolfe, and it accorded widespread support around the world. But the methods his administration adopted included a number of "highly immoral tactics and policies." Among these policies were "the rendition of suspects to countries with no regard for human rights and the use of torture at Abu Ghraib and Guantánamo Bay."[21] This is Wolfe's opinion. I am not trying to dissect the morality of these presidential actions. Rather, I am trying to illustrate the mechanism of self-justification and its relationship to violence. The pursuit of justice is just as deadly as the pursuit of injustice. "Evil begets evil," comments Wolfe accurately.[22] Justice kills, even while self-justification makes us feel better about it.

At this point, someone might respond: "Wait a minute! What's a US president to do? When foreign dictators are cruel to their people or when they harbor nuclear weapons, are Americans not justified in sending the military to take them out?" Yes, of course. But, this is

---

20. George W. Bush, "Address to the Nation," *PresidenticalRhetoric.com,* September 20, 2001, http://www.presidentialrhetoric.com/speeches/09.20.01.html.
21. Alan Wolfe, *Political Evil: What It Is and How to Combat It* (New York: Random House, 2011), 23, italics in original.
22. Ibid., 26.

just the point. Self-justification precedes violence. It justifies violence. War is the pursuit of justice, not injustice. When a nation pursues justice, people die. These are the facts. What I am after here is an understanding of the facts.

Here's another fact: not only does self-justification precede violence, but it can also occur while violence is being committed or follow after. On November 12, 2004, journalist Kevin Sites interviewed a Marine corporeal in Fallujah while under fire in the US war against Iraq. Sites asked the Marine whether killing people is difficult.

"No. I don't have a problem shootin' shitheads," he answered. By identifying Iraqis as shitheads—by cursing—this Marine is doing the world a favor by ridding us of them. He draws a line between good and evil, placing Americans on the good side of the line and shitheads on the evil side. This justifies shooting them.

"I shot six people in less than ten seconds," he reported. "I'm glad I'm here defending my country . . . I'm not here for the Iraqi people. I'm here for the American people. . . . I'm gettn' rid of terrorists. . . . I'm doing my job."[23] He's doing his job because he's loyal to the American people. President G. W. Bush, his commander in chief, sent this Marine to Iraq so that "justice will be done."

The message that patriotism communicates to our young soldiers preparing for war has two layers. On the top layer, we find justice—universal and eternal justice. On the layer just beneath, we find loyalty to one's nation as a substitute standard of justice. The moral universe of the top layer includes all persons, every human being regardless of nation. The subterranean layer includes only America, or whichever nation the soldier is loyal to. The top layer is ultimate, while the bottom layer is penultimate; but the distinction

---

23. Kevin Sites, *The Things They Cannot Say: Stories Soldiers Won't Tell You about What They've Seen, Done or Failed to Do in War* (New York: Harper, 2013), 32–38.

between the two becomes blurred. In fact, boot camp indoctrination deliberately blurs the distinction so that the soldier will shoot first and think about higher justice later. By renaming the people of Iraq "shitheads," no thinking is required before six trigger pulls in ten seconds.

Theologians Paul Tillich and Reinhold Niebuhr—along with their historian friend at Columbia University, John Herman Randall Jr.—describe patriotism and nationalism as demonic. Because the interest of the nation replaces allegiance to a justice that transcends national interests and includes the welfare of the enemy in its scope, these thinkers understand nationalism as a penultimate belief being treated as if it is an ultimate belief. To treat something as ultimate that is less than ultimate is to succumb to a demonic spirit. The result can only be damage and carnage.

Patriotism is a form of spirituality without religion, or perhaps more accurately, a substitute religion. "Whatever its origin and its ultimate value, patriotism is beyond doubt the most widespread social ideal of the day; it is the modern religion, far stronger than mere Christianity in any of its forms, and to its tribal gods men give supreme allegiance. Nationalism is almost the one idea for which masses of men will still die."[24] The patriot feels justified in his or her ultimate devotion to one country at the expense of others because his or her nation is allegedly blessed by God.

These three scholars saw the demonic force reap destruction in German Nazism, Japanese imperialism, Soviet communism, and the rising red star over China. In the era immediately following World War II, they worried about the possibility that this demonic spirit might take over the allies. Might the United States succumb? Had

---

24. John Herman Randall Jr., *The Making of the Modern Mind* (New York: Columbia University Press, 1976), 668.

these three lived into the second decade of the twenty-first century, what might they think?

Death and Eternity in China

In 1945, Mao Zedong emerged as leader of a Marxist China after a decade of bloodshed due to revolutionary fighting and World War II. Even though atheist and Marxist Mao might at first appear to be as anti-religious and anti-spiritual as one might get, watch how self-justification functions to create political community in what became Red China.

Because of the tensile strength of the dialectic between death and eternity, political rhetoric employing this dialectic is sure to draw rapt attention. When we can appeal to a good that is higher than death and identify ourselves with this higher good, we invoke perhaps the most convincing of self-justifications. Salvation comes through a purposeful death, or so we commonly assume. Do we have the power of salvation in our own self-justification?

In 1944, China's prospective leader identified himself with salvation and his army with a willingness to die to effect China's salvation.

All men must die, but death can vary in its significance.... The Chinese people are suffering; it is our duty to save them and we must exert ourselves in struggle. Wherever there is struggle there is sacrifice, and death is a common occurrence. But we have the interests of the people and the sufferings of the great majority at heart, and when we die for the people it is a worthy death. Nevertheless, we should do our best to avoid unnecessary sacrifices. Our cadres must show concern for every soldier, and all people in the revolutionary ranks must care for each other, must love and help each other.... From now on, when anyone in our ranks who has done some useful work dies, be he soldier or cook, we should have a funeral ceremony and a memorial meeting in his honor. This should become the rule. And it should be introduced among the people as well. When someone dies in a village, let a memorial meeting be held. In this way we express our mourning for the dead and unite all the people.[25]

Mao is prescribing the civic liturgy that will form the Chinese soul to fit a moral universe that places him, Mao, in a position of undisputed power.

Just how does this civic liturgy form the soul? A purposeful death is salvific, says Mao Zedong, and if the people are willing to support Mao, they will benefit from the salvation his sacrificial army accomplishes. It is right and salutary that they should honor the dead; and Mao is good because he teaches them to honor the dead properly and reverently. The unity of the Chinese people in honoring the dead transcends their death, and ours.

The extraordinary force of Mao's rhetoric is likewise exhibited in his parable of "The Foolish Old Man Who Removed the Mountains," a speech he gave on June 11, 1945.

> We must also arouse the political consciousness of the entire people so that they may willingly and gladly fight together with us for victory. We should fire the whole people with the conviction that China belongs not to the reactionaries but to the Chinese people. There is an ancient Chinese fable called "The Foolish Old Man who Removed the Mountains." It tells of an old man who lived in northern China long, long ago and was known as the Foolish Old Man of North Mountain. His house faced south and beyond his doorway stood the two great peaks, Taihang and Wangwu, obstructing the way. With great determination, he led his sons in digging up these mountains hoe in hand. Another greybeard, known as the Wise Old Man, saw them and said derisively, "How silly of you to do this! It is quite impossible for you to dig up these two huge mountains." The Foolish Old Man replied, "When I die my sons will carry on; when they die, there will be my grandsons and then their sons and grandsons, and so on to infinity. High as they are, the mountains cannot grow any higher and with every

25. Mao Zedong, "Serve the People," September 8, 1944, *Asia for Educators,* http://afe.easia.columbia.edu/special/china_1900_mao_speeches.htm#serve.

bit we dig, they will be that much lower. Why can't we clear them anyway?" Having refuted the Wise Old Man's wrong view, he went on digging every day, unshaken in his conviction. God was moved by this, and he sent down two angels, who carried the mountains away on their backs. Today, two big mountains lie like a dead weight on the Chinese people. One is imperialism, the other is feudalism. The Chinese Communist Party has long made up its mind to dig them up. We must persevere and work unceasingly, and we too, will touch God's heart. Our God is none other than the masses of the Chinese people. If they stand up and dig together with us, why can't these mountains be cleared away?[26]

Atheist Mao appeals here to the eternal deity. He also appeals to ancient Chinese tradition, which is nearly as eternal and much more racially specific. To support Mao is to touch God's heart and to further China's appointed destiny. With far less rhetorical eloquence but the same self-justifying force, Presidents George W. Bush and Barak Hussein Obama close their speeches with a variant of "May God bless these United States of America." Civic liturgy may appear to be secular, but in fact it is spiritual without being religious.

Excursus: Ting vs. Lo on Chinese Theology

When it comes to providing a theological analysis of Chinese culture in the wake of Mao's historical turn toward Marxist materialism, the question must be asked: If we look through the lens of justifying faith, can we see more clearly?

No, says Bishop K. H. Ting of the Protestant Church in China. Ting emphasizes that, as a teacher, Jesus stresses that God is love. This is the central Christian teaching, says the Chinese bishop. He adds that the doctrine of justification-by-faith has no relevance for

---

26. Mao Zedong, "The Foolish Old Man Who Removed Mountains," June 11, 1945, *Asia for Educators,* http://afe.easia.columbia.edu/special/china_1900_mao_speeches.htm#serve.

contemporary Chinese culture. First, Ting complains, the doctrine of justification-by-faith implies that God loves only those with faith and not the entirety of the human race. Second, the gospel understood in this doctrine removes the motive for moral living, separating grace from moral responsibility. Third, justification-by-faith emphasizes belief more than moral living. Thereby, it divides the world into a small group of believers and a large majority of moral individuals who are condemned to the flames of hell because they are not ranked among the believers. Those who support justification-by-faith would admit Hitler to heaven because he was a believer and deny heaven to Mao because he was an unbeliever. This seems unjust, says Bishop Ting.

Hong Kong systematic theologian Pilgrim Lo takes a different position from that of the Chinese bishop. Professor Lo is concerned about the interaction between Luther's theology and Chinese culture. "The God of Luther is the God and the Lord of culture," says Lo. "Luther should be an important subject in cultural studies."[27] Rather than sacrifice a traditional religious figure such as Martin Luther, a retrieval of Luther could enrich and expand contemporary Chinese Christianity.

Is it really a matter of culture alone? Or is it a critique of culture—every culture—that we should be concerned with? Here, I would like to add that Luther's insight regarding the contest between self-justification and justification-by-faith is relevant for any and every cultural analysis. Looking through the lens of justifying faith,

27. Pilgrim W. K. Lo, "Luther between Theology and Cultural Studies," *Lutherjahrbuch: Organon der Internationalen Lutherforschung,* ed. Christopher Spehr (Göttingen: Vandenhoeck & Ruprecht, 2013), 220–26. Exposition of Bishop Ting included here. Professor Lo invokes Luther in analysis of the Chinese context. "Asian scholars today are pursuing Luther studies by translating Luther's works, introducing and interpreting Luther's faith, teaching Luther's theology, and writing monographs on Lutheran doctrine, in order to rediscover and retain Lutheran identity." Pilgrim W. K. Lo, "Luther and Asia," chap. 45 in *Martin Luther's Theology,* ed. Robert Kolb, Irene Dingle, L'Ubomir Batka (Oxford: Oxford University Press, 2005), 614.

both Hitler the German Nazi and Mao the Chinese Marxist look quite similar. They both violate God's holiness by pressing an appeal to the divine into the service of their own self-justification and slaughter. We need something like the prophetic judgment that justification-by-faith offers in order to see the dangers lurking in civic spirituality.

Subtle and Not-So-Subtle Self-Justification

Self-justification is common in both civic spirituality and in our private thoughts. It's our default disposition. When challenged by either guilt or meaninglessness, a mechanism of self-justification clicks in—a process that applies to us both individually and collectively. "When someone kills in war there's a psychological triage that occurs," writes Kevin Sites. "The individual must find meaning in the act. Because killing is the ultimate refutation of our own humanity, there must be a justification to prevent the mind from defaulting to the judgment of murderer."[28] Because it is overwhelming to think of oneself as a murderer, the moral universe must somehow provide the criterion for judging the killer to be performing an act of justice. Would God approve?

As both Hitler and Mao recognized, appeal to divine justification is the strongest form of self-justification. The medieval theologian Bernard of Clairvaux understood this as well. On one occasion, Bernard delivered a eulogy for the Knights Templar. "The soldier of Christ is certain when he kills. . . . He kills with Christ, for he does not carry the sword without reason. He is a servant of God for the punishment of evil men and the praise of good men."[29] What more sublime justification for violence could a person ask for?

---

28. Sites, *The Things They Cannot Say,* xx.

Such subtle self-justification for war has a not-so-subtle biblical precedent. In the Deuteronomic History (found in the books of Deuteronomy, Joshua, Judges, 1 and 2 Samuel, 1 and 2 Kings), the priest fires up the troops just before the general takes his turn to dispense orders for battle. Deuteronomy 7:16: "You shall devour all the peoples that the Lord your God is giving over to you, showing them no pity," says the priest to the soldiers.[30] Curiously, the priest does not draw a line between good and evil; as a result, he cannot place the Israelites on the good side. Israel will win the war but only because of God's will and not because Israel is intrinsically good. Deuteronomy 9:6: "Know, then, that the Lord your God is not giving you this good land to occupy because of your righteousness; for you are a stubborn people." God gives victory to "a stubborn people."[31] On this point, the ancient Israelite priest differs from today's political leaders who tell their constituents how good and righteous and deserving they are. In ancient Israel, appeal to divine sanction for war did not include self-justification. But it certainly does today.

The visibility of religious justification for international violence has led many in our era to complain that religion is to blame for human warfare and terrorism. The corollary is obvious: if we can eliminate the practice of religion and convert to secularism or even

---

29. Bernard of Clairvaux, *De laude novae militiae ad milites templi,* 1 3 (*PL* 182.924); cited by Raymund Schwager, "The Theology of the Wrath of God," in *Violence and Truth: On the Work of Rene Girard,* ed. Paul Dumochel (Stanford, CA: Stanford University Press, 1988), 50.

30. The concept of *holy war* in ancient Israel differs from the terminology we use today. We think of a holy war as a battle between two religions. In ancient Israel, a holy war was understood as a war in which the God of Israel insured victory regardless of the ability of the soldiers to perform in combat. "Israel must not be afraid, for Yahweh is waging war with the help of miraculous phenomena: a mysterious discouragement, a divine terror, a kind of paralyzing confusion, will descend upon the foe." Gerhard von Rad, *Deuteronomy* (Louisville: Westminster John Knox, 1966), 69.

31. "Deuteronomy stresses Yahweh's election of an undeserving Israel . . . and the loyalty owed by Israel in return." Richard D. Nelson, *Deuteronomy* (Louisville: Westminster John Knox, 2004), 10.

atheism, then wars will cease and world peace will result. However, this is naïve logic. Even if, on the surface, this complaint appears to be accurate, a closer look shows that violence is a human problem, a universal human problem.[32] Mao's purge in China sought to eliminate religion—Confucianism as well as Christianity—in the name of Marxist atheism. Yet Mao appealed to a vague spiritual sensibility to justify his military pursuits. The fact seems to be this: with or without institutional religion, we can forecast that violence will recur, and recur again. What a religious or spiritual sensibility provides is transcendental rhetoric, employed to justify the pursuit of violence.

Political self-justification is spiritual without necessarily being religious. "Both Hitler and Stalin had little sympathy with organized religion and viewed the churches of their countries as potential enemies," writes Wolfe. These two dictators "were offering a competing system of meaning preoccupied with eternal questions of salvation and sacrifice."[33] Whereas established religious groups pose a threat to totalitarian governments, vague spiritual sentiments can easily be conscripted into support for the state. Jingoistic fervor accompanied by military aggression is perhaps the most formidable form that SBNR sentiment can take.

One point that Wolfe makes should not go by unnoticed: a SBNR has no leverage with which to render judgment against a rogue government justifying war. But religion does. A religious tradition with its institutional organization intact can rally criticism, prophetic judgment, and resistance. It would be premature to disqualify a Christian church or another religious institution from providing a moral compass to measure the direction taken by a secular state.

---

32. See William Rodriguez, "Is Religion the Cause of Violence," *Journal of Lutheran Ethics* (November 2013): http://downloads.elca.org/html/jle/www.elca.org/what-we-believe/social-issues/november-2d2013.aspx.htm.

33. Wolfe, *Political Evil,* 35.

A realistic doctrine of human nature—also called a theological anthropology—provides religious critics with the analytical tools needed to expose the Thrasymicus and Glaucon Principles at work among our political leaders.

Spiritual rhetoric on the tongue of a political leader is not particularly subtle. It is public and, to the critical eye, transparent and easily exposed. Nevertheless, we are often tempted to go along with this political self-justification without criticism; we are tempted to be complicit and cooperative.[34] Why? Because this mechanism of self-justification is secretly at work in each of us every day. It is our first line of self-defense. We invoke self-justification in our private moments as well as when interacting with family, friends, coworkers, and the public. Self-justification is as common as raindrops, seeping into every nook and cranny until nearly everything is wet with it. We draw an imaginary line between good and evil, and we place ourselves on the good side.

We want others to think well of us, just as Glaucon did. We also want to think well of ourselves. To be good, just, and true is to be eternal—or so we think. Even in moments when we might be feeling guilt or shame, we search for reasons to declare ourselves right. To be right is to be attuned, as Hitler says, to the "divine laws of existence."

Mere Rhetoric?

In the *Gorgias,* Socrates asks about the relationship between political rhetoric and true justice? If the speechmaker only wants to persuade us to vote or support a political party or policy, he or she is being

---

34. A guardian of words in the service of truth-telling, Marilyn Chandler McEntyre faults those who listen to the lies told by political leaders. "Indeed, we bear a heavy responsibility for allowing ourselves to be lied to. . . . The deceptions we particularly seem to want are those that comfort, insulate, legitimate, and provide ready excuses for inaction." *Caring for Words in a Culture of Lies* (Grand Rapids, MI: Eerdmans, 2009), 56–57.

disingenuous. Authentic rhetoric should make us hunger and thirst after truth, and truth demands absolute justice. "Will not the true rhetorician . . . aim . . . to implant justice in the souls of his citizens?" Socrates asks rhetorically and ironically.[35] We might imitate Socrates with reference to God: Will not the true rhetorician aim to implant faith in the true God in the souls of citizens? Whether we appeal to true justice or the true God, the rhetorician stands as much under that judgment as those listening to the speech.

When we reflect back on Hitler, Mao, or even the American presidents whipping up patriotic spirit to support their war plans, we should be suspicious. Were they actually attempting to plant justice in the souls of us as citizens, or, were they simply trying to appear to be pursuers of justice in our eyes? It could be the case that what appears to be oratorical justice is in fact less than actual justice. Rhetorical justice justifies the speechmaker, but it falls short of establishing or maintaining genuine justice in community.

One of the points I wish to press here is that when political or personal rhetoric appeals directly to ethereal justice or to Almighty God for justification, it appeals to something less than true justice or the true God. The true God transcends our image of God; the true God even transcends the concept of justice structuring our moral universe, no matter how we might place our trust in either the divine image or our concept of justice. When we self-justify in the name of God or in the name of justice, the concept of the divine or the just has usually been shaved and trimmed and minimized so as to fit our proposed program. In short, we shouldn't believe dictators or presidents when they justify their policies by appeal to a downsized moral universe.

---

35. Plato, *Gorgias* 504, in *DP*, 1:566.

My emphasis on using the transcendent for leverage against our projected substitute images is not foolproof. So intense is our propensity for self-justification that we can even prostitute divine transcendence for our own mundane purposes. Let me provide two examples, both dealing with justification of existing human hierarchy.

Blessing the Hierarchy: Static Violence

An appeal to transcendent order provides justification for civic or religious hierarchy—for keeping things the way they are even if the ways things are is oppressive. In India, for example, the law of karma justifies dividing society into multiple castes. The term for caste in Sanskrit is *varna*, which means "color." Indian society is arranged according to race and according to color, with the lightest on top and the darkest on the bottom. Below the caste system are millions of people previously known as outcastes or untouchables, now referred to as Dalits.

When modern Christian missionaries arrived in India, they repudiated the inequalities of the caste system. Before Christ, every man and woman is equal, the missionaries told the people. It is easy to understand why those who initially found Christianity most attractive were the lower castes and the outcastes. In the Christian Church, they found a dignity denied them by the prevailing social hierarchy. Generations later, Indian Christian leaders have developed a religious vision based upon their liberation from untouchability, Dalit Theology.

Even though the caste system is outlawed in modern India, it still governs with cultural force. Indian Old Testament scholar Monica Melanchthon feels the pain of exclusion experienced by so many. "The culture of our present-day society . . . produces persons who are excluded and barred from various arenas of life: economic, political, social, cultural, and religious [including] those who are poor, women, Dalits, indigenous peoples, people suffering from HIV/AIDS, and those whose human worth is negated and annulled by society's logic of separation and alienation." For Melanchthon, the message of grace provides a foundation for affirming human equality, regardless of one's status at birth. "In this context, the justice of God and the equality of human persons realized by the doctrine of divine grace is a sign of hope."[36]

This leads to my second example of justifying hierarchy: the Christian Church. Yes, Christians have long affirmed human equality and dignity granted each of us by the grace of God. Before the cross of Jesus, we are all sinners saved solely by God's grace. None of us are superior in the eyes of God. Yet nearly every generation of church leadership has found a way to justify hierarchy, patriarchy, and ecclesiastical power. Yale's Kathryn Tanner summarizes the logic: "God is to the angels as angels are to human beings, as the king to his vassals, as the lion or eagle is to the lowly grasshopper or snail, as a man is to a woman, as a father is to his household, as the head is to the other members of a living organism, as the soul is to the body."[37] According to this copy-the-heavenly-model method, we lower heaven low enough so that we can photograph it and print out copies here on earth.

The Christian Church remains *simul justus et peccator,* both justified in God's sight yet tarnished by sin. Despite our commitments to God's gift of grace, Cristina Grenholm reminds us that "we have to take into account that we are caste-, race-, and gender-driven cowards who resist the gift of life."[38] We are cowards because we

36. Monica Melanchthon, "The Grace of God and the Equality of Human Persons," in *GG*, 43.
37. Kathryn Tanner, *The Politics of God: Christian Theologies and Social Justice* (Minneapolis: Fortress Press, 1992), 133.

are unwilling to spell out the implications of our graced relationship with our saving God: the implication being that before God we are all equal and that this should apply to human community as well.

Have I now justified anti-hierarchicalism? Oops! My purpose here is not to justify any ism or ideology, even an anti-ideology ideology. Rather, I wish to show the subtle and incessant thrust of self-justification in our lives. Anti-hierarchicalism is not immune from self-justification and bigotry either. In fact, anti-hierarchicalism may be easier to proffer in our modern post-Enlightenment world with our public stress on human equality; hierarchicalists everywhere are in retreat. Confidentially, I relish watching hierarchicalists flee. But should I?

Nadia Sorts Out the Good Guys from the Bad Guys

Drawing the line between good and evil—between us and them—is tricky. Nadia Bolz-Weber, who writes the blog *Sarcastic Lutheran*, shows us just how tricky it is. Nadia reports that she had grown up in a fundamentalist church setting, where sorting between good people and bad people was routine. However, she later came to think that her fundamentalist churchgoer friends were hypocrites. So Nadia redrew the line between good and evil and placed her fundamentalist friends on the evil side. "As a teenager," she writes, "I began to question the Great Christian Sorting System. My gay friends in high school were kind and funny and loved me, so I supposed my church had placed them in the wrong category." With this in mind, Nadia reclassified her church friends. "Christians weren't good; people who fought for peace and justice were good. I had been lied to, and in my anger at being lied to about the containers, I left the church. But

38. Cristina Grenholm, "Grace, Transcendence, and Patience: A Response to Monica Melanchthon," in *GG*, 66.

it turns out, I hadn't actually escaped the sorting system. I had just changed the labels."[39]

Nadia's husband, Matthew, reiterates the point. "Nadia, the thing that sucks is that every time we draw a line between us and others, Jesus is always on the other side of it. Damn."[40]

Even Satanists Engage in Self-Justification

We have been observing our human propensity to draw a line between good and evil, at which point we usually place ourselves on the good side of the line. As shocking as it might sound, even worshippers of Satan justify their faith by identifying with what is good. One would think that veneration of the Prince of Darkness would affirm evil for the sake of evil. But even citizens in the kingdom of Satan may engage in self-justification.

Here's a case in point. In January 2014, the New York-based Satanic Temple submitted an application to the Oklahoma Capitol Preservation Commission. For what? To erect a monument on the Oklahoma state capitol grounds. What kind of monument? The proposed monument would be a seven-foot tall statue of Satan, depicted as Baphomet, the goat-headed figure with wings and horns sitting on a pentagram. The statue would include adoring children at Satan's side.

Why? In order to counter the influence of the Ten Commandments. At the time of the application, a monument to the Ten Commandments sat on capitol property, an inspiration to legislators. The Satanic monument application was facilitated by the Oklahoma chapter of the American Civil Liberties Union, which was suing the state of Oklahoma to remove the Ten Commandments

39. Nadia Bolz-Weber, *Pastrix* (New York: Jericho Books, 2013), 43.
40. Ibid., 57.

monument because "the state needs to get out of the business of endorsing religion." As a symbolic act in opposition to state support of the Ten Commandments, the ACLU facilitated the application of Satan worshippers to erect an alternative memorial.

Now, just what justifies the erection of a state-sponsored monument to Satan? Here is what a spokesperson for the Satanic Temple said. "More than anything, we feel our monument is meant to be a historical marker celebrating the scapegoats, marginalized and demonized minority."[41] Look at this justification carefully. Satanic Temple supporters support defense of victims, defense of those who have been victimized by scapegoating, marginalization, or demonization. If there is an ethical message to this book, it is that we should embrace such an ethic of caring for those who have been treated unjustly. We should cultivate a sensitivity to—and defense of—those who are victims of scapegoating, marginalization, and demonization. This motivation for action is just what Jesus sought to inculcate in each of our consciences. In short, these Satanists are justifying the erection of the monument on the grounds that it would garner support for the teachings of Jesus. Paradoxically, Satanists are good, just as Jesus is good.

An inversion is taking place here. While Satan is a symbol of evil—evil for the sake of evil—the line between good and evil has been redrawn by the Satanists. Accordingly, those who sponsor the Ten Commandments are now indirectly identified with evil, and the Satanic challengers identify themselves with the very virtues that most followers of the Ten Commandments embrace. The line between good and evil has been redrawn, and supporters of the Ten

---

41. Sama Hamedy, "Proposed Satan Monument Heats Up Debate in Oklahoma," *Los Angeles Times*, January 8, 2014, http://www.latimes.com/nation/nationnow/la-na-nn-satanic-monument-oklahoma-20140107,0,4198928.story#axzz2pqmpC9je.

Commandments have been placed on the evil side while supporters of Satan have placed themselves on the good side.

At minimum, this is curious. At maximum, it reminds us that self-justification serves the forces of evil. Evil dresses in clothes of virtue, and we need to sharpen our vision so that we can perceive the Pharisaic hypocrisy in self-justification. Hitler, Mao, Bush, and Obama—along with the New York Satanists—share something in common: they justify themselves because they stand on the good side of the line. Each of us is tempted to join this chorus and sing along.

The New York Satanists are members of a club to which we all belong. Human beings, writes Luther, "have been carrying on their mischief and violence under the lovely and excellent pretext and cover of doing it for the sake of righteousness. . . . They put up such a good front and use such beautiful words that they think even God himself will not know any better."[42]

The Pharisee Within

Jesus thundered judgment against the Pharisees of his time, using the term *hypocrite.* Matthew 23:27: "Woe to you, scribes and Pharisees, hypocrites! For you are like whitewashed tombs, which on the outside look beautiful, but inside they are full of the bones of the dead and of all kinds of filth." Jesus contrasts the outside with the inside. The outside looks moral and just and enviable. The inside, in contrast, reeks of death.

What if the difference between the inside and the outside is less radical? What if you and I try to conform our inside to the image we project on the outside? What if we take our own self-justification

42. Luther, *Sermon on the Mount,* in *LW*, 21:30.

seriously? Perhaps Jesus' thundering voice might sound like an alarm clock, waking us up.

John Sanford analyzes "the Pharisee in each of us." Like an actor, the hypocrite wears a mask, he says. "The mask is the person we pretend to be—the false outer personality that we turn to the world, but that is contradicted from within. . . . The destructive aspect of the mask is our tendency to identify with it, to think that we *are* the person we pretend to be, and thereby to remain unconscious of our real self." We lie, and then we believe the lie. "The result is spiritual and psychological stagnation."[43]

Through his denunciation of hypocrisy, Jesus means to shock us with judgment. But there's more to it than that. By announcing God's grace, we find we don't need to wear the mask any more. "If we would belong to the kingdom, this false outer front must go. . . . We must dare to be ourselves and must no longer hide behind a facade."[44] God's justification of us in faith liberates the soul from its felt need to pretend, its need to put on a mask colored by self-justification.

But watch out! The temptation to self-justify never goes away. We can all too easily listen to Jesus' denunciation of the hypocrites and identify ourselves with the humble anti-hypocrites. We can claim that justifying faith is a virtue we posses, and we can become proud that it is our faith alone that saves. Only humility can spare us from the delusion of moral superiority.

Our faith in the God who justifies takes the form of humility. Humility forms the soul. "For a person to have a soul," says Sanford, "he or she must relinquish egocentric identification with the outer mask and must be willing to face what is within."[45] If we realize that

43. John A. Sanford, *The Kingdom Within: The Inner Meaning of Jesus' Sayings* (New York: Harper, 1970), 70, italics in original.
44. Ibid., 71.
45. Ibid., 123.

we are held in the loving arms of a gracious God, then we can face the truth about who we are. This way of truth-facing is what creates an eternal soul.

Conclusion

The good news is that human beings are inclined toward the good. What we want is the good, and we justify virtually all that we do by appealing to what is good. It is rare that any of us will choose evil just because it's evil. Evil is a byproduct of the good. When Augustine sought to describe the inner workings of his soul, he recognized his yearning for what is good. His sin consisted of choosing the wrong good, of choosing a lesser good than the ultimate good. "My sin consisted in this, that I sought pleasure, sublimity, and truth not in God but in his creatures, in myself, and other created beings."[46] If we choose any good that is less than God, we choose division, conflict, violence, and destruction. That's the nature of sin.

The bad news is that we deny our sin. We think of our violence and destruction as good rather than evil because it is done in the service of justice. No matter how much havoc we wreak, it is justified.

The hinge on which everything in this book swings is the contrast between our self-justification, on the one hand, and God's gracious justification of us, on the other. The hinge verse continues to be Rom. 8:33b: "God is the one who justifies" (*theos ho dikaiosune*).

Marcus Barth (not Karl) suggests that even God engages in self-justification; but when God self-justifies, we creatures are the beneficiaries. God's act of justifying us is the act of giving us new life. "God justifies his work of creation and salvation . . . by showing

46. Augustine, *Confessions,* trans. Henry Chadwick (Oxford: Oxford University Press, 1991), 1.19.30, pp. 22–23.

that he is pleased with the man he has created anew. Resurrection, glorification, clothing over, renewal, changing a fleshly into a spiritual body—all these are designations for one and the same event: the public, glorious, incontestable, and irrevocable justification of man through God's grace."[47] Despite this unsurpassable and eternal gift, we follow the path of the fool and try to justify ourselves anyhow.

The thesis of this chapter is that we engage in self-justification in our daily lives. Declaring ourselves just is the default position taken by the psyche. Spirituality—whether religious or SBNR in nature—consists in forming the soul according to what standards we believe justice requires. We conscript the conscience into providing standards that we can attain, which provides us with the self-satisfaction that comes with our moral embodiments and achievements.

The problem is that frequently somebody gets hurt. Some of us get run over by innocent bus drivers. Soldiers march to the drumbeat of self-justifying political rhetoric. When drone strikes kill terrorists and their families, justice is done. Justice is a dangerous thing. It maims and kills and destroys. Yet under every circumstance, we want to think of ourselves as justified by justice.

It is all too human to draw a line between good and evil and place ourselves on the good side of the line. But what if we draw the line between good and evil and God places Godself on the evil side? We would declare ourselves good, and thereby separate ourselves from God. What then?

---

47. Marcus Barth, *Justification*, trans. A. M. Woodruff III (Grand Rapids, MI: Eerdmans, 1971), 82.

8

Ethics for Bold Sinners

The three most important norms, or mandates, for politics under
God are the preservation of justice for all people, the special
protection of the weak and marginal, and the imperative to treat
all humans as image bearers of God.

–Mark Noll[1]

It is better that a life should contract many a dirt-mark,
than forfeit usefulness in its efforts to remain unspotted.

–William James[2]

Suppose we draw a line between good and evil, and God places
himself on the evil side. What would happen to our attempts at self-
justification? They would be nullified. That's the downside of the
gospel message.

---

1. Mark A. Noll, "What Lutherans Have to Offer Public Theology," *Lutheran Quarterly* 22:2
(Summer 2008): 130.
2. James, VRE, 354.

This shocking reversal is what we Christians think God is addressing to us in the life, teachings, and death of Jesus of Nazareth. Rather than identify with the powerful Romans or the learned Pharisees, Jesus identified with the outcasts, the lepers, the blind, the deaf, the poor, and especially with those called "sinners" in the four Gospels. His parables pounded away at an important theme: the last shall be first, and the first shall be last. The most powerful words he spoke inhabit the performative realm of forgiveness rather than the spirited rhetoric of justice. He died unjustly, a victim of a system of retributive justice that failed to exact true justice.

One implication of the divine revelation in the cross is that we no longer look for God among the justified but rather among the victims of someone else's self-justification. We look for God not in the Nazi power structure but rather among the Jews and others suffering in the death camps. We look for God not among the triumphant Chinese Maoists but rather among the martyred and those who die in ignominy. We look for God not in the blessings of American prosperity but rather in the debris of the homes felled by American bombs in faraway villages. When we draw a line between good and evil and place ourselves on the good side, you can bet that God will not be found standing with us.

This is the bad news of the gospel. "Everyone of us is a broken, sinful human being," says Elizabeth Eaton, Presiding Bishop of the Evangelical Lutheran Church in America. "There are no degrees of who is more sinful than someone else."[3] This means that we delude ourselves with our attempts to draw fictional lines between ourselves and evil or sinful others. Among other things, the gospel reveals to us that we cannot get away with this fictional self-justification.

---

3. Elizabeth Eaton, "2013 Commencement Address at Trinity Lutheran Seminary," *Trinity Seminary Review* 34:1 (Winter/Spring 2014): 7.

That's the bad news. The good news is that God justifies us. Romans 8:33b: "God is the one who justifies" (*theos ho dikaiosune*). We can find justification in this mess, to be sure, but our justification is not something we accomplish ourselves. It comes to us as a gift of divine grace.[4] Until we get this truth through our heads, we will continue to reap violence and suffering in our vain attempts to make ourselves look and feel like we belong on the good side.

Curiously, this makes the discipline of ethics the most ungodly of human enterprises and moral leadership in the political domain the most suspect. What do ethicists or moral leaders do other than try to draw a line between good and evil and place their people on the good side? Ethics is the very form of human thinking that estranges us from God. Once we have heard the gospel message, should we still engage in ethics or try to live morally? Should bold sinners think ethically and act morally? If this discussion is too perplexing, pour yourself another cup of coffee, and then come back to the discussion that follows.

Adam and Eve, You and Me

As I have said, I believe our reliance on the moral order of the universe derives from an intuition. It begins when, as children, we first utter those words, "That isn't fair!" This intuition abides despite what we are taught by our families or social surroundings and persists whether or not it is reinforced by our religious training. Justice and goodness and truth and beauty are eternal. If we want to be eternal, that's where we want to be. Right?

---

4. "The gospel is not merely a doctrine about the nature of God, a high ethical standard, or the way to an enriched and refined spiritual life, or the like. The gospel is the proclamation of the work wrought by God when He sent Jesus Christ into the world." Anders Nygren, *Commentary on Romans,* trans. Carl C. Rasmussen (Philadelphia: Muhlenberg Press, 1949), 25.

This intuition concerning the moral order of the universe is at work in the Bible. My interpretation of the Adam and Eve story follows: *we each try to draw a line between good and evil and place ourselves on the good side of the line.* Or to say it another way, our first reflex in a moment of tension is to justify ourselves. The story of Adam and Eve in the Garden of Eden takes the form of an etiological narrative. It does not refer merely to a historical couple living in Iraq between the Tigris and Euphrates rivers. Rather, it describes all people of all times and all places, including the reader of this book and its writer. We all live in this garden—or perhaps more accurately, in the field of weeds just east of Eden.

As you might recall, Eve looks at the tree bearing the forbidden fruit. She likes what she sees. It appears "good" to eat. At that moment a serpent engages her in conversation. The serpent tells her not to hesitate—to eat the forbidden fruit—because something good will happen. "You will not die," says the serpent in Genesis 3:4-5, "for God knows that when you eat of it your eyes will be opened, and you will be like God, knowing good and evil." To have one's eyes opened, to gain enlightenment, to gain knowledge—now that sounds attractive! It sounds like the goal of a spiritual quest. To be like God! How could one turn down such an opportunity? Genesis 3:6-7: "So when the woman saw that the tree was good for food, and that it was a delight to the eyes, and that the tree was to be desired to make one wise, she took of its fruit and ate; and she also gave some to her husband, who was with her, and he ate." Eating the forbidden fruit was a good thing to do. At least, to Eve it appeared to be a good thing.

Both the man and the woman gained something: the knowledge of good and evil. Their eyes were opened. However, this involved some collateral damage. Suddenly, they realized something they had not noticed prior, namely, that they were not wearing any clothes. The biblical text continues.

> Then the eyes of both were opened, and they knew that they were naked; and they sewed fig leaves together and made loincloths for themselves. They heard the sound of the Lord God walking in the garden at the time of the evening breeze, and the man and his wife hid themselves from the presence of the Lord God among the trees of the garden. But the Lord God called to the man, and said to him, "Where are you?" He said, "I heard the sound of you in the garden, and I was afraid, because I was naked; and I hid myself." He said, "Who told you that you were naked? Have you eaten from the tree of which I commanded you not to eat?" The man said, "The woman whom you gave to be with me, she gave me fruit from the tree, and I ate." Then the Lord God said to the woman, "What is this that you have done?" The woman said, "The serpent tricked me, and I ate." (Gen. 3:7-13)

Note the chain of self-justification at work here. Adam basically says, "It's not my fault. Blame the woman you gave me." Eve follows, "It's not my fault. Blame the serpent who beguiled me. And God, while we're at it, who made the serpent?" Well, God, of course. God is guilty for creating a serpent who talks and lives in the Garden of Eden. It's God's fault for denying the man and woman the awareness of good and evil, therefore, God is really the guilty party. Adam and Eve draw a line between good and evil, and they put each other, the serpent, and even God on the evil side. We sheepish sinners are desperate to think of ourselves as good.

"Adam wanted to appear innocent, he passed on his guilt from himself to God, who had given him his wife. Eve also tries to excuse herself and accuses the serpent, which was also a creature of God," comments Martin Luther. "Here Adam is presented as a typical instance of all sinners and of such despair because of their sin. They cannot do otherwise than accuse God and excuse themselves."[5] Adam

---

5. Martin Luther, *Lectures on Genesis, LW*, 1:178–79.

and Eve draw a line between good and evil, and they place God on the evil side of that line.

We work with the assumption that goodness is eternal, and we are so desperate to identify ourselves with what is good that we will vilify God if necessary. We will judge God by a criterion that transcends God. On the surface, this seems like nonsense. Yet our intuitions sometimes invest us in nonsense or, more precisely, lies.

Actually, one could try to defend Adam and Eve. They don't exactly lie, at least not in the full sense of telling a false story. They simply emphasize certain points and perspectives belonging to the true story. Still, it is an attempt to deceive, is it not? They deceive themselves into believing they are good or right or just. But God is not fooled.

Why might we want to defend Adam and Eve? Might our motive arise from our own temptation to downplay deceit? Are we comfortable with our deceit? Perhaps it would be best to clean the deck and simply say it outright: it's a lie. "The lie is the specific evil which man has introduced into nature," says Buber.[6]

The father of lies is Satan, says Jesus. John 8:44: "When he [the devil] lies, he speaks according to his own nature, for he is a liar and the father of lies." So who is it? Did Satan or humanity introduce the lie into nature? Perhaps it doesn't matter who told the first lie. We now swim in a churning sea of lies.

Evil Ethics?

This interpretation of Adam and Eve makes ethics the most sinful of the human professions. The ethicist, like Adam and Eve, works hard to distinguish good from evil, right from wrong. The ethicist draws a

6. Martin Buber, *Good and Evil* (New York: Charles Scribner's Sons, 1952), 7.

line between good and evil, and then he or she tries to justify one or another action on this basis. Although the ethicist does not (usually) lie, the ethicist more than any other in our society keeps the human race closeted in the darkness of original sin.

Dietrich Bonhoeffer was an ethicist. He opens his widely read book on the subject with this: "The knowledge of good and evil seems to be the aim of all ethical reflection. The first task of Christian ethics is to invalidate this knowledge."[7] What? That's right! Bonhoeffer wants to "invalidate" our knowledge of the difference between good and evil. The problem is that our pursuit of the distinction between good and evil demonstrates that we human beings are no longer at one with our origin; we no longer belong to God. "Instead of knowing only the God who is good to him [humanity] and instead of knowing all things in Him [God], he now knows himself as the origin of good and evil. . . . He has become like God, but against God. Herein lies the serpent's deceit. . . . In becoming like God man has become a god against God."[8]

According to the ethicist within each of us (we each have a little ethicist abiding within us who is occasionally supposed to speak through each of our consciences), we try to draw a line between good and evil and place ourselves on the good side. Unfortunately, according to the gospel, when God draws a line between good and evil, God places the divine self on the evil side. In Christ, God became sin, subject to death. The great reversal in the story of Jesus is that God lands with both feet on the evil side of the line. If we, along with our private and public ethicists, work diligently to discern the good and then identify with the good, we end up on the wrong side of the line. We separate ourselves from God. And if we insist

---

7. Dietrich Bonhoeffer, *Ethics,* ed. Eberhard Bethge, trans. Neville Horton Smith, The Fontana Library (London: Collins, 1949), 17.
8. Ibid., 18–19.

vehemently that our side of the line is the good side, then we become demigods—gods against God. Our former friends and SBNRs refer to us as bigots.

Two things make it difficult for us to see God within the realm of sin and death. The first is that we don't expect to see God on that side of the line. This failed expectation leads to the "theology of the cross" (*theologia crucis*). Jesus Christ, who knew no sin, became sin. The power of God is revealed within weakness. The glory of God is revealed within humiliation. The life of God is revealed within death. If the fragile soul props itself up through self-justification and succeeds in establishing itself firmly on the good side of the line, it will be very disappointing to find that God has taken up residence on the other side. More on the Theology of the Cross later.

The second reason that we find it difficult to see God on the evil side of the line is that we have blinded ourselves. Our ethical reasoning turns off the lights. Engaging in self-justification is like placing a blindfold over our eyes so that we cannot even see what's in the mirror. Among the things we can no longer see is our sin. After all, we are safely situated on the good side of the line. We've left sin behind. Why bring up the nasty subject of sin again?

Sin blinds us in the same way that a lie blinds us. Without sight, we are unable to see God. In order to see God, we have to see ourselves realistically. "Luther rightly insisted that the unwillingness of the sinner to be regarded as a sinner was the final form of sin," comments Reinhold Niebuhr. He continues:

> The final proof that man no longer knows God is that he does not know his own sin. The sinner who justifies himself does not know God as judge and does not need God as Saviour. One might add that the sin of self-righteousness is not only the final sin in the subjective sense but also in the objective sense. It involves us in the greatest guilt. It is responsible for our most serious cruelties, injustices and defamations against our fellowman. The whole history of racial, national, religious

and other social struggles is a commentary on the objective wickedness and social miseries which result from self-righteousness.[9]

This blindness leads to violence.

Violence? The connection may not seem obvious, but then we've chosen to blind ourselves to reality, so even what is obvious becomes invisible.

More Evil Ethics

The problem with ethicists and moralists is that they provide rational justifications that, in effect, perpetuate the cycle of violence. They even provide a name for it: *retributive justice*. In more common terminology, we know it as revenge.

One prime example is the self-defense argument. If you hit me first, then I am morally justified in reciprocating with an equally forceful punch. It might be immoral for me to punch you first, but I'm certainly justified in extending the violence you have initiated. I am certainly justified in drawing a line between good and evil while placing you on the evil side. Thanks to the ethicists, hurting you has become morally acceptable.

One of the problems with the self-defense argument is that it covers up the human lie. The human lie is that it is important for me to be justified. This is so important that I always imagine myself to be the victim of the first punch. I would never admit that I'm the one who threw the first punch, that I am the one who initiated the combat. There is no time or place where I am unable to employ the morality of self-defense in my self-justification. While the truth is

9. Reinhold Niebuhr, *The Nature and Destiny of Man: A Christian Interpretation*, 2 vols. (New York: Charles Scribner's Sons, 1941), 1:200.

that before God neither you nor I need to be morally justified, we hire our ethicists to help us in our efforts at self-justification.

Literary critic René Girard alerts us to the blind alleys that ethicists and moralists may lead us into.

> Moralists . . . authorize us, at least tacitly, to reply to obvious provocations by the measured counterviolence . . . which seems to us always justified. . . . Our moralists have not succeeded to altering the familiar dynamics of violence in any way. They share the habitual illusions on the subject—which is precisely why their teaching pleases us. They reassure us of our innocence and encourage us in our pious regret of the widening scope of violence, without ever awakening in us the least doubt with regard to ourselves.[10]

Jesus tries to alert us to the complicity of ethics in our self-deception. He tries to awaken us and will not allow ethicists to bless us in our self-deceit, or even in our desire to harm those whom we deem harmful to us. In his Sermon on the Mount, he denies us any justification for perpetuating the cycle of violence by telling us to turn the other cheek. Matthew 5:38-41: "You have heard that it was said, 'An eye for an eye and a tooth for a tooth.' But I say to you, Do not resist an evildoer. But if anyone strikes you on the right cheek, turn the other also; and if anyone wants to sue you and take your coat, give your cloak as well; and if anyone forces you to go one mile, go also the second mile." Jesus has tacitly fired all ethicists and replaced them with an abiding relationship with God.

In his insightful interpretation of Jesus, Girard grants that those who poke an eye or slap a cheek or sue or rob us of our coats are genuine threats. Yes, they're out to get us. Jesus is not naive. He is aware that it is only natural for one's first thought to be of self-defense, or even retribution. Yet Jesus is alerting us to a danger. "We

---

10. René Girard, *The One by Whom Scandal Comes* (East Lansing: Michigan State University Press, 2014), 18.

are dealing with people who wish to infuriate us, to draw us into a cycle of escalating conflict," Girard cedes.

> They [our enemies] will do everything they can . . . to provoke a response that will justify them in retaliating in turn, to manufacture an excuse for legitimate self-defense. For if we treat them as they treat us, they will be able to disguise their own injustice by means of reprisals that are fully warranted by the violence we have committed. It is therefore necessary to deprive them of the negative collaboration that they demand of us. . . . Only the conduct enjoined by Jesus can keep violence from getting out of hand, by putting a stop to it before it starts.[11]

By being unethical, Jesus tries to put an end to the cycle of justified violence.

In the life of the saint, love trumps justice. Charity trumps self-defense. Kindness trumps getting even. Despite his criticism of the unhappy or melancholy consciousness of the fragile soul, William James cannot hold back his praise for the spiritual accomplishments of the saint. Human transformation is possible, and the saints demonstrate it. "The saints are authors, *auctores,* increasers of goodness. The potentialities of development in human souls are unfathomable. So many who seemed irretrievably hardened have in point of fact been softened, converted, regenerated. . . . We have no right to speak of human crocodiles and boa-constrictors as of fixedly incurable beings."[12] James has even witnessed the power of turning the other cheek. When non-resistance trumps retributive justice, transformatory power is let loose. "Non-resistance, when successful, turns enemies into friends; and charity regenerates its objects. These saintly methods are, as I said, creative energies."[13]

11. Ibid., 19–20.
12. James, *VRE*, 357.
13. Ibid., 358.

These saintly methods, as James calls them, respond to Jesus' admonition to turn the other cheek rather than to seek justice.

This may come as a shock: Jesus does not ask us to be ethical or moral or just. Jesus asks us to stop the cycle of violence. But if we are hell bent to justify ourselves by exacting violence in the name of self-defense, then violence will continue in perpetuity.

The Pharisee and the Tax Collector

Virtually everything in this book is an interpretation of a single parable in the Bible. The passage I have in mind is Jesus' parable of the Pharisee and the publican, in which Jesus hints at everything important about the concept of justification-by-faith. As a reminder, here is the passage in the New Revised Standard Version. Luke 18:10-14:

> Two men went up to the temple to pray, one a Pharisee and the other a tax collector. The Pharisee, standing by himself, was praying thus, "God, I thank you that I am not like other people: thieves, rogues, adulterers, or even like this tax collector. I fast twice a week; I give a tenth of all my income." But the tax collector, standing far off, would not even look up to heaven, but was beating his breast and saying, "God, be merciful to me, a sinner!" I tell you, this man went down to his home justified rather than the other; for all who exalt themselves will be humbled, but all who humble themselves will be exalted.

Whereas the Pharisee sought self-justification, the publican accepted God's justification. Jesus and Paul agree on Rom. 8:33b: "God is the one who justifies" (*theos ho dikaiosune*).

What might Nadia say? Nadia tells us that teachings like this from Jesus should come with a warning label: "*Caution! Contents may cause extreme discomfort if actually ingested.*" Nadia continues:

> This parable is a trap and the bait for this trap is our desire to figure out

the moral of the story. Because as soon as we reach for that delicious little one inch square piece of cheddar, convinced the point of the parable is that to be really righteous, to be really good in the eyes of others and in the eyes of God is to be humble, then we find the jaws of this parable snap around us because the very next thing out of our mouths can only be: *Thank you God that I am humble like the Tax collector and not a bragger like this Pharisee.* Trapped. Or in the words of Homer Simpson, D'uh![14]

Here is the trap: we can turn faith itself into a form of self-justification, one more mask that hides the truth. "Faith is not at all the supreme and true and finally successful form of self-justification," Karl Barth reminds us.[15] When this temptation to self-justify in the name of faith knocks at our door, we need to turn to the mirror and laugh at ourselves.

New Testament scholar David Brondos contends that St. Paul's notion of justification by grace through faith was taken from Jesus, especially teachings such as the parable about the Pharisee and the tax collector. There is shock value in what Jesus says because a reversal takes place. "This, then, is the paradox underlying Jesus' teaching and practice: *the real sinners are those who claim to be righteous, while the truly righteous are those who recognize they are sinners.*"[16] What we must first get straight is just who we are: we are sinners who engage in self-justification as an expression of our sinfulness. We are sinners who lie to ourselves. We are sinners who hire ethicists to help us lie to ourselves.

---

14. Nadia Bolz-Weber, "Reformation Day Sermon on How Jesus' Teachings Should Come with a Warning Label," *Sarcastic Lutheran* (blog), October 28, 2013, http://www.patheos.com/blogs/nadiabolzweber/2013/10/reformation-day-sermon-on-self-righteousness-and-humility/, (italics in the original).
15. Barth, CD, IV/1, 617.
16. David A. Brondos, "Borders, Boundaries, and Blessing: Mission as Converting Hypocrites into Sinners," *Dialog* 49:1 (March 2010): 38, italics in original. See David A. Brondos, *Redeeming the Gospel: The Christian Faith Reconsidered* (Minneapolis: Fortress Press, 2010), chap. 4.

Does this render the discipline of ethics irredeemable and moral leadership impossible? No, says Brondos. Curiously, the self-acknowledged sinner—the one who sins boldly—becomes the best ethicist.

> Hypocrisy breeds hypocrisy; and when those on top behave as hypocrites, they turn everyone else into hypocrites as well. In reality, only those who acknowledge their sin and injustices when these are pointed out to them, repent publicly of what they have done, and seek to mend their ways with help from others can defend what is right and just and exercise any type of moral leadership in relation to others. People who see themselves as just and righteous cannot practice justice and righteousness, only sinners can.[17]

What kind of an ethicist or leader might this approach produce? My answer: a non-hypocrite who feels blessed with God's justification as a gift of grace, who looks at ethics differently, and who sins boldly. Oh yes, the ethicist encourages the political leader and everyone else to pursue justice and righteousness. Yes, indeed. But for the justified sinner, a new spirit takes hold, a spirit that permits an accurate assessment of what is just rather than a self-serving spirit that desperately needs to be on the right side of the line between good and evil. Rather than self-justification for oneself, we pursue justice for the neighbor. We pursue justice and righteousness "in a spirit of *sinners helping other sinners to overcome their own sinfulness* rather than *accusing and condemning* one another."[18] Saved sinners make good ethicists because they sin boldly.

---

17. Brondos, "Borders," 41.
18. Ibid., 42 (italics in the original).

Loving Self, Loving Other

Christians of all stripes believe we should confess our sins and love our neighbor. Public false modesty combined with public commitment to neighbor-love can become the standard for minting new Christian Pharisees who proclaim, "I'm more caring than thou!"

What counts as confessable sin? Is loving the self a sin that prevents us from loving others? No. Jesus' love commandment includes love of self. Matthew 19:19: "You shall love your neighbor as yourself." Jesus does not say love either your neighbor or yourself. He says love both.

Sometimes self-love gets lost in Christian rhetoric because of our sustained emphasis on selfless love for others. We sometimes enunciate terms such as "ego" or "selfishness" with a sneer. We hint that the ego or the self might contaminate otherwise pure altruism. This can be misleading. Ignoring oneself or even hating oneself is not an admiral ethical idea.

His Holiness the Dalai Lama distinguishes between what we might call sinful arrogance and healthy self-confidence. "One sense of self, or ego, is concerned only with the fulfillment of one's self-interest, one's selfish desires, with complete disregard for the well-being of others. The other type of ego or sense of self is based on a genuine concern for others, and the desire to be of service. In order to fulfill that wish to be of service, one needs a strong sense of self, and a sense of self-confidence."[19] I cite a Buddhist because, curiously, even with an ontology of *anatta* or "no-self," he affirms the indispensible value of self-confidence. A robust sense of self with self-confidence is actually formed by one's "desire to be of service" and, reciprocally, is

19. Dalai Lama and Howard C. Cutler, *The Art of Happiness: A Handbook for Living* (New York: Penguin Putnam, 1998), 279.

requisite for loving one's neighbor. Can I be confident in saying, "I am a self who loves others"?

According to Christian feminist Cynthia Moe-Lobeda, we do not need to repent from our self-love when loving others. "*Agape weds other-love with self-love*," she writes. "As a feminist theologian, my reading of the gospels finds self-love inherent in the commandment to love neighbor as self."[20] If we are to sin boldly when pursuing ethical action, working out of a robust self-confidence does not count as a mortal sin.

I have just said that we should love our self and love our neighbor. The two arrive in a single package. However, let me proffer what may at first seem like a strange logic: we first love the neighbor and, in this loving of someone who is other, we love ourselves. It is not the case that we love the self first and then, after loving the self, we decide to bring the neighbor in on the deal. The reverse logic obtains.

Loving Other, Loving Self

Curiously, one's love for the neighbor—love for the Other in our life—makes it possible for one to love the self. Even more, without loving the Other, one cannot become a self; at least, one cannot become the self that is itself in relation to the eternal God.

Recall how, in chapter 1, I described the human soul as an empty vortex at the center of a swirl of activity, as the principle of centrality within an exocentric sphere of interactions.[21] This extended metaphor suggests that if you or I try to go it alone—if we try to establish ourselves as independent by cutting the self off from

20. Cynthia Moe-Lobeda, *Resisting Structural Evil: Love as Ecological-Economic Vocation* (Minneapolis: Fortress Press, 2013), 171 (italics in the original).

21. In Pannenberg's anthropology, we creatures are exocentric in that we are open to being centered by God's spirit. "Creaturely life has an eccentric character . . . it is referred to the divine power of the Spirit that works upon it." *ST*, 2:186.

the relationship we share with our external interactions—we would collapse into nothingness. However, if we engage in neighbor-love with the others in the external swirl of our daily lives, then we constitute ourselves as loving selves and, thereby, as selves in the first place.

Actually, when we first wake up in life and discover that we are conscious, we are already in relationship with our neighbor. That neighbor might be a parent or a sibling or a hospital nurse. This very relationship makes an ethical demand on us to love those with whom we are in relationship. If this is the case for us as human beings, then perhaps when we pursue theoretical ethics, we can rely on something like natural law, something like a universal human condition upon which to construct an ethics of love.

Did you follow me around this last corner? If not, let me try again. I'll explain with a brief reference to a philosophical discussion about the *Other*. It begins with Martin Heidegger. Recall that peculiar word he introduced, *Dasein*.[22] It combines being, *Sein*, with thereness, *da*. "To be" is to "be there," to be somewhere and not nowhere. Your or my existence is always existence somewhere and at sometime. We cannot be in the garage and in the dining room at the same time. Nor can we be in the dining room and perched on a cloud watching all things on Earth at the same time. To be is to be there, somewhere specific in space and in time.

We never experience being in the abstract. In every moment of our lives, we are contextual, living in relationship to our environment and in relationship to the neighbors who make up our life-world. We cannot be a self in the abstract sense. We can be who we are only in the concrete sense of being a specific person-in-relationship. *Dasein* cannot but be *In-der-Welt-Sein* (being-in-the-world), including

22. See Martin Heidegger, *Being and Time,* trans. John Macquarrie and Edward Robinson (New York: Harper, 1962).

Miteinandersein (being-with-others) and even *Miteinanderschaffen* (creating-with-others). Heidegger's students have drawn out the implications of this observation.

Among Heidegger's students, two deserve special mention here: Jewish philosopher Emmanuel Levinas and Lutheran philosopher Knud Løgstrup. We will look at each in turn, seeing what we might learn from them that would help us in constructing an ethic for hypocrites who must sin boldly.

Levinas does not deconstruct the human subject or self. That is to say, he does not anchor our attention in the empty vortex around which our relationships swirl. Rather, he contends that the subject is constructed within a primordial relationship to the Other, to the neighbor. We cannot be our selves except in relationship to the Other; and this otherness evokes within our subjectivity a sense of infinity. According to Levinas, the self must be "welcoming the Other, as hospitality; in it the idea of infinity is consummated."[23] In other words, "I am 'in myself' through others."[24] What Levinas is telling us, I think, is that our human consciousness begins in relationship to other persons, and this basic or primordial relationship demands that we love the other on the analogy of showing hospitality to our neighbors. Without serving the other in love, we cannot be a self at all, let alone our own selves. Further, loving the other person is not merely one option from among many that we might freely choose; rather, loving the other is an ontological necessity for us to be a self, to be a subject or especially a soul.

Turning to another of Heidegger's students, Danish philosopher Knud Løgstrup, we find a similar description of our fundamental situation as human beings. To be a human person is to be in a

---

23. Emmanuel Levinas, *Totality and Infinity: An Essay in Exteriority,* trans. Alphonso Lingis (Pittsburgh: Duquesne University Press, 1969), 27.
24. Emmanuel Levinas, *Otherwise Than Being, or, Beyond Essence,* trans. Alphopnso Lingis (Pittsburgh: Duquesne University Press, 1998), 129.

relationship with other persons such that they make the demand that we must serve them with unselfish love. According to Løgstrup, this is the *ethical demand*, a demand that belongs to our ontology as human beings. To be is to be a person-in-relationship, and this relationship entails the demand that we serve the well-being and the flourishing of the other party in that relationship. When we wake up to find ourselves in being, we find that we are not individuals first who add relationships later. Rather, we find that whatever individuality and responsibility we have derives from a prior world of concrete relationships. We are not independent but interdependent, and entailed in this interdependence is a silent yet potent command: love your neighbor!

Our responsibility is inescapable. "By our very attitude to one another we help to shape one another's world. By our attitude to the other person we help to determine the scope and hue of his or her world, we make it large or small, bright or drab, rich or dull, threatening or secure,"[25] writes Løgstrup. This philosopher, like Luther, believes each of us can serve as "daily bread" for those around us. Our impact on another person "may be a very small matter, involving only a passing mood, a dampening or quickening of spirit, a deepening or removal of some dislike. But it may also be a matter of tremendous scope, such as can determine if the life of the other flourishes or not."[26]

This is a philosophical argument. It derives merely from observation of the human condition. It does not require a theological commitment. "I am convinced that his [Løgstrup's] philosophical argument can, in fact, stand on its own without any specifically Christian presuppositions," comments Hans Fink.[27] Yet this

---

25. Knud Ejler Løgstrup, *The Ethical Demand* (Notre Dame, IN: University of Notre Dame Press, 1997), 18.
26. Ibid., 15–16.

description of the human situation seems like a philosophical wine bottle yearning for a theological cork. "The ethical demand is an aspect of the created order of life. In the final analysis he [Løgstrup] believes that life thus ordered be received as if it were a gift (*donum*) from a Creator."[28]

Danish ethicist Svend Anderson corks the bottle. "Ultimately, the idea of the demand and responsibility being justified in interdependency is one that Løgstrup takes from Luther's idea of the creation ordinances. 'The ethical demand' is Løgstrup's term for Luther's version of natural law. We are dealing with the universal ethics formulated by a Lutheran philosopher."[29] In sum, what we find is that "Løgstrup, in working out his ethics, shows himself to be a Lutheran philosopher."[30]

The human soul is a principle of centrality amid a surrounding swirl of exocentric relationships that include both the neighbor and God. Our openness toward the Other is simultaneously an openness toward God. Loving both neighbor and God are constituent to loving ourselves. This is an ontological given. It is also an ethical demand.

Proleptic Ethics

Just as faith seeks understanding, so also we need to seek understanding on moral matters. Ethics is the discipline of reflecting on morality, according to Moe-Lobeda. "*Morality* refers to the lived

---

27. Hans Fink, "The Conception of Ethics and the Ethical in K. E. Løgstrup's *The Ethical Demand*," in *Concern for the Other: Perspectives on the Ethics of K.E. Løgstrup*, ed. Svend Andersen and Kees van Kooten Niekerk (Notre Dame, IN: University of Notre Dame Press, 2007), 10–11.
28. Ibid., 21.
29. Svend Andersen, "In the Eyes of a Lutheran Philosopher: How Løgstrup Treated Moral Thinkers," in *Concern for the Other*, 51.
30. Ibid., 29.

dimension of life pertaining to doing and being—for individuals and groups (small and large)—in ways that are good, right, and fitting. *Ethics,* on the other hand, is 'second order discourse' reflecting on that dimension of life; ethics is disciplined inquiry into or study of morality."[31] Ethics is the "science of the moral," says Tillich;[32] and ethics deals "with the laws of free moral action," says Immanuel Kant.[33] Should bold sinners pursue the science of moral action? Yes, indeed.

Christian ethicist Aana Marie Vigen adds a subtle observation. "Ethics, as a discipline, does *not* simply relate to what one thinks about particular moral questions. Rather, it involves *how* one thinks about them. Ethics considers and reveals what sources or moral wisdom, methods of evaluation, and even blind spots are evident in how one approaches moral questions."[34] This means that ethics requires critical analysis. Ethics also works out of a vision of a world better than the one in which we currently find ourselves. "Create a constructive moral imagination," writes Vigen before she asks, "What vision do you offer?"[35] My answer: we begin with a creative vision of God's promised future.

My own approach is what I call *proleptic ethics.*[36] Proleptic ethics begins with a vision of God's promised future, which is symbolized as either the Kingdom of God or the new creation. According to

31. Moe-Lobeda, *Resisting Structural Evil,* 17.
32. Paul Tillich, *Morality and Beyond* (San Francisco: Harper, 1963), 21.
33. Immanuel Kant, *Groundwork of the Metaphysic of Morals,* trans. H. J. Paton, 3rd ed. (New York: Harper, 1956), 13.
34. Aana Marie Vigen, "Conclusion: Descriptive and Normative Ways of Understanding Human Nature," in *God, Science, Sex, Gender: An Interdisciplinary Approach to Christian Ethics,* ed. Patricia Beattie Jung and Aana Marie Vigen, with Jon Anderson (Urbana: University of Illinois Press, 2010), 242, italics in original.
35. Ibid.
36. Ted Peters, *God—The World's Future: Systematic Theology for a Postmodern Era, 2nd ed.* (Minneapolis: Fortress Press, 2000), chap. 12; Peters, *Science, Theology, and Ethics* (Aldershot, UK: Ashgate, 2003).

this vision, God's future will be characterized by justice—restorative justice imbued with divine love. This divine promise provides the theological foundation for ethical reflection. We can see the proleptic structure reflected in the concern for gender justice voiced by the Evangelical Lutheran Church in America when they formulated a statement on human sexuality. "For believers, it is hope in God's future, not in an idealized past, that inspires participation in God's changing, open, and inexhaustible creation. Christians believe that God's promised future includes the transformation of the whole creation (Romans 8:19-25). Guided by this vision, Christians anticipate and live out the values of God's promised future concretely in the present."[37] This, I recommend, is *how* we should think about ethical matters.

Now, you might be asking: Can one get on the wagon and still order a single malt Scotch during cocktail hour? Can Ted describe ethics as the epitome of self-justification and then proceed to cultivate a science of self-justification?

The transition from God's grace to human ethics begins from within the messy world in which we live. Pure, untrammeled acts of justice are impossible within the crisscrossing forces that engulf us. We can perform better or worse acts, to be sure, but we do not have the option of drawing a line between absolute good and absolute evil. Ambiguity is our inescapable daily reality. This led Luther to enunciate his fundamental ethical principle: *crede in Christum et fac quod debes*—that is, believe in Christ and do what you must. In other words, sin boldly.

Moe-Lobeda reiterates the challenge of ambiguity and the necessity of embracing responsibility within ambiguity. "In things

---

37. Evangelical Lutheran Church in America, "A Social Statement on Human Sexuality: Gift and Trust," *Evangelical Lutheran Church in America,* August 19, 2009, http://www.elca.org/en/Faith/ Faith-and-Society/Social-Statements/Human-Sexuality.

human—good and evil are intertwined. . . . human finitude renders our actions toward the good, including our acts of love and justice, imperfect. However, despite our imperfection and the intermingling of evil with good, we are called to move forward in justice-making love to the best of our ability."[38] Better to have loved imperfectly than never to have loved at all!

What does this acceptance of ambiguity and imperfection imply for ethics? *Ethics is the art of boldly sinning while pursuing the good*—the empirical or daily good that may be less than the pure, final, or eternal good. Ethics is the art of boldly sinning while pursuing a temporary justice that may be less than eternal justice. But don't flag in zeal! Better to practice daily goodness and temporary justice than their opposites.

Conclusion

Sadly, self-justification is our human default position. Unsatisfied with the vacuum in the center, where we think a self or soul should be, we try to form the soul by copying what we see in the moral universe that forms our worldview. We think we're building our souls according to the blueprint supplied by our moral universe. We delude ourselves with the assumption that if we're successful at constructing a just self, then this self will live forever.

Forming an eternally just soul sounds easy. But like wooden planks rotting on our dock, we fear stepping too hard and falling through. In those moments between daily consciousness and dropping off to a night's sleep, unbidden thoughts sometimes occupy us: *Maybe it's not true. Maybe it's a lie. Maybe it's a lie I'm telling myself. Oh well, if there's no god then it just won't matter.* In the next moment, sleep arrives.

---

38. Moe-Lobeda, *Resisting Structural Evil,* 164.

Or to say it another way, perhaps waking consciousness is a form of daytime sleep, and we experience this self-critical awareness for only those few seconds before the night's slumber ends it.

Our moral universe requires that we draw a line between good and evil. We place ourselves on the good side of the line. Our moral universe is constructed in such a way that this is possible. According to the criteria in our moral universe, we can self-justify. What we do we believe to be good, right, and true. Our moral universe defines the self as good. It keeps us sane. The problem, of course, is that the moral universe is idolatrous. It is a moral universe without the true God of grace. Without the true God of grace, our ethical deliberation consists of placing ourselves on the good side of every line we draw.

But whom do we place on the evil side? Answer: the scapegoat. To the scapegoat we now turn.

9

Scapegoats and Broken Souls

The cross is the revelation of a destabilizing truth.

–René Girard[1]

"My soul has fled."

"What do you mean?"

"It's gone. It fled my body. I felt it leave."

–US soldier speaking to Edward Tick[2]

From deep within our souls, we yearn to be just. We yearn for justification, whether we call it justification or not. Yet our pursuit of justification can have a dark and violent side. If we reject being declared just by God's grace—if we reject justification-by-faith—then

---

1. Girard, *The One by Whom Scandal Comes* (East Lansing: Michigan State University Press, 2014), 63. With genius of insight, Girard's scapegoat theory focuses on the invisible scapegoat. What Girard does not do that I do here is distinguish the visible from the invisible form scapegoating takes.
2. Tick, *War and the Soul: Healing Our Nation's Veterans from Post–traumatic Stress Disorder* (Wheaton: Quest Books, 2005), 12.

the only alternative is self-justification. When we pursue self-justification, we become dangerous to others.

Unconsciously or semiconsciously, we draw a line between good and evil, between what is just and what is unjust. And we place ourselves on the good side of the line, on the just side of the line. Sometimes this includes placing someone else on the evil side. Those whom we place on the evil side become our scapegoat. At that point, we can justify harming or even destroying our scapegoat because scapegoating is an act of self-purification. We purify ourselves by destroying the scapegoat who, figuratively, bears away our sins and leaves us in a justified state. This is a delusion, to be sure, yet it's virtually an everyday activity.

Because we enter the world of delusion when engaging in self-justification, the matter gets even more complicated. In our vain effort to purify ourselves, we sometimes sacrifice a scapegoat on the good side of the line. This scapegoat is innocent; yet we are willing to sacrifice the innocent because this sacrifice has purifying power, or so we think. Actually, we don't think. We just do it. The sacrifice of the innocent scapegoat is invisible to us, hidden beneath the delusion.

In this chapter, I will distinguish two types of scapegoats, the visible and the invisible. I will show how each purifies (justifies) us in a different way. We purify ourselves when cursing the visible scapegoat; but the invisible scapegoat dies to make us holy and blesses us with purification. The visible scapegoat is our enemy, whereas the invisible scapegoat is our friend. Finally, I will show how the cross of Jesus Christ bursts the delusion, shatters the scapegoat mechanism, and reveals the devastating truth about the violence wrought by the futile attempt to self-justify.

This chapter engages one more topic: the broken soul. The soul breaks when we lose our moral universe, when we lose the transcendental vision of what is eternally just and good and true. This can and does happen to our sacred victim. Our invisible scapegoat becomes victimized, confused, and despairing. The victim experiences soul loss, or what we refer to today as moral injury, which is frequently followed by suicide. Self-justification via scapegoating leads ineluctably toward someone else's death so that we might be purified.

The Purifying Power of the Scapegoat

Our ancestors in the archaic world practiced scapegoating—literal scapegoating. The role of ancient scapegoat practice was to cleanse, purify, or renew the community by banishing evil. In ancient Israel, the scapegoat bore the sins of Israel away on the Day of Atonement. Leviticus 16:16a, 21: "Thus he shall make atonement for the sanctuary, because of the uncleannesses of the people of Israel. . . . Then Aaron shall lay both his hands on the head of the live goat, and confess over it all the iniquities of the people of Israel, and all their transgressions, all their sins, putting them on the head of the goat, and sending it away into the wilderness by means of someone designated for the task." By cursing the living goat and sending the cursed animal into the wilderness, the "uncleannesses of the people of Israel" could be atoned for.

The scapegoat mechanism remains alive and well in today's human psyche, in group dynamics, and in civic liturgy. In our individual psyches, the ancient practice of scapegoating has been sublimated or transmogrified into an ever-present principle of soul-formation and social-construction. As we try to form the soul in light of our vision of cosmic justice, opportunities to scapegoat others tempt us with a spiritual shortcut, namely, self-justification. Today's scapegoats are still burdened with the task of carrying away our sins.

Of the mere handful of scholars in the world who have studied the scapegoat pattern, the most helpful, in my judgment, is Stanford literary scholar, René Girard. The term *scapegoat,* he avers,

> designates (1) the victim of the ritual described in Leviticus, (2) all the victims of similar rituals that exist in archaic societies and that are called rituals of expulsion, and finally (3) all the phenomena of nonritualized collective transference that we observe or believe we observe around us. . . . We cry "scapegoat" to stigmatize all the phenomena of discrimination—political, ethnic, religious, social, racial, etc.—that we observe about us. We are right. We easily see now that scapegoats multiply wherever human groups seek to lock themselves into a given identity—communal, local, national, ideological, racial, religious, and so on.[3]

Like the prophets in ancient Israel, we need to cry, "Scapegoat!," so that lies might be exposed as lies—so that blind eyes can see again.

The delusion nearly all of us buy into is a lie that covers up an uncomfortable truth: when we scapegoat we increase evil rather than rid ourselves of it. Scapegoating deforms the soul because the soul forms itself around a lie that feeds and grows off violence perpetrated against those whom we victimize. The bad news of the gospel is that Jesus identifies with the scapegoat—with the victim—not those for whom the scapegoat allegedly atones. If Jesus would have his way, there would be no more scapegoats. Jesus' death on the cross should be considered the last act of scapegoating; Jesus should be the final scapegoat. Regrettably, subsequent history is just as filled with scapegoats as the history that came before.

"The cross is a symbol, a reference to a historic act, and a conveyer of meaning," Martin Marty tells us.[4] One thing the cross means, I

---

3. René Girard, *I See Satan Fall Like Lightening,* trans. James G. Williams (Maryknoll, NY: Orbis Books, 2001), 160. Girard does not distinguish as sharply as I do between the visible and the invisible form the scapegoat takes.

4. Martin E. Marty, *Lutheran Questions, Lutheran Answers* (Minneapolis: Augsburg Fortress, 2007), 56.

contend, is that God places the divine self on the side of the scapegoat. When we find ourselves drawing a line between good and evil and placing a scapegoat on the other side, watch out! God is on the other side.

To Bully a Slut

Rehtaeh Parsons was gang raped following a party in November 2011. The fifteen-year-old girl living in Nova Scotia was taken to the party by a friend. She drank some vodka. Perhaps too much. While semiconscious, four boys raped her. To celebrate and brag about their accomplishment, they took a picture and put the photo on the internet. It went viral.

When a girl or a woman is raped, she feels violated. She feels dirty, tarnished, contaminated, and profaned. Here it is helpful to recall that our intuition about justice designates the body as holy, as a temple of the sacred. A rape victim feels polluted, which leads to the feeling of shame. Even though she commits no sin, she feels sinful. It is naive to think that the only form of sin is an act of free will. Being made unclean by someone else's sin is still sin. A victim may feel more shame than the perpetrator. This is the way Rhetaeh Parsons felt.

The local police did not prosecute. They could not sort out the "he said" from the "she said," they said. So, without a pending prosecution, a pattern of internet bullying began and continued. Rhetaeh was described as a "slut," which is a form of profanity; it designates a person as morally inferior. The person who uses the term *slut* is cursing, and to curse is to draw a line between good and evil and place the cursing person on the good side of the line. The alleged slut plays the role of scapegoat in someone else's self-justification.

"She walked into the school and everyone started calling her a slut," her mother reported. "This day changed the lives of our family forever. . . . Rhetaeh was suddenly shunned by almost everyone she knew. . . . She struggled emotionally with depression and anger."[5] On April 7, 2013, seventeen-year-old Rhetaeh hanged herself and later died in the hospital.

Cursing Creates Community

Clearly, Rhetah Parsons served as a scapegoat for the high school community. Her friends drew a line between good and evil, and they placed Rhetah on the evil side. By calling Rhetah a slut and shunning her, the high school community engaged in an act of self-purification.

The language employed in cursing comes in three basic forms: allusions to immorality, excrement, or weakness. We have just seen how the allusion to immorality—being a slut—provided the high school with an opportunity to declare itself moral by shunning the immoral one. When the community tries to purify itself by creating a visible scapegoat, it will most likely identify an enemy and declare this enemy to be immoral, making that person subject to the community's judgment and condemnation.

To be immoral is to be worthless, even damnable. Ascriptions of immorality come in a wide range of forms. Saddam Hussein was described by two presidents (named Bush) as a dictator who was cruel to his own people. As opposed to Rhetaeh Parsons, Saddam Hussein was probably guilty of such accusations, but actual guilt or innocence matters little here. What matters is the role the scapegoat plays in creating a self-justified community through cursing.

Community cursing is common. Individuals can be described as a bitch, a whore, a tyrant, unfaithful, lazy, or even insensitive. Other

5. Leah Parsons, "About Angel Rhetaeh," Facebook page, https://www.facebook.com/angelrehtaehofficial/info?tab=page_info.

races or ethnicities can be described as morally loose, promiscuous, business cheats, welfare cheats, or clannish Other nations can be described as backward, imperialist, godless, or reckless. Such descriptions establish distance. To take a stand against such an enemy is tantamount to taking a stand for what is moral, pure, right, just, and good. Taking such a stand places one in solidarity with others who also deem themselves morally upright. Self-justification binds us to a community at the point where the scapegoat is shunned or attacked or expelled. The sacrifice of the scapegoat establishes or maintains a community made up of persons who know they are right.

Homophobic discourse and racist discourse function to support an ongoing cultural curse. The selection and use of terms such as "fag" or "nigger" construct a mental model in which the non-fags and non-niggers live in a morally superior community. Such language justifies discrimination, perhaps even persecution of the class of persons being scapegoated. Mary E. Lowe, a self-identified queer feminist theologian, exposes such discourse as a form of sin. "Some discourses are sinful and distorting, and we sin when we actively or passively participate in them . . . the conservative religious discourse that lesbians and gays are unnatural can be considered sinful because it rejects the diversity of God's creation, it denies that all are *imago Dei,* it impedes the flourishing of all persons, and it claims that gender is God-given rather than acknowledge that beliefs about gender are constructed."[6] Our world of discourse provides the world of meaning within which we live, and if this world is shot through and through with the language of scapegoating, then someone is going to suffer social damnation. By uncovering and exposing just how our

---

6. Mary E. Lowe, "Sin from a Queer, Lutheran Perspective," in *Transformative Lutheran Theologies: Feminist, Womanist, and Mujerista Perspectives,* ed. Mary J. Streufert (Minneapolis: Fortress Press, 2010), 76.

linguistic world functions to establish and maintain a state of curse, Lowe hopes to dismantle it so that we can see sin for what it is.

The second family of curses alludes to excrement or, more generally, some form of contamination or pollution. To say a person is a piece of excrement convinces the speaker that this is true and, because it's true, it justifies the mistreatment that is about to follow. Just before a murderer pulls the trigger or stabs with the knife, he or she pronounces such a curse. We know this from testimony given by murderers after the fact. Recall the Marine quoted in the previous chapter; he did not kill *persons* in Iraq but "shitheads." Killers kill because they are defending what is pure from contamination by what is unclean.

Hitler and the Nazis described the Jewish community as a cancer, as a disease weakening the Aryan race. Hutus described the Tutsis as vermin, and they sought to eliminate the vermin through a genocide that took almost a million lives. American troops in Vietnam employed the command to "waste them" when referring to killing, the "them" being gooks. American troops fighting in the second Iraq war described the people living there as towelheads, ragheads, and hadjis. Such cursing depersonalizes and makes these victims anonymous. Once the curse is uttered, murder becomes justifiable.

Such military cursing is not spontaneous or haphazard. It's designed and inculcated. "In the modern science of war, military training strategies are directed purposefully at blocking empathy for those defined as the enemy. Stereotyping, de-humanizing, ridiculing, demonizing, discrediting—all are aimed at breaking down identification with the dangerous Other to promote efficient killing."[7]

---

7. Caroline H. Knowles, "Notes toward a Neuropsychology of Moral Injury," *Reflective Practice: Formation and Supervision of Ministry* 33 (2013): 77.

In addition to immorality and excrement, the third category of curse is weakness. To call someone weak is to curse them. How does this work? Of all the things we desire or covet, the most lusted after is power. Power may come in disguised forms, but it remains the single prize for which all others can be sacrificed. Cursing among those proud of their power includes appellations of weakness toward the one being cursed. In Homer's *Iliad,* for example, Menelaus tries to inspire the tired Achaean troops on the battle apron in front of the walled city of Troy. He takes the negative (or stick) approach. "You braggarts, you pitiful cowards—not men, but women—how can you let such bitter disgrace come upon us if not one man here stands up to fight against Hector?"[8] Note what counts as an insult: bragging, cowardice, and womanhood. To be a woman is weak. Menelaus wants to inspire strength, so he insults his men by associating them with weak women. This discourse, within which women are dubbed as disdainful, serves to sustain a state of curse for women in antiquity. My point is not that Menelaus cursed his soldiers; rather, we should see how the accepted pattern of Greek discourse functioned as a curse against women.

Some refer to such cursing discourse as *dehumanization* or even *demonization.* When cursing, we first ignore the humanity of our enemy and then describe the enemy as demonic. If the enemy is demonic, then we are justified when crusading for the elimination of the demon. "In order to create soldiers willing to kill and a citizenry willing to tolerate it," writes Edward Tick, "we must first depersonalize and demonize the other. To depersonalize portrays others as anonymous and less than human. To demonize is to take the process a step further by making the other a carrier of evil, an

---

8. Homer, *The Iliad,* trans. Stephen Mitchell (New York: Free Press, 2011), 7.95–96, p. 111.

incarnation of the devil."[9] Demonization is a form of curse; it justifies violence against the one cursed.

Christians Cursing Jews

The Jews of medieval Europe knew what it meant to be cursed by the dominant Christian community. According to Reformation scholar Kirsi Stjerna, the Holy Roman Empire incorporated "fragile communities," which the Empire scapegoated in order to ease their own insecurities. Christians saw Jewish people as a threat, as a menace to their own faith. So the dominant group ghettoized the minority in an attempt to insulate the two groups in separate regions. Frequently, Jewish families were expelled from Christian areas as a sort of religious cleansing. The cultural atmosphere was "poisoned with anti-Jewish laws, fears, jokes, and slander."[10] Such cultural cursing led to scapegoating. "In an age when life was precarious and catastrophes could visit a community at any time, the Christian mob did not need much kindling to react violently toward an individual or a group deemed to be the scapegoat; the Jew as a most vulnerable, convenient target."[11]

This was the ambient belief system Luther inherited and passed on to his heirs. On the one hand, Luther's reading of the Bible led him to admire the Jews for being the family of Jesus and his virgin mother, Mary. "We are but Gentiles, while the Jews are of the lineage of Christ. We are aliens and in-laws; they are blood relatives, cousins, and brothers of our Lord."[12] On the other hand, Luther's vituperations and invectives drew an untraversable line between the

---

9. Tick, *War and the Soul*, 81–82.
10. Kirsi I. Stjerna, "The Jew in Luther's World," in *Martin Luther, the Bible, and the Jewish People* (Minneapolis: Fortress Press, 2012), 18.
11. Ibid., 20.
12. Luther, *That Jesus Was Born a Jew* (1523), *LW*, 45:201.

insider Christians and the outsider Jews—a line between good Christians and the evil others. "They defame our Lord Jesus Christ, calling him a sorcerer and tool of the devil. . . . They may lie, blaspheme, defame, and murder whom they will, even God himself and all his prophets."[13] He even went so far to say, "They are our open enemies."[14] Luther tags Europe's Jews with names such as blasphemers, defamers, murderers, and enemies. After four centuries, this cultural stream became a raging torrent of prejudice, anti-Semitism, and genocide. In light of this dark history, the hero of the Reformation ought not become a candidate for sainthood.

Cursing is a form of self-justification that patches up a fragile soul. Cursing may lead to scapegoating, and scapegoating may lead to violence. Is there is a power in the gospel that can rid us of the need for self-justification, that can eliminate our need to curse? One might have hoped that Luther, of all people, would have experienced this power of transformation by grace. But alas, he could only point to it. He did not embody it.

The Visible Scapegoat Mechanism: Malign and Bind

Up to this point, most of what I have discussed pertains to the visible scapegoat, whom we malign in order to bind ourselves together. The visible scapegoat is the enemy whom we curse as evil; this cursing produces a spirit of unity among those who have taken a righteous stand against the evil one. In particular, a foreign scapegoat has a way of fostering unity at home, uniting us against a common enemy. As a result, divisions can quickly give way to a spirit of patriotism, nationalism, chauvinism, and jingoism when we picture a Satan or a Hitler across the border. This first kind of scapegoat is visible, even if

13. Luther, *On Jews and Their Lies* (1543), *LW*, 47:254, 260.
14. Luther, *An Admonition against the Jews* (1546), in *LW*, 58:458.

we shroud our scapegoating in self-righteous rhetoric. The more evil we paint the scapegoat, the more just and justified we feel in taking up arms. In sum, the visible scapegoat mechanism operates on the principle of malign 'n' bind.

The second kind of scapegoat is the product of a bigger lie we tell ourselves. Like the visible scapegoat, the invisible scapegoat also helps create community by binding us together. But, in place of *malign 'n' bind*, the invisible scapegoat combines *blind 'n' bind*. We become blind to the role played by the invisible scapegoat in uniting our social unit. We simply do not want to become aware of the scapegoat mechanism upon which we rely for social cohesion. In contrast, what happens becomes virtually invisible and remains invisible until we confess our lie and face the truth. Both kinds of scapegoats bind us together, but the second blinds us to why we are together. Whereas the visible scapegoat mechanism maligns and binds, an invisible scapegoat mechanism operates on the principle of blind 'n' bind.

Both types of scapegoating result in the scapegoat's death so that the self-justifying scapegoater will live. When it comes to petty gossip around the coffee pot, scapegoating takes the form of virtual or figurative death. When it comes to political gossip about foreign leaders and alien peoples, it leads to war and sometimes genocide. In the case of the invisible scapegoat, the victim frequently commits suicide. In general terms, we murder the visible scapegoat, and the invisible scapegoat takes his or her own life. Self-justification leads to scapegoating, and scapegoating leads to someone's death, either figuratively or literally. When the blood of the scapegoat is shed—even if only in our verbal imaginations—we feel justified and purified.

The Invisible Scapegoat Mechanism: Blind and Bind[15]

Maligning the visible scapegoat on the evil side of the line creates community on the good side of the line. The invisible scapegoat also creates community, though in a different way. By establishing what is sacred, it generates loyalty and faithfulness, ritual and reverence. In this way, the sacred centers our community. The invisible scapegoat blinds as it binds.

The sacred scapegoat relies on remembered death, especially sacrificial death. In the United States, the current scapegoat is the US soldier. "Now, wait just a darned minute!" you may object. "American soldiers didn't do anything wrong. What they did was brave, and right, and heroic! When we draw the line between good and evil, the soldiers are on the good side of the line."

Granted, all of this is true. Yet I still nominate the American soldier for the office of official scapegoat—the scapegoat that most profoundly unites American society. "The origin of any cultural order involves a human death and that the decisive death is that of a member of the community," observes Girard.[16] The member of our community whose death sanctifies our community is the wounded soldier. The dead soldier is immortalized in the rhetoric that ascribes to him or her the status of hero. The dead soldier allegedly "sacrificed" his or her life for "freedom," making his or her grave "holy ground." In fact, the near apotheosis of the fallen warrior buries the lie of self-justification deeper than the ascription of evil to our enemies.

What I am about to say may appear counterintuitive, even insulting. Understandably, the reader might be tempted to "Admit

---

15. In Jonathan Haidt, *The Righteous Mind* (New York: Vintage, 2012), Haidt says that, general speaking, morality blinds and binds.
16. René Girard, *Violence and the Sacred*, trans. Patrick Gregory (Baltimore: Johns Hopkins University Press, 1977), 256.

Nothing. Deny Everything. Make Counter Accusations." But please bear with me.

Soldiers Die So That We Might Live

At a civic liturgy honoring US soldiers on Memorial Day, 2011, President Barack Obama linked today's warriors and God's holy word to our first patriots in the Revolutionary War of 1776. "What binds this chain together across the generations, this chain of honor and sacrifice, is not only a common cause—our country's cause—but also a spirit captured in a Book of Isaiah, a familiar verse, mailed to me by the Gold Star parents of 2nd Lieutenant Mike McGahan. 'When I heard the voice of the Lord saying, "Whom shall I send? And who will go for us?" I said, "Here I am. Send me!"'"[17] Regardless of the specific text, the mere allusion to Holy Scriptures in a political speech connotes sacred presence, blessing, and reverence.

Observe the symbol theft. The president steals the power of the biblical symbol for his own political agenda. The call of God to the prophet has become transmogrified into the call of America to the soldier. Whereas the ancient Hebrew prophet answered God's call to deliver the divine word, America's soldier answers the same divine call to enter into combat. To fight for America is a holy calling, says the president.

With an ascending rhetorical crescendo, the president ritually recalls the sacrifices that founded his nation. Patriotic sacrifice stands on the same level as religious sacrifice. Or perhaps more precisely, patriotism becomes the spiritual bond.

That's what we memorialize today. That spirit that says, send me, no

---

17. Barack Obama, "Remarks by the President at a Memorial Day Service," May 30, 2011, White House website, http://www.whitehouse.gov/the-press-office/2011/05/30/remarks-president-memorial-day-service.

matter the mission. Send me, no matter the risk. Send me, no matter how great the sacrifice I am called to make. The patriots we memorialize today sacrificed not only all they had but all they would ever know. They gave of themselves until they had nothing more to give. It's natural, when we lose someone we care about, to ask why it had to be them. Why my son, why my sister, why my friend, why not me? . . . We remember that the blessings we enjoy as Americans came at a dear cost; that our very presence here today, as free people in a free society, bears testimony to their enduring legacy.[18]

To sacrifice for America's freedom is to offer the ultimate sacrifice. There is none higher. Americans today enjoy the blessings of the salvation wrought by our soldiers' sacrificial blood.

Symbol stealing is not restricted to the redemptive power of the soldier's sacrifice. It's routine. When one walks into the lobby of the headquarters of the US Central Intelligence Agency at Langley, one sees the CIA motto engraved in large letters: "Ye shall know the truth and the truth shall set you free," (John 8:32). In scripture, the *truth* refers to the truth about God—the gospel. Does the CIA really spread the truth of the gospel? In addition, recall the profound words of Sarah Palin, former governor of Alaska and presidential candidate, speaking before the National Rifle Association in Indianapolis in 2014. Referring to American contractors torturing prisoners in Iraq, she remarked, "Water boarding is how we baptize terrorists."[19] This remark precipitated the greatest amount of applause during her address. By plugging into the power of Christian symbols, political rhetoric energizes the spirituality of a secular nation.

Let's turn back to our discussion of the US soldier. The redemptive power of death expressed in today's patriotism represents a symbolic theft—the state's theft of what was once a Christian symbol, the cross.

18. Ibid.
19. Sarah Palin, "Waterboarding Is How We Baptize Terrorists," *CBS News* video, 12:23, April 27, 2014, http://www.cbsnews.com/videos/sarah-palin-waterboarding-is-how-we-baptize-terrorists/.

There is power in Christ's death on the cross, and there is power in the death of the Christian martyr who dies innocently as Christ did. But is this redemptive power transferrable to the secular soldier?

Roman Catholic theologian William T. Cavanaugh refers to what is happening here as a "migration" of religious valence from the church to the nation-state. Our modern nation-state is not secular; rather, by stealing Christian symbols such as providence to buttress its own messianic exceptionalism, America has become an idol. "The deepest theological danger inherent in American exceptionalism, then, is that of the messiah nation that does not simply seek to follow God's will, but acts as a kind of substitute god on the stage of history. When the concept of choseness becomes unmediated by the church and unmoored from the biblical narrative, the danger is that the nation will not only be substitute church but substitute god....Our freedom itself becomes an idol, the one thing we will kill and die for."[20] Just as ancient Christian martyrs died professing their faith in the universal salvation brought by Jesus Christ, today's soldier dies to sacralize America's messianic role in bringing freedom to the world.

Revered Reformed theologian Jürgen Moltmann dates the military's theft of the cross's symbolic meaning to the Roman Emperor Constantine in the fourth century. Today, nations with a Christian heritage adopt the Constantinian way of doing things.

> The first model of self-sacrifice was that of the Christian martyr in the times of Christian origins who gave his or her life for Christ and with Christ for the gospel and the faith. The martyr followed her or his conscience and, in discipleship of Christ, stood at the side of poor and oppressed people. The Constantinian change of affairs turned the Christian martyr into the Christian soldier. . . . The crown of the martyr was changed into the medal of honor for bravery and victory. In this way the death of the soldier received a religious halo, and it was

---

20. William T. Cavanaugh, *Migrations of the Holy: God, State, and the Political Meaning of the Church* (Grand Rapids MI: Eerdmans, 2011) 96.

sanctified and glorified by the understanding that they died that we may live. They died for us.[21]

Though Moltmann is referring here to the German military, his words apply to the American situation equally. The sacrificial death of the scapegoated soldier redeems the nation.

Even without the pivotal role played by Constantine in Western history, I believe that society's scapegoating of its own soldiers might take place in this form. What the Constantinian theft of Christian symbols provides is a way for American presidents to self-justify through persuasive civil rhetoric. The rhetoric of sacrifice blinds while it binds the American people. Blood gets shed in war after war after war to sanctify the "land of the free."

The Blinding and Binding Power of the Soldier-Scapegoat

In this chapter, I am trying to show not only how a scapegoat creates and sustains human community but also that a scapegoat is most effective at self-purification when invisible. In the example of the American soldier, we can see how the invisible scapegoat provides the glue that keeps American society from falling into disarray. The American soldier is functionally sacred; no one dares, by word or deed, to violate this sacredness or even expose its scapegoat dimension.

To illustrate the power of the civic liturgy, I turn to another of President Barack Obama's speeches. In doing this, I am not implying that this president is more guilty of self-justification through scapegoating than are other persons, and I am certainly not implying that I endorse a Republican Party agenda. Rather, I am simply trying

21. Jürgen Moltmann, "The Cross as Military Symbol for Sacrifice," in *Cross Examinations: Readings on the Meaning of the Cross Today*, ed. Marit Trelstad (Minneapolis: Augsburg, 2006), 261.

to demonstrate a universal human phenomenon—what Christians call *sin*—that has bedeviled civilization since the rise of city states three millennia before Jesus. Part of sin is hiding sin; bringing sin out in the open is awkward, to say the least.

During his "State of the Union" address on January 28, 2014, the otherwise lackluster speech was nearing its conclusion when President Obama turned his hand and pointed to someone sitting in the balcony. To the immediate right of the First Lady, Michelle Obama, sat a soldier in uniform, Sergeant First Class Cory Remsburg. Cory's father sat to his right, evidently providing support. The television cameras locked onto the threesome, with Cory in the middle, as the president's voice began to rise toward a grand finale.

At the podium, America's leader took the time to rehearse Cory's biography. On his tenth deployment to Afghanistan, this young soldier was nearly killed by a massive roadside bomb. When his comrades found him he was face down, underwater, with shrapnel in his brain. He was rushed to the hospital, where he remained in a coma for weeks. He recovered, though he is still blind in one eye and struggles to coordinate his left side of his body. The president lauded this valiant hero's courage, tenacity, and drive. "My recovery has not been easy," said the president, quoting Cory. "Nothing in life that's worth anything is easy." Then the floodtide of the president's passion erupted into a rhetorical crescendo.

> Cory is here tonight. And like the Army he loves, like the America he serves, Sergeant First Class Cory Remsburg never gives up, and he does not quit. My fellow Americans, men and women like Cory remind us that America has never come easy. Our freedom, our democracy, has never been easy. . . . The America we want for our kids—a rising America where honest work is plentiful and communities are strong; where prosperity is widely shared and opportunity for all lets us go as far as our dreams and toil will take us—none of it is easy. But if we work together; if we summon what is best in us, with our feet planted firmly

in today but our eyes cast towards tomorrow—I know it's within our reach.

Believe it!

God bless you, and God bless the United States of America.[22]

With this, everyone in the House chamber stood in thunderous applause. The standing ovation lasted for more than two minutes, the longest single applause of the evening. Even the Republican Speaker of the House, John Boehner, who had sat stone-faced through most of the president's remarks, stood and clapped vigorously for the entire two minutes. All eyes were directed to the uniformed hero standing next to the First Lady.[23]

Just what is going on here? Despite the animus and vileness of the rivalry between Republicans and Democrats that virtually and literally shut down the federal government during the president's second term, this moment of applause signalized unity, fraternity, and singleness. No one in that chamber would have even considered not participating in the applause. It was a sacred moment. The invisible scapegoat provided the foundation for the community's binding experience.

Who or what is the invisible scapegoat here? Not Cory the soldier. Cory is a visible hero. However, Cory does have a role as a scapegoat—a role that was drowned out and obscured by the laudatory applause. What is invisible is not the scapegoat per se, but rather the scapegoat mechanism by which we justify ourselves, our

22. President Barack Obama, "President Obama's 2014 State of the Union Address," full transcript and video, *Mediaite.com*, January 28, 2014, http://www.mediaite.com/tv/president-obamas-2014-state-of-the-union-address-full-transcript/.

23. "The war in Iraq, like the one in Vietnam, wasn't popular; but the troops, at least nominally, were—wildly so. (Just watch the crowd at a sports event if someone in uniform is asked to stand and be acknowledged.) Both sides of the relationship, if they were being honest, felt its essential falseness." George Packer, "Home Fires: How Soldiers Write Their Wars," *The New Yorker*, April 7, 2014, 70.

way of life, our structures of power, and the violence our nation perpetrates around the world. I have no doubt that Cory, as a soldier, is a hero and properly deserves the gratitude of his people; but his invisible role as an accomplice in patriotism, nationalism, and jingoism is unknown to himself, to his commander in chief, or to the American people. The invisible scapegoat is blinding while binding.

While enjoying the speech on television, I texted a friend to mention that we were looking at the invisible scapegoat mechanism at work before our eyes: Cory is the president's scapegoat, our nation's scapegoat. My friend zipped back a text, "Don't tell Cory!" My friend is right. As soon as the truth be told, the invisible scapegoat would lose its unifying power. No prophet could get away with exposing this national hypocrisy, though a comedian might. In the spring of 2014, news broke that forty veterans recently returned from the war zone died while waiting to get an appointment with a doctor at the Veterans Hospital in Phoenix, Arizona. They literally died while waiting to see a doctor. Medical services for this nation's heroes are limited due to budget constraints, yet the public lie prevents this from becoming widely known. Unless, of course, someone investigates the facts.

Upon further inquiry, it became known that veteran services in eight states were postponing appointments beyond fourteen days and cooking the books to conceal the practice. Television comedian Jon Stewart describes General Eric Shinseki and his executive colleagues at the Department of Veteran Affairs as suffering from PBSD, post-bureaucratic stress syndrome. Then Stewart launches into a diatribe saying that America was able to pack up and send three hundred thousand troops halfway around the world and conduct two wars at a cost of two trillion dollars, which was paid for "under the table," but that this nation could not provide health care for those soldiers who came home hurt from these wars. The only way to help our veterans, concludes Stewart, would be to "declare war on them."[24] The comedian's allusion to war paints a picture of unacceptable neglect on the part of the larger society against its soldiers. What the comedian almost but not quite reveals is how our soldiers are playing the role of scapegoat. Although, if the scapegoat is to purify, it must remain invisible.

Should Today's Prophets Expose the Civic Lie?

Should today's prophets expose the civic lie? It would be dangerous. It would first draw cursing and then perhaps crucifixion.

The threat of becoming cursed arises whenever one threatens the holy. In American civil religion, the holy is the US government, which is symbolized by the Pentagon, at least according to theologian Marilyn McCord Adams. We tread on holy ground when "we scapegoat someone, or when we offer young people for slaughter on the battlefields of war. Surely, they underlie our subliminal sensibility that the Pentagon is *holy* ground and not merely a useful social agency."[25] The Pentagon is not literally a sacred place, to be sure, yet it resonates with symbolic shock waves through the American psyche. The American suppliant prays to the Pentagon for safety or security while ceding to the Pentagon the power and right to take human life. And the human life it takes is that of our sons and daughters, whose lives are sacrificed in some far-off land in order to bless us with freedom. To disturb this sacrificial mechanism with prophetic criticism is to precipitate a protective reaction, to precipitate being cursed. Cursing the critic sustains community that

24. Jon Stewart, *The Daily Show with Jon Stewart*, "The Inexcusables," video, 4:41, May 19, 2014; http://thedailyshow.cc.com/full-episodes/r79kxv/may-19--2014---james-mcavoy, accessed 5/20/2014.
25. Marilyn McCord Adams, *Christ and Horrors: The Coherence of Christology* (Cambridge, UK: Cambridge University Press, 2006), 243 (italics in the original).

is oriented around the holy—which is to say, around the scapegoated victim. Cursing seems to be an effective form of spiritual duct tape that protects the fragile social soul.

Invisible scapegoating blinds as it binds. The social fabric is united by the mechanism of self-justification, and it must remain at least partially, if not completely, invisible for scapegoating to perform its community-uniting function. The prophet wants to reveal what's beneath the social lie so that society can repent. "One of the insidious characteristics of structural injustice (structural sin) . . . is its tendency to remain invisible to those not suffering from it. If we do not see the structural injustice in which we live, we cannot repent of it. Failing to renounce it, we remain captive to it," says Moe-Lobeda.[26] However, despite the prophetic impulse of Moe-Lobeda, the sad news about the human condition is this: once the scapegoat is revealed, the fragile social soul will panic and redirect its self-justificatory venom toward another victim. In the twenty-first century, Americans have buried their invisible scapegoat beneath multiple layers of self-justification: national security, liberation, freedom, and, of course, heroism. Should a prophet or social critic try to expose what lies beneath these layers, he or she can only expect to release a new barrage of cursing and maligning.

Comparing Visible and Invisible Scapegoats

Before shifting topics, note the difference between the visible and the invisible scapegoat. The visible scapegoat is someone we semi-consciously sacrifice in order to create or sustain our community. The invisible scapegoat gets sacrificed—either by the visible scapegoat or by our own bureaucracy—and in this sacrifice, the one scapegoated

---

26. Cynthia D. Moe-Lobeda, *Resisting Structural Evil: Love as Ecological-Economic Vocation* (Minneapolis: Fortress Press, 2013), 61.

provides a sacred center around which our community feels validated. In the case of the visible scapegoat, we malign to bind. In the case of the invisible scapegoat, we make ourselves blind to bind. But regardless of which type of scapegoat we choose, both kinds bind. Both types of scapegoat serve to create human solidarity through public self-justification.

For both types of scapegoat, we draw a line between good and evil; and in both cases, we place ourselves on the good side of the line. The difference is this: the visible scapegoat goes on the evil side of the line while the invisible scapegoat shares the good side with us. The soldier is one of us. While the soldier dies just like our enemy dies, the death of the invisible scapegoat sanctifies our community. Not only does the soldier's self-sacrifice unite us, it also makes us holy. Our land becomes sacred ground. Should a prophet dare to suggest that this system is a lie, we can safely predict the equivalent of another crucifixion. Recall Jesus' words in Luke 4:24, "Verily I say unto you, No prophet is accepted in his own country" (KJV).

VISIBLE SCAPEGOAT	INVISIBLE SCAPEGOAT
Outside Enemy or Target	Inside Friend or Partner
Evil	Sacred
Cursing	Celebrating
Malign and Bind	Blind and Bind

Jesus as the Final Scapegoat

Although it might sound like an exaggeration, we could think of the entire New Testament as a funeral eulogy for Jesus of Nazareth. But this eulogy differs greatly from those delivered by modern American heads of state. Jesus differs from the soldier in that he did not engage in national defense, or even in self-defense. He did not elect to perpetuate the cycle of violence that creates or sustains communal unity. Rather, the New Testament remembers his death as standing in judgment against those who would sacrifice a scapegoat. The Bible stands against declaring the scapegoat sacred and demanding peoplehood or nationhood or patriotism in his name. The Bible tries to remove the blindfold that blinds and binds.

What is key here is that the death of Jesus desacralizes the scapegoat. "Christ became a scapegoat in order to desacralize those who came before him and to prevent those who come after him from being sacralized," observes Girard.[27] The New Testament memory of Jesus dismantles any community oriented around the sacred by exposing the ugly truth regarding how this or any community is established or sustained. The death of Jesus makes visible what had been invisible. The death of Jesus shocks us with truth, with prophetic and revelatory truth.

Even though the Christian church through the centuries has remembered Jesus Christ as the victim of the scapegoating mechanism, in the Christian communion, Jesus does not function as one scapegoat or sacrifice among others. Even though we interpret the death of Jesus in light of the scapegoat model, the efficacy of Christ's saving work does not depend on the scapegoat mechanism. "Christ is not a divinized scapegoat," trumpets Girard. "Those who hold him to be God—Christians—are those who do not make him their scapegoat."[28] To speak of Christian unity does not require scapegoating, whether with a visible or an invisible scapegoat. One of the clear messages of the New Testament that becomes habitually garbled, muddied, and twisted in modern civic and moral rhetoric is this: No more scapegoats!

27. Girard, *The One by Whom Scandal Comes*, 44.
28. René Girard, *When These Things Begin: Conversations with Michael Treguer*, trans. Trevo Cribben Merrill (East Lansing: Michigan State University Press, 2014), 33.

Perhaps theologian S. Mark Heim can best sum it up for us. "Scapegoating is one of the deepest structures of human sin, built into our religion and politics. It is demonic because it is endlessly flexible in its choice of victims and because it can truly deliver the good that it advertises. Satan can cast out Satan, and is the more powerful for it."[29] We victimize others in the name of the good. Because we believe we are doing good, the evil we do becomes invisible to us. Our virtues reap as much violence as our vices.

We will now turn to the victims of our scapegoating. Sometimes the scapegoat does not fight back with counter-scapegoating or retributive justice. Sometimes the scapegoat merely suffers from our self-justification. Sometimes this suffering takes the form of soul breakage. Sometimes broken souls commit suicide.

Breaking the Soldier's Soul

Souls break. They break when the moral universe breaks. When the moral universe collapses, the soul disintegrates and falls into an abyss of meaninglessness. The soul either departs or gets lost, and we are left soulless.

Our inner souls and the outer moral order are correlated. The moral universe orders the soul, and we measure our inner lives according to what we believe is the order of ultimate justice. If ultimate reality is structured morally, then we feel sane. If that moral universe collapses, then we lose ourselves in the chaos of mania.

Some call this *anomie,* meaning that we live without law. When the shell of our Kosta Boda bowl shatters, its contents spatter. The vortex is lost, and so is the center; the periphery and the center are lost at the same time. The soul breaks with the bowl.

---

29. S. Mark Heim, "Saved by What Shouldn't Happen," in *Cross Examinations,* 217.

The broken soul can be experienced by anyone. But looking at American soldiers suffering from moral injury provides particularly illuminating access to the broken soul. Under fire in the war zone, some of our scapegoated soldiers have suffered acutely not only from physical injury but also from misunderstanding, confusion, betrayal, and guilt. In certain cases, their moral universe has collapsed. The soul's collapse follows, and suicide follows that. As of this writing, twenty-two US veterans per day commit suicide, a death rate higher than the combat rate.[30] With suicides at eight thousand per year, America now loses twice as many soldiers per year to suicide than it lost on the battlefield over ten years of combat. Soldier suicide is the exhaust pipe of America's military machine on the move.

Let me tender a diagnosis: these suicides are the result of an unresolved theodicy problem. Precisely, our word *theodicy* (combining God or *theos* and justice or *dikē*) refers to the justification of God in a world replete with injustice, evil, and suffering. Can a loving and powerful God exist in a world of injustice, evil, and suffering? If so, how can such a God be justified? That's the theodicy question. For the broken soul, a moral universe no longer exists by which God or anybody else can be justified.

---

30. Kevin Freking, "Veteran Suicide Rate at 22 Each Day, Department of Veterans Affairs Report Finds," *Huffington Post*, February 1, 2015, http://www.huffingtonpost.com/2013/02/01/veteran-suicide-rate_n_2599019.html.

Breaking the Soldier's Moral Universe

The human soul and the moral universe are correlates. To lose one is to lose the other.[31] The loss of one's moral universe breaks the soul and, on some occasions, precipitates suicide.

Irresolvable guilt can break a fragile soul—sometimes even just the feeling of guilt. For the soldier in combat, just seeing death can elicit as much guilt as causing someone's death. In his magisterial study, *On Killing*, Lt. Col. Dave Grossman tells us that "the combat soldier appears to feel a deep sense of responsibility and accountability for what he sees around him. It is as though every enemy dead is a human being he has killed, and every friendly dead is a comrade for whom he was responsible. With every effort to reconcile these two responsibilities, more guilt is added to the horror that surrounds the soldier."[32] During stage one of soul-breaking, the moral universe remains intact regardless of the difficulty the soldier encounters when trying to assess his or her reality.

Later, when the fragile soul is afflicted by so much guilt that self-justification cannot patch up the bowl, the soul breaks. In stage two, when the bowl breaks, one loses both the soul and its corresponding moral universe. The experience of a broken soul may begin with guilt, but soon the moral universe by which guilt is measured also begins to crumble. Losing a moral universe is a process.

31. The moral universe is a structure—whether imaginary or real—that provides order. When a civilian enlists in the military, he or she believes serving as a soldier reinforces the standards set by this moral universe. Tim O'Brien had been an opponent to US involvement in the war in Vietnam, but in 1968, he submitted himself to induction into the Army. He said he did not want "to upset the order I knew, the people I knew, and my own private world." Note the correlation between the "order" and his own private world. "It was not just that I valued that order. I also feared its opposite—inevitable chaos, censure, embarrassment, and the end of everything that had happened in my life, the end of it all." Despite the note of intimidation, O'Brien believed in an order to reality, and he feared the disruption of that order. Quoted by Packer, "Home Fires," 69. The soldier enters war with the moral order intact. Disorder comes later.
32. Lt. Col. Dave Grossman, *On Killing* (New York: Little, Brown, 2009). 74.

On some occasions, the moral universe breaks first. The soul is vulnerable to breaking when the moral universe fades or disappears. When we feel we can no longer rely upon cosmic justice, the justness within the soul loses its foundation. It collapses from within. Mass killing, selective murder, torture, and unstoppable dehumanization erode the props holding up one's moral universe. "Mass killings make modern war especially debilitating to the soul," says Edward Tick, who heads the *Soldier's Heart* program in Albany, New York.[33]

The moral universe—which makes the existence of the soul possible—sometimes evaporates. This breakdown carries us beyond guilt. The very criterion by which guilt can be measured disappears. One of my Berkeley colleagues, Herbert Anderson, observes how "veterans express their torment in many ways: 'I lost my soul'; 'How can I ever accept myself again, how can people ever accept me if they know what I've done, what I allowed to happen?'"[34] The moral universe and the soul are so mutually defining that the loss of one entails the loss of the other. "The spiritual and emotional foundations of the world disappeared and made it impossible for me to sleep the sleep of the just," writes Michael Yandell, a US veteran of the Iraq war. "What began to erode for me in Iraq in 2004 was my perception of good and evil. What I lost was a world that makes moral sense."[35] Without a moral universe, one can no longer draw a line between good and evil; nor can one belong to a community dedicated to doing the good.

To get at this phenomenon, a new term has been recently introduced into our vocabulary: *moral injury* (sometimes called *internal conflict* in military documents). This term opens up horizons

---

33. Tick, *War and the Soul,* 91.
34. Herbert Anderson, "Symposium on Moral Injury and Spirituality," *Reflective Practice: Formation and Supervision of Ministry* 33 (2013): 8.
35. Michael Yandell, "The War Within," *Christian Century,* January 7, 2015, 12.

for understanding soldiers within the larger category of PTSD, post-traumatic stress disorder. The PTSD diagnosis joined the register of disorders listed by the American Psychiatric Association in 1980 "to describe anew what therapists had always seen as a common consequence of war: the breakdown of the personality under the assault of unrelenting horror and fear."[36] In the Civil War, it was known as "battle fatigue," and in later wars, it was called "shell shock." Gradually, PTSD was employed to diagnose the aftereffects of other traumas such as rape, auto accidents, and natural disasters. The moral injury diagnosis applies to a subgroup within PTSD.

A veteran suffering from PTSD finds his or her thought processes and daily life disrupted. Typically, a military chaplain or a psychiatrist can recognize the symptoms of PTSD:

1. A stressor. A stressor is a traumatic event involving intense fear, helplessness, or horror. For a soldier, the stressor might occur during battle.
2. Intrusive recollection. The traumatic event is persistently reexperienced in recurrent memories. The veteran soldier experiences uncontrollable recall of the original trauma.
3. Numbing. The victim of PTSD engages in psychic avoidance of certain thoughts or conversations that may appear associated with the trauma. This leads to withdrawal, detachment, and estrangement.
4. Hyperarousal. Hyperarousal manifests itself as difficulty in falling asleep or remaining asleep, irritability with outbursts of anger, difficulty in concentrating, hypervigilance, or exaggerated startle response.

---

36. Sebern F. Fisher, *Neurofeedback in the Treatment of Developmental Trauma* (New York: W. W. Norton, 2014), 3.

This is PTSD. Moral injury overlaps with PTSD, but moral injury has its own characteristics as well.

The World Health Organization provides us with a similar diagnostic category: enduring personality change after catastrophe. EPCC symptoms are what one might expect: a hostile or mistrustful attitude toward the world, social withdrawal, feelings of emptiness or hopelessness, chronic anxiety, and estrangement. Jonathan Shay applies this to soldiers broken in combat. "A person broken by combat has lost the capacity for a sense of well-being, self-respect, confidence, and satisfaction—all attributes that we lump together in our concept of happiness."[37]

Moral injury can be more devastating than garden variety PTSD or EPCC. According to *Time* magazine, "Moral injury arises when a service member cannot reconcile what he has done, or experienced, in war with his worldview of him or herself prior to war. Commonly this involves killing, especially when the slain are non-combatants, often women or children."[38] Professional therapists offer this description: "Moral injury is often experienced as an intensely private, deeply sincere, and often distressing self-questioning and soul-searching. Specifically, many veterans experience cognitive, emotional, and spiritual consequences of war-related trauma that often lead them to ponder such basic theodicy questions as: 'Does God exist?' or 'Is God fair and just?' Many struggle with, or abandon, their spiritual faith or religion and many report feeling guilt and shame regarding their wartime behaviors."[39]

---

37. Jonathan Shay, *Achilles in Vietnam: Combat Trauma and the Undoing of Character* (New York: Scribner, 1994), 174–75; see also, 169.

38. Elspeth Cameron Ritchie, "Moral Injury: A Profound Sense of Alienation and Shame," *Time*, April 17, 2013, http://nation.time.com/2013/04/17/moral-injury-a-profound-sense-of-alienation-and-abject-shame/.

39. Kent D. Drescher, Jason A. Nieuwsma, and Pamela J. Swales, "Morality and Moral Injury: Insights from Theology and Health Science," *Reflective Practice: Formation and Supervision of Ministry* 33 (2013): 54.

The soul broken by moral injury is not simply a step in the decline of the fragile soul. It's a long jump. The soul may break completely under one or both of two kinds of assaults. The first is guilt over what one might have done or even seen done by others. In the case of guilt, the moral universe remains intact and provides the standard by which the guilt is determined. The second assault includes the dissolution of the moral universe itself. The moral universe dissolves in the midst of atrocity, meaningless death, and the futility of war. To put it another way, the moral universe dissolves when the soldier catches a glimpse of the truth: he or she is being used as the nation's scapegoat.

This moral shock causes fissures in the mixing bowl, fissures too destructive to mend with spiritual duct tape. The moral universe fragments, breaks, and shatters. The components that make up the self descend into chaos. When all has settled, there no longer exists a vortex, a center, a soul. Suicide frequently follows.

Soul Breaking in War

The term I use is *broken soul.* Here's a case in point. Gunnery Sergeant Leonard Shelton fought as a US Marine in Iraq during the first Gulf War. He saw death on the battlefield and was shocked by his experiences. He underwent a "shattering of his sense of self," according to journalist Kevin Sites. "Shelton had lost the thread of his own story, unable to tell it, because he was unable to comprehend it." As his moral universe fell into disarray, so did his sense of self. "I'm a demon in my own life," he writes, "destroying my own core." Cosmic justice and the self mutually define one another. When one fails, so does the other. "I stopped praying. I grew up in a Christian environment. But I didn't believe it anymore. Human flesh melting on steel?"[40]

Rev. Beth A. Stallinga, who served as a US military chaplain in Afghanistan, tries to understand the role that belief in God plays in soul fracturing. "While many people today see religion as irrelevant to their lives, it is still common that those with no previous religious identity blame God when they encounter suffering."[41] Blaming God is one thing; even more dramatic is the loss of the very moral universe that makes it possible to blame anybody.

Another chaplain, Marty Mendenhall, helps those of us who are not warriors to understand our friends and family members in uniform. "Having confronted real radical evil, the veteran is no longer able to accept the cultural assumptions which formed the basis of pre-combat life. Evil of this magnitude encompasses an almost total immorality into which the soldier is drawn. This creates moral pain on a scale incomprehensible to most noncombatants. The veteran's entire belief system collapses into angry, often lifelong nihilism. This is the most enduring and intractable element of combat trauma."[42] Combat trauma includes not only physical injury but moral injury as well.

Symbols play an important role in life's meaning, and in the loss of meaning. When the symbols break, so do our souls. Here is another case in point, reported again by Stiles. In December 1967, some US Marines shot and killed a North Vietnamese officer. When stripping him they found photos of his wife and children. "It made me realize we had killed a human being," reported First Lieutenant Thomas Saal. His buddies then made a cross and crucified the dead enemy. They hung him up for all to see. "They fucking crucified him," cries Saal. "My men crucified the soldier after they stripped him naked."

---

40. Kevin Sites, *The Things They Cannot Say: Stories Soldiers Won't Tell You about What They've Seen, Done or Failed to Do in War* (New York: Harper, 2013), 125.

41. Beth A. Stallinga, "What Spills Blood Wounds Spirit: Chaplains, Spiritual Care, and Operational Stress Injury," *Reflective Practice: Formation and Supervision of Ministry* 33 (2013): 17.

42. Marty Mendenhall, "Chaplains in Mental Health: Healing the Spiritual Wounds of War," *Annals of the American Psychotherapy Association* 12:1 (Spring 2009): 46.

This was a turning point in Saal's psyche. It marked the loss of his soul. "I knew that's where I left my soul . . . I lost my humanity. I saw it fly over my head. I'm sure there's a lot of souls like mine, flying over the Iwo Jimas and the Gettysburgs."[43] Whether we understand what is happening here as soul loss or soul breaking, such a trauma so shakes the soul loose from its foundations that its own integrity dissolves and disappears.

Edward Tick uses the term *soul wound* where I use *broken soul*. Within the category of PTSD, we find "a constellation of fixated experience, delayed growth, devastated character, interrupted initiation, and unsupported recovery. Many veterans . . . remain in a state of shock because of what they have seen and are terrified for their lives. . . . They cannot shape their new self into an identity that can give them inner order, strength, and meaning and help them find a place in society and the cosmos."[44] For the self to be centered and whole, it must be centered in the moral cosmos, or at least in our trust that the cosmos is ordered by a transcendent form of justice. To lose our moral universe is to lose the intactness of the soul. "Severe trauma shatters a sense of the meaningfulness of the self, of the world, and of the connection between the two," observes Shay.[45]

David Martin relies on the term *soul-loss*. "Soul-loss is the dethronement and incarceration of that which should be sovereign, the erasure of essential markings, the averting of the face from the summit of being, the atomization of integrity, the deterioration in the realm of spirit of vital presence, and a repulsive occupation by powers or turbulences making for destruction, darkness, and death."[46] Our veterans become bedeviled with "turbulences" that make for

---

43. Sites, *Things They Cannot Say*, 165–68.
44. Tick, *War and the Soul*, 107–8.
45. Shay, *Achilles in Vietnam*, 180.
46. David Martin, "Bedeviled," in *On Losing the Soul: Essays in the Social Psychology of Religion*, ed. Richard K. Fenn and Donald Capps (Albany, NY: SUNY, 1995), 40.

"destruction, darkness, and death" by murder and suicide. Warriors who killed so-called "shitheads" in Iraq have come home to kill themselves.

Moral Injury: A Theological Reflection

In this study, I have benefited from the sensitive work of two of my Berkeley colleagues, Rita Nakashima Brock and Gabriella Lettini. They write that "moral injury is the result of reflection on memories of war or other extreme traumatic conditions. It comes from having transgressed one's basic moral identity and violated core moral beliefs."[47] Consider this statement carefully. They are not referring merely to guilt; much more is at stake. If I transgress my moral identity, then I feel guilty. I should feel guilty. Nevertheless, my moral universe holds together, even if I am judged by it.

What is more dramatic and more serious, I think, is the crumbling of the very universe that makes moral judgment possible. Brock and Lettini bring us to this point. "Moral injury results when soldiers violate their core moral beliefs, and in evaluating their behavior negatively, they feel they no longer live in a reliable, meaningful world and can no longer be regarded as decent human beings. . . . The consequences of violating one's conscience, even if the act was unavoidable or seemed right at the time, can be devastating."[48] What I would like to focus on is the phrase, "they feel they no longer live in a reliable, meaningful world." Once the soul is broken, repair is difficult and must be sought before suicide eliminates the opportunity.

---

47. Rita Nakashima Brock and Gabriella Lettini, *Soul Repair: Recovering from Moral Injury after War* (Boston: Beacon, 2012), xiv.
48. Ibid., xv.

The term *soul* must be used here because this is how those who suffer from moral injury speak. The term does not commit us to a metaphysical definition, but it does refer us to the core or center of an integrated self. Recall how, in chapter 1, I use the term *soul* to refer to our inmost essence as an individual self. Using the term *spirit,* which overlaps with *soul,* I refer to our capacity to relate with one another and with God. While the word *soul* connotes who each of us is as an individual, the word *spirit* connotes that dimension of personal reality that unites us with others and with God. To speak of soul reminds us that as embodied creatures we have a center of identity—a centered self—which develops in spiritual relationships. When the self disintegrates as a result of moral injury, the soul seems to depart. Only spirit can retrieve the soul.

A Vietnam veteran tells how he sat in the hut of a cowering family in a small village. Through the open hut door, he could see other American soldiers pushing around the elderly as well as children, giants among diminutives of another race. The Americans set fire to family homes, one after the other. Watching this happen, the vet says he was filled with rage at his comrades, who were heartlessly destroying the livelihood of people they had never known or would never understand. The question of good and evil ran through his mind, and he judged that the Americans were evil. At this point, his soul was caught in a conflict it could not win. "At the very moment I found my soul," he reports, "at the very moment it woke up and I could see the truth for the first time in my life, at that very second when I knew we were evil, it fled. I lost it."[49] His soul did not exactly break. It flew away.

It is the soul that gets broken or lost or wounded. Chaplains and therapists who invest themselves in the healing process of veterans

___

49. Cited by Tick, *War and the Soul,* 111–12.

find that they must rely upon the word *soul*. All other words seem shallow in comparison. "The soul is the nexus of our deep connection with all that is good, true, and beautiful: our connection with the rest of creation, and our connection with God. [Moreover,] soul wounds result in a diminishment of everything meaningful to the person. They erode the human capacity for connection, trust, gratitude, appreciation, creativity, playfulness, compassion, forgiveness, peace, hope, love, and zest for life."[50] When the soul breaks, so does everything else. Suicide begins to look attractive to the person with a broken soul because death invites escape from unendurable psychic pain. "Many combat veterans think daily of suicide," Shay reports.[51]

In my earlier discussion of the fragile soul, I pointed out the correlation between the self and the world, between the soul and the moral universe. The actual moral universe we grow up with provides the horizon of values according to which we structure our daily lives. This original moral universe is accompanied by a vague intuition that there exists an ultimate justice, a final cosmic order, which establishes our moral universe. We grow up living in confidence that the actual moral universe that frames the meaning of life is sufficient and trustworthy. The unbearable shock that our moral universe has been shattered leads to the shattering of the soul. Without a world of meaning, the ears of the broken soul hear the siren call of suicide.

Refining the Concept of Moral Injury and the Broken Soul

If we suffer from guilt, the moral universe remains intact and provides the criterion by which we measure our failure to live up to the

---

50. John Sippola, Amy Blemenshine, Donald A. Tubesing, and Valerie Yancey, *Welcome Them Home, Help Them Heal: Pastoral Care and Ministry with Service Members Returning from War* (Duluth, MN: Whole Person Associates, 2009), 43.
51. Shay, *Achilles in Vietnam*, 179.

standards of justice. When the moral universe disintegrates and evaporates, so also does the metaphysical criterion by which justice can be measured. This distinction is key, I believe, to understanding the black hole into which the broken soul falls.

Because of this distinction, I must refine the concept of moral injury as developed by an otherwise insightful commentator, Robert Emmet Meagher. Meagher blames today's high suicide rate among American veterans on the Christian concept of Just War. The concept of the Just War arose in the context of Emperor Constantine's military campaigns and St. Augustine's theology. Without going into the details of this complex theory, the idea of the Just War distinguishes between murder and killing. Murder is sinful, whereas killing in war is justified by Just War Theory. When a soldier kills for the sake of his or her country, such killing is justified by the alliance of "God and Country." The moral universe is convincingly articulated by both theologians and politicians alike. In principle, soldiers who kill should feel no guilt for their actions on the battlefield. Meagher objects to admitting Just War Theory into our moral universe.

Meagher's prescription is that our modern society rid itself of justifying perpetual war through Just War Theory. "Just War Theory is a dead letter," he writes; "It was never more than a theory, and at its worst it was a lie, a deadly lie."[52] Meagher asks society to cease its justification of perpetual war and its victimization of otherwise innocent soldiers.

Here is the problem, as Meagher sees it. Just War Theory seems convincing to the soldier right up until the moment he or she kills. But, when the non-killer first becomes a killer in combat, something dies within the soldier. "All killing kills something in the killer,"

---

52. Robert Emmet Meagher, *Killing from the Inside Out: Moral Injuyr and Just War* (Eugene, OR: Cascade, 2014) xviii.

reports Meagher.[53] This experience of killing oneself from within leads to what Meagher understands by moral injury. The term *moral injury* "designates the violation, by oneself or another, of a personally embedded moral code or value resulting in deep injury to the psyche or soul. It is what used to be called sin."[54] I cannot fully agree. Meagher here presumes that the moral universe–"personally embedded moral code"–remains intack and that the soldier's activity is judged sinful by this moral code. Even though this undoubtedly applies in many cases, it falls short of understanding moral injury that accompanies the broken soul.

The soul breaks because the moral universe disintegrates and evaporates. The atrocities which our soldiers commit or watch are so overwhelming that belief in a moral universe loses its credibility. Witnessing the writhing and terror of the victims of torture, sniping, massacre, drone bombing, and wanton murder destroys both the metaphysical justice above and the moral soul within. The result is anomie, anarchy, mania, disintegration, and finally suicide.

PTSD can come in the form of guilt. But, the soul broken by moral injury is not undergoing guilt over one's sin; rather, the soul is overwhelmed by the loss of even the criterion by which guilt could be measured.

---

53. Ibid., xviii..
54. Ibid., xvi–xvii.

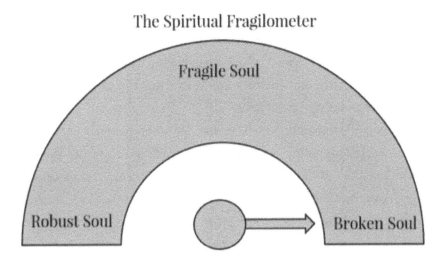

The Spiritual Fragilometer

Demythologizing the Myth of War

Edward Tick gets it. As a psychotherapist working with war veterans suffering from PTSD, he gets it. The experience of war is an experience of ultimacy. Each moment is riddled with the tension of life and death, and this tension bespeaks a transcendent valuation, a contest between ultimate good and ultimate evil. To fight in war is to embody a transindividual archetype; it is to live in the realm of myth. To fight in war is to join with the heroes in the battle of Troy, to join with the heroes who have fought in war after war over time immemorial. "Every war is the Trojan war; every war is Armageddon," Tick writes.[55]

Tick can see through the lies that those of us in the larger society tell ourselves, the lies that provide divine justification for pursuing international violence. But they are not merely lies of our own making, he says. Rather, our self-justifications seem to be a response to a call from beyond, an urgent demand made upon us by the

55. Tick, *War and the Soul,* 42.

gods, who call us to fight against the "axis of evil," to use the phrase of George W. Bush, or "the evil empire," to use Ronald Reagan's description of the Soviet Union. Invisible to us in our passion to pursue war is that our enemies are answering the same siren call. "War is an archetypal force that creates a larger-than-life arena into which we are irresistibly pulled. In war we embody and wrestle with god powers. The politics and hostilities of warfare rise from the gut of the war god. War evokes in us an altered state of consciousness. Odin, Ares, the Lord of Hosts, Lord Krishna possess us. We are their servants . . . What is most difficult to see, however, is that all sides make this same claim and that *everyone's* beliefs are manifestations of the same universal myth."[56] As members of the human race, we are like cattle being driven by sadistic divine wranglers toward an ineluctable slaughter. En route to having our throats cut, we moo myths, especially the myth of the hero warrior.

The myth of the warrior—what I dub a *mythologeme*, because it is a fragmentary plot that appears in many myths—is an archetype, and the archetypal law affects us as much as the law of gravity. We disobey it at our peril. As people of faith, we must engage the myth head on, consciously trying to disarm it of its destructive power. Unless we disarm this myth, it will rule our psyche like Genghis Kahn ruled Asia. "We must somehow support the manifestation of the warrior archetype and live the myths. . . . We have choices in *how* we engage these archetypes, how consciously we repeat them, how we direct their energies, and what types of outcome we seek."[57] We have no choice but to live *in* the myth, but we do have choices regarding how to mitigate the damage the myth wreaks on our psyches and our society. Those of us who have viewed the scapegoated Son of God hanging on the cross may have gained sufficient insight to

56. Ibid., 41, italics in original.
57. Ibid., 66, italics in original.

demythologize the myth of war and resist baptizing the heroism of the warrior.

Let me proffer the following hypothesis: the mythologeme of the warrior conflicts fundamentally with our assumptions regarding a just universe. Before combat, the modern solder deludes himself or herself into believing that the latter justifies the former. Under fire, the soldier cannot have both, but in the midst of atrocity, the soldier loses both. This is the cruel joke the myth plays on us. Yet this is our destiny as the human race, whether we morally approve or not. We are in bondage to the myth of the hero warrior, and we cannot free ourselves. The opportunity for choice in the matter arises only at the point where we offer integrated healing to the morally injured.

I say Tick gets it because he can see what most of us fail to see, namely, that our enemies are just like us because we both engage in mutual scapegoating. We are all caught up in the same "universal myth": we all tell ourselves that our pursuit of war is justified. This realization should lead us to pause. Just what is going on here? Has our moral universe been constructed so that we deem ourselves just and our enemies unjust? No, that can't be the case. One standard of justice applies to friends and enemies alike. So does our division of the human race into allies and enemies constitute a distortion of our moral universe? Has national self-justification deformed or perverted our moral universe? Just how do we get out from under this conundrum? Clearly, we need to demythologize our own belief system.

The moral universe that frames our belief system seems both sturdy and fragile at the same time. It seems sturdy because we imagine it is grounded in the divine, in one god or another. How could the gods be wrong? But the fragility of the moral universe unveils itself in those moments when we ask: How does it look from the point of view of the enemy? When the enemy finds himself or herself in our position (only in reverse), are there two moral universes? Of course not. At this point, the mind begins to split. The wall of self-justification we lean on begins to crumble. The myth is disintegrating, and we are falling. Just how far will we fall? Where's the bottom?

Healing a Broken Soul

From a therapeutic point of view, preliminary observations suggest that healing for veterans suffering from PTSD, EPCC, or moral injury requires meaningful relationships. Propping up an already failed moral universe or appealing to a still higher form of metaphysical justice is not a cure that corresponds to the diagnosis. Rather, to the extent that a cure exists it will be found in non-judgmental relationship with others who understand.

Sharing experiences with others who understand the trauma is necessary, although it may not be sufficient. Some success is reported when these veterans are drawn into public service projects. In *Time* magazine, Joe Klein reports that a 2009 study shows that ninety-two percent of recent veterans expressed a desire to continue serving in some way alongside those who understand their experience. Leaders in this movement want to modify the GI Bill so that it will also pay for a year's worth of public service.[58]

From a theological point of view, my first message to Reformation theologians is this: a forensic version of justification-by-faith will not directly fix this problem. If you're a barber, then everyone you see looks like they need a haircut. If you're an aspirin salesman, then everyone you see looks like they have a headache. If you believe justification-by-faith is the cure, then everyone you meet looks like

---

58. Joe Klein, "Can Service Save Us?," *Time*, June 20, 2013, http://nation.time.com/2013/06/20/can-service-save-us/print/.

they suffer from works-righteousness. *Make sure the cure fits the disease.* Justification-by-faith will provide comfort and healing to those of us suffering from the fragile soul, but not necessarily the broken soul. The elegant doctrine of justification-by-faith squarely addresses our human propensity for self-absorption, self-justification, legalism, absolutism, rigidity, works righteousness, moral pride, and scapegoating. It addresses those of us with our moral universe intact, those of us who suffer from the tyranny of the conscience.

For the broken soul, the moral universe is no longer intact; it's shattered. The once-centered self must alone face the terrifying darkness of eternity, which comes roaring up like a dragon to seize the soul and drag it down into the abyss. Luther labeled this experience *Anfechtung*, and he knew it personally. No set of pious Band-Aids can heal what requires major surgery.

The crucified Jesus also knew personally the loss of his moral universe, as well as the depth of despair. From the cross, he cried out, "Eloi, Eloi, lema sabachthani?" (Mark 15:34), which means, "My God, my God, why have you forsaken me?" Israel's God and the prophecies of that God seemed to fail the Son of God in the moment of crisis, the moment of death. Is this Jesus, the crucified Jesus, present in our justifying faith? If so, then perhaps the broken soul should come to know that he or she is not alone. *Anfechtung* and the broken soul have become essential to the divine life.

We dare not approach the gashes left by life's tragedies with too small a bandage. It is clearly inadequate to jump to the conclusion that "everything's really okay" because our nation won this war. Each soldier's moral universe is capable of rendering a judgment against our nation. However, in the event that it is unable to render this judgment, it crumbles and loses its ability to judge anything. In the latter case, the self crumbles right along with the world. No bandage or spiritual duct tape can provide quick healing.

While the hope for healing such moral injury before suicide might seem as effective as a rain dance in drought, spiritual leaders such as military chaplains have learned a great deal about what is helpful. Chaplains seem to agree on one key item: the broken soul needs the company of other broken souls who have shared the experience. A caregiver such as a chaplain or therapist or pastor needs to surround the healing situation with comrades, with domesticated battle buddies. To put this in theological terms: the broken soul can only find repair through relationship with a wounded healer, through shared spirit.

As in other traumatic situations, a trustworthy and empathic bond between the caregiver and the morally wounded soldier is requisite. However, the promise of confidentiality is only minimally requisite. "More than any other requirement, safety is essential if healing is to begin. In almost every case of severe trauma what suddenly makes the world feel so unsafe is the shattering of two of the most fundamental existential beliefs: the world is fair and the world is safe," advises Stallinga. "A war can be just and still be perceived or experienced as evil. If nothing else, it represents a failure in government diplomacy and a breakdown in the human capacity for a reasoned compromise."[59]

Next, the pastor or therapist must be willing to enter into the moral darkness by listening as empathetically as possible to the particular story of grief where the wounds hurt most. Patient presence and unconditional acceptance is requisite for working through shame. Deep empathy within the shame has the potential for providing a healing moment of grace. Even when we feel powerless over a past that cannot be changed, we have access to one tool for control: lament. Lament can permeate Christian spirituality because it combines human realism with an implicit hope. "It is in lament

59. Stallinga, "What Spills Blood," 21.

that the experience of being abandoned, or forsaken, or ignored by God is given voice, and where the problem of *Deus absconditus,* the hidden God, emerges in the sharpest form," writes Brooks Schramm. "Lament as such does not attempt to justify suffering or derive meaning from it—it only wants God to relieve it or take it away. It wants God's compassion."[60]

Shared lament. God's compassion. Hope. "We often think of irrational guilt as needing to be relieved; it is a pathology to be fixed. But for many soldiers guilt has a redemptive side. It can be inseparable from empathy for those who have been harmed and from a sense of responsibility and duty—the desire to make reparations—even when the harm was unintentional."[61] Moral darkness is not the final reality. And while such soul repair is labor-intensive and time-consuming, it is worthwhile because each temporal soul is of infinite value.

Stallinga enters the darkness bearing grace for the wounded soul.

> At this stage the chaplain, whether rabbi, priest, imam or minister, embodies the possibility of a gracious connection and the hope that the sufferer might come to understand his or her distress in relation to centuries of human history and within a community of faith that points to something greater than the current misery. The origin of evil and the presence of suffering in life is a mystery for which listening silence is often the only appropriate response. . . . But the larger part will be the task of companioning the warrior through despair and hopelessness all the while representing the possibility of reconnection with all that gives life hope and meaning.[62]

In addition to shame, grief can plague the heart and mind of the veteran. Certainly, grief is an expected response to death, and in the case of combat trauma, it comes in two forms: grief for lost comrades

---

60. Brooks Schramm, "Lament's Hope," in *Spirituality: Toward a 21st Century Lutheran Understanding,* ed. Kirsi Stjerna and Brooks Schramm (Minneapolis: Lutheran University Press, 2004), 69–70.

61. Stallinga, "What Spills Blood," 21.

62. Ibid., 23.

and grief for the loss of a moral universe. A moral universe has been shattered, and trust has been betrayed. "Long after the event, many traumatized people feel that a part of the self has died and the most profoundly afflicted wish that they were dead . . . They are spiritual injuries that manifest in grief, loss, guilt, shame, lack of forgiveness, loss of meaning and purpose, loss of hope, loss of faith, and a search for restoration and wholeness. They impact every facet of the veteran's life."[63] The caregiver must walk bravely into the grieving quicksand that surrounds the veteran; in doing so, he or she risks sinking as well. Thankfully, this trip through the tomb of Good Friday leads to Easter's resurrection.

Conclusion

"War begins in illusion and ends in blood and tears," writes George Packer.[64] Of what relevance is justifying faith, we might ask? I hope that my analysis of self-justification over against justification-by-faith helps us to grasp what is going on in the illusion of war and the shedding of both blood and tears.

My analysis begins with the scapegoat and ends with the broken soul. When cursing the visible scapegoat, to malign is to bind. The invisible scapegoat is more insidious: it blinds as it binds. Both types of scapegoat are associated with violence that manifests itself in verbal and military forms. Furthermore, the New Testament can be read as a prophetic message: no more scapegoats! When we see the Son of God scapegoated, the scapegoat mechanism collapses. In place of self-justification, the gospel invites us to rely upon justification-by-faith.

However, I have hinted that the doctrine of justification-by-faith is too small a bandage to apply to the existential hemorrhage

63. Ibid., 20.
64. Packer, "Home Fires," 69.

experienced by the broken soul. Perhaps I should qualify this. If we limit justification-by-faith to a strictly forensic rendering, it will not suffice because forensic rendering relies upon a moral universe that remains intact. What the person undergoing moral injury is experiencing is the loss of a moral universe, even the loss of a will to live.

As the broken soul contemplates death, suicide appears as a welcome relief from the unbearable weight of soul loss. Chaplains on the pastoral firing line have learned that presence heals, especially the presence of those who share the experience. The key is trust. Often, the suffering soldier feels that he or she can trust another veteran who shares the experience. In our congregations, we need patience combined with presence to allow this trust to build so that the veteran with a broken soul can take the time to heal in a trusted and trusting environment.

This leads us to another dimension of justifying faith—namely, the real presence of the suffering and dying Jesus and the resurrected Christ. Drawing on Luther, Danish theologian Regin Prenter writes that this is what justification-by-faith means. "In inner conflict man is completely in the power of death. Nothing of his own righteousness is effective. The groaning of the Spirit toward God is a real raising from death, a new creation."[65] The Holy Spirit places the suffering Jesus within each soul. Our groans rise up with his to heaven. Simultaneously, the Holy Spirit places within the soul the resurrected Christ, Easter's power over death. Even in the experience of a broken or lost moral universe, the redeeming God of the true universe is present.

65. Regin Prenter, *Spiritus Creator: Luther's Concept of the Holy Spirit* (Philadelphia: Muhlenberg, 1953), 185.

10

Faith as Belief

There is only one proof that the Eternal exists: faith in it.

–Søren Kierkegaard[1]

We all live with faith. We all trust something, whether we think about it or not. We could not negotiate our world on a daily basis without trusting most of what makes up our world. When driving, we trust that the driver coming in the opposite direction will not cross the median and hit us head-on. The child trusts that the ropes on the swing will not break. The scientist trusts that the natural world is rational; and this trust makes experimentation and the pursuit of new knowledge possible. Faith as trust provides an unconscious prop for the theater of daily consciousness.

Theologians call this basic trust *animal faith* or *basic faith* or *primordial faith.* Schubert Ogden, for his part, relies upon "a basic faith in the meaning of life, or in the meaning for us of ultimate reality."[2] Faith as trust is virtually universal, indispensable, and understandable.

---

1. Søren Kierkegaard, *Purity of Heart,* trans. Douglas V. Steere (New York: Harper, 1938), 84.
2. Schubert M. Ogden, *The Understanding of the Christian Faith* (Eugene, OR: Cascade Books, 2010), 24.

Any act of trust invests us in something or someone beyond ourselves, in the object of our trust. The structure of trust indicates that the self cannot be itself unless it transcends itself. To say it another way, trust liberates the self from narcissism. Trust opens the self to friendship with God. "Basic trust is directed to an agency that is capable *without limitation* of protecting and promoting the selfhood of those who trust in it," writes Pannenberg. "God is the true object of trust even in its beginnings."[3]

Luther recognizes the role faith as trust plays in the constitution of the human self. He asks: In what or in whom do we place this trust? In functional terms, the object of our trust is our god. The issue is whether we trust the real God or a substitute. Recall how Luther says, "It is the trust and faith of the heart alone that make both God and an idol. If your faith and trust are right, then your God is the true one."[4] Do we trust the real God or an idol? One implication of this observation is that in conversion we never move from unfaith to faith. We always move from faith to faith, from one object of trust to another. Unless, of course, we start with a broken soul.

For both the fragile soul and the broken soul, trusting the real God could make daily living better—much better—because we are less likely to sin. In faith, the eternal grace of God is present, providing justification so that we don't need to engage in self-justification. Romans 8:33b: "God is the one who justifies" (*theos ho dikaiosune*). A justifying faith is justifiable.

Here's the key: If we realize that God justifies us, then we don't have to justify ourselves. If we don't have to justify ourselves, then we have no need to scapegoat others. In fact, we will find it quite easy to

---

3. Wolfhart Pannenberg, *Anthropology in Theological Perspective,* trans. Matthew J. O'Connell (Louisville: Westminster John Knox, 1985), 231, italics in original.
4. Luther, Large Catechism, *BC,* 386.

love and care for others, especially the scapegoats among us. We may even find ourselves crusading on behalf of justice for the scapegoats.

However, there is a great deal more to understanding what *faith* actually means. Faith as trust is only one aspect of faith. The other aspects provide faith with good reasons to trust God. Faith is not blind, even though a person of faith cannot see everything clearly.

In this chapter, I would like to analyze our faith in a trustworthy God, faith in the God of grace. I would like to give attention to seven features of faith, seven marks that distinguish faith in the God of Jesus Christ from faith in alternative objects:

1. Faith responds to God's Word.
2. Faith recognizes that God is gracious.
3. Faith believes.
4. Faith trusts.
5. Faith experiences the risen Jesus Christ dwelling in one's soul.
6. Faith sins boldly in love.
7. Faith seeks understanding.

I will attend to the first three features of faith in this chapter. In chapter 11, I will discuss trust (number 4), and in subsequent chapters I will attend to the final three features on the list. Follow me as I look briefly at each.[5]

1. Faith Responds to God's Word

Recall how the term *justifying faith* prompts two questions. First, can we justify embracing faith in a secular or non-religious society? Second, can we find justification before God in our faith? Here I

---

5. Some of this chapter is drawn from a previous article, Ted Peters, "Atheist Stimulus and Faith Response," *Trinity Seminary Review* 30:2 (Summer/Fall 2009): 87–102

will deal with the first question: Is it foolish or wise to embrace faith in God through Jesus Christ? My answer: it is wise because it is justifiable to embrace faith. However, the reasons that justify faith are a bit tricky and less than straightforward. They require listening for God to speak in disguised form.

Faith is not something we invent. Our faith is a response to God's stimulus. It is a response to what we have heard or what we have read about God's gracious activity in the life and work of Jesus Christ. Because we have heard the story of Jesus, we respond by living the life of faith. We do not generate our faith as a heroic act of will. Rather, our faith is a response to God's Word. St. Paul writes that "faith comes from what is heard, and what is heard comes through the word of Christ" (Rom 10:17, NRSV). What we hear is the story of Jesus, and when this story becomes our own personal story we respond with faith.[6] "The Word is the gospel of God concerning his Son, who was made flesh, suffered, rose from the dead, and was glorified through the Spirit who sanctifies," trumpets Luther. "To preach Christ means to feed the soul, make it righteous, and set it free, and save it, provided it believes the preaching. Faith alone is the saving and efficacious use of the Word of God."[7]

From where does God speak a divine word to us? From the Bible or a sermon?

This is why we continually teach that the knowledge of Christ and of

---

6. *Sola scriptura* is a Reformation watchword. "If Scripture is our primary language of faith, then biblical fluency implies that we know the Bible well enough to dream in its language—with visions of biblical stories, laws, prophecies, letters, gospels, and prayers dancing in our lives and inviting us to see, to know, and to be known by God." Diane L. Jacobson, "Book of Faith: Retrospective and Prospective," *Currents in Theology and Mission* 41:3 (June 2014): 159.

7. Luther, *The Freedom of a Christian*, *LW*, 31:346. "The gospel is the Reformation label for that promise which, if true at all, is unconditional: the promise made in the name of one who has already satisfied the condition of death and therefore has all the future in his gift," writes Eric W. Gritsch and Robert W. Jenson. "The gospel tolerates no conditions. It is itself unconditional promise." *Lutheranism: The Theological Movement and Its Confessional Writings* (Minneapolis: Fortress Press, 1976), 44.

faith is not a human work but utterly a divine gift; as God creates faith, so he preserves us in it. And just as He initially gives us faith through the Word, so later on He exercises, increases, strengthens, and perfects it in us by that Word. Therefore the supreme worship of God that a man can offer, the Sabbath of Sabbaths, is to practice true godliness, to hear and read the Word. On the other hand, nothing is more dangerous than to become tired of the Word.[8]

For Swiss theologian Karl Barth, who thinks much like Luther does, the Word of God is an event of revelation that prompts and protects faith. It comes to us in three forms: (1) the incarnate Word in the person of Jesus Christ, (2) the Bible, and (3) the living proclamation that takes place within the Church. "The revelation attested in Holy Scripture is the revelation of the God who, as the Lord, is the Father from whom it proceeds, the Son who fulfils it objectively (for us), and the Holy Spirit who fulfils it subjectively (in us)."[9] On the one hand, the Word of God is spoken to us. On the other hand, the Word of God becomes revelation only when it lodges within the soul, only when it is received.

God speaks. We listen. God declares that our sins our forgiven. We accept God's judgment and we celebrate our forgiveness with gratitude. "Faith means to take God's judgment on oneself: to trust in his promise and to accept his forgiveness."[10] Faith begins with God's word objectively addressed to us, and it concludes with our subjective response.

---

8. Martin Luther, *Lectures on Galatians*, 1535, *LW*, 26:64.
9. Karl Barth, *CD*, I/2, 1. As faith responds to God's word, it expresses itself in the construction of a religious tradition, Christianity. God transcends and even judges this religious tradition. Distinguishing divine transcendence in this way humanizes and de-absolutizes our understanding of the Christian religion. This interpretation stands in contrast to that of Lutheran dogmatician John Theodore Mueller, who speaks of "perfection" in reference to the Christian religion. "Christianity is a God-made religion; all others are man-made." *Christian Dogmatics* (St. Louis: Concordia, 1955), 28.
10. Hans Joachim Iwand, "The Righteousness of Faith According to Luther," *Lutheran Quarterly* 21:1 (Spring 2007): 35.

God's Word is objective and our faith is subjective—right? Well, it certainly looks that way superficially. Yet if we press deeper, we find that it is more nuanced. This is the tricky part. Our subjective reception is due to the work of the Holy Spirit deep within us; the Holy Spirit prompts us to listen to the Word of God, to hear the divine Word as addressed to each one of us. John Calvin calls this the inner witness of the Holy Spirit. "For as God alone is a fit witness of himself in his Word, so also the Word will not find acceptance in men's hearts before it is sealed by the inward testimony of the Spirit."[11] On the one hand, God's Word comes objectively as a word addressed to us. On the other hand, God works from within our subjectivity to seal the contract, so to speak, to establish anfd maintain our relationship.

In principle, Christians will not concede to atheist critics that faith is one's own invention, merely a projection of one's wishes onto an imaginary spiritual realm. We Christians believe that we have heard God speaking to us, and our faith is a response to what we have heard. Do we have wishes that we project onto God? Of course. However, God is not reduced to merely a product of our imaginary projections. Our gracious God has invited us to project our images of benevolence onto the divine screen.

If justifying faith is worthy of our commitment, we must take seriously the atheist challenge. According to *The New Encyclopedia of Unbelief:* "Philosophically, atheism is justified in two different ways. Negative atheists attempt to establish their position by showing that the standard arguments of the existence of God are unsound. Positive atheists attempt to show that there are good grounds for disbelieving in God."[12] The justification of atheism depends on the success or

---

11. Calvin, *Inst*, 1:79.
12. Michael Martin, "Atheism," in *The New Encyclopedia of Unbelief,* ed. Tom Flynn (Buffalo: Prometheus, 2007), 89.

failure of arguments. What do atheists argue about? That they do not need to appeal to a divine rational creator of the natural world in order to pursue scientific knowledge. That's it. Nothing more. If the atheist wins the argument, a rational creator deity—a prime mover, so to speak—does not exist. If the theist wins the argument, all that exists is a prime mover. Nothing about the character or personhood or distinctiveness of God is addressed in such argumentation. Unfortunately, whether or not God is gracious is not even a question in the public debate.

I can imagine a person of faith saying, "I just don't care who wins the atheist debate. Even if the theist wins, the existence of the God of grace has not been addressed." The question of whether or not God is gracious, I think, is more important than whether or not a prime mover exists. If there is a deity who exists but is not gracious, who cares? In the Word of God, we find the God of grace addressing us. Faith in this God of grace is our response.

This brings us to the next complexity: How do we know that God is gracious? Reformation Protestants try to spell this out by connecting what is revealed about God with the event of the crucifixion of Jesus Christ. When we refer to the *theology of the cross,* we are alluding to the paradox within special revelation—namely, that God is revealed in, with, and under what is not divine. Specifically, the event of the cross reveals God in a most unexpected and mysterious way. In the cross, we see tragedy, defeat, suffering, and death. And yet, to the eyes of faith, the God of meaning, victory, salvation, and resurrection is present. In, with, and under the weakness of the cross, the power of God is present. In, with, and under the degradation of Jesus, the glory of God is present.

Luther writes, "The manifest and visible things of God are placed in opposition to the invisible, namely, his human nature, weakness, foolishness. . . . it does [a theologian] no good to recognize God in his glory and majesty, unless he recognizes him in the humility and shame of the cross. . . . 'Truly, thou art a God who hidest thyself' (Isa. 45:15)."[13] The heart of God and God's willingness to share the sufferings of the world God so loves come to articulation in the event of the cross. Just as it is hard to see ourselves for what we are because of self-justifying lies, it is hard to see the presence of God in the scapegoat on the cross.

Much more could be said about this difficult insight. However, let's take another look at the debate between theists and atheists. Today's aggressive atheists challenge people of faith, saying that the idea of God is incompatible with the scientific or materialist view of the natural world. Therefore, atheists argue, no God exists. Oxford's Richard Dawkins is the most vivid example. In his book, *The God Delusion*, Dawkins considers what he calls the "God Hypothesis." He analyzes the hypothesis scientifically and concludes "most probably that God does not exist." He claims this is a scientific conclusion, and on this basis he describes the content of Christian belief as "a pernicious delusion."[14]

13. Luther, *Heidelberg Disputation* in *LW*, 31:52–53. In an unpublished paper by David Tracy, "Martin Luther's *Deus Theolgicus*" (2014), we see a marvelously comprehensive yet penetrating review of Luther's understanding of the gracious God who is both revealed and hidden. On the one hand, Luther's reliance on a theology of the cross leads to a God who is revealed yet still mysterious—a God revealed under the opposite (*sub contrario*) and even under a contradictory opposite (*sub contradictario*) that nullifies any deity demonstrated in the conclusion of a rational argument. Here revelation and faith are pitted against reason. On the other hand, when by heartfelt faith (*fides cordis*) we become grounded in the hidden God, reason as faith-seeking-further-understanding is unleashed anew. "Faith also redeems reason for newly illuminated theological use," observes Tracy. "This much is clear: Luther is undoubtedly original in his model for *Deus theologicus*, i.e., in his unique and epoch-making description of the two forms of God's Hiddenness. By that double move, Luther does interrupt and, to a certain extent, disrupt the earlier traditions on adequate God-language by his singular—and, in my judgment, persuasive—concept of the double Hiddenness of God both in and beyond revelation. At the same time, Luther's logically developed Trinitarian theology is not discontinuous." In sum, Luther both innovates and recalibrates the Latin tradition of theology's knowledge of God.

14. Dawkins, *The God Delusion* (New York: Houghton Mifflin, 2006), 31. I provide a more thorough exposition and reply to Dawkins in chapter 1 of *The Evolution of Terrestrial and Extraterrestrial Life* (Goshen, IN: Pandora, 2007). It is important to note that the scientific method does not lead to any conclusion regarding the existence or nonexistence of God.

In light of the theology of the cross, I recommend we concede this point: the idea of God does not fit easily within a narrowly scientific or reductionist view of the world. While the idea of God is certainly not incompatible with science, the God of grace cannot be uncovered through investigation of the God hypothesis or strictly rational proofs. In fact, if we look for God there, we should not be surprised not to find him. It's like looking through a telescope for a cell of an organism when we should be using a microscope. No wonder we don't see what we're looking for.

God is present *under the contrary*, not in the conclusion to an empirical investigation. Where we see death, God is present with the promise of life. Where we see deterioration and dissipation, God is present with creativity and newness. Where we see natural law and contingency, God is present with faithfulness and openness. Where we see survival of the fittest, God is present in solidarity with the unfit. Attempting to prove the existence or non-existence of a prime mover by projecting a God hypothesis in a so-called scientific manner can never admit the kind of evidence found in the cross.

The event of the cross, toward which the scriptures direct our eyes, is an event of revelation. Yet this mode of revelation cannot be placed in the same categories of knowledge with which a scientist might work. To study the natural world scientifically is to examine our world with microscopes and telescopes and other measuring devices, after which the scientist cautiously reports what is confirmable knowledge. The paradoxical and mysterious dimension of the cross event simply cannot be turned into subject matter for empirical

"Science chooses not to invoke supernatural explanations to fill gaps in naturalistic explanations. This of course does not rule out the *possibility* of supernatural intervention. Operational science takes no position about the existence or nonexistence of an omnipotent god." Charles M. Wynn, Sr., "Scientific Methodology and Its Religious Parallels," *The Skeptical Inquirer* 38:4 (July/August 2014): 56. For Dawkins to rest his atheism on science is fallacious. Many devout believers in God are numbered among the world's most revered scientists.

research. It should come as no surprise to a theologian of the cross that an atheist is unable to verify the so-called God hypothesis based upon what one construes as empirical evidence.

Christians who place their faith in the God of grace—revealed in, with, and under the cross of Jesus Christ—are unaffected by the reductionism implied in the God hypothesis for two reasons. First, the God who Dawkins is testing for is not exactly the same God revealed in the cross. Don't get me wrong. Yes, we are talking about the omnipotent God of theism who is responsible for the creation of the world, the prime mover. However, what Christian faith discerns in the cross is that God is gracious, and this cannot be discerned when asking about the creative power behind natural phenomena.

Secondly, the two pathways to knowledge are not consonant. To set out to confirm or disconfirm a scientific hypothesis is to look for relevant evidence that supports or challenges the hypothesis. All such evidence is evaluated positively. In contrast, revelation through the cross provides negative knowledge, or at least paradoxical knowledge. We see weakness, but power is revealed. We see defeat, but victory is revealed. We see sin, but forgiveness is revealed. We see disgrace, but grace is revealed. The truth or falsity of this Christian claim cannot be adjudicated by an appeal to scientific research. That today's atheists do not even hypothesize about God's graciousness is no surprise, but it signifies that they do not address what is at the heart of distinctively *Christian* belief in God.

As creator of the universe, God is a topic for debate in the dialogue between science and religion, between atheism and theism. Even though aggressive atheists find they cannot confirm this deity's existence by studying the God hypothesis, the existence of a divine creator would still be consonant with scientific knowledge of the world. What is unique and not subject to scientific discussion is the knowledge that God is gracious. To learn this, we must attend to what is revealed in the cross of Jesus Christ and addressed to us in the Word of God.

2. Faith Recognizes That God Is gracious

Our faith is in God. However, not just any old divine being will do. The particular God in whom the Christian invests faith exhibits the unique and decisive attribute of grace. But what is grace? Bishop Carder's description is a fine start: "Grace is doing on our behalf what we could never do for ourselves—create ourselves in the image of God, reconcile ourselves to God whose life we have denied and distorted, restore the divine image in humanity, and transform ourselves and creation into the likeness of Jesus Christ. Grace is Jesus Christ!"[15] Cathleen Falsani trumpets boldly:

> Justice is getting what you deserve.
> Mercy is not getting what you deserve.
> And grace is getting what you absolutely don't deserve.[16]

God loves us graciously. Regardless of what we deserve, God loves us graciously. Even if we human beings find ourselves estranged or alienated from the divine, God overcomes this alienation by graciously loving us, accepting us, justifying us, saving us. Romans 3:21-24: "But now, apart from law, the righteousness of God (*dikaiosune tou theou*) has been disclosed,[17] and is attested by the law

---

15. Kenneth L. Carder, *Living Our Beliefs,* rev. ed. (Nashville: Discipleship Resources, 2009), 77.

16. Falsani, *Sin Boldly: A Field Guide for Grace* (Grand Rapids, MI: Zondervan, 2008), 14.

17. Arland Hultgren contends that this "is the most provocative statement in the entire letter [Romans]—indeed in all of Paul's letters—concerning the redemptive work of God in Christ." Arland J. Hultgren, *Paul's Letter to the Romans: A Commentary* (Grand Rapids, MI: Eerdmans, 2011), 151. He adds that the "righteousness of God (*dikaiosune tou Theou*), now revealed, is not God's justice. . . . The righteousness of God is God's saving activity, setting the relationship right between humanity and himself" (ibid., 154). In the book that launched the neo-orthodox revolution, *The Epistle to the Romans,* Karl Barth announces that "the Judge pronounces His verdict according to the standard of His righteousness only. Unlike any other verdict, His

and the prophets, the righteousness of God through faith in Jesus Christ for all who believe.[18] For there is no distinction, since all have sinned and fall short of the glory of God; they are now justified by his grace as a gift, through the redemption that is in Christ Jesus."[19]

By grace, God's justice becomes our justice. By God's grace, we sinners find ourselves forgiven. By our own reason or strength, we are unable to fulfill the demands of justice or accomplish our own forgiveness; yet these become ours in faith as a gift of God's grace. "All grace comes from above," writes Korean martyr Ju Gi-Cheol.[20]

Perhaps no recent theologian emphasizes the role of divine grace more forcefully than the late Gerard Forde. "To the age old question, 'What shall I do to be saved?,'" Forde offers this shocking answer: "Nothing! Just be still; shut up and listen for once in your life to what God the Almighty, creator and redeemer, is saying to his world and to you in the death and resurrection of his Son! Listen and believe!" To shut up and listen to the divine Word—and then believe it—results

verdict is creative. He pronounces us, His enemies, to be His friends." Barth, *The Epistle to the Romans,* trans. Edwyn C. Hoskyns, 6th ed. (Oxford: Oxford University Press, 1968), 93.

18. We have previously asked whether our justification-by-faith is due to our faith in God or God's faith in us. Paul's phrase, *dia pisteuo,* leaves us with this ambiguity because "through faith" appears in the genitive case. Rather than refer to our faith "in" Jesus Christ, Paul could be saying that we are justified "through the faith of Jesus Christ." This is the interpretation elected by Herman Waetjen. "There is no evidence in Paul's letters that he proclaimed, exhorted or encouraged 'faith in Jesus Christ.' Nowhere does he speak of 'believing in Jesus.' . . . To make Jesus the object of faith on the basis of 3:22a—and elsewhere in Paul's letters—as Luther and Calvin did, and as many current interpreters of Romans and Galatians continue to do, is a mistaken and flawed interpretation of this genitive construction." Herman C. Waetjen, *The Letter to the Romans: Salvation as Justice and the Deconstruction of Law* (Sheffield, UK: Sheffield Phoenix, 2011), 113.

19. "Sin is more than an inner state; it is an objective power of corruption which has man in its clutch," remarks Anders Nygren in his interpretation of this decisive passage (Rom. 3:21). This means that, contrary to Socrates's *just soul,* our justice is a gift from God, not our own moral achievement. Nygren declares that "righteousness is solely a property of God"; so it follows that "it is truest to translate *dikaiosune Theou* as 'righteousness *from* God.'" Anders Nygren, *Commentary on Romans,* trans. Carl C. Rasmussen (Philadelphia: Muhlenberg Press, 1949), 146–47 (italics in original).

20. Ju Gi-Cheol, *Essential Writings,* ed. Korea Institute for Advanced Theological Studies, trans. Yang Sung-Hyun (Seoul: KIATS Press, 2008), 115.

in a faith that is aware of God's grace. "The faith by which one is justified is not an active verb of which the Old Adam or Eve is the subject; it is a state-of-being verb. Faith is the state of being grasped by the unconditional claim and promise of the God who calls into being that which is from that which is not."[21] You and I are as dependent upon God for our faith as we are for our being called into being.

This awareness that the God of grace has entered our human soul constitutes the liberating power of faith. In addition to the objective knowledge that God is gracious, the grace of this God can become subjectively present to us in our faith, giving faith its liberating power. "Faith . . . involves liberation from the drive for self-assurance and therefore from uncertainty," writes Oswald Bayer. "It means liberation from the search for identity and its attempted discovery. In prayer I am led away from myself. I am torn away from self and set outside the self with its abilities and judgments."[22] Grace liberates. Faith frees.

I ask once again: What role does this emphasis on divine grace play in the current debate over the existence of God? Unfortunately, it plays no role at all.

We have already depicted the argument over the existence of the creator god as the prime mover. Even if grace is not being debated, something else is. Atheists contend that the deity in whom Jews, Christians, and Muslims place their trust fosters violence. Religion is violent. Religion must be stopped.

What does their argument entail? Atheist Sam Harris argues that "the biblical God is a fiction, like Zeus and the thousands of other dead gods whom most sane human beings now ignore."[23] What

21. Gerhard O. Forde, *Justification by Faith—A Matter of Death and Life* (Minneapolis: Fortress Press, 1982), 22.
22. Oswald Bayer, *Living by Faith: Justification and Sanctification,* trans. Geoffrey W. Bromily (Grand Rapids, MI: Eerdmans, 2003), 26.

Harris fears is the immoral and violent behavior perpetrated by religious persons. "Competing religious doctrines have shattered our world into separate moral communities, and these divisions have become a continual source of human conflict."[24] Elsewhere he writes, "religious faith perpetuates man's inhumanity to man."[25] In short, if we believe in a god such as Zeus, we will foster hatred against other religious groups and prosecute violence against those who believe differently. Harris would prefer that we give up our belief in the God of Israel, affirm a rationalist's approach to human living, and put our trust in humane values.

Before proceeding, let's pause for a moment to recall the relevance of what I've been saying about sin as self-justification. Whether we belong to an organized religion or not, we human beings are inclined to draw a line between good and evil and place ourselves on the good side. This frequently leads to placing a scapegoat on the other side—a human propensity that seems to describe precisely what Harris is

23. Harris, *Letter to a Christian Nation* (New York: Alfred A. Knopf, 2006), 55–56.
24. Ibid., 79.
25. Harris, *The End of Faith: Religion, Terror, and the Future of Reason* (New York: W. W. Norton, 2004), 15. Atheists who claim to ground their anti-theism in science contend that religion is so violent that we should rid the world of religion. Is this reasonable? Even though so-called scientific studies of religion and violence have not been conducted, there are studies that show that regular churchgoers tend to engage in less crime and engage in more socially responsible activities such as altruism, charity, and aiding the poor. "The widely advanced hypothesis that the world would be better—more humane—without religion is entirely reasonable, and it should continue to be debated by thoughtful scholars. Contrary to the forceful assertions of some prominent atheist authors, . . . the data consistently point to a negative association between religiosity and criminal behavior and a positive association between religiosity and prosocial behavior." Scott O. Lilienfeld and Rachel Ammirati, "Would the World Be Better Off without Religion? *The Skeptical Inquirer* 38:4 (July/August 2014), 35. I would like to make two points. First, sociologically speaking, religious people tend to exhibit ethical integrity and social responsibility. Second, the atheist complaint against religion works with a narrow understanding of what religion is. As a result of the purported scientific mindset of atheists, their concept of religion is limited to people affiliated with religious institutions. They are deaf and blind to spiritual sensibilities, to multilevel symbolic understanding, and to the sublimated and disguised import of religious sensibilities into science itself as a cultural phenomenon. Atheistic religiosity is just as religious as the enemies it opposes. In this book, it is not my task to defend religion against its attackers; rather, I mean to understand human nature in light of what has been revealed by God in Jesus Christ.

attributing to historical religions. Religions foster scapegoating and violence because their adherents see themselves as dogmatically right while judging all others to be wrong. Belief in a god such as Zeus fosters rigidity, absolutism, and murder.

Now, back to the question of God's existence.[26] The Olympian Zeus, with all of his temper tantrums and lightening bolts, is not a god who attracts Christian belief. Once Christians have heard the news that the God of Israel—the God who created our cosmos—is gracious, they are likely to lose interest in all other candidates running for the office of head divine being. It would be quite a disappointment if someone proved the existence of a god such as the prime mover or even Zeus, only to discover that this god is not gracious. A non-gracious divine being, whether existent or not, would be unworthy of Christian appreciation or praise.

What is central to Christian faith is the affirmation that the God of Jesus Christ is the wellspring of divine grace. God loves us, even when we are unworthy of that love. Grace is the most important divine attribute. Perhaps we might say: *for Christian faith, the gracious character of God means more than the mere existence of a divine being.*

Allow me to present two implications. We are constantly tempted to create God in an image that serves our self-justification or even to deny God's existence if it serves our self-justification. What faith does is permit God to be God. And God is gracious. Simon Peura draws this first implication, arguing that a faith that allows God to be gracious actually fulfills the first commandment, namely, to worship

26. Our zealous atheists frequently repeat two arguments against those of us who have faith in God. First, God does not exist. Second, religion is violent. In principle, these are separate issues. "The question of whether the world would be better off without religion has no logical bearing on the ontological question of God's existence. . . . the question of God's existence is logically and factually independent of the question of whether belief in God's existence is beneficial for the human species." Lilienfeld and Ammirati, "Would the World Be Better Off without Religion?," 31. In this book, I wish to justify our faith, to be sure; but this does not include proving the existence of God. Unless God is gracious, the simple issue of the existence or nonexistence of the kind of God the atheists set out to disprove is virtually irrelevant.

the true God rather than an idol of our own making. "The faith fulfills the First Commandment, because it lets God be the Giver."[27]

The second implication is this: if we place our faith in a gracious God, then we are likely to behave graciously in our world. We are likely to respect and perhaps even love those who are *other* to us, to those who disagree with our dogmas. We are not likely to shatter the peace over doctrinal disputes nor persecute those who believe differently than we do.

The complaint that Harris and other aggressive atheists raise against religion is that religion fosters violence. Perhaps we should concede this point. However, we should point out that violence is a generic human trait that we share with non-religious and post-religious and anti-religious people. In earlier chapters, we have seen how secular governments create their own civic spiritualities and manipulate millions of people into marching off to war. Secularism or sustained opposition to institutional religion provides zero protection from self-justification, scapegoating, and violence.

At the very least, faith in Jesus Christ is justifiable because it offers an opportunity to face realistically the truth about the human condition, our own condition. The truth is that our confused contortions, which are spawned by self-justification, alienate us from one another and even from ourselves. The presence of God in the scapegoated Christ reveals a truth about ourselves that is difficult to uncover in other ways. The best we get from the roaring and bellowing and squawking atheists is their own version of self-justification; they draw the line between good and evil and then place themselves on the good side with religious nincompoops on the evil side. This justifies the elimination of religion, even with nuclear

---

27. Simon Puera, "What God Gives Man Receives: Luther on Salvation," In *Union with Christ: The New Finnish Interpretation of Luther,* ed. Carl E. Braaten and Robert W. Jenson (Grand Rapids, MI: Eerdmans, 1998), 84.

weapons if necessary. What atheists cannot see from within their own logic is our shared human condition. What faith in Jesus Christ offers is truth about ourselves, which is accompanied by something even better—the realization that God loves us graciously.

3. Faith Believes

Do beliefs matter? The SBNRs (spiritual but not religious) say no. What matters is experience, not belief.[28] Listing one's beliefs in a creed only divides people between irreconcilable opinions, and SBNRs decry such divisions. They encourage spiritual unity that overcomes dogmatic divisions. Diana Butler Bass points us to a "Belief Gap." The belief gap is not a rejection of every belief but only those beliefs that seem to separate or divide. "Christianity is moving from being a religion *about* God to being an experience *of* God," she writes.[29] "Doctrine is seen as not only divisive, but as contrary to the message Jesus himself taught. Many people stumble on the creeds, thinking them to be a sort of doctrinal test for church membership. . . . In the minds of many, dogma deserves to die."[30] In response, I would ask: If Christian churches allow their creeds to die and then bury them, can we be confident that spiritual harmony will reign?

Do beliefs matter? In contrast to the SBNRs, the atheists say yes. "Unbelief serves as a liberating gateway to a more fulfilled life," advertises Richard Dawkins.[31] According to atheists, it appears that we're in a contest between belief and unbelief. I contend that a more

---

28. If William James were alive today, he would agree that experience, not belief, is the foundation of religion. "The fact is that those arguments [theological beliefs] do but follow the combined suggestions of the facts and of our feeling. They prove nothing rigorously. They only corroborate our pre-existent partialities." *The Varieties of Religious Experience*, Gifford Lectures Series 1901–2 (London: Longmans, Green, 1928), 439.

29. Bass, *Christianity after Religion* (New York: Harper, 2013) 110, italics in original.

30. Ibid., 111–12.

31. Richard Dawkins, foreword to *New Encyclopedia of Unbelief*, 10.

accurate description is a battle between competing beliefs. Which belief is more justifiable—belief in God or belief in no God? Which belief is more fulfilling? It is my considered judgment that belief in the God of Jesus Christ is more justifiable and more fulfilling.

Without beliefs as codified in the Apostles' Creed and Nicene Creed, the Christian faithful would find themselves unarmed against this atheist attack. If the atheists wish to attack Christian beliefs, then the Christians need beliefs for the attackers to target. Surrendering beliefs in the name of SBNR experience would leave faith's citadel undefended.

Both the Apostles' and Nicene Creeds begin with the affirmation, "I believe" (*credo*). What we affirm when we confess in this manner is that we have heard the story of Jesus; we respond by believing what the story of Jesus tells us about the God of the universe. We treat God's Word as truthful. We treat God's Word as truthful, even if we sometimes doubt our own partial formulations of God's Word.

What we Christians believe is that the life, death, and resurrection of Jesus of Nazareth reveals to us a truth about the whole of reality. All that is real comes from God's creative and redemptive will. The God who raises the dead can only be the God who creates the world.

Faith as belief in the God who creates and redeems the world requires a modicum of knowledge and understanding. "Faith rests not on ignorance, but on knowledge,"[32] contends Calvin. Christian faith requires knowledge of the story of Jesus as well as understanding of how one fits into the big picture of reality that God is drawing. Pentecostal Amos Yong places the pursuit of understanding at the earliest stage of faith, at the point where God's Word elicits our response: "Revelation is received by humble faith seeking understanding."[33] Some level of understanding is required at the

---

32. Calvin, *Inst.,* 3.2, 1:545.

beginning of faith if faith is to be intelligible. Faith builds on a prior knowledge that incorporates respectful understanding. One cannot be coerced by dogma or sword to believe what is unbelievable. "Faith without understanding is not faith but coercion,"[34] writes Løgstrup.

Contemporary atheists attack Christian faith on the grounds that belief relies upon ignorance rather than knowledge. "Faith is an evil precisely because it requires no justification and brooks no argument,"[35] says Dawkins with derision. Dawkins and other atheists believe that scientific reason provides all the knowledge we need. Because scientific reason cannot prove the existence of a creator God, we should abandon belief in such a God. Trust science, not religion, Dawkins would say.

Those who hold Christian beliefs defend their position in opposition to atheism, arguing that faith is based upon knowledge. This knowledge includes the objective history of Jesus plus its subjective appropriation in faith. In Article 20 of the Augsburg Confession (written in 1530), we find: "'Faith' here does not signify only historical knowledge . . . it signifies faith which believes not only the history but also the effect of the history, namely, this article of the forgiveness of sins, that is, that we have grace, righteousness, and forgiveness of sins through Christ."[36]

A faith that believes is justified by appealing both to the story of Jesus that we find in God's Word and to reason. Reason supports faith, even if this support never completely expunges all doubt.

33. Amos Yong, *The Spirit Poured Out on All Flesh: Pentecostalism and the Possibility of a Global Theology* (Grand Rapids, MI: Baker Academic, 2005), 298.
34. Knud Ejler Løgstrup, *The Ethical Demand* (Notre Dame, IN: University of Notre Dame Press, 1997), 2.
35. Dawkins, *God Delusion,* 306.
36. *BC,* 57. "Simple historical knowledge, then," comments Pannenberg, "needs to be supplemented by confident trust (*fiducia*) that grasps the true meaning, the effect of the history of Jesus, namely, the forgiveness of sins . . . On this matter Luther's judgment was the same as Melanchthon's." Wolfhart Pannenberg, *ST,* 3:143.

Scientific reasoning provides helpful knowledge of the created world in which we live, to be sure, but its method restricts itself to looking for natural causes. Modern science is blind to transcendent reality and deaf to things sacred. This blindness is not proof that transcendent reality does not exist, just as deafness is not proof that our world is strictly profane. People with strong Christian faith can work quite happily in scientific research, appreciating the beauty and intricacy of the natural world; but science is not the final court of appeal regarding the existence or non-existence of the divine—either as the prime mover or the God of grace. Atheism has no exclusive patent rights to scientific reason.

Belief requires prior knowledge, but this knowledge may fall short of certainty. Knowledge grows, even knowledge of the God whom we cannot see. Because we begin with a knowledge that falls short of certainty, faith cannot help but include doubt. "When Jesus speaks of faith," writes John Sanford, "he is speaking of a certain capacity of a person to affirm life in spite of what life may bring, and even in the face of doubts: 'Lord, I believe; help thou mine unbelief' (Mark 9:24, KJV)."[37] Once we believe in God, the intellectual battle between doubt and faith continues. "Faith is not possession but pilgrimage," warns Paul Sponheim. "Therefore, it is not strange that the word of confession is 'I believe, help my unbelief!'"[38]

In our era, no honest believer can escape the challenge of doubt. Arguments by atheists to reject belief in every god along with arguments by pluralists to respect every belief in every god challenge our claim to believe as true what the Church says about Jesus Christ. It is virtually impossible to avoid holding multiple alternative, if not

37. Sanford, *The Kingdom Within: The Inner Meaning of Jesus' Sayings* (New York: Harper, 1970), 123–24.
38. Paul R. Sponheim, *Faith and the Other* (Minneapolis: Fortress Press, 1993), 162.

contradictory, ideas in one's mind at the same time. Such doubt is internal to faith, yet doubt need not weaken faith.

Although it is frequently overlooked, the concept of justification-by-faith applies to the faith versus doubt interaction. Paul Tillich tells us how the doctrine of justification-by-faith mitigates the pain of doubt. "The principle of justification through faith refers not only to the religious-ethical but also to the religious-intellectual life. Not only he who is in sin but also he who is in doubt is justified through faith. The situation of doubt, even of doubt about God, need not separate us from God. There is faith in every serious doubt, namely, the faith in the truth as such, even if the only truth we can express is our lack of faith."[39] It is the object of our faith—Christ—who justifies us; it is not our faith in itself that justifies us. Still, God is truth, and God welcomes our intellectual commitment to truth, even when our truth-commitment entails skepticism and criticism. Because of our commitment to truth, doubt within faith is a healthy critical component to faith. The dialectic between belief and unbelief within us can actually testify to the strength of faith.

The bad news, so to speak, is that "believers are in perpetual conflict with their own unbelief," according to Calvin.[40] However, there is good news here as well. Belief resides deeper within us than doubt does. Belief remains home; doubt only visits on occasion. "Unbelief does not hold sway within believer's hearts, but assails them from without."[41] Despite the perpetual struggle between doubt and faith, faith will triumph because it relies upon the presence of Christ within the human heart at a level deeper than the doubts that assail us.

39. Paul Tillich, *The Protestant Era* (Chicago: University of Chicago Press, 1948), x.
40. Calvin, *Inst.,* 3.2, 1:562. Paul Tillich writes, "Every theologian is committed *and* alienated; he is always in faith *and* doubt; he is inside *and* outside the theological circle." *SysT*, 1:10, italics in original.
41. Calvin, *Inst.,* 3.2, 1:567.

Even with the confidence Calvin tries to elicit in us, it is still a struggle to answer the question, "What should I believe?," with certainty. Philosopher of religion Paul Holmer lays the responsibility for working through this struggle at the feet of the theologian. The theologian's struggle is exacerbated by the context in which God is said to be either dead or non-existent. "*Post mortem dei.* We are told by so many today that God does not exist and that the word *God* itself is therefore dead almost beyond revivifying."[42] As Holmer sifts through the subtleties regarding the content of Christian beliefs, he goes to the root of believing itself, namely, the possibility of personal faith in God. Rather than provide us with a set of beliefs that we may declare a "revelation," the theologian should attend to the basic capacity for belief itself. "Perhaps it is the task of theology not to be God's revelation but only to help people again to believe in God. . . . Seeking God with one's whole heart is no joke, especially if it might be the only way to find him."[43] Note how Holmer moves from the mind to the heart, from belief to trust.

Before we move to the heart, we need to ask honestly: Are beliefs of any value to the person of faith? Yes, they are. Beliefs help form the soul. Beliefs give shape to daily life. "Beliefs function in the service of character formation, faith development, missional engagement, and evangelization," writes Carder. "Beliefs are to be lived; doctrine to be practiced."[44] David Tracy adds, "I do believe in belief. . . . I believe in God. It is, I confess, that belief which gives me hope."[45] What connects our beliefs with our life is trust—trust in the truth of our beliefs and, more importantly, trust in the God who transcends those

---

42. Paul L. Holmer, *The Grammar of Faith* (San Francisco: Harper, 1978), 41.
43. Ibid., 51.
44. Carder, *Living Our Beliefs,* 10.
45. David Tracy, *Plurality and Ambiguity: Hermeneutics, Religion, Hope* (New York: Harper, 1987), 110.

beliefs and who welcomes us into a personal relationship through grace.

Does belief in the right thing produce justification? No. Does belief without doubt produce justification? No. At this point, you might complain, "Just wait a darned minute! Then what do you mean by faith in *justification-by-faith*?" Lundensian theologian Anders Nygren tries to answer this nuanced question. "Faith is not a subjective quality which must be present [in us] if the gospel is to be able to show its power. It is truer to say that one's faith is evidence that the gospel *has* exercised its power on [us]. It is not [our] faith that gives the gospel its power; quite the contrary, it is the power of the gospel that makes it possible for one to believe."[46] Justification is a gift to us from God, not a product of our believing.

Faith is a response to the gospel, and the gospel announces an objective fact: we have been offered salvation by God as a free gift in Jesus Christ. Faith is our subjective response to God's objective offer. Believing is a natural component to this response.

Belief is an activity of the human mind. When we turn to faith as trust, we turn not only to the mind but also to the heart and to all that we are. "Justifying faith is not intellectual assent to revealed truth," comments Alister McGrath. "Rather, it is trust (*fiducia*) in the promises of God, supremely the promise of forgiveness, coupled with the resulting union of the believer with Christ."[47] To faith as trust we now turn.

46. Nygren, *Commentary on Romans,* 71.
47. Alister E. McGrath, "Justification," in *The Oxford Encyclopedia of the Reformation,* ed. Hans J. Hillerbrand, 4 vols. (Oxford: Oxford University Press, 1996), 2:363.

11

Faith as Trust

The person lives by the future in which its trust is placed.

–Wolfhart Pannenberg[1]

Christian faith does not add a dispensable religious dimension to human life but rather transforms its existential mode from a self-centered to a God-open life that puts its ultimate trust not in any human institution, whether religions or non-religious, but in the creative presence of God's love."

–Ingolf Dalferth[2]

In the previous chapter, we looked at how—in faith—we give attention to God's Word, perceive that God is gracious, and believe selected doctrines to be true. If we wanted to be persnickety, we might dub these acts of faith *works*. It takes work on our part to

1. Pannenberg, *Anthropology in Theological Perspective*, trans. Matthew J. O'Connell (Louisville: Westminster John Knox, 1985), 527.
2. Ingolf U. Dalferth, "Post-secular Society: Christianity and the Dialectics of the Secular," *Journal of the American Academy of Religion* 78:2 (June 2010): 339.

believe in the truth of doctrines. If it takes work to have faith as belief, then we might rightfully ask: How can our faith be saving faith if it is a form of work? Faith as belief looks like one more way to climb the spiritual ladder, right? What happened to grace?

This is a problem only if we hold that our own faith is the cause of our justification—only if we assert that human faith is a mechanism that compels God to reward our faith with salvation. Instead, we must maintain that our justification and hence, our salvation, is a gift of God's grace. Our faith is a placeholder, so to speak, that identifies the intersection where God's grace and our consciousness connect. It is divine grace that saves, not our faith per se. What we are called to do in faith is trust in this gospel truth or, more personally, to trust in the God who bestows grace and promises resurrection into the new creation.

4. Faith Trusts

Like a saloon door that swings between two meanings, the New Testament word for faith, "πίστις, can mean not only faith in the sense of 'trust' in someone or something (Mark 2:5; Rom. 4:5), but also a person's 'belief that' certain things are true (Matt. 17:20), and hence 'the faith' meaning a body of doctrine (2 Tim. 4:7). It also has the sense of 'faithfulness' which is itself the ground of others' trust (Rom. 3:3)."[3] In the previous chapter, we looked at faith understood as belief. We now turn to trust and trustworthiness.

---

3. Morna D. Hooker, "Faith—III. New Testament," in *Religion Past and Present*, ed. Hans Dieter Betz, Don S. Browning, Bernd Janowski, and Eberhard Jüngel, 14 vols. (Leiden, Neth.: Brill, 2007–14), 5:15. "The God 'who justifies the ungodly' (Rom. 4:5) establishes his reign not because of our faithfulness to the Torah but because of his [God's] faithfulness to his [God's] promise in Christ." Johann Christian Beker, *Paul the Apostle* (Minneapolis: Fortress Press, 1981), 269.

The person of faith trusts God. Faith places us within the strong hands of God where we trust that, no matter what happens, God will keep a safe hold on us. When all that is finite and ephemeral has disintegrated and fallen, the God in whom we trust will bear us beyond the debris into the kingdom of salvation. We are told by Article 20 of the Augsburg Confession: "In the Scriptures the word 'faith' is to be understood not as knowledge . . . but as trust that consoles and encourages."[4] Our faith consoles and encourages us.

Just as joy gives rise to a smile, trust gives rise to hope. Faith orients us in the present, while hope orients us toward the future. Calvin exclaims, "Faith believes God to be true, hope awaits the time when his truth shall be manifested . . . faith believes that eternal life has been given to us, hope anticipates that it will sometime be revealed; faith is the foundation upon which hope rests, hope nourishes and sustains faith."[5] A hopeful person is an energetic person, a creative person, a cheerful person.

Atheism rejects this hope. "Atheism rejects the existence of God as a fiction devised by men desperate to keep on living in spite of the inevitability of death," writes Michel Onfray in an *Atheist Manifesto.*[6] Onfray's accusation is that our belief in God is a fiction we human beings have devised to give us comfort in the face of the cold prospect that we will cease to exist—that we will die. This is a provocation worthy of a response. Yes, indeed, we Christians find comfort in trusting that God will raise us from the dead, just as he resurrected Jesus on Easter as "the first fruits of those having fallen asleep" (1 Cor. 15:20). Now, which came first: our subjective desire to beat death or our response to an objective message we heard regarding God's

---

4. *BC*, 57.

5. John Calvin, *Ins*, 3.2, 1:590.

6. Michel Onfray, *Atheist Manifesto: The Case Against Christianity, Judaism, and Islam*, trans. Jeremy Leggatt (New York: Arcade, 2005), 15.

promise? Such a question is inescapably important, even decisive, and it poses a challenge that requires a response.

In doing so, I'd like to appeal to what Pannenberg says. "Faith as a personal act of trust is referred to God alone. Yet this personal relation of faith to God comes through the historical self-revelation of God and through our knowledge of it. Only herein is it fully defined. Christian faith in God is thus faith in the heavenly Father and in his Son Jesus Christ who overcame death and sin for us."[7] In short, the historical knowledge of Jesus' Easter resurrection provides the stimulus to which our trust in our future resurrection is a response. We have heard the gospel—the story of Jesus told with its significance—and because of the gospel, we trust God.

Now, let's turn to the dynamics of faith as trust. The existential question we must repeatedly ask ourselves is this: In whom are we actually placing our trust—in the true God or something less than God? "Faith," writes Paul Tillich, "is the state of being ultimately concerned."[8] Our ultimate concern is the value beyond all other values that orients our entire human life. If the material world is thought to be all that exists, then the material world could become that which we value ultimately. If, on the one hand, material possessions and profits enlist our focused energies and dedication, then wealth has become our ultimate concern, our *de facto* god. Furthermore, if we allow our consciousness to become absorbed by the market or our profit within the market, we are subject to the self-destruction that comes with idolatry. If, on the other hand, the true God is our ultimate concern and we daily trust God, then our faith orients all other values toward God, and we enjoy living in

7. Wolfhart Pannenberg, *ST*, 3:152–53.

8. Paul Tillich, *Dynamics of Faith* (New York: Harper, 1957), 1. Richard A. Rosengarten applies Tillich's description of faith as ultimate concern to the moral struggles we face in our global economy in "Letter from the Dean," in the University of Chicago Divinity School newsletter, *Circa* 31 (Winter 2009): 1.

hope regardless of the vicissitudes reaped upon us by the market or other such external forces.[9] Understanding faith in terms of ultimate concern helps us discern within ourselves just what has captured our trust. If the only worthy God—the God of grace—has captured our trust, then we live the robust life of a dynamic faith. The fragile soul becomes a robust soul.

Rather than say that our faith grasps grace, we might say that we are grasped by faith. What's the difference between being grasped by faith and grasped by grace? Hong Kong theologian Simon Chow reminds us that "faith is not simply human belief, but, more important, the faithfulness of God towards the believers."[10] God can have faith in us just as we can have faith in God. It's God's faith in us that justifies. This divine faithfulness triggers trust within us. God's faith grasps us in our faith.

Living daily out of a disposition of trust guides our eyes to see metaphors of God's grace in the world around us. Composer Herbert Brokering, for example, perceives a sign of God's promise of our resurrection in the emergence of the butterfly from the cocoon.

> O silent one, your wings will find the sunshine
> Our hearts now bow in butterfly delight.[11]

This trust influences the self; it forms the soul. "In faith we abandon ourselves to trust in God," writes Eberhard Jüngel. "Through this faith, the ontic self of the new person is constituted. In this sense, justifying faith is the ongoing differentiation of the individual . . .

---

9. "The bubble giveth and the breaking of the bubble taketh away. It is a bit comforting to know that the big run-up in our pension funds in the 90s and early 2000s was partly due to the bubble produced by the three causes I mentioned above. We enjoyed the bubble's fake prosperity which was then forfeited when the bubble broke. This means that my gains and losses were both a bit illusory." Robert Benne, "Reflections on the Economic Downturn," *Journal of Lutheran Ethics* 9:3 (March 2009): http://search.elca.org/Pages/Results.aspx?k=economic downturn&filter_by=1

10. Simon Chow, "Justification by Faith Reconsidered," *Theology and Life* 27 (2004): 131.

11. Herbert Brokering, "O Butterfly," *Trinity Seminary Review* 30:1 (Winter/Spring 2009): 46.

from his or her works, which makes it clear that the individual is more than the sum of these works."[12] Faith forms the soul. This is crucial: faith forms the soul.

Excurses: A Phenomenology of Faith

Let's pause for a moment to look phenomenologically at how human consciousness is structured and just how faith as trust affects our self-understanding. If you are allergic to philosophy, then I recommend you jump to the next chapter and avoid wheezing and sneezing at what I'm about to say.

Without pausing long enough to provide detail, let me confess my philosophical location: I work out of a hermeneutical matrix. Hermeneutics is the philosophy of interpretation. The field is named after Hermes, the Greek messenger deity. At every level, our human consciousness involves interpretation—one thing interpreting another in the service of constructing a worldview that bears meaning. Something within us wants to live in a world of meaning, and hermeneutical philosophers try to track this impulse. In the paragraphs that follow, I'd like to connect three dimensions of faith—belief, trust, and indwelling—with the dynamics of human consciousness.

In the tradition of Martin Heidegger, Hans Georg-Gadamer, and Paul Ricoeur, I affirm that human consciousness is rooted inextricably in our sensory interaction with our physical world. At the level of primary or first interaction with the world, babies grow into understanding (*Verstehen*). As we grow up, we never leave this realm of interactive understanding; we only expand it through accumulated experience. Here is what's important at this primary level: we

---

12. Eberhard Jüngel, "Justification: Dogmatics," in *RPP*, 7:126.

understand our relationship to the things of this world at the preconscious level of interaction with our immediate environment. As we mature into toddlers, consciousness begins to focus. Our maturing consciousness draws out of the panoply of sensory reports about the external world a selection of these reports that, in turn, orients our consciousness. We may focus on what we see while we allow other sensory reports to slip out of focus into subconsciousness. For example, we hardly notice the sound of the wind perceived by our ears; we ignore the smell of the flowers perceived by our nose; we talk over the aftertaste of our lunch perceived by our taste buds; or we shove out of our awareness the hardness of the floor perceived tactually by our feet. By filtering such co-present perceptions out of our awareness, we can focus our attention on a single object.

We react to our environment with all of our senses, even if our consciousness focuses solely on what we are looking at or thinking about. At the level of consciousness, we select, categorize, and evaluate what we perceive. In effect, our consciousness interprets (*Auslegung*) what we already understand at the preconscious level and, through this interpretative process, we develop our subjectivity. We become a subject, a centered self, so to speak, standing over against the realm of objects that surround us. It is "I" who is looking at whatever the object is. It is "I" who hears, smells, tastes, feels, and such. This "I" or centered self is the product of our own interpretation process. We have no conscious experience that is not already interpreted experience. What counts as human experience is always already at the level of interpretation.

At this second level (the level of interpretation), we human beings take advantage of language. Language comes to one's consciousness preformed. We inherit our particular language, our mother tongue (*Muttersprache*), from the environment within which we grow up. This language is already filled with historically bequeathed meaning even before we learn to speak it (*lange* is our inherited language system, whereas *parole* is our particular speech within this language). This inherited vehicle for historical meaning influences, if not determines, our interpretation of our more primary sensory understanding. Meaning is a synthesis of sensory perception with inherited historical connotation coming to us within the language we are beginning to speak.

The language that becomes internal to our subjectivity is a set of symbols that we share with the subjectivities and cultural history of our family, tribe, nation, and ethnic group. We understand ourselves intersubjectively. Intersubjective understanding with multivalent symbols and a shared history makes meaning possible because one can see oneself embedded within a story—within a history—that is self-involving. There is no meaning that is not subjective and self-involving.

Please get this picture: each of us is embedded inextricably in an interactive relationship with the physical environment. From the many sensory signals we receive from this interaction, we interpret some by organizing them into a meaningful pattern, and that pattern is largely determined by the symbolic language within which we express ourselves. Even though each of us becomes an individual self, our self-understanding is the result of an intersubjective relationship to our linguistic community and its history, replete with meaning embedded in this history. Our self-understanding as a product of imbibing the language of our particular historical community is called effective-history (*Wirkungsgeschichte*).

To sum up our progress so far, we have risen from our individual understanding in-the-world to a symbolic interpretation that enables us to distinguish the self from-the-world while belonging to this world. Symbolic self-understanding at the level of intersubjective interpretation has made this possible. However, we don't remain at this phase. A third phase in consciousness follows: knowledge (*Erklärung, Erkenntnis*). Knowledge is attained by abstracting ideas and concepts and interrelating them through rational thought. To gain knowledge requires something beyond primal sensory understanding and beyond interpretive self-understanding. It requires abstraction, that is, the isolation of objective ideas and the measurement of them according to external reality or against each other. To measure ideas against external reality is called *reference*, and to measure them against each other within a conceptual scheme is called *coherence*. If an idea passes either the reference or the coherence test, we think we have gained some knowledge.

Please flag here a very important feature of knowledge. Knowledge is objective. Almost by definition, what counts as knowledge is objective knowing divorced from subjective involvement. If the objectivist gaze is divorced from subjective participation, then it cannot have meaning for the subject. If we want meaning in life, we do not find it in objectivist knowing.

Let's follow this trail again. How do we move from linguistic self-world meaning to abstraction? The language of our mother tongue is multivalent. Each word or phrase can have multiple meanings. Therefore, meaning is not fixed. It is fluid. It is equivocal. This permits the development of worldviews (virtual worlds?) that are built entirely out of language; in addition, it permits rhetoric, poetry, history, and jokes. The multivalency of our inherited language (what linguistic philosophers call *ordinary language*) permits symbolic power, symbolic meaning. Our religious language is ordinary language with considerable multivalency and strong symbolic power. It is prerational—that is to say, not yet rational.

How do we move from the prerational to the rational? Via abstraction. Abstract knowing requires that we pause to select certain words or concepts and assign them a single meaning. Of the many meanings a single word might emit, rational knowledge requires univocity, that is, singularity and precision in reference. Ordinary language is multivalent or equivocal, while rational thought is monovalent or univocal. We move from the connotative to the denotative. This signals to us that rational knowledge is an abstraction from linguistic interpretation that, in turn, is an abstraction from sensory understanding of the physical world. Rational thought is abstract thought two steps removed from our primary sense experience.

To say it another way: the prerational is not irrational. The prerational is a form of linguistically influenced understanding that is already interpretive, symbolic, connotative, self-involving, and meaningful. The rational selects from the pre-rational interpretation certain ideas on which to focus, defines them univocally, and then tests them for their truth value. Both multivalent symbolic interpretation and abstract rational ideation belong within the larger phenomenon of human consciousness.

This description of levels within human consciousness has implications for what we mean by faith and what we mean by theology. Theology is reflection on faith. Faith comes first, at the level of interpretation of sensory input and with the help of inherited linguistic symbols. Faith is existential or personal trust aimed at God, but we understand our own trusting at the symbolic and multivalent level of consciousness. Theology, on the other hand, consists of rational or objective reflection that is abstracted from our concrete daily life in faith. We must avoid confusing which is the dog and which is the tail. Our daily life in faith is the dog, which occasionally wags a theological tail. We trust God with our entire being. When we think abstractly about trusting God, it's called *theology*.

Whew. If you've read this far without wheezing or sneezing, congratulations! But let me warn you, there's more. (You might wish to reconsider jumping to the next chapter.) If you're willing to follow me further into the philosophical thicket, hang on.

With this three-step hermeneutical scheme in hand, let's remind ourselves of the grammar of the language that we Westerners have inherited. Each Western mother tongue has inherited from our Greek- and Latin-speaking ancestors a specific grammar that structures our subjectivity and, inescapably, our sense of self. Whether one grows up speaking English or German or a Romance derivative such as French, Italian, or Spanish, the structure of one's subjectivity and its relation to the world shares much in common. As our sensory interaction with the material world rises up toward consciousness through the process of symbolic interpretation in language, three options open up for our internal consciousness. These options are the product of first, second, and third person grammatical constructions. In the first person, we say, "I am" or, in the plural, "we are." In the second person, we say, "I-you (thou)" or "we-you" or "you are." In the third person, we say "I-it" or "we-they" or "he, she, or it is."

Now, let me ask the question again: How should we handle faith? We have three options: faith as belief, faith as trust, and faith as the indwelling presence of Christ. Where in consciousness does each of these dimensions of faith contribute to soul formation?

Let's take them in reverse order. Faith as belief clearly belongs at the level of third person grammar and objective knowledge. Belief in what creeds say or in doctrinal formulations belongs in the category of rational judgments. This is the realm of abstract, monovalent, denotative, and objective ideas as well as truth-testing. Faith as belief takes the form of a third person assertion; we say such and such is true about objective reality. "God exists" or "God is gracious" are examples of third person constructions. The Apostles' Creed and the Augsburg Confession are third person constructions. They state objective facts that "we believe" to be true. Concepts of the divine—whether monotheism, pantheism, panentheism, polytheism, henotheism, or atheism—are just that: concepts that may or may not be true. Their truth depends on whether they refer to a reality that corresponds accurately to the concept or if they belong to a system of rational ideas that renders them coherent. Truth is determined by either *reference* or *coherence*—or both. Faith as belief expresses faith in the third person at the level of abstract ideas.

In contrast, faith as trust operates in the second person at the symbolic level of consciousness. We address God directly: "I'm speaking to you, God." This second person discourse is identified by Buber as befitting the "I-Thou" relationship that we share with God, as well as with other persons whom we treat with dignity. It is self-involving discourse. When we pray, we address God directly, in the second person: "Dear God . . ." or "Our Father, who are in heaven . . ." Our language is connotative. When we ask God to "give us our daily bread," we do not literally mean a loaf of Wonder Bread. The word "bread" connotes all that is needed for our welfare.

Our consciousness is aroused by second person symbolic meaning during liturgical worship, hymn singing, and in the reception of the sacraments. When we are baptized, the "water and the Word" are addressed directly to us—personally to us—even by name. When we receive the bread and wine during the "Sacrament of the Altar" (Luther's term), we commune with the body and blood of Jesus Christ himself. This I-Thou or We-Thou interaction stirs the consciousness at the prerational or symbolic level of second person discourse. It bears meaning, multilevel meaning.

When we pray, we are speaking in one or another language, which indicates that we are experiencing meaning at the level of language, at the level of mutlivalent symbol. Faith as trust takes the form of testimony to God's faithfulness in petitionary prayer, which is followed by living our days and nights in confidence that the gracious God who hears our prayers is present in providential care, in our daily bread. "Thank you God, for giving me this day."

When we turn to faith as the indwelling of Christ, we turn to first person grammar and to introspection, meditation, reflection, awareness enhancement, and self-inquiry. In earlier chapters, I suggested that if we turn our attention inward in search of the soul or the self, what we see is an empty vortex around which our sensory interaction with the world swirls. This swirl also includes our moral universe. At the center is emptiness. We would like to see a rock solid self or an immortal soul, but that's not what we see. We see a center, yes, but not a substance. The inextricable relation our empty center has with our environment is something we understand intuitively, even if we cannot find a discreet "I" or "ego" there to do the seeing.

"I am" is the way we begin many sentences. "I am slung here in existence between birth and death." The "I" is temporary, ephemeral, and dependent on the swirl that surrounds us. The interaction between the swirl (including our moral universe) and the vacuous center is only temporary; it is slated for dissolution.

Unless, of course, the eternal comes to dwell within us. Faith as the indwelling of Christ is that dimension of faith wherein the Holy Spirit places the resurrected one—the Easter Christ complete with our future in God's promised new creation—in the empty vortex where the soul or self should lie. The indwelling Christ fills the empty vortex with an eternal presence—with a promise that we, along with our redeemed swirl, will rise into the new creation.

First person discourse may not even be discourse at all. It could take the form of prelinguistic or extralinguistic meditation. St. Paul alerts us to the speaking of the Holy Spirit from within us at levels too deep for us to control, or even understand for that matter. St. Augustine reminds us that God is closer to us than we are to ourselves. It can be an exhilarating moment when we relax our focused concentration, when we do an end run around subject-object third person discourse and even abandon prayerful second person discourse by simply allowing our consciousness to sink into an appreciation of the presence of the divine within. This is mindfulness or awareness enhancement that imbues every dimension of our consciousness with an appreciation for the presence of divine grace in all things. It evokes within us an uncanny sense of the beauty of creation, the precious value of each moment of life, and the realization of our intimate connectedness with all of reality.

When it comes to justifying faith in the face of attacks by materialists and atheists, we need to note this important distinction: the language of attack is almost always in the third person, and it is almost always an alleged inference from objective argumentation. Belligerent atheists accuse religious persons of being irrational, of finding meaning in an objectively meaningless material universe. What they actually intend without knowing it is that religious language is symbolic, multivalent, connotative, and self-involving. What frustrates an atheist—who wants third person univocity—is that a religious or spiritual person can swim joyfully in this ocean of ambiguity, multivalency, and richness of symbolic meaning.

From the atheist point of view, atheism is superior to religious faith because atheism can face up to reality—that is, reality described in third person objectivist terms. But third person objectivist terms are fundamentally meaningless. While they may be contextually meaningful, they are existentially meaningless because they are impersonal. To be personal, they would have to appear in first or second person discourse. Therefore, the only philosophy third person discourse alone can support is nihilism, the belief that meaning cannot be discerned within our objective gaze. What goes unnoticed is that nihilism is a necessary product of third person discourse, which by its structure eliminates the self-involving dimension of the human subject. In sum, eliminative materialism or atheism speaks in third person rational discourse that excludes meaning in an attempt to criticize religious discourse at the first person or second person level where meaning resides.

To say it another way: third person objective discourse is, by its nature, meaningless. It's not meaningless in the sense that it fails to make sense. It makes good, rational sense. But as third person discourse, it deprives the subject of involvement in the object. It deprives the subject of existential meaning, of personal meaning, of historicized contextual meaning, of multivalent symbolic meaning. Third person discourse denies self-involvement, and without self-involvement, existential meaning is impossible. This is neither good nor bad. It's simply the nature of discourse within the objectivist gaze.

If I may recap (in the third person): I recommend we use the term *soul* to refer to our inmost essence as an individual self and use the term *spirit,* which overlaps with *soul,* to refer to our capacity to relate with one another and with God. Even though the soul is our essence (*esse*), it is not a substance (*substantia*). Rather, it is a linguistic construction.

Our God is the God of the eternal Word. God creates all things with the Word, and God can declare your and my eternal relationship by the Word. (The word *Word* is multivalent.)

While the term *soul* connotes who each of us is as an individual, the word *spirit* connotes that dimension of our personal reality that unites us with others. Our soul is formed by the spirit—the Holy Spirit—who places us in an eternal relationship with the Easter Christ. To speak of soul as our inmost essence suggests that, as embodied creatures, we have a center of identity, a centered self. However, our centeredness is actually dependent on our relationships, and our eternal centeredness is dependent on our eternal relationship to God.

Conclusion

As I said above, belief is an activity of the human mind at the level of third person discourse about abstract ideas. Trust involves more. Trust is an activity of the entire self: mind, heart, feelings, body, and activity. Trust is existential. Trust enlists the whole of a person's being when that person is living the life of hope. Trust engages God in an I-Thou relationship. Trusts forms the soul. Let me repeat: it is not our acts on behalf of justice that form the soul; it is faith as trust that gives form to the soul.

More than an intellectual belief, justifying faith centers our energy. It unifies, integrates, and radiates. Justifying faith, says William James, "is something not intellectual but immediate and intuitive, the assurance, namely, that I, this individual I, just as I stand, without one plea . . . am saved now and forever."[13] Faith operates at all three stages of consciousness: understanding, interpretation, and knowledge. It also operates in all three grammatical constructions: first person, second person, and third person.

If I may add one more point. It is not faith as belief or trust that justifies us. It is God's faith dwelling in us—not our faith in God—that justifies us. Faith is a human work or a human virtue. It is admirable, to be sure, it does not in itself have the power to save. Calvin and Barth press this often misunderstood point: "Faith as such cannot contribute anything to our justification: *nihil afferens nostrum ad conciliandum Dei gratiam*."[14] It is God who justifies us. Faith marks the spot where this takes place.[15]

13. James, *VRE*, 246.
14. Calvin, *Inst.* 3.13.5; Barth, *CD*, IV/1, 617.
15. "Faith is just this and nothing but this: the confidence of sinful man in the demonstration of the undeserved faithfulness of God as given in Jesus Christ, a demonstration in which he finds that his sins are forgiven," exclaims Karl Barth (*CD* IV/1, 626). On the one hand, we need to believe that the gospel message is true. On the other hand, we need to trust that this is true, and this trust breeds confidence in daily life.

What, then, does faith do for us? It expresses our humility before God. "Faith . . . is wholly and utterly humility," says Barth.[16] In faith, we say thank you to God for the gracious gift of justification and, with it, salvation. Our humble trust in God readies us for an interactive relationship with God that will last for eternity. To be sure, the soul-forming effect of faith includes belief and trust, but the decisive dimension of faith is the indwelling presence of Christ. To this we turn in the next chapter.

16. Barth, *CD* IV/1, 618.

12

Faith as the Indwelling Presence of Christ

The Christian Faith says nothing more than that we have been called into the immediacy of the mystery of God . . . this mystery gives itself to us in unspeakable nearness . . . in the Son of Man, who is the presence of the eternal Word of God among us.

–Karl Rahner[1]

Soul, adorn yourself with gladness, leave the gloomy haunts of sadness, come into the daylight's splendor, there with joy your praises render. Bless the one whose grace unbounded this amazing banquet founded; Christ, though heav'nly, high, and holy, deigns to dwell with you most lowly.

–Johann Franck (1618–77)[2]

The spiritually healthy soul is a strong soul, a robust soul. Its strength

1. Karl Rahner, *TI* 5:21.
2. Johann Franck, "Soul, Adorn Yourself with Gladness," in *Lutheran Book of Worship* (Minneapolis: Fortress Press, 1978) 224.

comes from God, from the presence of God within. The emptiness in the self's vortex becomes filled with the person of Jesus Christ, who is placed there by the Holy Spirit. Christ in both natures—the suffering humanity and the resurrected divinity—are present. Like a dynamo spreading power to light a city, this presence provides power that emanates from eternal life.

The Spiritual Fragilometer

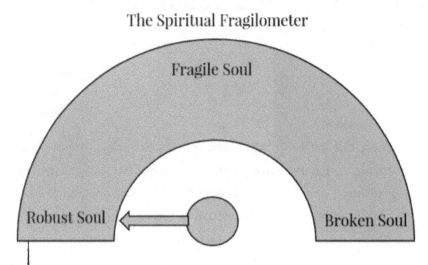

However, we must remember that it is not our faith, as such, that has justifying power. Faith empowers daily life, to be sure; but in itself, human faith does not save. "Because faith is obedient-humility, abnegation, it will and must exclude any co-operation of human action in the matter of man's justification," stresses Karl Barth.[3] When we speak of justifying faith, the faith that justifies is God's faith in us, not our faith in God. God's faith in us is placed in us by the Holy Spirit—the very presence of Jesus Christ in the human soul.

---

3. Barth, *CD* IV/1, 627.

5. Faith Experiences the Risen Jesus Christ in One's Soul

Faith justifies the sinner because Jesus Christ becomes present in the soul of the believer. It is the work of the Holy Spirit that unites three temporal moments: the Easter resurrection of yesterday, the resurrection God promises us in the future, and the presence of Christ in our faith today. The vortex at the center of life's daily swirl is no longer empty; it is filled with the living Christ.

Faith is more than mere believing or trusting. Faith includes the mystical presence of the living Christ. Luther tries to express this somewhat awkward yet indispensable dimension of faith. "It [faith] takes hold of Christ in such a way that Christ is the object of faith, or rather not the object but, so to speak, the One who is present in the faith itself."[4] Calvin says flatly, "Christ is not outside us but dwells within us."[5] This indwelling presence of Christ in the person of faith is the work of the Holy Spirit, adds Calvin. "The Holy Spirit is the bond by which Christ effectually unites us to himself."[6]

Theologian Regin Prenter stresses that the correct interpretation of Luther's "realism of revelation" is to see that the Holy Spirit makes the resurrected Christ present in the person of faith. Christ is not merely an idea we think about, not merely a historical figure we remember. Rather, the living Christ is truly present. "The Holy Spirit is God himself present in us," writes Prenter, "but in such a way that his presence takes Jesus Christ out of the remoteness of history and heavenly exaltation and places him in the midst of our concrete life as a living and redeeming reality which constantly calls upon both the groaning of faith and the work of charity. The relation of Jesus Christ to the work of the Holy Spirit . . . is a personal relationship of faith."[7]

4. Luther, *Commentary on Galatians* (1535), in *LW*, 26:129.
5. Calvin, *Inst* 3.2, 1:570.
6. Ibid., 3.1, 1:538.
7. Regin Preneter, *Spiritus Creator: Luther's Concept of the Holy Spirit* (Philadelphia: Muhlenberg, 1953), 92.

The Holy Spirit prompts the new life of Christ from within the person of faith. Commenting on Luther, Reformation historian Scott Hendrix emphasizes this point: "The new birth and the new connectedness to Christ come only through the operation of the Holy Spirit. Luther's spirituality is indeed Christocentric, but it is not Christomonist; it neither ignores nor neglects the third person of the Trinity."[8]

One of the delights to come out of the New School of Luther Research at the University of Helsinki in Finland is its stress on the importance of Christ dwelling within the person of faith. "Faith means the presence of Christ and thus participation in the divine life," writes Tuomo Mannermaa. "Christ 'is in us' and 'remains in us.' The life that the Christian now lives is, in an ontologically real manner, Christ himself."[9] The heart invites the living Christ into the soul; curiously, we discover Christ has already been there.

In my observation, the real presence of the living Christ in the soul is one of the dimensions of faith most overlooked and ignored by our theologians and preachers. The forensic model of salvation that depicts the relationship between grace and faith attempt to explain our justified relationship to God without referencing this key dimension. In my judgment, this is a mistake. If the Holy Spirit places the living Christ deep within us, then it seems that we should be able to draw from this wellspring of divine presence on a daily

8. Scott Hendrix, "Martin Luther's Reformation of Spirituality," in *Harvesting Martin Luther's Reflections on Theology, Ethics, and the Church,* ed. Timothy J. Wengert (Grand Rapids, MI: Eerdmans, 2004), 252.

9. Tuomo Mannermaa, *Christ Present in Faith: Luther's View of Justification* (Minneapolis: Fortress Press, 2005), 39. At least one critic says that "the key problem in the Finnish interpretation . . . is that of being and act, or essence and attributes." Duncan Reid, "Luther's *Finnlandisierung*: A Recent Debate about Salvation in Reformation Thought," in *Sin and Salvation,* ed. Duncan Reid and Mark Worthing (Adelaide, AU: ATF Press, 2003), 200. For the Finnish position on real presence to succeed, says Reid, the essence of God must be isomorphic with the Trinity because Christ is present to the person of faith by the Holy Spirit. There must be an "identity of God's inner Trinitarian being with God's Trinitarian actions *ad extra*" (Luther's *Finnlandisierung*, 201).

basis. Awareness of Christ's abiding presence could become the most comforting and inspiring gift of God's grace.

Tillich tries to help us out by coining the phrase, "justification by grace through faith." He objects to the Pauline and Lutheran phrase, justification-by-faith, because "it gives the impression that faith is an act of man by which he merits justification."[10] Tillich hoped his reformulation might clarify matters. However, Tillich's criticism and re-rendering are misleading. Tillich seems to assume that grace is something God does and faith is something we do. This misses the point I am making here: Jesus Christ is actually present to us in faith. To say "justification-by-faith" is to affirm God's gracious presence as a component to faith. Faith is already a gift of divine grace.

In light of the Socrates Principle elaborated in Chapter Three, the theology of Christ's real presence can be stated in the following way. Jesus died as a just person. He is in himself just, so he does not need any kind of Glaucon-like self-justification. When the Holy Spirit places the just Jesus within our faith, Jesus' justice becomes our justice. He has justified us, so to speak. If in our faith we are justified by Christ, we have no need to self-justify and, hence, no need to scapegoat others. Our justification is a divine gift, not the product of our self-deception.

Furthermore, the Christ present in our faith is the crucified and resurrected one. The eternity of the resurrected one is present within us, an eternity that transcends even our most sublime vision of the moral universe.

Who's Faith Saves? Before departing from this topic, I'd like to re-ask the question: Who's faith are we talking about? Is it God's faith in us? Is it your or my individual faith? Is it the faith inhering in the life of the Christian Church?

10. Tillich, *SystT*, 2:179.

The Formula of Concord recognizes that faith is a gift. "Faith itself is a gift of God."[11] All well and good. Yet faith can seem like a condition, like something we need to accomplish before we merit justification. "There is no true, saving faith in those who have no contrition and sorrow and who have the evil intention to remain and continue in sins. Instead, genuine contrition comes first, and true faith is found in and with true repentance."[12] Here's the rundown: 1) contrition, 2) repentance, 3) faith, and 4) justification. Whew! That's a lot of work. Is it meritorious work on our part?

Note how the Formula of Concord presumes that lack of contrition implies that we "have the evil intention to remain and continue in sins." This presumes naively that we have conscious control. This presumes that we, who sin, maintain a Pelagian sort of self-honesty and equanimity when making either right choices or wrong choices. But how might this apply if we lie to ourselves? How might this apply if we self-justify and scapegoat while deceiving ourselves? This habit of self-justification and self-deceit is common to both the unbaptized and the baptized, to both those with faith in Christ and those who lack it. Of all denominational groups, Lutherans should be aware of this subtle yet inescapable dimension of human existence. Why? Because Lutherans describe the person of faith—the saint—as one who is both saved and sinner at the same time, *simul justus et peccator*. What this implies is that even for the Christian with faith in Christ, sinning appears on the daily menu of activities.

Self-justification is the opposite of contrition. Scapegoating is an act committed by someone who has not repented. Self-justification and scapegoating are pursued only by people committed to the good, not by those with the "intention to remain and continue in sins." Therefore, the Formula of Concord is simply unhelpful for

11. Formula of Concord, Solid Declaration, art. 3, *BC*, 564.
12. Ibid., 566.

illuminating the most prevalent problem within the Christian community, let alone the wider world. Contrition and repentance are good things, to be sure. However, by making them prerequisite to faith and justification, the gospel of grace can no longer penetrate our pharisaic facade or uncover our self-protective mask.

If faith is a gift God gives us only as a conditional response to our prior contrition and repentance, then we are in trouble. We are without hope. Perhaps, the sequence functions differently. Could we think of faith as something that God gives first? After receiving the gift of faith, we begin experiencing contrition and taking repentant action. Eventually, we undergo renewal and transformation as well. But initially, in the moment of faith, what we receive is the indwelling of Jesus Christ placed within each of our souls by the Holy Spirit.

By emphasizing the real presence of the living Christ in, with, and under our faith, I think that we can cut through this conundrum bequeathed us by the Formula of Concord. Did I say "our faith"? Did I mean to put that in the plural form—*our* faith? Let's look at this again.

If we affirm that Christ is present within faith, are we talking about each person's individual faith? If this is the case, then we might worry: What if my faith isn't strong enough? Will Christ then absent himself? What if my contrition falls short of complete self-honesty? Will Christ flee? Does the Holy Spirit make Christ present only to individuals who pass a proper contrition and repentance test? Just how much faith must I possess to guarantee the divine presence?

Let's return briefly to the New Testament bomb that exploded into the Protestant Reformation. Romans 1:17: "For in it the justification of God (*dikaiosune tou Theou*) is revealed through faith for faith (*ek pisteus eis pistin*); as it is written, 'The one who is just will live by faith (*ho de dikaios ek pisteus zesetai*).'" Is it clear whose faith St. Paul is talking about? Is it our faith in God? Or is it God's faith in us? God's justification is revealed through faith, but it could just as well be God's faith. Regardless, note that the justifying of God (*ho dikaiosune tou Theou*) is *revealed* through faith, for faith; it is not the faith that accomplishes the justification. Faith is the conduit, so to speak, by which God's justifying work is revealed. In other words, it is not faith that justifies; it is God who justifies.

What does this imply? It implies that our faith in God does not trigger God's presence. Nor does our faith accomplish the work of justification. God elects to be present in God's own faith, and wherever God is present, the divine work of justification is also present. Faith may look like it belongs to us, but in a mystical way, perhaps our faith in God is at the same time God's faith in us.

Imagine the following. As a young college graduate, you migrated to San Francisco from some other part of the world. Originally, you were attracted by guitar music, flowers in long hair, and the opportunity for meaningful friendship, experimentation, and creativity. Perhaps you had just discovered that you belong in the LGBTQ (lesbian, gay, bisexual, transgender, and queer [or questioning]) community, and you hoped to meld with those who would accept you and affirm you in your sexual identity. Now that decades have passed and your body has deteriorated from substance abuse, exposure to the elements (from sleeping under bridges), and lack of medical attention to your feet and your teeth, everything hurts. By day, you beg. By night, you struggle to find a warm, dry nest. Some of your homeless friends seem to have lost their mental faculties, while others have died from AIDS. Your own mind seems chaotic; you're unable to focus, unable to engage others in lengthy conversations. No longer do you have the inner strength to possess anything like faith, let alone courage or initiative.

About two o'clock on a cold rainy night, you find a pastor from the San Francisco Night Ministry program sitting next to you. He asks you questions. He arranges for a nurse to come to where you are and clean your infected feet, bandage them, and give you a clean pair of socks. He demands nothing of you. He offers to pray with you and for you. You, in turn, can hardly comprehend what is happening, let alone respond.

Is Christ present? If yes, then where? In whose faith? In your individual faith? In the faith of the pastor and the nurse? In the faith of the church who supports this night ministry? I suggest that it is God's faith working through the church and through those of us in the church that bears the presence of both the crucified and risen Christ.[13]

6. Faith Sins Boldly in Love

Faith prompts love, genuine and authentic love. William James empirically confirms this in his studies of religious experience. "There is veritably a single fundamental and identical spirit of piety and charity, common to those who have received grace: an inner state which before all things is one of love and humility, of infinite confidence in God, and of severity for one's self, accompanied with tenderness for others."[14] This is love as a disposition, as an orientation to life, as a feeling of "tenderness for others." Yet tenderness in action may become strategic, carefully planned, and directed toward specified ends. The souls of those saved by grace are sensitive toward victims of scapegoating, beginning with the revelatory scapegoat, Jesus Christ. They are able to discern the visible and invisible

---

13. "The Christian church is that community of persons who 'got the hint,' and they thus refuse to be content with human pain and suffering." James H. Cone, *A Black Theology of Liberation* (Philadelphia: J. B. Lippincott, 1970), 228.

14. James, *VRE*, 260.

scapegoats among us. The person of faith who sins boldly in love will find a special place in his or her heart for the victims of scapegoating.

Today's atheists do not see Christians in this way. They attack Christians and others with religious faith when it comes to the matter of love. Religious faith is said to reap dogmatism, rigidity, narrow-mindedness, belligerence, violence, and war—all characteristics of the fragile soul. Onfray lets the big cannons loose. In reference to Christianity, Judaism, and Islam, he writes: "The religion of the one God . . . seeks to promote self-hatred to the detriment of the body, to discredit the intelligence, to despise the flesh, and to prize everything that stands in the way of a gratified subjectivity. Launched against others, it foments contempt, wickedness, the forms of intolerance that produce racism, xenophobia, colonialism, wars, social injustice. A glance at history is enough to confirm the misery and the rivers of blood shed in the name of the one God."[15] In order to build a bridge across the rivers of shed religious blood, Onfray calls us into a battle between religion and anti-religion: "We must fight for a post-Christian secularism, that is to say atheistic, militant, and radically opposed to" the three monotheisms.[16] Atheists draw a line between good and evil; they place atheism on the good side and religion on the evil side of the line. Atheism can marshal its fragile souls for visible scapegoating just as well as religion can.

Let's pause a moment to think this through. Is Onfray accurate? Has the broken dam of religious bigotry flowed into rivers of blood? Unfortunately, yes. Some chapters of history tell precisely this tragic story. Believers in God need to listen to Onfray's criticism and welcome the judgment therein. Next, we need to ask: Is spilling the

---

15. Onfray, *Atheist Manifesto: The Case Against Christianity, Judaism, and Islam*, trans. Jeremy Leggatt (New York: Arcade, 2005), 67.
16. Ibid., 219.

blood of those who disagree with us the appropriate expression of our faith in Jesus Christ? No, of course not. Then what is?

Faith acts in love. The faith I am talking about here performs works of love. When the gracious love of God in Jesus Christ becomes present within us, that outward-moving love energizes and directs and empowers the person of faith and the community of faith.

"Because the Holy Spirit is given through faith, the heart is also moved to do good works," the Augsburg Confession tells us.[17] Thus, faith "is more of the heart than of the brain,"[18] as Calvin reminds us. From the heart of faith issues love. St. Paul writes, "The only thing that counts is faith working through love" (Gal. 5:6b). When asking whether love precedes faith or whether faith precedes love, Calvin trumpets: "It is faith alone that first engenders love in us."[19] Faith alone saves, but the faith that saves is never alone. Living faith is loving faith. In James 2:26b, we read that "faith without works is . . . dead." In short, faith can be understood only as a source for love and service.

Here is a subtle point that differentiates the Reformation take on justifying faith from the medieval theology that preceded it. St. Thomas Aquinas and other scholastic theologians describe faith being formed by love, which is undoubtedly a healthy description of the Christian life. Yet the medieval theologians assert that it is a faith formed by love (*fides caritate formata*) that justifies. In contrast, the Reformers distinguish between faith and love without separating the two. Faith justifies, and love follows from faith in our daily life. The Reformers' concept of faith includes the presence of God in Christ, which they curiously describe as God's faith-in-us. "The faithfulness of God Himself, the *pistis tou Theou*, which cannot be destroyed by

17. *BC*, 56.
18. Calvin, *Inst.* 3.2, 1:552.
19. Ibid., 3.2, 1:589.

any unfaithfulness of man (Rom 3:3), is the foundation of the *pistis* in which he himself lives and which he proclaims," announces Barth.[20] What I wish to stress is that God has faith in us and places that faith *in* us. Your or my faith is not merely your or my faith; it includes God's faith in the form of God's presence. Therefore, we can affirm that faith alone (*sola fide*) justifies. Beyond God's presence, nothing can be added to turn a non-justifying faith into a justifying one. As Christians, we want our lives to take the shape of "faith formed by love" (*fides caritate formata*), to be sure. The Protestants among us simply wish to point out that it is the *fides* (more precisely, God's presence in the *fides*) rather than the *formata* that justifies.[21]

The love that forms our lives is neighbor-love. Loving one's neighbor is inextricably connected to loving God. Matthew 22:37-39: "He [Jesus] said to him, 'You shall love the Lord your God with all your heart, and with all your soul, and with all your mind.' This is the greatest and first commandment. And a second is like it: 'You shall love your neighbor as yourself.'" Are these two commandments really two different commandments? Or, for all practical purposes, are they only one? Maximus the Confessor would say two. He writes, "Love is a holy state of the soul, disposing it to value knowledge of God above all created things."[22] He then adds, "He who loves God will certainly love his neighbor as well."[23] Karl Rahner, on the other hand, suggests that these two commandments function as one: "Love for neighbor is the concrete way in which

---

20. Barth, *CD* IV/1, 532.
21. "This faith justifies without love and before love." Luther, *The Freedom of a Christian* (1520), in *LW*, 31:137.
22. Maximus the Confessor, "First Century on Love," in *Phil*, 2:53.
23. Ibid., 2:55.

we love God."[24] The arithmetic does not matter. What matters is that loving God and loving neighbor come in a single package.

Neighbor-love (*Nächstenliebe*) is a key term in the Lutheran vocabulary for identifying the direction that faith's love follows. Whether the neighbor is a friend next door or someone unknown on another continent, faith looks for the neighbor's needs and responds in loving service. Martha Ellen Stortz captures the mood of the term: "To a community of pickpockets, all the world is a pocket. More soberly, to a community of Lutherans, all the world is filled with neighbors."[25]

What is so important here is the specific Lutheran emphasis on love for the sake of the other, not for the sake of one's own spiritual development or progress. What orients the love that follows faith is the needs and interests and welfare of the neighbor. Luther announces that we "should be guided in all . . . works by this thought and contemplate this one thing alone, that [we] may serve and benefit others in all that [we do], considering nothing except the need and advantage of [our] neighbor. . . . [we willingly serve] another without hope of reward."[26] We love not to become more loving; rather, we love so that the neighbor becomes loved. We love not to become sanctified; rather, we love so that the neighbor becomes loved.

Despite this Lutheran emphasis, Lutherans are by no means alone on this important point. Elizabeth Johnson, the award winning Roman Catholic theologian at Fordham University, measures our love for God with our love for our neighbor by a social justice yardstick. "In a time of growing solidarity on a global scale," she

24. Karl Rahner, *Foundations of Christian Faith,* trans. William V. Dych (New York: Crossroad, 1978), 447.
25. Martha Ellen Stortz, "Practicing Christians," in *The Promise of Lutheran Ethics,* ed. Karen L. Bloomquist and John R. Stumme (Minneapolis: Fortress Press, 1998), 60.
26. Luther, *The Freedom of a Christian,* in *LW,* 31:365.

writes, "work for justice is stimulated by the Spirit of Jesus, for whom the neighbor's good has an incomprehensible value, commensurate with the love of God poured out upon them."[27] The pursuit of global justice is the pursuit of the welfare of many persons whom we may never personally get to know. Our pursuit is for their welfare, not our own. This constitutes the godly life.

Like a meadow flower blossoming with the rising sun, the godly life blossoms with the welling power of love. It is not too much To say that we can fall in love with God is not an overstatement; like erotic passion, our passion for God can penetrate and imbue and exude every dimension of our waking life. Jesuit giant Bernard Lonergan fell in love with God, and he describes how intellectual love overflows into compassionate love. "As the question of God is implicit in all our questioning, so being in love with God is the basic fulfillment of our conscious intentionality. That fulfillment brings a deep-set joy that can remain despite humiliation, failure, privation, pain, betrayal, desertion. That fulfillment brings a radical peace, the peace that the world cannot give. That fulfillment bears fruit in a love of one's neighbor that strives mightily to bring about the kingdom of God on this earth."[28] Loving the God who loves us leads seamlessly and naturally to mission.

Christians embrace a mission to make the world a better place through sharing faith and works of neighbor love. Our "mission is the true influencing power aiming at changing the world,"[29] according to Steve Sang-Cheol Moon. This mission anticipates a transformed future, a redeemed creation. "The promise and vision of God's future set the course for faith active in love striving in hope and

27. Elizabeth A. Johnson, *Quest for the Living God: Mapping Frontiers in the Theology of God* (New York: Continuum, 2007), 46.
28. Bernard J. F. Lonergan, SJ, *Method in Theology* (New York: Herder and Herder, 1972), 105.
29. Steve Sang-Cheol Moon, "The Spiritual Influence of Korea: The Movement and Task of Korean Mission," *KIATS Theological Journal* 2:1 (Spring 2006): 176.

seeking justice," writes theologian and ethicist James Childs.[30] We seek to make this world a better place by first sharing the gospel of God's grace and by attempting to replace injustice with justice.

Even if motivated by love and charitable expressions, the person of faith needs courage along with insight to work for social change. Much of the injustice that victimizes large swaths of human population is systemic, institutional, habitual, and reinforced by dominant economic and political interests. This certainly is the case when it comes to our inability as a global culture to take the steps necessary to slow climate change and cultivate planetary health. "Commitment to ecological wholeness in partnership with a more just social order is the vocation which best corresponds to God's own loving intent for our corner of creation," argues Johnson, a Roman Catholic.[31] Similarly, Moe-Lobeda (a Lutheran) affirms faith active in love, but then she calls for more. "My point is this: Where suffering is caused at least in part by societal or systemic factors, rather than singularly individual factors, charitable service aimed at meeting the needs of individuals and groups without *also* challenging those systemic factors may build social consent that perpetuates the suffering's powerful systemic roots."[32]

For Luther's disciples, the point is clear: faith is not idle. "For the believer has the Holy Spirit; and where He is He does not permit a man to be idle, but drives him to all the exercises of devotion, to the love of God, to patience in affliction, to prayer, to thanksgiving, and to the practice of love toward all men."[33] This love for all persons includes enemies as well as friends. "He does not distinguish between

30. James M. Childs, "Ethics and the Promise of God," in *Promise of Lutheran Ethics,* 106.
31. Elizabeth A. Johnson, *Ask the Beasts: Darwin and the God of Love* (London: Bloomsbury, 2014), 285.
32. Moe-Lobeda, *Resisting Structural Evil: Love as Ecological-Economic Vocation* (Minneapolis: Fortress Press, 2013), 90, italics in original.
33. Luther, *Commentary on Galatians* (1535), in *LW,* 26:255.

friends and enemies or anticipate their thankfulness or unthankfulness, but he most freely and most willingly spends himself and all that he has, whether he wastes all on the thankless or whether he gains a reward."[34]

Luther goes on to liken the person of faith to a tree that grows and bears loving fruit. "Thus he is a doer of the Law who receives the Holy Spirit through faith in Christ and then begins to love God and to do good to his neighbor. Hence 'to do' includes faith at the same time. Faith takes the doer himself and makes him into a tree, and his deeds become fruit."[35] To state this another way: the person justified by faith works for justice in an unjust world. As Korean-American theologian Paul Chung says of the German Reformer, "Luther's theological thinking of God regarding justification is enmeshed with his social and economic thinking of God's justice."[36] This pursuit of economic justice is accompanied by a presupposition of human equality—a point made by Monica Melanchthon. "The justice of God and the equality of human persons realized by the doctrine of grace is a sign of hope."[37] Justice, equality, and the pursuit of human dignity constitute the social direction that a faith active in love follows.

In the previous paragraphs, I write in the third person at a high level of abstraction. It is easy to speak of love in general or justice as a universal ideal. However, when we turn to concrete situations, things get messy. In our daily lives, issues are ambiguous. Clear lines between what is loving and what is not loving are difficult to draw. The pursuit of distributive justice for one faction might result in injustice for another. The pursuit of retributive justice might result

---

34. Luther, *The Freedom of a Christian*, in *LW*, 31:367.
35. Luther, *Commentary on Galatians* (1535), in *LW*, 26:255.
36. Paul S. Chung, *Christian Mission and a Diakonia of Reconciliation: A Global Reframing of Justification and Justice* (Minneapolis: Lutheran University Press, 2008), 43.
37. Monica Melanchthon, "The Grace of God and the Equality of Human Persons," in *GG*, 43.

in someone's death. In concrete daily experience, honesty tells us that clear lines between good and evil are seldom possible. Blurry lines, ambiguity concerning the "good," and situations in which we must choose between the lesser of two evils are far more routine. Yet the life of love presses forward, inspired by faith. The life of love requires that we sin boldly.

If atheist critics of the Christian religion perceive in us an intolerance that leads to violence, then this stimulus deserves an appropriate response. It is possible that this criticism is a result of eyes that have not seen love. However, if the criticism is accurate, confession, repentance, and renewal within the Christian communion are in order. We need to ask ourselves honestly: Have we been true to our divine calling? Has our faith been truly active in love? Members of the church of Jesus Christ are called to love, not decimate, our enemies.

7. Faith Seeks Understanding

Faith seeks understanding (*fides quaerens intellectum*) contend St. Augustine of Hippo and St. Anselm of Canterbury, two of our precedent-setting ancient theologians. This seeking appears twice—first in the justification of faith and second in the expansion of the faith once established. Earlier, when I described faith as belief, I pointed to the first stage, the knowledge of the story of Jesus conveyed by God's Word to which faith responds. Now we will look at the second stage in which established faith builds upon itself as it tries to understand more and more of reality. "Faith is not settled belief but living process," wisely comments Catherine Keller.[38]

---

38. Catherine Keller, *On the Mystery: Discerning God in Process* (Minneapolis: Fortress Press, 2008), xii.

Faith leads to reflection on faith; and reflection on faith leads to theology. The theologian not only digs deeply to search out foundational understandings but also pursues knowledge of the created world in ever-expanding circles of understanding. The theologian borrows wisdom to better understand human nature because the ecumenic (not ecumenical) task of Christian theology is to understand and explain all things in reality in light of their origin and destiny in the God of grace. Every person of faith cultivates a private little theologian within his or her mind.

Faith is never naked; it comes dressed in understanding. I would like to try on five types of understanding in which faith might dress itself.

The first is *symbolic self-God-world understanding.* This is existential or personal understanding at its near primordial level, the level at which our sensory perceptions are interpreted meaningfully by language just prior to becoming abstract. As persons of faith, we understand ourselves to be united to God by the indwelling of Christ, tied to the world around us by the mandate to love. This basic understanding rises up into articulation through symbolic speech in first and second person discourse and in the form of action. First and second person faith discourse combined with action includes the hymns we sing during worship, the prayers we offer to God, the gospel message we share with others, our acts of kindness or charity, and the organizations we choose to support for making our world a better place. Our self-world relationship is implicitly understood in light of our understanding of God as our creator and God's abiding presence. The theologian will ask us to pause and ask: Just how might we reflect further on this more basic self-God-world understanding?

Second in our lineup of theological apparel is *interpretation.* From bottom to top, theology is interpretation. We interpret the basic symbolic self-God-world understanding of the Bible in meaningful ways that are context-dependent. We contextualize ancient symbols in light of our contemporary situation or social location, which suggests that symbolic self-understanding can shift or change according to context. Take the cross for example. Marit Trelstad shocks us with dramatic differences. "When one views the imperialistic tendencies of a whole nation or overall environmental abuse of the earth, one may hold the cross to be an antidote to pride. When one views the personal effects of domestic violence and sexual abuse, one may say the punitive image of the cross furthers the abuse. . . . Simply put, the vantage point from which one sees the cross influences one's interpretation significantly."[39] Theological understanding requires self-understanding within one's respective context. This sorting out of the various meanings of multivalent symbols is the task of hermeneutical theology.

The third garment in which faith's understanding gets clothed is *technical mastery,* a form of understanding specific to our modern and emerging postmodern context. Darting fingers texting a friend on an iPad or iPhone demonstrate a mastery of the technology that we find ready-to-hand. This activity takes place at the level of second person discourse, an I-you relationship to the computer and through the computer to the world. We daily negotiate our urban existence with its global network of communication in a near subconscious awareness of how much we understand. This is a functional understanding, not an intellectual or conceptual one. It is a secular understanding, not an inherently religious one. It appears to be a value-neutral understanding that does not demand ultimate concern. Yet technical mastery adorns faith when we seek more elevated understanding. "Theology is expected to contribute constructively to many central issues of our time," observes Sweden's Archbishop

39. Trelstad, "Introduction: The Cross in Context," in *Cross Examinations: Readings on the Meaning of the Cross Today*, ed. Marit Trelstad (Minneapolis: Augsburg, 2006), 4.

Antje Jackelén. "Good solutions in many areas require cooperation between the best scientific, technological, and theological knowledge and skills."[40] As stewards acting out of faith, we may wish to pause occasionally and query ourselves: Just how can our technical mastery become a servant to faith acting in love?

The fourth article of theological clothing is *scientific explanation*. Science shines light into the darkness of ignorance, illuminating the world of nature. Microscopes and telescopes reveal wonders and truths invisible to the naked eye. Science is like a pot of boiling water as research bubbles to the top, bursting with new knowledge. Theological understanding in the form of third person explanation expands as science expands. A faith that seeks understanding will be attracted to science like a child to a Christmas toy. As the size and complexity of our wondrous cosmos grows, so also does our appreciation of the gracious God who created and sustains it. Yet scientific knowledge is penultimate, not ultimate. We should ask questions of ultimate concern from time to time. Does the natural world explain itself? Does what we know about nature require a transcendental explanation—an explanation that requires positing God as its creator and sustainer? Should we revisit Dawkins's God-hypothesis as we consider whether it enhances our understanding of the universe to know that it is the creation of a loving God?

Fifth, and finally, *maturing wisdom* is a form of understanding that a person of faith should don. Even though scientific explanation might contribute to wisdom, wisdom is a much more comprehensive and synthetic form of understanding that incorporates explanation within a web of insights born of accumulated experience. The Akamba and other tribal peoples of East Africa wait until a person is thirty-five

40. Antje Jackelén, "The Dynamics of Secularization, Atheism and the So-Called Return of Religion and Its Significance for the Public Understanding of Science and Religion: Some European Perspectives," in *Churrasco: A Theological Feast in Honor of Vitor Westhelle,* ed. Mary Philip, John Arthur Nunes, and Charles M. Collier (Eugene, OR: Pickwick, 2013), 26–27.

years old or older before allowing such a person to become an elder (a member of the ruling council). Similarly, in Asian cultures, senior family and community members are respected, especially when seniors provide wise counsel and insightful judgment. Such wisdom comes naturally, yet it seems miraculous because so few among us exhibit it. Though such understanding is not automatic in regard to Christian faith, it is worthy to seek at any age.

One manifestation of maturing wisdom is moral discernment. The contemporary moral difficulties we face are ambiguous; they may not yield immediately to black-and-white analysis. Insight and discernment are called for. Expressed as wisdom, faith can lead to a more insightful understanding. "Faith may broaden our vision and enable us to see what might otherwise have remained hidden to sight," writes ethicist Gilbert Meilaender. "It may enrich and enlarge our understanding of the moral life, and this enlarged understanding is, in principle at least, able to be shared with anyone and everyone."[41] Faith actually expands and deepens our understanding, if we let it.

A person of faith might ask: How does the following apply to me?

The beginning of wisdom is this: Get wisdom,
and whatever else you get, get insight. (Prov. 4:7)

Faith *Forms* the Christian Self

Before turning to our next topic, let's pause to draw out the implications of justifying faith for the soul. Listen carefully to what Paul writes in Gal. 2:19-20: "For through the law I died to the law (*apethanon eis ton nomon*), so that I might live to God. I have been crucified with Christ; and it is no longer I who live, but it is Christ

41. Gilbert C. Meilaender, *Faith and Faithfulness: Basic Themes in Christian Ethics* (Notre Dame, IN: University of Notre Dame Press, 1991), 127.

who lives in me (*ho Christos ze en emoi*). And the life I now live in the flesh I live by faith in the Son of God (*zo te pistei tou giou tou Theou*), who loved me and gave himself for me." Luther explodes: "Here Paul is the most heretical of heretics; and his heresy is unheard-of, because he says that, having died to the Law, he lives to God. . . . This supports the declaration that the Law does not justify, but that only faith in Christ justifies."[42] Yet more is going on here than a change to the status of the law. Paul is proffering a new understanding of the human self, of the soul in relation to God. God lives within the soul. Therefore, the self becomes an expression of the living God because the Son of God is living within the self. One's self becomes a new self because of the divine life present in the soul.

Luther Seminary's Guillermo Hansen develops Luther's notion that, in faith, God creates the soul. God establishes each of us as a person, as a new kind of self. Not an ego self but a loving self. If a scientist outlined the long history of biological evolution in which our physical past gave rise to our present subjective consciousness, it would appear that nature began with bodies and then added subjectivities. Luther's picture reverses this direction: God tackles our subjectivity through faith, and then we become persons who, in the body, love our neighbors. We are reborn as selves that subvert the world of the ego—what Luther calls "the Law" and I call the fragile soul—in order for us to grasp our true vocation in the gospel. In short, the law addresses the ego while the gospel gives rise to a new self, a new and robust soul.[43]

42. Luther, *Commentary on Galatians* (1535), in *LW*, 26:156. "For Luther, faith newly constitutes the actual person," writes Wolfhart Pannenberg, *Systematic Theology*, trans. Geoffrey W. Bromiley, 3 vols. (Grand Rapids, MI: Eerdmans, 1991–98), 3:163.

43. Guillermo Hansen, "Luther's Radical Conception of Faith: God, Christ, and Personhood in a Post-Metaphysical Age," *Dialog* 52:4 (Fall 2013).

A "sense of enlargement of life" is characteristic of what James calls the "*Strength of the Soul*... Fears and anxieties go, and blissful equanimity takes their place."[44]

The robust soul of faith is not the excellent soul of Socrates, which becomes just by conformity to the moral universe—by works of the Law. Rather, the soul of faith becomes just by the justness of the crucified-yet-living Christ whom the Holy Spirit places within the soul. The crucified Christ is also the resurrected Christ. In faith, God is placing eternal life within the soul, and this eternal life springs forth in the robust life of the renewed self.

Conclusion

Why might we waste our valuable psychic energy pursuing the arduous task of self-justification if we learn in faith that we have already been justified by God? The presence of the just Christ in our faith is the presence of divine justification, even if we are unjust. In this case, graced justice trumps earned justice.

In this book, we have engaged in justifying faith by providing good reasons to place our trust in the God who raised Jesus Christ from the dead. Trusting this gracious God will make our lives better. I have shown how justifying faith justifies us so that we can safely leave behind our previous habits of self-justification. The fragile soul need not break. Trusting God is more effective than legalistic duct tape.

Faith forms the soul. Certainly Martin Luther thought so. He distinguished between inner and outer personhood. We have "a twofold nature," he writes, "a spiritual and a bodily one. According to the spiritual nature, which men refer to as the soul, he is called a

---

44. James, *VRE*, 273, italics in original.

spiritual, inner, or new man. According to the bodily nature, which men refer to as flesh, he is called a carnal, outward, or old man."[45] Note that Luther does not make a metaphysical commitment or a Cartesian claim that we are divided into two substances, one spiritual and the other bodily. Rather, he makes the phenomenological observation that we have inner and outer dimensions. The inner dimension becomes consolidated or shaped by our faith; our personhood becomes established by the effect faith has on us.

Not long ago, I was preparing to teach a seminar. Arriving students were milling around, placing their laptops and coffee cups on the table. Into my classroom walked my friend and colleague, Bob Russell. Bob is the founder and director of the Center for Theology and the Natural Sciences. "Can we talk for a few minutes before class?" he asked.

"Certainly," I answered. He waved me to follow him into his office, right across the hall from the classroom. We entered. He closed the door. I sat, waiting to find out what was on his mind.

"I've been reading the debate between Luther and Erasmus on free will," he announced. "What do you think about it?"

"Er, uh, Bob, what do *you* think about it?"

"It's really complex."

"Yes, it really is," I murmured, trying to buy time to gather my thoughts.

"I don't get it," he went on. "Can you explain it to me?"

"Well, to be honest, Bob, it's been a few years since I read it, so I don't remember the details."

"Would you read it again, please? Then we can talk more."

"Okay," I responded. I had bought some time. Whew.

---

45. Luther, *The Freedom of a Christian* (1520), in *LW*, 31:344.

The next morning I was finishing breakfast while sitting at my desk staring at a text on my computer screen. The phone rang. It was Bob. "I stayed up late last night rereading Luther," he said. "And I think I get it now."

"Oh, good. Just what did you get?" I asked.

He answered, "There is nothing I can do to lose it. There is nothing I need to do to gain it." The "it," of course, refers to God's saving grace.

"Would you please repeat that Bob?"

"Yes. *There is nothing I can do to lose it; there is nothing I need to do to gain it.* Ted, it's beautiful. I finally get it. I feel like I've been born again."[46]

When my friend Bob said, "I get it," he meant he had been grasped by the gospel: *there is nothing I can do to lose it; there is nothing I need to do to gain it.* In St. Paul's words: "God is the one who justifies" (*theos ho dikaiosune*, Rom. 8:33b).

---

46. One of the more insightful analyses of Luther's treatment of free will is offered by Paul Hinlicky in chapter 5 of *Luther and the Beloved Community: A Path for Christian Theology after Christendom* (Grand Rapids, MI: Eerdmans, 2010). Hinlicky's analysis of the human self as ecstatic is similar to mine; however, his emphasis on our external relationship to God nearly disregards what I deem important, namely, the gift of a new centering of the human self that results from the indwelling presence of Christ. Apart from this slight demure, I believe Hinlicky's treatment of the problem of the human free will turned-in-on-itself is as elegant as it is subtle. Faith reconstitutes the self by turning the self outside the self, by turning it toward God. "This is the ecstatic love of Spirit-wrought faith, not the self-seeking centeredness of free-will, which uses God and all creatures only for its own purposes" (ibid., 143). To be born with a will turned-in-on-itself and then to be visited by the Holy Spirit with a will turned-by-God-toward-others is, in effect, to be reborn into the divine life.

13

The Joint Declaration on the Doctrine of Justification

"Justified by faith" means . . . tried by the faithful God, sentenced conformably to the appearance, death, and rising of the obedient and loving Son, acquitted and set free in a manner identical with new creation and recognizable only with rejoicing and thanksgiving.

–Marcus Barth[1]

Luther's insight and conviction led to a theological eruption that resulted in a religious lava flow. For five centuries, it flowed down the medieval mountainside, increasing in speed until it crashed into the ecclesial hierarchy and hardened into the Protestant Reformation of the sixteenth century. The medieval edifice underwent a torrent of change as new rivulets divided the mountain; these divisions came to include the Lutherans, the Reformed, the Anglicans, and the radicals (or Anabaptists). Eventually these groups fractured further, giving rise to the Quakers, Methodists, deists, and revivalists. To change

1. Marcus Barth, *Justification*, trans. A. M. Woodruff III (Grand Rapids, MI: Eerdmans, 1971), 68.

metaphors, like Humpty Dumpty falling to pieces, Western Christendom lay strewn across the landscape in fragments and chards on the eve of the modern age. Could anyone put Humpty Dumpty back together again?

In the wake of the Second World War, Christians in both the East and the West began to pick up the pieces and contemplate reassembly. The Second Vatican Council during the 1960s provided a plan for reconstruction. In the latter decades of the twentieth century, earnest and indefatigable theologians dedicated themselves to putting Humpty together again. Reassembly became the task of ecumenical theology. According to Martin Marty, *ecumenical theology* "refers to the efforts that developed among Christian theologians in and after the twentieth century to meet specific needs of the divided churches that made up the whole Church."[2]

In my own vocabulary, I like to distinguish between ecumenic and ecumenical theology. *Ecumenic theology* places theological reflection into dialogue and even creative mutual interaction[3] with domains of human experience or knowing outside the Christian Church. The whole of reality becomes the theologian's *ecumené*, so to speak. This leads the theologian into multireligious dialogue, analysis of worldviews in various cultures, engagement with new religious movements (NRMs), exploration of the natural sciences, participation in fine arts, and prophetic interaction with philosophy as well as politics, economics, and social analysis.

That's *ecumenic theology*. If we add *al,* we get the term *ecumenical theology,* which refers to the responsibility of the Christian theologian to work in an edifying manner with all arms of the Body of Christ.

---

2. Martin E. Marty, "'Ecumenical Theology,'" chap. 67 in *The Routledge Companion to Modern Christian Thought,* ed. Chad Meister and James Beilby (London: Routledge, 2013): 772.

3. Creative mutual interaction or CMI is a term coined by Robert John Russell. See his *Cosmology from Alpha to Omega* (Minneapolis: Fortress Press, 2008), 22, 132.

What I will here call *JDDJ* (*The Joint Declaration on the Doctrine of Justification*) represents an exercise in ecumenical theology.

JDDJ: Calvary in My Soul

The scaffolding for ecumenical reassembly was erected on October 31, 1999, with the signing of *The Joint Declaration on the Doctrine of Justification*. Initially a product of Lutheran and Roman Catholic theologians in partnership, Reformed and Methodist scholars later contributed their glue in an effort to reconnect disparate views. Throughout the process, the watchword has been *dialogue.* According to the recent ecumenical document, *From Conflict to Communion*, "Ecumenical dialogue means being converted from patterns of thought that arise from and emphasize the differences between the confessions. Instead, in dialogue the partners look first for what they have in common and only then weigh the significance of their differences. These differences, however, are not overlooked or treated casually, for ecumenical dialogue is the common search for the truth of the Christian faith."[4]

In light of the new dialogue, just how should we understand the concept of justification? After restudying what the Bible says and rereviewing the disputes during the sixteenth century, these conscientious and magnanimous theologians tried to articulate their areas of agreement. Let's take a moment to consider a couple of the items they deem to be essential.

In §15 of the *JDDJ*, the authors affirm that "in faith we together hold the conviction that justification is the work of the triune God. The Father sent his Son into the world to save sinners. The

---

4. Lutheran-Roman Catholic Commission, *From Conflict to Communion: Report of the Lutheran-Roman Catholic Commission on Unity* (Leipzig: Evangelische Verlagsanstalt, 2013), §34, http://www.lutheranworld.org/sites/default/files/From Conflict to Communion.pdf.

foundation and presupposition of justification is the incarnation, death, and resurrection of Christ."[5] Objectively, atonement happened on Calvary in the Christ event. Subjectively, you and I appropriate Christ's atoning accomplishment in the faith that justifies, in justifying faith. This statement places justification within the life of the believer, and it places the life of the believer within the larger framework of God's saving work in Jesus Christ. This is how Calvary gets into one's soul.

Continuing in the same paragraph from the *JDDJ*: "Justification thus means that Christ himself is our righteousness, in which we share through the Holy Spirit in accord with the will of the Father. Together we confess: By grace alone, in faith in Christ's saving work and not because of any merit on our part, we are accepted by God and receive the Holy Spirit, who renews our hearts while equipping and calling us to good works." The phrase "by grace alone" connotes the Lutheran emphasis, though it must be said that Roman Catholics don't deny divine grace here, to be sure. Pre-Reformation Catholics viewed grace as working cooperatively with human will—strengthening the human will—to perform good works worthy of eternal merit and, thereby, worthy of meriting salvation. It is this cooperative or double activity that is at stake. The Lutherans want to emphasize that God's grace is the sole actor in justification; we sinners are passive. Justification is a gift that we receive. That's what is meant by *sola gratia,* by grace alone.[6]

---

5. This and other quotes come from Lutheran World Federation and the Catholic Church, *Joint Document on the Doctrine of Justification,* 1999, http://www.vatican.va/roman_curia/ pontifical_councils/chrstuni/documents/rc_pc_chrstuni_doc_31101999_cath-luth-joint-declaration_en.html.
6. Karl Rahner, a Roman Catholic theologian, interweaves the elements while specifying the decisive priority of divine grace within human action. "The future which man creates by his own action is never the only factor justifying man as he really is. For man is always already justified by God through the decree by which God in his holy, incomprehensible and unspeakable infinity pledges himself to man so that every action of man, right down to the last,

JDDJ is careful to make the Lutheran position crystal clear by reiterating it in §26. "According to Lutheran understanding, God justifies sinners in faith alone (*sola fide*). In faith they place their trust wholly in their Creator and Redeemer and thus live in communion with him. God himself effects faith as he brings forth such trust by his creative word." Note that trust is the dimension of faith referred to here, not creedal confession or dogmatic belief, although these are important, to be sure. What is significant is that our response to the news of our justification by grace is one of trusting God. "For Paul," writes a commission of biblical scholars interpreting *JDDJ*, "faith is basically a fundamental trust in God that shapes the totality of a person's life."[7]

Are we saved by our trusting? No. We are saved by the presence of Christ placed within us by the Holy Spirit—at least according to the Lutherans.

Justification and Transformation

JDDJ §26 continues.

> Because God's act is a new creation, it affects all dimensions of the person and leads to a life in hope and love. In the doctrine of justification by faith alone, a distinction but not a separation is made between justification itself and the renewal of one's way of life that necessarily follows from justification and without which faith does not exist. Thereby the basis is indicated from which the renewal of life proceeds, for it comes forth from the love of God imparted to the person in

---

consists in the acceptance of God's action on him." *TI* 5:191. While this is not Lutheran *sola gratia*, it's close to it.

7. *The Biblical Foundations of the Doctrine of Justification: An Ecumenical Follow-Up to the "Joint Declaration on the Doctrine of Justificatio,"* presented by a task force from the Lutheran World Federation, the Pontifical Council for Promoting Christian Unity, the World Communion of Reformed Churches, and the World Methodist Council (New York: Paulist Press, 2012), 82.

justification. Justification and renewal are joined in Christ, who is present in faith.

Note how a "distinction but not a separation" can be made between justification and sanctification. No separation! Score one for the Catholics. Still, sanctification is a "response" to justification. Score one for the Lutherans![8]

Section 27: "The Catholic understanding also sees faith as fundamental in justification. For without faith, no justification can take place. Persons are justified through baptism as hearers of the word and believers in it." Unless one hears God's Word and believes it, justification does not apply. Because believing faith is prerequisite to justification, the event of justification takes place in the life of the believer. Justification is not the product of an objective atonement that takes place on Calvary; rather, justification takes place in the subjectivity of each believer, one believer at a time. Now, let's discuss the implications.

This statement indirectly precludes a doctrine of universal salvation. In principle, one could construct a defense of universal salvation by placing unilateral saving grace in Christ's atoning act on Calvary. If in atonement God declares all creation to be forgiven and reconciled, and if grace alone applies at this point, then salvation is universal regardless of any response on the part of the creature. Some late nineteenth-century Protestants developed this position, declaring that God's saving grace is eternal and coextensive with the

---

8. Not all Lutherans were happy with a score that falls short of total victory. From September 25 through November 11, 1999, 250 out of 300 German professors of theology prepared and signed an open letter rejecting the *JDDJ*, especially the "Official Common Statement" (OCS). The Lutheran professors complained about the "lack of consensus in the JDDJ regarding the significance of word and faith for justification" and "the significance of good works for salvation." As I have tried to show here, the respective Lutheran and Roman Catholic positions were adumbrated distinctly simply because there is no consensus, even though there may be more overlap or even harmony on the role of divine grace than is commonly assumed. See the detailed analysis by Richard Schenk, OP, "The Unsettled German Discussions of Justification: Abiding Differences and Ecumenical Blessings," *Dialog* 44:2 (Summer 2005): 153–164.

entire creation. This option is being rejected in *JDDJ*. The Roman Catholic position within *JDDJ* holds that God's unilateral declaration of justification applies personally to an individual with faith, one believer at a time. The result is double destiny: some humans spend eternity in heaven and others spend it in . . . the other place.

JDDJ §27 continues with a turn toward renewal and transformation:

> This new personal relation to God is grounded totally on God's graciousness and remains constantly dependent on the salvific and creative working of this gracious God, who remains true to himself, so that one can rely upon him. Thus justifying grace never becomes a human possession to which one could appeal over against God. While Catholic teaching emphasizes the renewal of life by justifying grace, this renewal in faith, hope, and love is always dependent on God's unfathomable grace and contributes nothing to justification about which one could boast before God (Rom. 3:27).

It is important for Protestants to clearly understand this point: Roman Catholics are as committed to the necessity of grace as the Protestants are. Any differences between the two parties have to do with the way grace works, not the absence or presence of grace.

During the Counter-Reformation, the Roman Catholic Council of Trent (1545–63) explicitly rejected both the Pelagian doctrine of works righteousness and the Lutheran version of justification-by-faith alone (*sola fide*). The Council describes faith primarily as assent to revealed doctrine rather than trust. It also asserts that justification is grounded in Christology by affirming that human beings are grafted into Christ. Further, the grace of God in Christ is necessary for the entire process of justification, although the process does not exclude natural dispositions for grace or the collaboration of free will. The Council declares that the essence of justification is not constituted by the remission of sins alone; rather, justification also includes the "sanctification and renovation of the inner" person by supranatural charity—that is, by effective justification. The formal cause of justification is "the justice of God, not that by which He Himself is just, but that by which He makes us just," and the final cause or purpose of justification is "the glory of God and of Christ and life everlasting." Faith, says the Council, is the "beginning, foundation and root" of justification. The Council of Trent affirms that eternal life is a gift of grace, not merely a reward for merit.[9] In sum, according to the sixteenth-century Council, justification is a process that includes sanctification; at the conclusion of that process, the product is eternal life. For Tridentine Catholics, justification is the prize the believer receives at the end of the race; for Lutherans, justification is the prize given before the starting gun is fired.

To what extent do Roman Catholic theologians in the twenty-first century reiterate the Tridentine position? The Roman Catholic party continues to disagree with the Lutheran party on this matter, even after *JDDJ*. Curiously, the Lutherans disagree among themselves. Their party can be divided into two caucuses, the forensic and the indwelling To this difference we now turn.

Forensicist Lutherans vs. Indwelling Lutherans

If you listen carefully to the sounds in a meadow on a hot summer's evening, your ears will distinguish the chirrups of the crickets from those of the frogs. Listening to Lutherans is similar. Some chirrups come from *forensicists* and others from *indwellers*. Might one caucus or the other be better attuned to the Roman Catholic concern for effective justification—that is, post-sanctification? Let's listen.

---

9. Council of Trent, Fourth Session, April 8, 1546, Decree Concerning the Canonical Scriptures; and Sixth Session, January 13, 1547, chap. 7. See *From Conflict to Communion*, §82.

The forensicist caucus within the Lutheran camp, led initially by Philip Melanchthon, employs a forensic or legal model to explicate justification. The name comes from *forum*, referring to the marketplace or courtyard where justice was decided in ancient Rome. According to the forensicists, we sinners are pronounced just or righteous in the heavenly court (*in foro divino*) even if, on Earth, we remain sinners.

The forensic model is well described in a predecessor dialogue dating to the 1980s. "Lutherans describe justification as the imputation to sinners of a righteousness which is that of Christ himself (*iustitia aliena*), received in faith. Justification therefore is the forensic act whereby God declares the sinner just; it is an act performed outside of us (*extra nos*) by which faith is accounted as righteousness."[10] The commitment to underscore how unilateral divine action excludes human participation leads the forensicists to place the event of justification outside of us. Justification imputes an alien justice. Our justification consists of a word spoken over us that changes our status before God, *corem Deo.*

So far, I have been reporting how the forensicists emphasize that justification is a divine act that takes place outside of us (*extra nos*). It is worthwhile to note another trait in the forensic model, namely, that it relies on the maintenance of the moral universe. The forensic model may have spiritual traction with the fragile soul but not with the broken soul. For the fragile soul, the news that Christ saves *extra nos* comes as good news; it means that the fragile soul is gifted with forgiveness while the moral universe remains valid. In contrast, the broken soul experiences anomie—that is, the absence of law. The moral universe has been shattered. Any announcement of grace that

---

10. H. George Anderson, T. Austin Murphy, and Joseph A. Burgess, eds., *Justification by Faith: Lutherans and Catholics in Dialogue VII* (Minneapolis: Augsburg, 1985), 50.

depends upon the now broken moral structure misses the mark. Like using a hammer where a screwdriver is called for, forensic justification cannot repair a broken soul.

As we can imagine, a Lutheran forensicist would like what article 3 of the Formula of Concord says: "The word 'to justify' . . . means 'to absolve,' that is, 'to pronounce free from sin.'"[11] This amounts to a court verdict, a verbal declaration of forgiveness or absolution. It amounts to a change of status *corem Deo,* before God. We are justified because God declares this to be the case. We are just not because we ourselves possess or exhibit justice; we are just solely in our status before God. Simultaneously, we are sinful in ourselves yet justified before God. Regeneration (*regeneratio*) and vivification (*vivicatio*) are separated from justification.[12] God is disposed to justify us in this way because God is gracious. *Grace* refers to God's disposition to treat us with favor. This is the heart of the forensicist view.

The late Gerhard Forde is a Lutheran who draws the contrast sharply between the sixteenth-century Lutheran and Catholic positions. His chirp sounds like a forensicist. "Above all," he writes,

---

11. *BC,* 495.

12. Friedrich Mildenberger worries that the Formula of Concord may be flawed because the sharpness of the distinction between justification and sanctification is dulled by a dependent relationship between them."The Formula of Concord assumed the burden of the almost-irresolvable problem of distinguishing justification and sanctification. Justification was now described as coming from outside the believer through the gospel. Faith receives the righteousness of the gospel. This is accompanied by a process of sanctification or renewal that is based on the capacity to do the good which the Spirit has given in the regenerate believer. The idea is that the believer will become an observably better person. The Formula of Concord was very conscious that this could raise serious problems about the certainty of salvation . . . it [sanctification] can never be separated from justification. Justifying faith can never coexist with an evil intention." *Theology of the Lutheran Confessions,* trans. Erwin L. Lueker (Minneapolis: Fortress Press, 1983), 165.I concur with Mildenberger that the Formula risks returning to a legalism that sacrifices the security of salvation in faith. The problem, as I have been describing it in this book, is the persistence of original sin. Even justified and baptized believers in Christ engage in that dimension of sin we refer to as self-justification and scapegoating. This is serious sin because it is a tacit rejection of justifying faith—a rejection common to the most devout Christian believers. Describing a Christian believer as *simul justus et peccator* is much more realistic than asserting that no justification is present when no sanctification has been achieved.

"the *simul justus et peccator* [simultaneously justified yet sinful] brings with it an understanding of sin that undermines all ordinary ideas of progress according to moral or legal schemes. The *iustitia* exists *simultaneously* with the *peccatum*. . . . There must be, as Roman Catholics like to say, a real progress, a real transformation. . . . So there is a real stand-off here."[13] On one occasion Forde came to my home for a barbeque. He was wearing a tee shirt that read: "I don't believe in Sanctification." I presumed someone bought it for him as a gift. Nevertheless, Forde wore it with pride.

Indwelling Lutherans vs. Forensicist Lutherans

Forensic chirping is not the only sound in the Lutheran meadow. The indwellers make their own distinct sounds. Whereas the forensic caucus holds that justification takes place *extra nos*, "outside of us," the indwelling caucus holds that justification takes place *intra nos*, "within us."

The indwellers refer more to the so-called *real* Luther than to the Formula of Concord.[14] In addition to God's grace, we the believers receive a gift—Christ's presence in faith. *Grace* refers to God's disposition toward favor, whereas *gift* refers to what the sinner

---

13. Forde, *Justification by Faith—A Matter of Death and Life* (Minneapolis: Fortress Press, 1982), 43.
14. The Formula of Concord deliberately rejects the indwelling position held by Lutheran Reformer Andreas Osiander. The Formula rejects the position that Christ "dwells in the elect through faith and impels them to do what is right and is therefore their righteousness." Solid Declaration, 3.2, in *BC*, 562. Evidently, the indwelling position propagated by Osiander relies metaphysically on Neoplatonism, whereas the Formula authors follows Luther's understanding of the creative power of God's word. "Osiander failed to see what Luther saw in the Old Testament texts they both loved: that God works through his Word, and that that Word is not some ontological category but rather a speaking that creates reality in relationships. Because Osiander sought reality in eternal ontological substances, he failed to see reality where Luther saw it, in God's creative action through his Word." Charles P. Arand, Robert Kolb, and James A. Nestingen, *The Lutheran Confessions: History and Theology of the Book of Concord* (Minneapolis: Fortress Press, 2012), 225. Is God actually present in, with, and under the Word of God?

receives, namely, the renewing and transforming power of God's love in the indwelling Christ. According to the indwellers, both grace and gift belong to the event of justification.

This real-presence or indwelling-of-Christ model of justification has been celebrated recently by the Finnish School of Luther Research in Helsinki, which has been seeking dialogue between Lutherans and the Orthodox. "Faith means justification precisely on the basis of Christ's person being present in it as favor and gift. *In ipsa fide Christus adest:* in faith itself Christ is present, and so the whole of salvation," writes Mannermaa.[15]

Helsinki theologian Simon Peura believes that he can draw out an ecumenical concordance by emphasizing the union with Christ enjoyed by the person of faith. Peura is critical of the Lutheran voice heard in the *JDDJ* because it relies too narrowly on the forensic model of justification. What is ignored is the indwelling dimension, he charges. To formulate the problem: if the Lutherans emphasize only the forensic aspect of justification and the Roman Catholics only the effective aspect, then the two communions are left unconnected. If, however, the Lutherans emphasize the dimension of real presence, then the connection can be reestablished. "According to Luther it is possible to connect the forensic aspect and the effective aspect of justification to each other with the help of the concepts of *unio cum Christo* and *inhabitatio Christi.* If these ideas are taken into account, Lutherans can without difficulty argue that a Christian is both made righteous and also deified as a partaker of divine nature."[16] Although Peura does not jettison the forensic model, his indwelling-of-Christ model accomplishes more than the forensic model alone can. The

15. Tuomo Mannermaa, "Why is Luther so Fascinating? Modern Finnish Luther Research," in *Union with Christ: The New Finnish Interpretation of Luther*, ed. Carl E. Braaten and Robert W. Jenson (Minneapolis: Fortress Press, 1998), 14–15.
16. Simon Puera, "Christ as Favor and Gift: The Challenge of Luther's Understanding of Justification," in *Union with Christ*, 67.

indwelling model comes much closer to what Roman Catholics accept, as well as what the Eastern Orthodox proffer. One can see why Peura and his Helsinki colleagues simultaneously see this as a soteriological and ecumenical move.

In America, Carl Braaten is favorably impressed by Peura's thesis. "I am convinced that the christological (*unio cum Christo*) treatment of justification is essential, and that only on its basis is it possible to stress both aspects of justification, while observing the proper distinction between the gracious mercy of God as the forgiveness of sins for Christ's sake, on the one hand, and the lifelong process of renewal and sanctification in the Holy spirit, on the other hand. Both are necessary; they belong together and must not be separated, neither should they be confused."[17] In sum, the indwelling model of justifying faith comes closer to both the Orthodox and the Roman Catholic models than does the forensic model.

Ecumenically minded non-Lutherans, such as South African Reformed theologian Alan Spence, would like to blend Roman Catholics and Lutheran Protestants into a single Christian blend. But to make this blend taste good, he needs to slightly alter the recipe. Where Roman Catholics would advocate sanctification, Spence advocates striving for social justice. "Our determination to strive for justice is motivated by love and it is expressed in a humility that befits those who have themselves failed so badly and continue to do so. We find that it is only as we become great lovers overwhelmed by the Spirit of Jesus that we start to satisfy the righteous demands of the law."[18] The motivation of selfless love motivates us to strive for justice, and this striving for justice in turn makes us just. However, this is not merely a matter of brute will power. The Holy Spirit inspires and empowers the person who loves.

---

17. Carl E. Braaten, "Response," in *Union with Christ*, 75.
18. Alan J. Spence, *Justification: A Guide for the Perplexed* (London: T&T Clark, 2012), 151.

This sounds like a chirp from the Formula of Concord. "After a person has been justified by faith, there then exists a true living 'faith working through love' (Gal. 5:6). That means that good works always follow justifying faith and are certainly found with it, when it is a true and living faith. For faith is never alone but is always accompanied by love and hope."[19] Yes, Lutherans of both the forensic and indwelling caucuses affirm faith active in love, but both would also affirm *simul justus et peccator* to an extent that Spence overlooks. The Spence blend tastes like a mixture of beer and chocolate; while each taste tantalizes on its own, the two do not belong together.

The Indwelling Presence of Christ in the Person of Faith

Let's go back for a moment to *JDDJ* §26. "The justification of sinners is forgiveness of sins and being made righteous by justifying grace, which makes us children of God. In justification the righteous receive from Christ faith, hope, and love and are thereby taken into communion with him." Communion? Yes, communion. This relationship between the person of faith and the indwelling Christ is frequently overlooked in discussions of justification. Nevertheless, it is decisive. "Christ is not outside but dwells within us," says Calvin.[20] This is not figurative but literal language. If one must appeal to mysticism to make the indwelling model coherent, then so be it.

Let's travel back past *JDDJ* to Martin Luther for a moment. Faith is not simply an act of belief; it is a grasping of the indwelling Christ. Or, in reverse, faith is being grasped by Christ. Luther likens Christ's presence to paint on a wall. "Faith takes hold of Christ . . . He is the form that adorns and informs faith as color does a wall." Luther

---

19. *BC*, 496.
20. John Calvin, *Institutes of the Christian Religion* (1559), ed. John T. McNeill, 2 vols. (Louisville: Westminster John Knox, 1960), 3.24, 1:570.

stumbles for words. Faith "takes hold of Christ in such a way that Christ is the object of faith, or rather not the object but, so to speak, the One who is present in the faith itself."[21]

Luther then turns mystical, as I have shown. "Therefore, faith justifies because it takes hold of and possesses this treasure, the present Christ. But how He is present—this is beyond our thought; for there is darkness . . . Where the confidence of the heart is present, therefore, there Christ is present, in that very cloud of faith."[22] The allusion to the *Cloud of Unknowing* does not, in itself, place Luther into the garden-variety camp of medieval mystics. Luther is not joining a club or a school of mystical thought. Rather, he is struggling to make the point that "the Holy Spirit *places the resurrected Christ into the life of the person of faith. Luther's view differs radically* from the mystics in that the recovery of true humanity is attained *not through the deification of man, but through the humanity of God.*"[23] Rather than a human ascent into the realm of the divine, the divine takes the initiative and enters the mundane life of the human. Instead of our climbing the spiritual ladder to the top, God descends the ladder and meets us at the bottom.

Luther appreciated the mystical tradition he inherited, but his theology of indwelling depends more upon his own particular experience than it does generic mysticism. "Luther's reflections on the condition of a justified sinner reckon with a world beyond the historical and the objective, experiences as the Presence of the mystical Christ," writes Bengt Hoffman. "Through the mystical experience—prayer included—the non-rational is infused into the rational. . . . The inspiration for such reflection is mystical and therefore trans-logical. In this sense the criteria of scientific

---

21. Luther, *Commentary on Galatians* (1535), in *LW*, 26:129.
22. Ibid., 26:130.
23. Hans Joachim Iwand, "The Righteousness of Faith According to Luther," *Lutheran Quarterly* 21:1 (Spring 2007): 50 (italics in the original).

knowledge must be inadequate for theological reflection."[24] Third person abstract discourse at the level of theology must be founded on first person internal experience or second person I-Thou experience.

Recall how Prenter proffers that divine presence in faith explains how justification-by-faith is effective. Without Christ's indwelling, the forensic model becomes nothing more than an abstract idea, a nice theological thought. "The doctrine of justification in its extreme forensic form threatened to become an abstract doctrine, which operated by the weight of the law, and which made Christ a mere idea."[25] In faith, however, Christ is more than an idea, more than a theological doctrine. Christ is a living presence. "For Luther the work of the Holy Spirit always means a relationship to the truly present crucified and risen Christ."[26] Before the indwelling Christ can become an abstract theological model, the indwelling presence is an I-Thou relationship.

Pannenberg, among others, elects to join the indwelling caucus. He complains that the forensic model is much weaker than the real-presence model. Whereas the indwelling of Christ—sealed for eternity in us by baptism—is secure, the external forensic judgment must logically be repeated again and again. This repetitive requirement leaves the sinner insecure in God's grace. "If the forensic justification is separated from the basic intuition of 'mystical' participation in Christ by faith, then a peculiar *actualism* (or *extrinsicism*) results: We must accept the promise of divine forgiveness again and again, because we slide back into sin again and again. The shift toward such actualism occurred as early as in Melanchthon, whose rational sobriety had little access to the more profound

24. Bengt R. Hoffman, *Luther and the Mystics* (Minneapolis: Augsburg, 1976), 220.
25. Regin Prenter, *Spiritus Creator: Luther's Concept of the Holy Spirit* (Philadelphia: Muhlenberg, 1953), 63.
26. Ibid., 28.

mystical roots of Luther's thought. It vitiated the function of baptism (as constituting a continuous new life in Christ), because in spite of baptism sinfulness remains and divine forgiveness is needed again and again."[27] The indwelling model relies upon mystical presence, whereas the forensic model does not.

Advocates of forensic justification do not intend to leave the person of faith in the insecure position described by Pannenberg. Pannenberg's criticism of the forensic position may be excessive. Nevertheless, he is correct in showing how the forensic model fails to embrace all that can be found in the indwelling model. Might we be able to interpret the forensic model as a once-for-all occurrence that provides comfort for the sinner before God? God's Word is eternal; therefore, God's pronouncement of our forgiveness is an eternal pronouncement. If this is what the forensicist intends, then Pannenberg's criticism of actualism misses the mark.

But is the forensic model compatible with what Luther himself says? No, and yes. On the one hand, because Christ is actually present in the person of faith, it would not be accurate to describe the event of justification as strictly *extra nos,* "outside of us." Christ is inside, not outside. On the other hand, it is the righteousness of Christ and not our own righteousness that defines us as justified, so speaking of *iustitia aliena,* or "alien justice," fits Luther.

Could we combine the two models? Suppose we imagine a scenario that looks something like this. In a divine courtroom, we (you and I) are the defendants. The evidence of our offenses is presented. The case is clear: we are guilty. At the moment the gavel is being lowered, however, the judge looks at the defendants' box. The judge sees the innocent Christ standing there, not us. When the gavel comes down, we are declared innocent and acquitted. Our innocence

---

27. Wolfhart Pannenberg, *Christian Spirituality* (Louisville: Westminster, 1983), 21 (italics in the original).

is the gift of the present Christ. This declaration is final. We cannot be tried a second time.

Because the person of Christ is present in the person of faith, the so-called "happy exchange" takes place. "By this fortunate exchange with us He took upon Himself our sinful person and granted us His innocent and victorious Person."[28] Or, as Calvin puts it, the "indwelling of Christ in our hearts—in short, that mystical union . . . so that Christ, having been made ours, makes us sharers with him in the gifts with which he has been endowed."[29] Within the human soul, an exchange takes place: Christ's salvation replaces our condemnation. Christ's innocence becomes our innocence. Christ's resurrection unto everlasting life becomes our resurrection to eternal life.

Here, I would like to borrow Plato's language to describe this exchange in terms of justice and justification. Jesus Christ would himself be a just soul. Jesus suffered injustice rather than perpetrating injustice, and his justness has eternal effect. Christ's eternal justness becomes our justice in the happy exchange that takes place in faith. This is justification by grace.

One more thought. Does justification-by-faith apply solely to the individual baptized person, or does it apply communally to the Church as well? According to Michael Welker, justification-by-faith applies to both. "God gives human beings faith, in which they—both individually and communally—enter into relationship with God."[30]

Let's ask again: does *simul justus et peccator* apply to the Church as well as to individuals? Take off the rose-colored glasses and look around. The Church of Jesus Christ is by no means sanctified; yet, it still points to the Kingdom of God. "The church is the heart of the

---

28. Luther, *Lectures on Galatians,* 1535, *LW*, 26:284.
29. Calvin, *Inst.,* 3.10, 1:737.
30. Michael Welker, *What Happens in Holy Communion?* (Grand Rapids, MI: Eerdmans, 2000), 173.

present in proleptically anticipating the future," says Hans Schwarz rightly.[31] Now, in this age while the Body of Christ is pointing to God's future fulfillment, the One Holy Catholic and Apostolic Church may rightly be described as *simul justus et peccator*. As such, the Church too is called to sin boldly.

Real Presence and Real Transformation

The separation of justification from sanctification does not please critics of either Lutheran party. Regardless of the declarative statement, justification needs to be effective, at least according to Roman Catholic critics. In "The Decree on Justification" issued on January 13, 1547, the Council of Trent describes justification as both an event and a process: believers are declared righteous due to the work of Christ, but they also engage in the process of actually becoming righteous through the ongoing work of the Holy Spirit. According to the Council, however, the latter comes before the former. Regeneration along with sanctification precede justification. "Justification of the sinner may be briefly defined as a translation from that state to which a human being is born a child of the first Adam, to the state of grace and of the adoption of the sons of God through the second Adam, Jesus Christ our Savior." This means that we as sinners actually become just before we can be declared just. In order to avoid ambiguity, canon 11 makes clear what is being rejected. The Council of Trent condemns anyone who teaches that justification takes place "either by the sole imputation of the righteousness of Christ or by the sole remission of sins, to the exclusion of grace and charity . . . or that the grace by which we are justified is only the goodwill of God." For

---

31. Hans Schwarz, *The Christian Faith: A Creedal Account* (Grand Rapids MI: Baker Academic, 2014), 167.

Tridentine Catholics, the term *justification* includes what Protestants think of as both justification and sanctification.

As we saw above, Calvin, like Luther, is a member of the indweller caucus. Christ is actually present in the faith of the believer. However, Calvin thought of this a bit differently than Luther did (not to mention Melanchthon). Christ's indwelling emits a "double grace," Calvin claims. In addition to a declaration of justification, *corem Deo,* Christ's presence becomes the power of the Holy Spirit for transformation. The first grace leads to a forensic declaration of justification. The second grace leads to a renewing or transforming work of sanctification. Reformed theologians who follow Calvin place both justification and sanctification as sub-doctrines under the more inclusive doctrine of reconciliation. Reconciliation includes both justification and sanctification. For a sinner to be reconciled with God, both declarative justification and effective sanctification are required.

Following the Council of Trent and sympathetic to Calvin, Alister McGrath objects to the Lutheran party on the grounds that this sixteenth-century position deviates from the classical Christian commitment. According to Augustine and the tradition, argues McGrath, *justification* means that the sinful person becomes transformed—turned from sinfulness to righteousness. To McGrath's chagrin, Melanchthon apparently denies this classical commitment. The Lutheran position "marks a complete break with the teaching of the church up to that point. From the time of Augustine onward, justification had been understood to refer to both the event of being declared righteous and the process of being made righteous. Melanchthon's concept of forensic justification diverged radically from this understanding."[32] Does this critique elicit fear and

---

32. McGrath, "Justification," in *The Oxford Encyclopedia of the Reformation,* ed. Hans J. Hillerbrand, 4 vols. (Oxford: Oxford University Press, 1996), 4:364. Alister McGrath contends that the

trembling among Lutherans? No, not at all. Neither the forensicist nor the indwelling caucuses within the Lutheran party are intimidated by the complaints of the Council of Trent, Calvinists, or McGrath. Lutherans, no less than other Christians, press the believer forward toward works of love.

Even though justification is for sinners, sinners respond in love. *JDDJ* §37: "We confess together that good works—a Christian life lived in faith, hope and love—follow justification and are its fruits. When the justified live in Christ and act in the grace they receive, they bring forth, in biblical terms, good fruit. Since Christians struggle against sin their entire lives, this consequence of justification is also for them an obligation they must fulfill. Thus both Jesus and the apostolic Scriptures admonish Christians to bring forth the works of love." Indeed, both Lutherans and Catholics, along with Calvinists, stress that the justified believer should embody St. Paul's "faith active in Love" (Gal. 5:6).

The life of love links justification with sanctification. "Justification and sanctification differ insofar as Paul develops the idea of justification in the context of conversion and the genesis of faith, while, when speaking about sanctification, he directs his attention to leading a Christian life."[33] Here, the Lutherans add a slightly cynical accent, distinguishing between sanctification for the lover and authentic love aimed at the beloved. Love, by Christian definition, is not self-serving. Love orients itself to the needs of the

---

Reformation truncated the Pauline meaning of "justification" and, thereby, left out much that is important in the Christian message. "The *concept of justification* and the *doctrine of justification* must be carefully distinguished," writes McGrath. "The *concept of justification* is one of many employed within the Old and New Testaments, particularly the Pauline corpus, to describe God's saving action toward his people. It cannot lay claim to exhaust, nor adequately characterize in itself, the richness of the biblical understanding of salvation in Christ." Alister McGrath, *Iustitia Dei: A History of the Christian Doctrine of Justification from 1500 to the Present Day*, 2 vols. (Cambridge: Cambridge University Press, 1986), 1:2 (italics in the original).

33. *Biblical Foundations*, 75.

neighbor, not the lover. Jesus' own self-sacrifice and self-emptying (*kenosis* in Phil. 2) becomes the model for the follower of Jesus. If this is the nature of love, then a true disciple ought not march on a path toward self-improvement, self-sanctification, self-perfection. A selfless orientation in love contradicts a purposeful attempt to make oneself holy. Although Lutherans use the word *sanctification,* they don't mean it. What Lutherans emphasize is love of neighbor for the sake of the neighbor, not for one's own purification or moral self-improvement.

This is subtle, but more than any other point, it distinguishes the Lutheran position from all others, be it Roman Catholic or Reformed. For the Lutheran, love of neighbor is for the sake of the neighbor and solely for the sake of the neighbor. The purpose of loving one's neighbor is not to define the person doing the loving as a loving person. To press neighbor-love (*Nächtstenliebe*) into the service of sanctifying the person of faith prostitutes an otherwise disinterested love. It makes love of neighbor into a means toward a selfish spiritual end rather than an end in itself. As the beneficiary of the Christian's love, the neighbor is the moral end; there is no further end. The Christian's sanctification cannot in itself be the moral end that makes neighbor-love a means. This would be contradictory. If a Christian believer is already justified-by-faith, then he or she does not need sanctification to enjoy a blessed relationship with the God of grace. To my reading, no other Christian sub-tradition gets this.

Certainly, Lutherans were not the first to discover this tension between sanctification and disinterested love. They inherited it from insightful ascetics in medieval Europe. When faith is active in love, the benefits go to the loved, not the lovers.

Good Works

This brings us to the matter of good works. For whose benefit are good works oriented? The Lutherans will stamp their feet and grimace: good works are solely aimed at the benefit of the person whom we love! Good works are not performed to increase the merit of the lover. Mary Lowe puts it this way: "Through God's grace we recognize ourselves as sinful subjects before God, and in the liberation that comes from justification we are freed to love the neighbor. This implies an ought—an obligation to the other. But this service is not done as a work of merit but as an act of love."[34] This is reminiscent of a point Luther makes again and again. "So, also, our works should be done, not that we may be justified by them, since, being justified beforehand by faith, we ought to do all things freely and joyfully for the sake of others."[35] For the sake of others!

Yet the *JDDJ* discussion marches on, falling just short of clarity on this matter. §38: "According to Catholic understanding, good works, made possible by grace and the working of the Holy Spirit, contribute to growth in grace, so that the righteousness that comes from God is preserved and communion with Christ is deepened. When Catholics affirm the meritorious character of good works, they wish to say that, according to the biblical witness, a reward in heaven is promised to these works. Their intention is to emphasize the responsibility of persons for their actions, not to contest the character of those works as gifts, or far less to deny that justification always remains the unmerited gift of grace." This is distinctively Catholic.

In contrast, a *JDDJ* Lutheran will not grant "growth in grace" if it suggests more grace. Total grace has already been offered and

---

34. Mary E. Lowe, "Sin from a Queer, Lutheran Perspective," *Transformative Lutheran Theologies: Feminist, Womanist, and Mujerista Perspectives,* ed. Mary J. Streufert (Minneapolis: Fortress Press, 2010), 82.
35. Luther, *The Freedom of a Christian,* in *LW*, 31:368.

effected in justification, which is the equivalent of total salvation. When the gallon jug is already full, no additional milk will make it more full. Nor will a Lutheran grant that our works are meritorious before God because Christ's merit more than suffices for any merit that we can earn. Section 38 remains a distinctively Roman Catholic contribution that is not shared with *JDDJ*'s Lutheran partners.

Will Lutherans and Catholics ever come to a rapprochement? The answer depends on which Lutherans you ask. I do not expect to see rapprochement in my lifetime.

Is Justifying Faith Irrelevant Today?

Has the sixteenth-century volcano cooled? Is this theological discussion an anachronism or a religious antique? Should it be placed in the historian's museum of outdated ideas? "How can the message of justification speak to people who no longer seem to ask that question?"[36]

Some scholars think that issues surrounding justification are meaningless in our twenty-first century context. Spence, for example, fences the doctrine of justification within a sixteenth-century context. "The doctrine of justification is dependent on an understanding of the human predicament in terms of sin, guilt, and judgment. We could say that they are related to one another as a medicine is to the disease for which it serves as a cure."[37] Accordingly, because we modern and emerging postmodern people no longer suffer from sin, guilt, and judgment, the therapy of justifying faith will not cure us from anything. "We now live in an age in which these ideas [sin, guilt, judgment] are not significant. . . . Such an assumption, however, is not entirely correct."[38]

36. *Biblical Foundations,* 112.
37. Spence, *Justification,* 146.

How should we assess this? It is one thing to jump from context to context. Yes, of course, our contemporary context differs from sixteenth-century Europe in significant ways. But we must remember that what we think about justifying faith is rooted in the biblical witness to God's grace that dates a millennium and a half earlier. This biblical revelation of God's grace helps to illuminate human nature, which expresses itself in every historical and cultural context. "The theology of justification offers the deepest insight into the human condition before God. . . . Our incapacity as human beings to do anything to restore the broken communion with God becomes apparent only through the recognition that God has already done all that is necessary to reconcile us with him."[39] I wonder if it might be premature to give up so quickly on the illuminative capacity of the doctrine of justification. To see God as gracious and ourselves as justified might make our modern and emerging postmodern souls look different.

I have been trying here to convey our reality as fragile and broken souls. In each model, the centered self gains its shape from the moral universe that contains the swirl of everyday activities. The center borrows its shape from the periphery. In the case of the fragile soul, we ask our moral universe to draw a line between good and evil so that we can stand firmly on the good side. We deceive ourselves into thinking that God stands on our side, which justifies treating those on the other side as scapegoats deserving of destruction. In the case of the broken soul, the moral universe is crumbling and losing its shape. As the moral universe disintegrates, so also does the soul who depends on it for its own shape. Escape from the dissolving self appears possible through suicide.

38. Ibid.
39. *Biblical Foundations,* 109.

The gospel promise that the Holy Spirit places Jesus Christ in the vortex of the human soul has dramatic implications. By placing the suffering Christ on the cross within us, we suddenly become aware of the destructive consequences of our efforts at self-justification. We become aware that our participation in eternal life is not the product of constructing a just soul; rather, it is a gift from the resurrected Jesus Christ. Justifying faith becomes justified as faith.

Conclusion

There is nothing I can do to lose it; there is nothing I need to do to gain it.

14

Gift

We have come to know "the astonishing experience of gift."

–Pope Benedict XVI[1]

When I hear the gospel, that I have been accepted and adopted by God for the sake of Jesus Christ in the Holy Spirit, I am radically passive. I receive that which is given to me as a "categorical gift."

–Oswald Bayer[2]

Can we refer to justification in the human soul as a gift? If the concept of grace (*gratia*) refers to God's disposition of mercy toward us, and if the concept of gift (*donum*) refers to what is given to us, we must ask: Are there any strings attached? Is this gift of grace unconditional, or does it come with obligations? If the gift comes

---

1. Pope Benedict XVI, *Caritas in Veritate* [Encyclical on Integral Human Development in Charity and Truth], Vatican Website, June 29, 2009, sec. 34, http://www.vatican.va/holy_father/benedict_xvi/encyclicals/documents/hf_ben-xvi_enc_20090629_caritas-in-veritate_en.html.
2. Oswald Bayer, "With Luther in the Present," *Lutheran Quarterly* 21:1 (Spring 2007): 11.

with obligations, does this make it a conditional gift or even a non-gift?

Consider the statement offered by the emeritus Methodist bishop Kenneth Carder: "Our identity as children of God is God's gift to us; living in the world as redeemed sons and daughters of God is our gift to God."[3] The question arises: Does this reciprocal gifting imply that God's gift to us comes with strings attached? Some of today's theologians and philosophers are engaged with this question as well.

As background, I must point out how Luther seems to distinguish grace from gift. "Grace must be sharply distinguished from gifts," he writes. "A righteous and faithful man doubtless has both grace and the gift. . . . but the gift heals from sin and from all his corruption of body and soul. . . . Everything is forgiven through grace, but as yet not everything is healed through the gift. . . . for the gift there is sin which it purges away and overcomes."[4] Because God's justification declares a person just while still in a state of sin, the person of faith begins the arduous process of overcoming that sin. The sin prior to and following justification is the same, argues Luther, but our status before God is different. Prior to justification, sin warrants wrath, condemnation, and death. Subsequent to justification, sin is not counted (so to speak). While we strive to purge sin from our daily life, "it is called sin, and is truly such in its nature; but now it is sin without wrath, without the law, dead sin, harmless sin, as long as one perseveres in grace and gift."[5] Note Luther's wording: "as long as one perseveres in grace and gift."

Elsewhere, Luther equates grace and gift. "But 'the gracr of God' (gratia Dei) and 'the gift' (donum) are the same thing, namely, the very

---

3. Kenneth Carder, *Living Our Beliefs*, rev. ed. (Nashville: Discipleship Resources, 2009), 90.
4. Luther, *Against Latomus*, in *Luther's Works*, American ed., vols. 1–30, ed. Jaroslav Pelikan (St. Louis: Concordia, 1955–67); vols. 31–55, ed. Helmut T. Lehmann (Minneapolis: Fortress Press, 1955–86), 32:229.
5. Ibid.

righteousness (*Iustitia*) which is freely given to us through Christ."[6] Just where do you stand, Dr. Luther? Make up your mind, please!

Whether grace and gift are identical or different is not an issue that bothers contemporary theologians. What has become an issue, however, is whether or not the gift of grace come with strings attached. Does it necessarily imply reciprocity? Does the declaration of forgiveness in justification-by-faith necessarily imply effective transformation? I recommend that we use the term *grace* to refer to the divine disposition to give. I recommend that we use the term *gift* to refer to what God gives and we receive. I further recommend that we use the term *agape* to refer to gracious love—that is, love that asks for nothing reciprocal in return. Our theological question will be: Does the gift of grace come with strings attached? If so, do the strings disqualify it as a gift?

Reciprocal Altruism

"In all societies gifts have reciprocal character," Sammeli Juntunen asserts.[7] There is no free lunch. Anthropologists make it clear that reciprocity clings to the gift like barnacles to a ship's hull.

The strings attached to a gift may be invisible, at least at first. Hospitality is a form of gift-giving with threads so fine they are invisible, until you bring them into focus under the philosopher's magnifying glass. This leads theologian Risto Saarinen to aver, "There is no free gift. If somebody offers you a gift, this person is increasing his or her social status and putting you in his or her debt. It belongs to the idea of gift that this is not said but, on the contrary,

---

6. Luther, *Romans*, in *LW*, 25:306.
7. Sammeli Juntunen, "The Notion of Gift (*donum*) in Luther's Thinking," *Luther between Present and Past: Studies in Luther and Lutheranism*, ed. Ulrik Nissen, Anna Vind, Bo Holm, and Olli-Pekka Vainio (Helsinki: Luther-Agricola-Society, 2004), 55.

explicitly denied."[8] Here is the lie again. When we give, we deny that strings are attached, yet our reputation is enhanced in the eyes of the recipient not only by the gift itself but also by our denial of the strings attached. If we are the recipients, we contribute to the self-justification of the gift-giver.

The phenomenology of gift-giving introduces a dilemma, or aporia, which philosophers such as Jacques Derrida point out. The dilemma looks like this: If I give you a gift, then I look good and put you in my debt; but if this is to be a genuine gift, there must be no reciprocity, return, exchange, countergift, or debt.[9] The concept of the gift implies that you return nothing to me. However, in giving you the gift, my social standing increases, and you are required to respond with gratitude. The mere recognition of the gift by the receiver nullifies the gift as gift. Within the economy of exchange, the very condition that makes gift-giving what it is includes strings even while, by definition, it denies the strings.

By necessity, the next question becomes: Does this observation regarding gift-giving in the economy of exchange apply to the gift given in the gospel? No, says German theologian Oswald Bayer. "God's coming into the world and his existence in it is *contrary* to human experience and corresponding expectations" for reciprocity.[10] No strings attached.

Not so fast. Danish theologian Bo Holm sees strings when he interprets Luther's understanding of the gospel through an economic lens. What is the economy of justification? It requires a component of reciprocity, mutuality, and exchange. In response to God's love,

8. Risto Saarinen, *God and the Gift: An Ecumenical Theology of Giving* (Collegeville, MN: Liturgical Press, 2005), 18.
9. Jacques Derrida, *Given Time: 1. Counterfeit Money* (Chicago: University of Chicago Press, 1995), cited by Saarinen, *God and the Gift*, 24.
10. Oswald Bayer, "Gift: Systematic Theology," in *Religion Past and Present*, ed. Hans Dieter Betz, Don S. Browning, Bernd Janowski, and Eberhard Jüngel, 14 vols. (Leiden, Neth.: Brill, 2007–14), 5:431, italics in original.

we love. We participate. "Justification is the opening of reciprocity, making realized reciprocity itself the gift of grace."[11] Grace stimulates; we respond. Holm likes the sentence that Luther uses to connote economic reciprocity: *"Deus dat ut dem, et do ut des* (God gives that I may give, and I give that you may give)."[12]

However, if we look through the lens of new creation rather than today's economy, gift looks different. The indwelling Christ is God's gift to us, which amounts to a creation, a new creation. It is Christ from within the new creature who motivates our life of loving service. Luther likens the justified person to a tree that sprouts leaves. Is the tree obligated to sprout leaves? No. The process of sprouting leaves is natural to the tree. Similarly, Luther likens the justified person to the sun. Do we have to demand that the sun shine? No. The sun shines spontaneously. Likewise, the person of faith who has spontaneously been given the living Christ loves the neighbor. In sum, this particular gift does not involve a reciprocal or obligatory character, which leads Juntunen to conclude: "I think that the idea of the *donum* being comparable to creation makes it clear that all reciprocity between the giver and the receiver is excluded."[13]

Even without strings, argues Peura, the indwelling Christ leads to transformation, to effective justification, and even to deification. Puera believes that Luther includes "participation, change, and deification. The aim of justification is actually a complete transformation in Christ."[14] This transformation follows from the real presence of Christ in faith. "Luther's understanding that God the Father is favorable to a sinner (*favor Dei*) and that Christ renews a sinner (*donum Dei*) is based on the idea of a *unio cum Christo*. This

---

11. Bo Holm, "Luther's 'Theology of the Gift,'" in *GG*, 85.
12. Ibid., 86.
13. Juntunen, "Notion of Gift," 61.
14. Peura, "Christ as Favor and Gift," in *Union in Christ: The New Finnish Interpretation of Luther*, ed. Carl E. Braaten and Robert W. Jenson (Grand Rapids, MI: Eerdmans, 1998), 60.

same idea explains why grace and gift are necessary to each other. Gift is not only a consequence of grace, as is usually emphasized in Lutheran theology, but it is in a certain sense a condition for grace as well."[15] According to Peura, we now have a "condition for grace." Does this condition amount to the completion of the gift-giving—a completion that requires our response, participation, and achievement? Are these the strings?

Might we compare the gift of grace to a Christmas gift, wrapped in such a way that the contents are hidden? We may shake it, but our shaking will not reveal precisely what the contents are. We must open the gift. Once it is open and we can identify it, then we will put it on, or use it, or in some way integrate it into our other possessions. The gift may be a stimulus, but it becomes a gift in the full sense only when we respond. No giver would give an expensive gift without expecting it be enjoyed through usage. This response does not amount to reciprocity, to be sure, yet the gift giver feels a sense of accomplishment only when the gift is opened, used, and appreciated. But does gift analysis help us understand the gospel?

The Basic Gift of Existence

Philosopher Martin Heidegger analyzed human consciousness. According to Heidegger, we sort of wake up at some point in our life and realize that we are here. We are here, and our being-here is not the result of our own decision or action. We're just here in this time and this place. We are *Dasein* (being-there or being-here and not somehwere else). This being-here has the feel of having been thrown. We feel we have been thrown from non-existence into existence. We live with a sense of "thrownness," *Geworfenheit*.[16] Might we think

15. Ibid., 56.

of our basic having-been-thrown-into existence as a gift? Jean-Luc Marion considers this and remarks: "*The gift delivers Being/being.*"[17]

On this matter, the way our language works is informative. In English, we simply say "there is" when identifying something that exists. The same is true in French: *il y a.* But note what happens in German: *es gibt.* When we say "there is," we literally say, "it gives." Marion comments, "No one more than Heidegger allowed the thinking of the coincidence of the gift with Being/being, by taking literally the German *es gibt,* wherein we recognize the French *il y a,* there is . . . we would understand the fact that there should be (of course: being) as this fact that *it gives, ça donne.* Being itself is delivered in the mode of giving."[18] "To be is to be gifted," say philosophers such as Heidegger and Marion. "To be is to be graced," theologians respond.

But who threw us into existence? Who is the giver when we say *es gibt?* Is our very existence best understood as a gift? If so, how can we pay back the giver? We can't. Reciprocity is not possible. No economy of exchange is at work. The basic gift of our existence is radical, brute, impenetrable.[19] Here, the philosophers seem to stop with givenness. Might there be a giver? Is it too soon to say the giver is God?[20]

16. Martin Heidegger, *Being and Time,* tr. John Macquarrie and Edward Robinson (New York: Harper, 1962).

17. Jean-Luc Marion, *God without Being,* trans. Thomas A. Carlson (Chicago: University of Chicago Press, 1991), 101, italics in original.

18. Ibid., 102.

19. Marion places both feet in the pure givenness or pure giftedness of existence without relying on the being of the giver. Thereby, Marion can think of God without being. Critics such as John Milbank want to deny Marion this move. When we recognize the givenness and hence giftedness of our very existence and respond in gratitude, this counts as reciprocity. It implies a divine giver. See John Milbank, *Being Reconciled, Ontology and Pardon* (London: Routledge, 2003) and the discussion by Saarinen, *God and the Gift,* 30–33.

20. What we are looking at here is the phenomenology of human experience, which raises the question of transcendence and the question of God. "This realization that one's existence is completely dependent upon factors beyond one's control—factors unified by the mind's instinctive drive toward simplicity, coherence, oneness—issues in the theological concept of

Another philosopher of Heidegger's ilk, Eric Voegelin, suggests that we are thrown into existence and then retrieved by the same source. While we exist between birth and death, we experience estrangement. If we give attention to the giftedness of our existence, we become attuned to the being—the ground of being—from which our existence is estranged. "Attunement, therefore, will be the state of existence when it hearkens to that which is lasting in being, when it maintains a tension of awareness for its partial revelations of the order of society and the world, when it listens attentively to the silent voices of conscience and grace in human existence itself. We are thrown into and out of existence without knowing the Why or the How, but while in it we know that we are of the being to which we return."[21] As a philosopher, Voegelin uses the word *being* where a theologian might use the word *God*. Both Heidegger and Voegelin tell us that if we simply stop for a moment to reflect on our thrownness into existence, we will catch the first glimmer of grace in our creation. In, with, and under our very being-here is grace.

As I mentioned in chapter 8, two of Heidegger's disciples—Lutheran philosopher Knud Løgstrup and Jewish philosopher Emmanuel Lévinas—begin their phenomenological analysis of the human condition by looking at the givenness of the basic human situation. According to Løgstrup, "life has been given to us. We have not ourselves created it." When we wake up to realize that we have been given a life that we did not create, we further realize that we are not alone. Someone who is other is present. We find ourselves already in relationship with other persons, persons

God's sovereignty. When it is compounded with gratitude for the goodness of this life which God's sovereignty has effected and is continuously sustaining we have the germ of the concept of grace; God's free and unstinted gifts to man which not only have made his life possible but sustain and enable it at every point along the way." Huston Smith, *The Religions of Man* (New York: Harper, 1958), 103.

21. Eric Voegelin, *Israel and Revelation*, in *Order and History*, 5 vols. (Baton Rouge: Louisiana State University Press, 1956–87), 1:5.

whom we trust and to whom we owe moral responsibility. The other person is other; and our relationship is already characterized as love for the other. "Man's relationship with the other is *better* as difference than as unity: sociality is better than fusion," writes Lévinas. "The very value of love is the impossibility of reducing the other to myself." To summarize, what we have been given is existence, and this is personal existence-in-relationship-to-the-other. This relational existing is basic, fundamental. It is the givenness with which we begin to understand ourselves as individuals.[22]

Is identifying our given state of existence sufficient? Not for Luther. Luther would not stop here. He would go on to identify the giver as God, prompting within us a sense of gratitude for God's gracious gifts. He opens his commentary on the creed in the Small Catechism with the lines, "I believe that God has created me together with all that exists. God has given me and still preserves my body and soul: eyes, ears, and all limbs and senses; reason and all mental faculties . . . And all this is done out of pure, fatherly, and divine goodness and mercy, without any merit or worthiness of mine at all! For all this I owe it to God to thank and praise, serve and obey him. This is most certainly true."[23]

What Luther says here deserves special attention. The first thing to note is the priority of you and me as individual persons over the universe and everything that exists. Your and my subjective identity and awareness come first; everything else follows. God is personal. The self or the soul provides the point of orientation from which we look out upon the world, which includes the physical as well as the moral universe.

---

22. See citations and discussion of Løgstrup and Lévinas on gift in Hans S. Reinders, "Donum or Datum? K. E. Løgstrup's Religious Account of the Gift of Life," in *Concern for the Other: Perspectives on the Ethics of K. E. Løgstrup,* ed. Svend Andersen and Kees van Kooten Niekerk (Notre Dame, IN: University of Notre Dame Press, 2007), 177–206.

23. *BC,* 354–55.

Second, God's grace in creation comes with strings attached. On the one hand, we are not responsible for our existence. We have been placed here by "divine goodness and mercy, without any merit or worthiness" of our own. On the other hand, we "owe (*schüldig*) it to God to thank and praise, serve and obey him." We are obligated to show gratitude for the gift of existence. Whether we show gratitude or not does not change the fact that God is gracious, that God is merciful and good. But is it necessary for us to show gratitude to God if our existence is to be a gift? Is this reciprocal response necessary for this basic gift to actually be a gift?

The reformers leave us with an unresolved problem. While they stress that the gifts of God's grace are utterly independent of any merit or worthiness on our part, they also say that God's gifts are concrete and specific to us in our daily lives. This specificity implies participation and even soul formation. This participation implies a response on our part, an active living out of the gift. Does this amount to merit or worthiness after the fact?

Justifying Faith, Loving Neighbors, and Sinning Boldly

Is justifying faith the same as the gift of being-here? Is the anonymous *es gibt* the model for the divine gift of justification? Are all people of all times and all places automatically justified because of some eternal divine decree? Does justification come automatically with creation?

Not according to Saarinen. Justifying faith is personal, he contends. For any gift to be given, there must be a receiver; the receiver is a participant in the gift-giving interaction. This applies especially to the gifts of God's grace in faith. "Faith does not signalize a cooperative act, but a personal participation in the reciprocity of giving and receiving. A gift cannot be given if the receiver is not there." Saarinen then teases out the implications for the means of grace—the sacraments. "At least four requirements can be read from the Lutheran Confessions: (1) that the recipient is alive, (2) is faithful, (3) is a person and (4) is not just anybody, a placeholder or a representative of a larger group, but the very person to whom the sacrament is physically given."[24] Reception makes it possible for giving to result in a gift.

Does the very fact that a receiver is present for the gift to be a gift entail reciprocity? Not precisely. That is to say, no reciprocity is required according to the economy of exchange in which we would be obligated to pay God back for his gracious gifts. Our gratitude does not accrue directly to God's advantage; rather, our gratitude comes to expression as our love for our neighbor.

This is the point where Saarinen, following Luther, develops the notion of agape love in the Christian life. "In Luther's account, Christians are called to imitate the divine love in such a manner that they fulfill the needs and wants of others."[25] Agape attends to the needs of the needy, not to one's needs as a lover of the needy. "A pure love would require a person who is not seeking his own profit but would act altruistically. Giving a completely free gift would be an example of pure love and altruism."[26] Frankly, at this point, I need to ask: Is it possible that agape love defined in this way is possible in the human economy of exchange?

The answer is no, for two reasons. First, as adumbrated above, all gift-giving in the economy of exchange is a disguised form of reciprocity. There are no gifts without strings attached. Would this apply to a gift God gives? Let's work with the hypothetical "yes" to see where it might lead.

24. Saarinen, *God and the Gift*, 11.
25. Ibid., 56.
26. Ibid., 52.

The second reason has to do with theological anthropology. According to the Augustinian tradition on human nature (the tradition to which Luther belongs), the human ego cannot in this life be decentered. Everything that we do—whether we are baptized or unbaptized—is an expression of the ego for the sake of the ego. There can be no human action that is totally selfless or ego-free. Every one of our attempts to love our neighbor with agape love is compromised if not contaminated with a self-serving motive. Even the pursuit of a just soul would betray a self-serving motive, thereby disqualifying what action we take as pure agape. Pure agape is impossible for us.

"Luther shares this skepticism with regard to pure love and genuine altruism. For Luther, human reason is inevitably egoistic and thus incapable of pure giving," comments Saarinen. "Luther is always and tirelessly making the point that all human efforts to do good and to live a good life are contaminated by egoism."[27] If this skepticism obtains, then why ask us to respond to God's grace by graciously loving others? Are we being asked to do the impossible?

Adumbrating all of these strings makes me feel like I've just dumped a bowl of spaghetti over the head of the faithful Christian. The noodles are mixed and messy. Attempting to unravel it in order to find a single strand of pure, self-sacrificial love would be both tedious and unnecessary. Plunge ahead, Luther would say. Sin boldly. Don't let the spiritual spaghetti tie us up and restrict our bold attempts at loving our neighbor.

Preliminary Conclusion: This Is a Pseudo Problem

It appears that we have a philosophical problem, an aporia. If we define a gift as what is given without any strings attached, then, in

27. Ibid.

the ordinary economy of human exchange, no pure gift-giving can practically exist. Every gift implies a gain given to the gift-giver—a gain due to the obligation of the receiver to offer thanks and to define the gift-giver as someone who is a gift-giver. To be defined as a gift-giver is to be noble, generous, and good. In short, the act of gift-giving—which includes its reciprocal response—serves the function of self-justification for the gift-giver. If this obtains, then the command to love God and love our neighbor with agape love becomes a fiction, an impossible demand. In daily life, loving and gift-giving without strings attached simply does not take place, at least not in a pure form.

I would like to suggest that this is not a real problem. It is a pseudo problem. The difficulty arises from the fallacy of misplaced concreteness, to use the term of Alfred North Whitehead.[28] There is confusion here between what is abstract and what is concrete. To say it another way, the apparent impossibility of pure reciprocity-less gifting or pure selfless loving confuses the ideal with the practical; it confuses the dog with the tail.

Recall how I suggested we define our terms: *grace* should refer to the divine disposition to give; *gift* should refer to what God gives and we receive; and *agape* should refer to gracious love. Each of these is an ideal definition, an abstraction, an idea that refers to a concept. None of these describe with precision what actually happens in our daily lives. Nor do any of these describe with precision what actually happens in God's relationship to us. We need to begin with what actually happens—*the concrete*—and then reflect theologically—*the abstract*—on what happens. What happens is the dog; our mental waggings represent the tail. The tail should point us to the dog, not the reverse.

---

28. Alfred North Whitehead, *Process and Reality: An Essay in Cosmology,* corrected ed., ed. David Ray Griffin and Donald W. Sherburne (New York: Free Press, 1978), 7.

In this case, the dog is the event of Jesus Christ. What does this event mean? It means that God has entered the created order, become present in our souls, forgiven us our sins, justified us by grace. In turn, we have begun to live with faith, hope, and love. An interaction has taken place in the history of the world and in the biography of our individual lives. That's the dog, the concrete dog.

The dog's wagging tail is our attempt to understand the dog abstractly by proffering theological ideas and religious descriptions about what the dog means. Our theological attempt to define terms such as *grace, gift,* and *agape* is tail wagging. Let's avoid confusing the tail with the dog, confusing the abstract descriptions with the concrete reality toward which they point.

God's interaction with the world and with our individual souls is messy. It's not neat. It's ambiguous. On the one hand, God comes with grace and beauty and glory; God comes in light. On the other hand, the world greets God with selfishness and ugliness and tragedy; the world's darkness snuffs out the light. We find ourselves at the point of collision, experiencing two realities at once. To posit pure concepts such as grace, gift, or agape is to posit abstractions, to imagine ideals that simply do not exist in our everyday world. Such purities do not exist either for us or for God.

Part of the mission of St. Paul's letters to the Romans and Galatians is to persuade us that our justification is the result of God's grace rather than our works. The Reformation took up the same mission, reiterating that we are saved by God's grace and not by any merit on our part. So far, so good. Once this point has been made, what does it add to speak of a divine gift that is so pure that it avoids contamination by reciprocity? What does it add to speak of agape love that is so pure that no ego or self is involved? Speaking this way only adds *abstractions that may become distractions.* In a world messy with ambiguity, we respond to God's love with our own love. This observation led Luther to throw in the towel on the purity question and simply say, "Sin boldly."

The debate over the purity of the gift or the purity of agape opens us up to the risk of using spiritual duct tape to patch up a fragile soul. As I suggested earlier, *reine Lehre* (pure doctrine) tells us less about the content of the doctrine and more about the fragility of the theological position it attempts to protect. If we allow the essence of grace, gift, or love to haunt us because we cannot conceive, let alone live, according to the impossible standard it sets, then we might overlook the otherwise messy domain within which our God actually shares our lives.

Inadvertent Passivity

A word of caution. If we overstress the idea of gift to the extent that we inculcate a sense of passivity in the person of faith, we may distort the life of faith. The life of faith is not passive. It is active. The Holy Spirit empowers us to be ourselves, to become ourselves. Galatians 5:22-23: "The fruit of the Spirit is love, joy, peace, patience, kindness, generosity, faithfulness, gentleness, and self-control." The Holy Spirit forms our souls. If the gift of Christ's presence is a seed, then the seed comes to harvest in our lives as these fruits. We would not want the passivity concomitant to the giftedness of justification-by-grace to obviate this spiritual activity.

Overstressing giftedness can blunt a healthy sense of self-worth and destroy our initiative to pursue social justice. For centuries, the standard critique of the Lutheran branch of the Reformation is that the overemphasis on unilateral divine grace has led to quietism—to unresponsiveness in the face of social injustice. In recent times, feminists have criticized the larger atonement tradition for its lack of support for women who, in the face of sexism, need to stand up for their rights. "Jesus' vicarious suffering becomes critiqued as an appropriate theological or anthropological model since it could disable one's own ability or confidence to stand up to oppression," comments Marit Trelstad.[29] If a divine gift disables rather than enables us, we've made a mistake in our interpretation of it.

Gift language helps us explicate the meaning of our fundamental biblical symbols, such as the cross or Pauline affirmations of justification-by-faith. But the latter are not slaves to the former. While the concept of gift illuminates God's gracious action, divine action comes first; our theological reflection in light of the concept of gift comes second. When the Holy Spirit places the living Christ in our souls, we can expect power, excitement, transformation, and vigorous activity—fueled by love—on behalf of our neighbor.

Conclusion: God as Giver and Gift

In order to stress the graciousness of God, Luther generously slathers the concept of gift over many theological expositions. Take the Trinity, for example. The three persons of the Trinity give themselves to one another, making each of them a giver and a gift within the divine life (*ad intra*). In turn, each person gives to us, making the divine both giver and gift for us (*ad extra*). "The Father gives himself to us," writes Luther. "But this gift has become obscured and useless through Adam's fall. Therefore the Son himself subsequently gave himself." It does not end there. "The Holy Spirit comes and gives himself to us also, wholly and completely."[30] Saarinen comments that this amounts to a specifically Lutheran

29. Trelstad, "Introduction: The Cross in Context," in *Cross Examinations: Readings on the Meaning of the Cross Today*, ed. Marit A. Trelstad (Minneapolis: Augsburg, 2006), 7.
30. Luther, *Confession concerning Christ's Supper* (1528), in *LW*, 37:366.

emphasis: "The trinitarian creed is rewritten from the perspective of God's self-giving."[31]

In parallel fashion, the Mass or the Sacrament of the Altar must be understood as a divine gift to us and for us. The reformers rejected the idea that on the church's altar a sacrifice is performed that propitiates God's wrath and renders satisfaction on our behalf. The priest at the altar cannot offer a sacrifice as a gift to God because Christ's death on the cross has put an end to all human sacrifices. Rather, it is God who renders satisfaction in Christ and offers the benefits to us. "For the passion of Christ was an offering and satisfaction not only for original guilt but for all other remaining sins," reads the Augsburg Confession. "Likewise, Scripture teaches that we are justified before God through faith in Christ . . . The Mass, therefore, was instituted so that the faith of those who use the sacrament should recall what benefits are received through Christ . . . For to remember Christ is to remember his benefits and realize that they are truly offered to us."[32] Every leak in the bottom of the spiritual boat is plugged by reference to God's self-giving and our receiving.

When it comes to justification-by-faith, we must avoid seeing faith as an efficacious product of human achievement. Rather, faith is a gift. Perhaps better said, faith is our act of unwrapping the gift that the Holy Spirit gives, namely, the presence of Christ. The indwelling Christ consists of both the giving of Christ and Christ as gift. "Through receiving Christ by faith, we have union with Christ. The gift is given for us, but also to us," says Saarinen rightly.[33]

In summary, the generous use of the language and conceptuality of gift becomes one of the ways we emphasize the priority of God's grace in our creation, redemption, and daily lives. There is no pill

---

31. Saarinen, *God and the Gift*, 46.
32. Augsburg Confession, art. 24, in *BC*, 71.
33. Saarinen, *God and the Gift*, 51.

we need to take to relieve the intellectual constipation brought on by the philosophical debate over the nature of gift. The employment of gift language is an attempt to explicate the significance of the gospel message, not pare down the gospel to fit a predetermined concept.

15

Sanctification by Grace

Because you have taken hold of Christ by faith, through whom you are righteous, you should now go and love God and your neighbor.

–Martin Luther[1]

Love is precisely the truest climax of what takes place in faith.

–Karl Rahner[2]

Christian theologians are accustomed to speaking of human loving as empowered and guided by God. We love because God first loved us. First John 4:11 reads: "Since God loved us so much, we also ought to love one another." But atheists and SBNRs might object to this. Human love doesn't depend on divine love, does it?

We all know atheists and agnostics who exhibit personal integrity and even give time and money to charity. It appears that their inclination to perform good works is built in to their common

1. Luther, *Commentary on Galatians*, 1535, *LW* 26:133.
2. Rahner, *TI*, 4:203.

humanity, not dependent on their religious affiliation or even religious beliefs.

Is religious belief superfluous? If it's human nature to love others, then why do we need religion? At first glance, this seems to make sense. A SBNR can appreciate an ethic of loving one's neighbor without belonging to a church, especially a church that illegitimately claims a patent on charity.

As we look at this more closely, I would like to offer two observations. First, let's make a distinction overt religious belief and divine inspiration. Might it be possible for a person who disavows religious belief to still respond to divine inspiration? A separation from institutional religion does not necessarily mean a separation from God. God can work within the unwilling or even the undiscerning.

The second observation requires a more detailed analysis. The most profound form of love—love in the form of self-sacrificing service to others—requires more than our given humanity can supply. In Christian vocabulary, this form of love is known as *agape.* Agape love seeks the welfare of the neighbor without regard to one's own benefit. While agape is more of an ideal than an actual practice, it's the ideal toward which followers of Jesus aspire. Even if those who strive to love in agapeic fashion fall short, they keep pressing forward. Pressing forward is the path that bold sinning takes.

In most situations, reciprocal altruism is the form in which we experience love. In a closed social unit, individuals help others and receive appropriate help in return. On the surface, good works look self-sacrificial. Upon closer examination, reciprocal altruism is a positive version of eye-for-an-eye or one good turn deserves another. Reciprocity is what philosophers once called *enlightened self-interest.* Service to others is still service to oneself, only indirectly. Certainly, there is nothing immoral about reciprocal altruism; our social groups require it to survive. However, we need to filter reciprocity out of the definition of agape love.

Agape love serves the other as other without regard for reciprocity. But as we discovered in our discussion of gift in chapter 14, a philosophical question is necessary: How is this possible? If we define ourselves as autonomous individuals who make willful decisions in order to pursue our self-interest, how can we divorce ourselves from ourselves in service to another person? How can a morally free person become subordinated or even submissive to the needs of someone else? We see unexpected acts of kindness almost every day. Therefore, our concern ought not to be whether it's possible for human beings to act lovingly, but rather how to explain what actually happens.

May I present my candidate and explanation? God is secretly at work within the human will to make it possible for us to transcend ourselves. That's right: it's God again. There may be some who don't want to use the term *God* here, but we must admit that some force or draw or lure lifts us up and beyond ourselves and places us in the service of the other.

Philosopher William Desmond ponders this mystery taking place before our very eyes. "Acting on the call of agapeic service is not sustainable by our will alone," he writes. "It is not enacted by autonomous will deliberately setting out to be beyond itself in service for the other. Transcending desire discovers that, in being fully itself, it is more than itself and called forth by transcendence as more than itself, transcendence as superior to it. . . . That is why I speak of a willingness before and beyond the will, or any will to power."[3] The philosopher then uses the "G" word to explain this transcendence. "The life of agapeic service is impossible if we are alone and without

---

3. William Desmond, *The William Desmond Reader,* ed. Christopher Ben Simpson (Albany, NY: SUNY 2012), 81.

the sustaining power of the good as other. . . . the familiar word (and I think best word) for transcendence itself is 'God.'"[4]

What does the theologian think about this? The theologian's work is not necessarily a matter of prescribing what we ought to believe. Sometimes the theologian can simply point to what is already there.

Augustine: For the Love of God

Here is how Augustine points to what I have been describing. By nature, we are born with the type of free will we understand as the ability to choose. We are free to choose whether we will eat pie or ice cream for desert; we are free to choose to vote for either a Democrat or a Republican; we are free to choose whether we will be spiritual or religious or atheistic. Regardless of which choice one makes, the object of the choice serves the desires and needs of the self. We are self-oriented. We are hopelessly ego-oriented. This self-orientation means freely made choices unavoidably express what we want, demand, or pursue. In our Enlightenment-based society, this natural free will is called *liberty* or, more commonly, *freedom.* By *freedom* or *free will*, I mean self-expression, ego-expression, or self-determination, which affects the world around us. We are born with it, and it is the responsibility of our government to protect and further it.

Augustine's observation here is key: natural free will is conscripted into the exclusive service of the self. All decisions are made on behalf of me. My good. My happiness. My welfare. My share in distributive justice and my revenge in retributive justice. We love, to be sure; but our love is fundamentally *amor sui,* love of oneself. Love of oneself is also known as pride, or *superbia,* the first on various lists of the

---

4. Ibid., 82.

seven deadly sins. What the natural self is unable to do is liberate itself from itself and pursue the good for the sake of the good. God is the ultimate good; on our own, the only god we can serve is *numero uno, me.* What is commonly thought to be liberty—self-expression—is actually bondage to the self and to the self's interests.

What happens in faith, says Augustine, is that the Holy Spirit visits us and reorients the self so that we can appreciate the good for its own sake. The Holy Spirit liberates us from ourselves, so to speak. It liberates the will to choose the good as the good, regardless of its benefit or lack of benefit for the self. In this way, the inner soul gains a new foundation, a divine foundation, and the will gains a secondary freedom: the ability to choose God for God's sake rather than the self's sake. In the case of agape love, we gain freedom from the self to choose the welfare of the neighbor for the sake of the neighbor.

As Augustine describes it, "The human will is divinely assisted to do the right in such manner that, besides man's creation with the endowment of freedom to choose, and besides the teaching by which he is instructed how he ought to live, he receives the Holy Spirit, whereby there arises in his soul the delight in and the love of God, the supreme and changeless Good. This gift is here and now, while he walks by faith, not yet by sight."[5] In faith, we delight in the ultimate good, in the true God who transcends the deity lodged in our moral universe. In our minds, we may not be clear on just how to imagine or picture or describe this transcendent God, but our

---

5. Augustine, "The Spirit and the Letter," in *Augustine: Later Works,* trans. John Burnaby, Library of Christian Classics 8 (Louisville: Westminster John Knox, 1955), 197. Hans Schwarz is not persuaded by Augustine's treatment of free will and human responsibility. "Despite Augustine's assertion that humans themselves are responsible for their sinfulness, this was not thought through so thoroughly as to overcome all contradictions in relation to human freedom and responsibility. It is no wonder, therefore . . . [that] his opponent Pelagius even imagined himself a confederate of Augustine." Hans Schwarz, *The Human Being: A Theological Anthropology* (Grand Rapids, MI: Eerdmans, 2013), 182–83.

ultimate concern is now lodged with God. We walk by faith, not yet by sight. Sight will come later.

I must stress how very important this singular insight of Augustine is. He introduces an alternative understanding of freedom that probably seems strange to our modern mindset. We accept natural freedom or what we call *free will*—that is, we rely upon our freedom to choose between alternatives. For most of us, this is the only definition of freedom we know. Hidden behind or underneath this freedom is another form of freedom—*Christian freedom*. This second freedom takes the form of *liberation from the self*. In natural freedom, we do not have the option of denying the self on behalf of either God or our neighbor. Every choice we make extends the self-interest of the self making the decision. In the modern world, we celebrate self-expression, self-promotion, and self-expansion. But self-expression can become a chain that binds us to the very narrow-minded pursuit of our own desires. How can we liberate ourselves from our selves? We cannot. The Holy Spirit has the power to liberate us from within, says Augustine. With the power of the Holy Spirit, we can be liberated from self-interest and self-expression and begin to appreciate the good for the sake of the good and love the neighbor for the sake of the neighbor. Nowhere in a civic liturgy will you hear a rally cry for Christian freedom; nevertheless, it is a human possibility because of God's gracious presence in the human soul.[6]

One thing I find disappointing among the medieval scholastic theologians and even the Reformers is that they reformulate Augustine's concept of Christian freedom to include the so-called *infusion of grace*. The term *infusion* seems too impersonal, in my

---

6. Please note that in the civic discussion of human freedom, what is always meant is self-expression or self-determination. The Christian understanding of freedom—*freedom from* self-expression and *freedom for* loving the neighbor—is utterly and totally ignored. Even many churches ignore the distinction between the civic and the Christian understandings of freedom.

judgment. In contrast, I think the term *grace* describes something so personal that it's deeper than personal, if this can be said. The idea of infusion of grace connotes a spiritual hypodermic needle descending from heaven and inoculating us against infection. But grace isn't a substance that can be squeezed and shot into us. Grace is a loving disposition, a personal trait of God. The Holy Spirit is a divine person. Having made my position clear, let's take notice of the language Augustine employs here. Instead of infusion, he tells us that the Holy Spirit becomes present to us in faith. The divine indwells within the human. The spirit unites with the soul. Grace connotes a relationship God has personally established with us. The self moves over, so to speak, to make room in the soul for a second self, the divine self. Each of us has but one soul, to be sure, but God is spiritually present, affirming without nullifying the personal self that each of us is.

There is more to this: our personal relationship with this loving God results in God's love working through us. "Free choice alone, if the way of truth is hidden, avails for nothing but sin; and when the right action and the true aim has begun to appeal clearly, there is still no doing, no devotion, no good life, unless it be also delighted in and loved. And that it may be loved, the love of God is shed abroad in our hearts, not by the free choice whose spring is in ourselves, but through the Holy Spirit which is given us."[7] Note that the personal presence of the Holy Spirit is "not by free choice." Rather, the Holy Spirit "is given us." The presence of the Holy Spirit liberates the self from the self so that as a self we can love the other—the good as other, God as other, and our neighbor as other. Because of the presence of the Holy Spirit, loving our neighbor is not a product of one more selfish choice. Rather, the Holy Spirit is "shed abroad" in our hearts,

7. Augustine, "Spirit and the Letter," 197–98.

says Augustine, so that we find our souls reoriented toward what is divine and ultimately good.

As we have seen, numerous interpreters of the Reformation try to drive a wedge between the Lutherans and Augustine. Those who want to say that the Reformers abandoned the traditional view—the infusion of grace effects justifying transformation—may not have given sufficient attention to what Augustine is actually saying here. By *grace*, Augustine means the indwelling of the Holy Spirit and the reorientation of the human self toward the transcendent good beyond the self. Luther, who began as an Augustinian monk, believes justifying faith marks the same transition with the same dynamics. Before we move on to delineating the Reformers' alleged departures from Augustine, let's pause to notice what happens during this important concurrence in the human soul: the indwelling presence of the Holy Spirit creates a new self that is oriented toward the good, including love for both God and neighbor.[8]

Comparing Roman Catholics, Lutherans, Reformed, and Methodists

JDDJ (*Joint Document on the Doctrine of Justification*) is a document produced by theologians who love to polish antique doctrinal jewels that are surgically incised and precise in their meaning. But as sociologist of religion Peter Berger complains, what sparkles for theologians is dull to most lay people. For the world's masses, theological gems are indistinguishable from costume jewelry. "Most

---

8. Harry J. McSorely, CSP, has produced a detailed study of Augustine and Luther on the question of free will. On the questions of natural free will in every day decisions and the enslaved will in relation to God, McSorely says that Augustine and Luther agree. This applies to the passive and active dimensions of grace as well. "Man's will is at times described as being purely passive, but this is explained in such a way as to admit an active response by man." *Luther: Right or Wrong? An Ecumenical Theological Study of Luther's Major Work, The Bondage of the Will* (New York and Minneapolis: Newman Press and Augsburg Publishing House, 1969), 361.

people, lay people, couldn't care less," comments Berger. "The denominational divisions basically define theology, and for most lay people, the theological distinctions are not terribly real."[9] The agenda of this book has been to polish arcane theological gems so that they glisten with illuminating reality, even the reality of a lay person's daily life.

Having acknowledged this, we must admit that when the theologians finally get their say, sometimes the discussion gets stubbornly complicated. Just how do theologians put together justification and sanctification? Let's discuss four alternatives: Tridentine Catholics, the Lutherans, the Reformed, and the Methodists. A careful review will be illuminative for understanding the dynamics of a life lived in gratitude to God for grace.

A measure of precision is in order here. The Council of Trent contends that infused righteousness is the formal cause of justification. To say it another way, the believer travels the road toward sanctification; having arrived at sanctification, he or she is ready for justification and salvation. According to the Council, the person of faith first sheds sin and performs works of love—a growth process that concludes with sanctification and, hence, justification. Justification is the product of the process of sanctification, which is fueled by an infusion of divine grace. If you run the sanctification race and win, then justification is your prize.[10]

9. Cited in Gregor Thuswaldner, "A Conversation with Peter L. Berger: 'How My Views Have Changed,'" *The Cresset* 77:3 (Lent 2014): 21.
10. In §121 of *From Conflict to Communion*, we find: "according to the Catholic reading, Luther's doctrine of 'forensic imputation' seemed to deny the creative power of God's grace to overcome sin and transform the justified. Catholics wished to emphasize not only the forgiveness of sins but also the sanctification of the sinner. Thus, in sanctification the Christian receives that *justice of God* whereby God makes us just." Lutheran-Roman Catholic Commission, *From Conflict to Communion: Report of the Lutheran-Roman Catholic Commission on Unity* (Leipzig: Evangelische Verlagsanstalt, 2013), http://www.lutheranworld.org/sites/default/files/ From Conflict to Communion.pdf. Rahner is a bit more nuanced, but he also emphasizes the divinizing power of God's active grace. "For God's salvific action on man is not merely a forensic imputation of the justice of Christ. And it is not merely the announcement of a purely

According to the Lutheran mind, and in contrast to the Council of Trent, justification comes first. We get the prize, and then we run the race. Justification is a unilateral act of God, solely a gift of divine grace (*sola gratia*). The justified person is *simul justus et peccator,* simultaneously justified and sinful. Full salvation is granted at this point. The life of loving follows justification, and within this life, works of love represent the freed expression of the justified believer. "Lutherans also affirm the reality of sanctification and good works, but they regard these effects as fruits rather than parts of justification itself. In this sense the Lutheran doctrine of imputed righteousness is intended to safeguard the unconditional character of God's promises in Christ."[11] Justification by grace in faith prompts the life of agape love, which Kristin Johnston Largen emphasizes: "Justification is the work of God through and through, and humans can neither contribute nor add to what God has done in Jesus Christ. All that is left is the joyful response by the believer, and the life of love, inspired by faith."[12]

For their part, Reformed theologians such as John Calvin follow the Lutherans in distinguishing justification from sanctification. Similarly, they hold that justification comes first; the justified person has been elected by God, an act of divine grace alone. But the Reformed insist with greater vehemence than the Lutherans that sanctification is necessary for salvation. The justified believer must

future act of God. Nor is it constituted merely by man's faith, however this is to be further interpreted. It is a true, real, creative action of God in grace, which renews man interiorly by making him participate in the divine nature" *TI,* 4:257.

11. H. George Anderson, T. Austin Murphy, and Joseph A. Burgess, eds., *Justification by Faith: Lutherans and Catholics in Dialogue VII* (Minneapolis: Augsburg, 1985), 50. "Grace is an event . . . the individualistic setting of the debate about *gratia imputata* versus *gratia infusa* (imputed vs. infused grace) bypasses Paul's basic [cosmic] intent." Johan Christian Beker, *Paul the Apostle* (Minneapolis: Fortress Press, 1981) 265. Regardless of just how God's grace is present in the individual believer's faith, God's grace intends a healing of the entire creation.

12. Kristin Johnston Largen, *Finding God among Our Neighbors: An Interfaith Systematic Theology* (Minneapolis: Fortress Press, 2013), 212.

respond by pursuing growth in personal holiness in order to avoid jeopardizing his or her justification. Salvation becomes associated with full reconciliation. Both justification and sanctification are components of a more comprehensive achievement—reconciliation. The starting gun announces justification, but the race is not over until the believer has reached sanctification.

Following Calvin, the Reformed have contended that the Christian receives a twofold grace of Christ (*duplex gratia Christi*), both justification and sanctification. In the words of Randall Zachman, "The grace of justification is the foundation and basis of our adoption by God, for God can only regard us as God's children if God forgives us our sins and reckons us as righteous. However, the grace of sanctification is the purpose and goal of adoption, for God adopts us so that we might actually become God's gratefully obedient children."[13] This emphasis on the dual gifts of grace led the Reformed to a place where the concept of reconciliation became inclusive of both justification and sanctification.

Methodist followers of John Wesley speak of justification as a relationship change. Justification places a person in relationship with God through Jesus Christ. By a divine act, God forgives one's sin. However, in justification alone, no real change in the believer has yet taken place. Sanctification—the pursuit of Christian perfection—follows as a fitting response to justification. The deepest desire of the Methodist is "our actual moral renovation," which happens over time.[14] Conversion, regeneration, and renewal are decisive steps in the process. According to Colin Williams, "Methodism insists that no man can drift into a right relationship to God and that the varieties of Christian experience must be marked

13. Randall Zachman, *The Assurance of Faith: Conscience in the Theology of Martin Luther and John Calvin* (Minneapolis: Fortress Press, 1993), 11.
14. Randy L. Maddox, *Responsible Grace: John Wesley's Practical Theology* (Nashville: Kingswood Books, 1994), 169–70.

by a conscious acceptance of the love of God brought within man's reach in Christ. It is this fundamental truth which the Methodist emphasis on conversion seeks to safeguard."[15] Inner renewal and transformation are what excites Methodist spirituality. Like the Reformed, the Methodist hears the starting gun announcing justification, but the race is not complete until the believer crosses the finish line marked by perfect sanctification.

Bishop Carder tells us precisely what the Methodist thinks about sanctifying grace. "God's goal for humanity is the complete restoration of the divine image and the total conformity of all creation to the image of Jesus Christ. Sanctification (from *sanctus*, holy) denotes the process by which the believer is made holy following justification."[16]

John Wesley's Christian Perfection

As long as we're attending to the Methodists, let's go back to the eighteenth century and discuss John Wesley for a moment. Wesley distinguishes justification from sanctification. "But what is it to be justified? . . . it is not the being made actually just and righteous. This is *sanctification*, which is indeed in some degree the immediate *fruit* of justification, but nevertheless is a distinct gift of God, and of a totally different nature. The one implies what God *does for us* through his Son, the other what he *works in us* by his Spirit."[17] Wesley's distinctive contribution to the Christian tradition is his detailed emphasis on sanctification.

---

15. Colin W. Williams, *John Wesley's Theology Today* (Louisville: Abingdon, 1960). 202.
16. Kenneth Carder, *Living Our Beliefs*, rev. ed. (Nashville: Discipleship Resources, 2009), 81.
17. John Wesley, Sermon 5, "Justification by Faith," §2.1, in *The Bicentennial Edition of the Works of John Wesley*, ed. Frank Baker, 35 vol. (Nashville: Abingdon, 1984), 1:87, italics in religion.

Wesley asks: "What is it to be sanctified?" He answers: "To be renewed in the image of God, in *righteousness and true holiness*." This implies that the person of faith loves God with all his or her "heart, and mind, and soul." Then Wesley connects sanctification with justification. The latter gives birth to the former. "When does inward sanctification begin? In the moment a [person] is justified. Yet, sin remains in him; yea, the seed of all sin, till he is *sanctified throughout*. From that time a believer gradually dies to sin, and grows in grace."[18] In short, when we are justified, we are still *simul justus et peccator,* justified yet sinful. Even so, because God's love is within us, we respond by pursuing a life of loving. We press forward toward transformation, toward becoming a person who becomes totally disposed toward loving both God and neighbor.

Perfection is the goal. To live in perfection, says Wesley, is to wake up in the morning with the sole motive of loving God and loving neighbor. The goal of Methodist sanctification in this life on earth is the perfect disposition toward love. "'Faith working by love' is the length and breadth and depth and height of Christian perfection," say John and brother Charles.[19]

John Wesley is quick to point out that Christian perfection does not exempt one from error. A sincerely loving person may very well make mistakes from time to time. We may be "filled with pure love, and still be liable to mistake."[20] Therefore, he adds, "*sinless perfection* is a phrase I never use."[21] Perfect sincerity in loving is possible in this life, even if exculpation from all sin is not. We may limp on occasion

---

18. John Wesley, *A Plain Account of Christian Perfection* (London: Epworth, 1952), 33, italics in original.
19. John and Charles Wesley, *Hymns and Sacred Poems* (London: Straham, 1739), viii, https://divinity.duke.edu/sites/divinity.duke.edu/files/documents/cswt/04_Hymns_and_Sacred_Poems_(1739)_mod.pdf
20. Wesley, *A Plain Account,* 42.
21. Ibid., 45, italics in original.

because of residual sin, yet our response to justification is to run the race toward sanctification.

Without being silly by exaggerating human capacities, realistic Methodists hold out a goal toward which we can aspire: perfect loving. "Perfect love, then, is an unmixed love. It is purposeful and intelligent concern for the will of God and the welfare of one's fellow human beings."[22] If we find ourselves on the road toward perfection, we will find ourselves with a daily disposition to love our neighbor for the sake of the neighbor. This is the sanctification process.

My treatment of the topic of sanctification entails a tension over two concerns that requires attention. The first concern is the process of moral improvement, which involves becoming more holy or more godly. The shape of our lives becomes formed by love. The second concern is the nature of that love, agape. Both Catholics and Protestants agree without equivocation that this love orients itself toward a transcendent good, which is expressed as the good of the neighbor. Loving God and loving neighbor are functionally equivalent, and both are distinguishable from loving self (*amor sui*) and from pride (*superbia*). Are these two concerns compatible? If I set as my goal the sanctified life and pursue it directly, I am trying to make myself holy or godly. In essence, this form of spiritual process extends my self-orientation—my self's wants and desires. As such, the pursuit of holiness produces spiritual narcisisssm and replaces agape love with self-love. The challenge is this: Does love of neighbor for the sake of the neighbor require the sacrifice of my own selfish desire to become sanctified? Is the race toward perfection doomed to failure at the starting line?

The two goals—the pursuit of sanctification and the pursuit of agape love—are affirmed together by most Christian groups in the

---

22. Wilber T. Dayton, "Entire Sanctification," in *A Contemporary Wesleyan Theology,* ed. Charles W. Carter, 2 vols. (Grand Rapids, MI: Francis Asbury, 1983), 1:533.

conversation: Roman Catholics, Reformed, Methodists, and others. The belief that these two goals are incompatible—and that neighbor love without regard to one's own personal sanctification takes priority—is the position taken by the Lutherans alone. In place of Christian perfection, the Lutherans insert the directive to sin boldly in the service of neighbor-love. Instead of complete sanctification, the Lutherans understand the end as neighbor-love, with bold sinning as the means.

Well, almost all Lutherans. A minority within the Lutheran camp yearn for such a process spirituality too. According to Michael von Brück, Luther's emphasis on justification should include "more than a forensic act: it now becomes a transformation through the power of the Spirit. While justifying grace is still *iustitia impartata,* it is also a process which changes our life."[23] Saarinen, whom I cited earlier on the nature of gift, follows a similar path. "Coming from the new Finnish school of Luther studies, I believe that justification is both forensic and effective."[24] While these two do not represent the dominant Lutheran view, the question of the relationship between justification and sanctification will not go away.

What causes the gears to grind out of sync is the Lutheran emphasis on realism. To be realistic, we must admit that daily life is a moral mess. Pure love with pure effect is not possible. On a daily basis, we find ourselves in conflicted situations, both within and without. What should we do? Sin boldly.

23. Michael von Brück, *The Unity of Reality: God, God-Experience, and Meditation in the Hindu-Christian Dialogue* (New York: Paulist, 1991), 110–11.
24. Risto Saarinen, "Living *Sola Fide:* Features of Religious Recognition," *Dialog* 52:3 (Fall 2013): 207.

Sin Boldly

Relatively few people in our century know much about Martin Luther. They have heard of Martin Luther King Jr., but who is this other guy? If Martin Luther is known, he is most often quoted for saying, "Sin boldly," which is usually accompanied by a chuckle.

Yet, "sin boldly" ranks as one of the most illuminating of Luther's spiritual insights. In no fashion is Luther advocating anti-nomianism or eudemonism. He's not removing all restraints on pride or narcissism or pleasure-seeking. In fact, he has something quite different in mind. The Reformer recognizes that we find ourselves frequently in moral dilemmas. If we are conscientious and want to pursue the right path, we may find that the right path leads to collateral damage. In some situations of conflict, a lack of action may even yield moral damage. Damned if you do; damned if you don't. In such a dilemma, Luther reminds us that grace covers us. So make a decision. Take some action. We do not have to justify ourselves because we have already been justified by God. Therefore, sin boldly.

"Actually, to put Luther's sexy quote in context (if anything about Lutheranism can be considered sexy), surely it has to be this nearly 500-year-old theological sound bite," writes Falsani.[25] So what is the context of this oft-quoted phrase? The sexy theological sound bite recalls some advice Luther gave to his colleague, Philip Melanchthon.

> If you are a preacher of grace, then preach a true and not a fictitious grace; if grace is true, you must bear a true and not a fictitious sin. God does not save people who are only fictitious sinners. Be a sinner and sin boldly, but believe and rejoice in Christ even more boldly, for he is victorious over sin, death, and the world. As long as we are here [in this world] we have to sin. This life is not the dwelling place of righteousness, but, as Peter says, we look for new heavens and a new earth in which righteousness dwells. It is enough that by the riches of

25. Cathleen Falsani, *Sin Boldly: A Field Guide for Grace* (Grand Rapids, MI: Zondervan, 2008), 105.

God's glory we have come to know the Lamb that takes away the sin of the world. No sin will separate us from the Lamb, even though we commit fornication and murder a thousand times a day. Do you think that the purchase price that was paid for the redemption of our sins by so great a Lamb is too small? Pray boldly—you too are a mighty sinner.[26]

Sin boldly!

Preach a true, not fictitious, grace!

Believe boldly!

Rejoice boldly!

Make moral decisions carefully but courageously!

In sum, if sinful action is unavoidable, be honest and follow the best path your judgment can discern. Make moral decisions carefully but courageously!

Might such moral logic apply to a secular situation? On May 22, 2013, President Barack Obama addressed the student body at the National Defense University at Fort McNair. He appealed to just war criteria to justify his use of drones to bomb terrorist targets in foreign countries. "America's actions are legal. We were attacked on 9/11. Within a week, Congress overwhelmingly authorized the use of force. Under domestic law, and international law, the United States is at war with al Qaeda, the Taliban, and their associated forces. We are at war with an organization that right now would kill as many Americans as they could if we did not stop them first. So this is a just war—a war waged proportionally, in last resort, and in self-defense."[27] A war that is proportional, a last resort, and in self-defense is a just war. Furthermore, it's legal because it is congressionally authorized. Just war theory among Christian ethicists has, for centuries, provided us with an application of the sin boldly principle. To perpetrate

26. Luther, Letter to Philip Melanchthon, August 1, 1521, in *LW*, 48:281–82.
27. "President Obama's Speech on the Future of the War on Terror," *Washington Post*, May 23, 2013, http://www.washingtonpost.com/blogs/wonkblog/wp/2013/05/23/read-president-obamas-speech-on-the-future-of-the-war-on-terror/.

violence in war leads to evil and suffering, pure and simple. Even in a justified war, countless people die. The pursuit of justice is violent—that's an inescapable reality. Make no mistake: justice kills.

In addition to this appeal to legality, Obama's justification also appealed, in part, to what Luther might call the mandate to sin boldly. The president had to confront a situation in which non-action would also be deadly. He had to weigh alternatives that led to either more or fewer deaths. Drone killing saves lives, he argued. This rhetoric was not a smoke screen; the president actually believed what he said to be true. Because all persons—both Americans and non-Americans—possess dignity, it is the president's moral obligation as commander in chief to reduce as much as possible the death toll of collateral damage. Working out of a secularized variant of the Just War Theory, the president said: "Before any strike is taken, there must be near-certainty that no civilians will be killed or injured—the highest standard we can set."

Next, he weighed the alternatives: Should we attack or not? This last point is critical, because much of the criticism about drone strikes—at home and abroad—understandably centers on reports of civilian casualties. . . . It is a hard fact that U.S. strikes have resulted in civilian casualties, a risk that exists in all wars. For the families of those civilians, no words or legal construct can justify their loss. For me, and those in my chain of command, these deaths will haunt us as long as we live, just as we are haunted by the civilian casualties that have occurred through conventional fighting in Afghanistan and Iraq.[28] Of all the alternatives, one of which is doing nothing, the alternative that best preserves human lives includes using drones in counter-terrorism attacks, which may result in civilian casualties.

This American president's appeal to a stripped-down Just War Theory provides us with a secular example of the logic behind

28. Ibid.

Luther's directive to "sin boldly." In this world, the sanctified life is not possible, even for a person justified by God in his or her faith. Even if just action is motivated by pure love, the effect will encompass more than what we intend. No matter which way we turn, collateral damage will be part of the fallout. The person of faith has no choice but to live simultaneously as saint and sinner, *simul iustus et peccator.* To be sanctified in this situation is to return again and again to our gratitude to God for justification. "The *simul* makes all such schemes of progress impossible. The justification given is a total state, a complete, unconditional gift. From that point of view true sanctification is simply to 'shut up and listen!' For there can be no *more* sanctification than where every knee bends and every mouth is silent before God, the Holy One."[29]

In summary, the concept of boldly sinning presupposes two inescapable realities: the impossibility of pure moral action devoid of self-interest and the acknowledgement that moral action frequently takes place within a contextual situation where non-action is morally problematic. If the moral agent need not concern himself or herself with self-justification *corem Deo*, then he or she is liberated to render the best practical judgment and act accordingly.

We turn next to ethics. As I have already said, the ethicist focuses energy on doing the very thing that takes us the farthest away from God; the ethicist draws a line between good and evil and tries to place himself or herself on the good side of the line. The ethicist engages in direct and unmitigated self-justification. Yet, when it comes to modern institutional life, without ethics it is impossible for people of faith to love the world and to love their neighbors. All people of faith must be ethicists. Sin boldly.

---

29. Gerhard O. Forde, *Justification by Faith—A Matter of Death and Life* (Minneapolis: Fortress Press, 1982), 50, italics in original.

More on Ethics for Bold Sinners

Perhaps the most courageous form of sinning boldly is the commitment to ethics.[30] I previously described ethics as the most sinful of human activities because it constitutes the most sophisticated form of self-justification. Ethical justification by itself estranges us from God because God alone has the job of justifying. Despite this, I am promoting the discipline of ethics. I honestly believe conscientious ethicists make our world a better place. They cannot make our world a perfect place, but they can foster what is better over what is worse. To pursue ethics is to sin boldly.

Ethics is a theoretical discipline that considers how can we love the neighbor effectively in a world of intersecting conflicts. It tries to draw practical lines between good and evil, between just and unjust, between right and wrong, and, of course, between better and worse. Because this moral line drawing is the task of ethics, the ethicist commits the sin of self-justification. As I have discussed throughout this book, the pursuit of virtue does damage just like the pursuit of vice. The Christian can only breathe a sigh of relief for divine grace and continue to pursue the ethical life by sinning boldly.

Justification yields justice. In other words, those of us who respond to God's gracious justification of us become motivated to pursue justice for others in this unjust world. Saarinen affirms that "justified sinners are called to care for justice in their families, communities,

---

30. At risk of overstatement, Lutheran spirituality tends toward living ethically on behalf of the need of the neighbor, in contrast to the pursuit of sanctification or personal holiness for the Christian with justifying faith. In the Reformed tradition, sanctification (as a human response to justification) is necessary for reconciliation to attain completion. In somewhat enigmatic fashion, Hans Küng seems to recognize this. "The Catholic understands by 'sanctification' primarily the objective and ontological holiness (*heiligkeit*) achieved in man by God. The Protestant emphasizes the subjective and ethical sanctification (*heiligung*) brought about by man. Both are valid provided the differences are seen in their unity." *Justification: The Doctrine of Karl Barth and a Catholic Reflection* (Louisville: Westminster John Knox, 1981), 268.

societies, and in the world as a whole."[31] Deliberating over this pursuit of justice is best identified with the term *ethics.*

What is the foundation for ethics? Many in the Reformation tradition appeal to the analogy of the good tree bearing good fruit. Accordingly, the person of faith becomes the good tree by virtue of justification by grace; and this good tree then bears works of love that lead to moral accomplishment. Forde provides an example of this logic. "The good tree will bear good fruit. But we are concerned here with what makes the tree good so that it *can* bear fruit. The Christian life must be seen as a faith, a vision, a hope, a basic hold on life effected by God's act in Jesus Christ, which leads subsequently to attitudes and actions in the world for others."[32] Faith gives us the attitude of love, and this love bears moral fruit.

George Forell explains what is behind the good tree analogy. "Luther brought a complete change in the generally accepted definition of love. . . . Now Luther defined Christian love as self-giving, spontaneous, overflowing as the love of God. . . . It is on the basis of this definition of love as overflowing, spontaneous love that Luther's ethical principle must be understood. . . . For Luther, the love which is faith active towards the neighbor was a gift of God."[33] Peura similarly emphasizes that our love is actually divine love working from within us. "It is actually God himself who extends through our lives his love toward all of those who need his love and want to be saved. We, like all other creatures, are the hands and all of

31. Risto Saarinen, "Ethics in Lutheran Theology: The Three Orders," *Seminary Ridge Review* 5:2 (Spring 2003): 37–53.
32. Gerhard Forde, "Christian Life," *Christian Dogmatics,* ed. Carl E. Braaten and Robert W. Jenson, 2 Vols. (Minneapolis: Fortress Press, 1984), 2,397, italics in original.
33. George W. Forell, "Martin Luther: Theologian of the Church," *Word and World* 2 (1994): 27.

the means of God's unselfish love."[34] The tree that bears good fruit is God's tree, so to speak.

The difficulty with the good tree analogy is that it restricts itself to motivation. The good tree is motivated by God's love to bear luscious fruit for those in the vicinity who are present to pick it. What this model fails to take into account is sober analysis, sound judgment, effective cooperation, institutional channels, and creative action. Much of our ethical thinking and moral action in contemporary society takes institutional form, wherein the loving disposition of individuals becomes invisible amid the flurry of policies, procedures, and programs.

A positive fruit of the good tree analogy is that it places moral responsibility on the shoulders of the person, not on the person's code of ethics or moral law. Meilaender reminds us of a point I made earlier in this book: "God addresses us and calls us to himself [and this call] constitutes us as persons."[35] We make moral decisions and take ethical actions as persons, as selves, as souls. As persons, we are determiners of how we act and, to some degree, we determine what happens as a result of our actions. What we experience as human freedom is better understood as the fact that each of us is a person who determines what happens. Self-determination is what we mean by freedom, at least freedom of the will. A person of faith acts out of faithfulness, contends Meilaender. The person of faith loves other persons. "Our task is nothing less than this: to achieve within human life the love that is a dim reflection of the life of God."[36]

34. Peura, "What God Gives Man Receives: Luther on Salvation," in *Union in Christ: The New Finnish Interpretation of Luther*, ed. Carl E. Braaten and Robert W. Jenson (Grand Rapids, MI: Eerdmans, 1998), 95.
35. Gilbert C. Meilaender, *Faith and Faithfulness: Basic Themes in Christian Ethics* (Notre Dame, IN: University of Notre Dame Press, 1991), 45.
36. Ibid., 48.

The most distinctive motive of the loving soul is generosity. "Generosity is kindness or munificence that goes beyond the moral minimum to do no harm, to fulfill one's obligations, or simply to refrain from defrauding or stealing from others. It is a readiness to share liberally," says Childs.[37] Generosity rides up and out of the justified soul on the agape escalator, rising higher than any moral prescription can demand.

This focus on faith's motivation makes ethical theorizing and moral living complicated in secular institutions when devout Christians take up a common cause with a plurality of individuals possessing a wide variety of motivations. The love expressed by an individual is subject to many translations and emendations and alterations before the neighbor benefits. "We do not need to wait for the whole world to be converted to justification by faith in Jesus Christ before we can work together with our non-Christian friends for earthly justice against hunger, homelessness, oppression, exploitation, racism, sexism, and other evils," says Forell.[38]

This common cause draws together Roman Catholics, Protestants, and others in cooperative concert. Pope Francis paves the path for believers and atheists to join hands and trod the path together. "The Lord created us in His image and likeness, and we are the image of the Lord, and He does good and all of us have this commandment at heart: do good and do not do evil. All of us." In a homily delivered May 22, 2013, the pontiff pressed for an open mind so that Catholics could partner with non-Catholics on ethical agendas.

> Good works are grounded in creation, not redemption. Therefore, Christians should acknowledge good works wherever they are performed, by Catholics or non-Catholics. This applies even to atheists. 'Father, this is not Catholic! He cannot do good.' Yes, he can . . . The

---

37. James M. Childs, Jr., "Generosity," *Dialog* 52:1 (Spring 2013): 1.
38. Forell, "Martin Luther," 213.

Lord has redeemed all of us, all of us, with the Blood of Christ: all of us, not just Catholics. Everyone! 'Father, the atheists?' Even the atheists. Everyone! We must meet one another doing good. 'But I don't believe, Father. I am an atheist!' But do good: we will meet one another there.[39]

Regardless of how one comes down theologically on justification and sanctification, the Holy Father encourages mutual respect combined with enthusiastic cooperation between believers and non-believers in performing good works. The ethicists can help us by weighing better and worse alternatives so that we can choose.

The Third Use of the Law

Ethical theorizing and neighbor love require giving attention to the law. In previous chapters we looked briefly at the law. Whether the law comes to us as revealed in the Ten Commandments or in the form of natural law or even in the form of wisdom gained by our elders, it is one law, and it functions in three different ways. Directly or indirectly, we think that God's law is responsible for the construction of our moral universe.

The first use of the law is the political or civil use, as I have already said. According to the first use, we try to build and maintain a community organized around fairness, justice, and peace. We use the letter of the law and even the spirit behind the letter as the template for the community in which we live. We strive to emulate on earth the moral universe we believe originates in heaven.

The second use of the law is the pedagogical or theological use. According to the second use, we allow the law to judge us. Like looking at ourselves in a mirror, the law reveals to us who we are.

---

39. "Pope Says Atheists Who Do Good Are Redeemed, Not Just Catholics," *Huffington Post*, May 23, 2013, http://www.huffingtonpost.com/2013/05/22/pope-francis-good-atheists_n_3320757.html.

Measured according to the law's standards, we find ourselves missing the mark and coming up short. To our chagrin, we discover that we are sinners.

The second use is much more difficult for us than the first. As I discussed earlier, we innately love justice. We pursue justice. But when the standards of justice judge us for failing, we resist this judgment and engage in the fruitless effort of self-justification. We pretend to others and to ourselves that we are just, regardless of the truth. The second use of the law is to reveal to us a truth we want to deny.

The gospel provides the dialectical counterpoint to the law in its second use. Whereas the law accuses, the gospel forgives. Whereas the law condemns, the gospel saves. Whereas the law declares us unjust, the gospel declares us just.[40] One might say that law and gospel come together like birthday cake and ice cream.

Is there a third use of the law? What role does the law play in the life of someone who has heard the gospel message and responded with faith? Once the sinner is forgiven and declared just, does the law gain a new function? Once one enjoys a personal relationship with the God of Jesus Christ that transcends the law in grace, does one's conscience change?

Some Protestants proffer a third use of the law. Here's how Calvin puts it: "The third and principal use . . . finds its place among believers, in whose hearts the Spirit of God already lives and reigns. . . . The law is to the flesh like a whip to an idle and balky ass, to arouse it to work. Even for a spiritual man not yet free of the weight of the flesh, the law remains a constant sting that will not let him

---

40. "Because sin remains a reality in their life, Christians constantly need both law and gospel; law, to lead them to repentance *and* to guide their life in the Spirit; and gospel, to forgive their repeated failure to live perfectly according to God's will even with the Spirit at work in their life." Günther Gassmann and Scott Hendrix, *Fortress Introduction to the Lutheran Confessions* (Minneapolis: Fortress Press, 1999), 62, italics in original.

stand still."[41] Now, just a minute, Mr. Calvin! Didn't I describe the person of faith who trusts God and in whom the person of Christ is present as one who spontaneously expresses God's love? Didn't I describe faith as active in love? If this is the case, why would we need to beat ourselves with the whip of the law like a jackass who refuses to work? There seems to be some incongruity here.

The Solid Declaration of the Formula of Concord tries to clarify this apparent incongruity. Because the person of faith is *simul justus et peccator,* the *peccator* still requires the law as both guide and disciplinarian. The New Adam, Christ, has not yet fully expunged the Old Adam. The law still applies to the person of faith. "Therefore, in this life, because of these desires of the flesh, the faithful elect, reborn children of God need not only the law's daily instruction and admonition, its warning and threatening. Often they also need its punishments."[42] Like Calvin, the Solid Declaration wants the law to kick the believer in the . . . donkey.

The entire mood imbuing the concept of the three uses seems unnecessarily negative, in my judgment. Article 6 of the Formula of Concord identifies the three uses with just a tad less negativity than Calvin. "The law has been given for three reasons: first, that through it external discipline may be maintained against the unruly and the disobedient; second, that people may be led through it to a recognition of their sins; third, after they have been reborn—since nevertheless the flesh still clings to them—that precisely because of the flesh they may have a sure guide, according to which they can orient and conduct their entire life."[43] What is important here is the delineation of three uses of one divine law. Yet why must it refer to God's law in such negative terms? Where's the joy? This description

---

41. Calvin, *Inst,* 2.7.12, 1:360.
42. *BC,* 588.
43. Ibid., 502.

fails to recognize the innate love for justice that motivates so many of us. As human beings, we are fundamentally oriented toward what is good, just, and true. We welcome the divine law in its first use, even if the second use twists us in knots. If and when the gospel does its work, we become liberated from self-justification and are able to more robustly embrace the divine law in its first use.

What function does the law in its third use perform? I think that it is more helpful to think of the law as a guide than a whip. However, I seem to be out of sync with the Calvinists and the Lutherans on this point because all advocates of a third use point to the Old Adam or the residual flesh rather than to the spontaneous motive to love the neighbor as God loves.

I would like to suggest that the third use is a return to the first use. Instead of understanding the law strictly in the negative sense as a disciplinarian, we could think positively by turning our attention toward our natural thirst for justice and our innate delight in what is good. The third use would encourage us to slake our thirst for justice by pursuing justice in its distributive, retributive, and restorative forms. If a person of faith is supposed to be the New Adam but the Old Adam is still haunting him, then the third use of the law would provide guidance and wisdom for the New Adam to pursue love of neighbor. As I see it, the problem in Calvin and the Solid Declaration is that both ascribe the need of the law's third use to the Old Adam. This is a *non sequitur* if the third use is aimed at the New Adam. I believe the justified person of faith will spontaneously retrieve his or her natural appreciation for the good as well as his or her inclination to pursue the law in its first use so as to structure our society according to the principles of justice. Put the whip back in the buggy shed.

The Law Needs Ethical Interpretation

What exactly does the law in its first and third use say? Let's ask the ethicists. In our modern and complex world, we need to rely upon ethical theorists to interpret the law and show us the way justice will lead. Ethicists cannot simply repristinate inherited laws, even biblical laws. Rather, ethicists need to be creative because the complex context in which we live daily confronts us with new challenges requiring new responses. We cannot rely upon a set of laws formulated in the past to provide moral guidance, at least not detailed moral guidance. As atheist Bertrand Russell frequently remarked, he had no trouble with the tenth commandment because he was never tempted to covet his neighbor's ass—most likely because he lived in the city and his neighbor didn't have a donkey. If the tenth commandment is to make sense today, it needs a bit of interpretation. Let's ask the ethicists to help us with the interpretation.

To obey God's law—that is, to employ ethical deliberation to guide one's service to the world as our neighbor—requires that we be creative. Love requires creativity. Recall Jesus' parable of the Good Samaritan who found a man, beaten and robbed and lying on the side of the road. No existing law prescribed in detail what he ought to do. He acted creatively. Luke 10:33-34: "But a Samaritan while traveling came near him; and when he saw him, he was moved with pity. He went to him and bandaged his wounds, having poured oil and wine on them. Then he put him on his own animal, brought him to an inn, and took care of him." In response, we might ask why the Samaritan took the injured man to an inn Why didn't he take the patient to the nearest Good Samaritan hospital? There's one in virtually every city. Oh, that's right! Good Samaritan hospitals did not exist then. Could it be that the historical establishment of Good Samaritan hospitals is a creative action taken by people of faith who love their neighbors?

As modern urban life becomes increasingly complex, no inherited set of laws or moral prescriptions can cover all the challenges we face. We find ourselves in situations where we must make decisions, and ours is an era of choice. What a person motivated by love requires is the courage to take responsibility for choice and make creative decisions. Pannenberg contends that our very commitment to love leads to ethical choices. "Even to discover the plight of those I encounter on my way through life requires an act of creative imagination. . . . A situation is never by itself clearly ethical; it is so only when confronted by a person who makes ethical decisions. Only the creative imagination of love discovers in a situation a need and at the same time the means for meeting it."[44]

In its third use, the law applies to much more than merely restraining the flesh or disciplining the Old Adam within us. Instead, the law provides an inspiration and guide for pursuing love of neighbor and love of the world God has created to house our neighbors. The law in its third use—which is actually the first use—facilitates the positive expression of God's love at work within the person of faith.

The first or political use of the law may be the form that a bold sinner adopts to express love, yet no use of the law can fully encapsulate the propelling motive: faith active in love. Meilaender reminds us eloquently that law "cannot capture successfully one of the great themes of the Christian life: self-giving and even self-sacrifice on behalf of the neighbor, done with a glad and willing heart."[45] The practical product of faith active in love is social justice, which is what the first use of the law sponsors. "Faith must be active in love, and love, in turn, must seek justice for the neighbor."[46]

44. Wolfhart Pannenberg, *Ethics*, trans. Keith Crim (Louisville: Westminster, 1981), 65.
45. Meilaender, *Faith and Faithfulness*, 123.
46. Ibid., 147.

In content, the third use of the law is identical to the first. If anything is added, it's the freedom and encouragement to love creatively, imaginatively, and aggressively.

The Law, the Gospel, and Soul Formation

God's law in its second use risks retarding healthy self-actualization and, thereby, squelching the soul. All by itself, the law demands self-obliteration by conforming the self to a heteronomous standard, by structuring the inner life solely according to an outer measure, by prompting guilt for missing the mark. Translating the law into the demand for self-giving love on a daily basis makes even the love commandment seem oppressive.

To be sure, God's law is not alone in wreaking havoc on one's inner life. Social standards set by media advertising—including athletic prowess, slim waist lines, celebrity profiles, luxurious lifestyles, happy families, and entrepreneurs' success—tear apart our inner souls with feelings of inadequacy. Whether overcome by the sublime law of God or by the images dominating today's media, the fragile soul writhes in self-doubt and psychic pain.

Fragile souls come in two types according to feminist theologians Catherine Keller and Lisa Dahill. The first type, the *separative self,* refers to the autonomous male, who is an independent soul separated as much as possible from the demands of others. In its fragility, the separative self may require firm, even rigid, ego boundaries. We've met him in our military unit or on the athletic field or in the board room: the braggart, the self-aggrandizer, the windbag. He displays his medals, fondles his trophies, and broadcasts his accomplishments. At first glance, he appears self-confident; but the soft underbelly reveals a desperate need to fulfill the cultural image of the man as a man—strong, independent, and triumphant. Without this introjected self-image, he fears the threat of non-being, of insipient nothingness.

The second type, the *soluable self,* characterizes the much more relational female. While the soluable woman complements the separative man, this may not in itself be healthy for the woman. Keller describes soluability this way: "Women's tendency to dissolve emotionally and devotionally into the other is a subjective structure internalized by individual women, but imposed by the [patriarchal] superstructure. Woman is to wait: for her very self, her self-definition, and the advent of the hero who will bring her joy."[47]

We met the soluable woman in Jane Wyatt, who starred in the now antiquated television series, *Father Knows Best.* Her identity is established by her "Mrs.," and her success is measured by the success of her children. The self gets swallowed up in the swirl and abandons its center. Without the swirl of relationships, she fears the nothingness at the center.

It does nothing to bolster the fragility of the separative or the soluable self by demanding change or transformation. We can demand that men cease hiding behind patriarchic protections—that they become more relational, more connective, more vulnerable. We can demand that women become more assertive, more independent, more self-reliant. After all, this is what social justice demands. Perhaps this is even what God demands. We might even refer to this demand as God's law in its first use.

But this demand for social justice and healthy self-actualization can easily slip into the law in its second use. It provides a mirror for us to measure ourselves, a measure revealing that we are missing the mark. Some of the males among us might find it difficult to surrender patriarchy, and some females might find they cannot separate their

---

47. Catherine Keller, *From a Broken Web: Separation, Sexism and Self* (Boston: Beacon, 1986), 13.

identities from their families. What then? Condemnation? Guilt? Shame? Will our selves have failed to become fulfilled souls?

Dahill is concerned about social justice, especially women who are victims of abuse. Because most victimized women suffer at the hands of men, the split between the separative self and the soluable self exacerbates the injustice endured by abused women. It is our responsibility as Christians to identify with the victim, to look at the matter of self-development from the underside. "This view from below has explosive potential for the structures of self, faith, and society; yet the dynamite it packs is not that of destruction but of the Gospel itself," she writes. "And I am claiming it [the gospel] as well for those on the underside of selfhood, and more broadly for the despised or wounded aspects of the selves of all human beings."[48] For the fragile soul made fragile in part by a soluable self enduring abuse, Dahill offers the gospel as the presence of the crucified Christ and the presence of those of us who have been called as Christ's disciples. The movement of divine grace, according to Dahill, takes the form of other selves—God's self or the self of another faithful person—becoming present to the underdeveloped if not abused self of the victim. Gospel means presence, divine presence, and this presence makes a self where previously a self may have been underdeveloped or unrelational.

The content of the law is not found in its content. Whether we read the Ten Commandments, Jesus' teachings, Civil Rights legislation, UN treaties, or the Scout Law, we find that literal laws require nuanced interpretation. Application requires interpretation. This is what our ethicists help us do. Thank God for the ethicists!

48. Lisa E. Dahill, *Reading from the Underside of Selfhood: Bonhoeffer and Spiritual Formation* (Eugene, OR: Pickwick, 2009), 225.

The Breath of the Holy Spirit in the Church

Along with the gospel and a life motivated by love, the law in its first, second, and third uses is more than an individual matter. Each of us thirsts for the profound personal transformation promised in the Christian message, but we don't have to go it alone. We share the company and encouragement of others in our faith community: the one, holy, catholic, and apostolic church.

What is the church? Rahner sings a melody sweet to Lutheran ears: it is word and sacrament that defines the essence of the church. "Word and sacrament constitute the Church. Or, to put it more exactly: the power to preach the word of God by the authority of God and of his Christ, and the power to administer the sacraments to men are the two basic powers of the Church which are constitutive of its essence."[49] God is present in the preached word and sacraments. This presence collapses into itself both the remembrance of the past and the expectation of the future.

"The gospel of Christ knows of no religion but social; no holiness but social holiness," say John and Charles Wesley repeatedly."[50] Each individual becomes who he or she is in Christ through the shared life of the Christian community—through hymn singing, communal prayer, and the life of service, in addition to word and sacrament. Marilyn McCord Adams, who has made a study of horrendous evils such as massacres and genocides, locates the church metaphysically, right between the soul and the cosmos.

> My approach from horrors identifies Christ as the One in Whom all things hold together, the One Who becomes the center of the macrocosm by hypostatically uniting Godhead to the microcosm. It also identifies Christ in the hearts of all people, laboring as Inner Teacher to become the center of each and every individual self. It remains to say

---

49. Rahner, *TI*, 4:254.
50. John and Charles Wesley, *Hymns and Sacred Poems*, viii.

something about the intermediate level, about the *mediocosm* which is the Church![51]

Adams is telling us that the church functions as the mediocosm that synthesizes soul and cosmos, self and universe, the Easter anticipation and the eschatological consummation.

The church is like an arc sparking between two temporal terminals: Jesus' Easter resurrection of yesterday and the advent of God's promised new creation tomorrow. The gospel as justification, new creation, and proclamation electrifies our souls and energizes our community of souls. God's voltaic tomorrow gets discharged today in our lives of faithful loving. We can feel the galvanizing power when we find ourselves among our friends in faith.

In addition to our friends-in-faith, who provide the power of proleptic living in light of God's promise, the Holy Spirit empowers us. "The Holy Spirit gives the church its narrative identity as a Spirit-breathed people, in whom the Spirit breathes new life, life that is experienced not only existentially through the gift of faith but also through the lived-out reality of forgiveness of sins and transformed relationships. This is a community that grows in holiness because the Holy Spirit is at work within and through its members," writes Cheryl Peterson.[52] The galvanic power of the Holy Spirit applies to the church catholic, including Roman Catholics, Lutherans, Presbyterians, Methodists, and all those who worship at the foot of the cross. Oswald Bayer adds the indispensable eschatological

---

51. Marilyn McCord Adams, *Christ and Horrors: The Coherence of Christology* (Cambridge: Cambridge University Press, 2006), 200. The individual is the microcosm, and the universe the macrocosm. "The gospel proclaims the new state of affairs that God has initiated in Christ, one that concerns the nations and creation. Individual souls and their experience are only important within that worldwide context and for the sake of the world. Christ as the object and content of the gospel is not simply the means for individual holiness and private experiences." Beker, *Paul the Apostle,* 8.

52. Cheryl M. Peterson, *Who Is the Church? An Ecclesiology for the Twenty-First Century* (Minneapolis: Fortress Press, 2013), 128.

anticipation when he avers, "The Christian church is not some minority group, but the renewed humanity, 'a new creation' (2 Cor. 5:17)."[53]

Conclusion

"The content of the gospel, its understanding, and its appropriation fuse in the interpretive act, inasmuch as the gospel aims directly at the *Amen* of the obedience of faith."[54] Does the obedience of faith imply that we should sin boldly? Yes.

In terms of a spiritual time line, Lutheran Protestants place justification first, followed by sanctification. But is this the way it actually happens? Is there really a temporal distinction, or is it a logical distinction? For those of us blessed with a birth and baptism into a Christian family and a Christian church, we find ourselves well on the road to sanctification long before we realize that grace has already gifted us with justification. Justification may logically precede sanctification, even if this isn't the case psychologically.

The Reformation emphasis on the priority and exclusivity of divine grace in justification makes this point: it is God who justifies and saves. When we wake up and realize this, it's time to say "thank you" to God. For the person who has realized the presence of divine grace, an attitude of gratitude increases.

This attitude of gratitude can appear in our lives at any time. It does not matter which milestone we have just passed on the road toward full sanctification. The living Christ can breathe love through us whether or not we are aware of his presence. In fact, we might

53. Oswald Bayer, "Preaching the Word," *Lutheran Quarterly* 23:3 (Autumn 2009): 252.
54. Beker, *Paul the Apostle,* 121. "The message of justification and the doctrine of justification are *explications of the gospel,*" says Harding Meyer, "The Text—The Justification of the Sinner—in the Context of Previous Ecumenical Dialogues on Justification," in *Justification by Faith: Lutherans and Catholics,* 75, italics in original.

experience a moment when we look back and realize that this has been happening for some time. In fact, sanctification or neighbor-love might be fully operative before we become aware of it or make a conscious commitment to full trust. We should thank the theologians for clarifying the difference between justification and sanctification, though these differences are conceptual abstractions. In day-to-day life, we live with a messy mixture. Sin boldly.

16

The Life of Beatitude

Let thy religion be the religion of the heart. . . . at the same time [let] all which is in thee [be] athirst for God, the living God, longing to awake up after his likeness, and to be satisfied with it. Be thou a lover of God and of all mankind.

–John Wesley[1]

The future comes first. Then the present. Who you and I will be in God's future kingdom influences, if not determines, who we are today and even who we have been in the past. Trust and hope in life of beatitude forms us into robust souls.

Who We Will Be Determines Who We Are Now

Our present and our past are defined by our future, by God's future. This makes the human soul's identity contingent, dependent on what

---

1. John Wesley, Sermon 25, "Sermon on the Mount," §5, in *The Bicentennial Edition of the Works of John Wesley*, ed. Frank Baker, 35 vol. (Nashville: Abingdon, 1984), 1:570–71.

we will yet become. The end of the story will retroactively determine the meaning of all previous chapters in this story.[2]

Let me repeat what I said earlier—who we are is constituted by our entire biography, by our whole narrative, which awaits completion. Now, it is likely that you may have forgotten many parts of your story, events that have drifted away and are no longer retrievable by your active memory. You may even think that much of your past is no longer relevant, no longer meaningful. However, all of what you have been is lodged in God's memory and is being readied for transformation at resurrection. The Christian promise of resurrection includes a holistic transformation of all that makes you you. The advent of God's everlasting kingdom does not cancel the past; it redeems and heals the past by integrating all of the parts into a comprehensive and meaningful whole.

The eschatological future will not be just one more new day in a long sequence of days. Rather, the eschatological transformation will be a consummation. As consummation, God's future gathers up and reassembles all events of the past and re-relates them according to a healed pattern. Each one of us will undergo a resurrection of our entire biography with connections to all of our relationships. Even if you or I occasionally forget the past, God will not. Moreover, the way God remembers heals.

Will our resurrection into God's everlasting kingdom consist of a soulectomy? Will God simply yank your spiritual soul out of your body and airmail it to heaven, leaving your physical body for the

---

2. As we explicate the concept of *beatitude*, I wish to integrate the tensile relationship between the future and the present. Johanne Stubbe Teglbjærg Kristensen at the University of Copenhagen illuminates this integration in her study of hope. "The resurrection of Christ constitutes the origin of theological hope . . . the future is in some way integrated into the present as a decisive aspect of hope or even regarded as the condition for the experienced present." *Body and Hope* (Tübingen: Mohr Siebeck, 2013), 5.

worms on Earth? No. The idea of such a soulectomy does not seem to cohere with the notion of eschatological consummation.

Theologians these days seldom if ever separate the soul from the body or spirit. They customarily speak of salvation for body, soul, and spirit together, holistically.[3] In light of what I have just said, I might as well add the time span of our life that is, body, soul, and spirit together as a biography, even biography-in-relationship. If salvation is healing, then full healing implies a healing of the whole with all of its parts, even its temporal parts. Still more awesome is the thought that God's eschatology provides a consummation for all of physical and cosmic history, the advent of a new creation within which we play a part. This advent of eschatological healing is the moment of our soul's final constitution. We can come to know our own souls ahead of time—now, today—by recognizing the presence within us of the resurrected Christ, who is placed there by the Holy Spirit. God's eschatological tomorrow retroactively defines our souls today. In other words, our faith in God's tomorrow makes us who we are today.

"It is from the future that the abiding essence of things discloses itself, because the future alone decides what is truly lasting," writes Pannenberg.[4] It is God's promised future that gives being to our souls, lasting definition.

Faith and Fulfillment

It takes faith in God's future to become a robust person. As you may recall, the center of the swirling is a virtual vacuum. It's empty. It

---

3. "There is a unity in the dimensions of human existence—the whole man is called to salvation—and there is an inner dynamism of grace by which it becomes effective in a healing, sanctifying, and divinizing way in all the dimensions of man." Rahner, *TI*, 5:105.

4. Pannenberg, *Anthropology in Theological Perspective*, trans. Matthew J. O'Connell (Louisville: Westminster John Knox, 1985), 525.

lasts only as long as the surrounding winds continue to blow. When a hurricane expires, so does the eye of the hurricane. Yet God offers the promise of a fulfillment to come, a divine granting of being to the soul in everlasting relationship. If we embrace today that promise for tomorrow's reality, our souls form around that promise, and we become what we trust. This is because the one in whom we place our hope is trustworthy.

By affirming "the becoming of the human as person" in light of God's promise, says Dominican theologian Richard Schenk, our very trust in that promise yields a robust fulfillment of personhood.[5] We hope that grace over time will show that we really are freed for freedom towards God, capable of receiving a gift of hope in more than what we can provide ourselves. The "more than" what we can provide becomes a distinctive part of one's very self.

In a previous chapter, I asked: How does the person justified by God's grace in faith become sanctified and effectively just? From this question, let's turn to an even more difficult one. How do we transform the nothingness of the empty vortex into a substantial self, an essential soul? How does the "hypothetical point" become an eternal reality? How does the soul become formed or reformed according to our vision of God's future salvation?

What has been implicit we now make explicit, namely, God's grace gives each of us a centered self, an essential soul. To say this a bit differently: we are who we are because of our relationship with God, a relationship bestowed upon us by God's Spirit. Still more precisely, we are who we are because of who we will be in God's promised future. To trust God now transforms us into our future selves ahead of time. If we reverse the terms, to trust God now means

5. Richard Schenk, "Von der Hoffnung, Person zu sein. Theologische Überlegungen zur Diskontinuität von Verheißung und Vertrauen," in *Kontinuität der Person: Zum Versprechen und Vertrauen,* ed. Richard Schenk, *Collegium Philosophicum,* Band 2 (Stuttgart-Bad Cannstatt: Friedrich Fromman Verlag-Günther Holzboog, 1998), 176.

that today we enjoy some of who we will be tomorrow. One's soul and hence one's personhood exist at the metaxy, the point of tension between the present and the ultimate future.

At this point, you may want to exclaim: "Wait just a darned minute! I'm already autonomous. I've got a self right now, thank you very much! I don't need to ask God to add another one." Well, that's not exactly what I am saying here. Recall the contrast between the human and the divine, which I pointed out earlier: God's perimeter is nowhere, and God's center is everywhere. God's center does not compete with ours; rather, it complements and fulfills our center. Tillich calls this relationship between one's centered self and God's eternal sustenance *theonomy,* a spiritual presence of holiness that affirms without negating the finite self. It is a state of fullness within a world of fragmentation.[6] From within us, God's presence establishes, bolsters, and strengthens the individual self by providing a transcendental foundation for it.

Our very personhood is determined by God through our faith, not by what we do.[7] Faith structures the soul. Faith actually constitutes the personhood of an individual. As the justified person, we are the person meant by God. Not only the Christian but also the human being as such can virtually be defined through justification-by-faith.[8]

I follow Pannenberg here, who incorporates the eschatological self into the present anticipatory self. "The 'inmost self' is not to be equated with the ego of the so-called 'natural man.' Rather, it is the human person as seen in the light of that person's destiny

---

6. Tillich, *SysT,* 1:54.

7. Schwobel follows Luther, "der Glaube macht die Person: *fides facit personam.*" Christoph Schwobel, *Gott im Gespräch* (Tübingen: Mohr Siebeck, 2011), 84.

8. "Faith constitutes the personhood of an individual (*fides facit personam*) . . . who as the justified person is the person meant by God; it is not only the Christian but the human being as such that can virtually be defined through justification by faith." Eberhard Jüngel, "Faith: IV. Systematic Theology," in *Religion Past and Present,* ed. Hans Dieter Betz, Don S. Browning, Bernd Janowski, and Eberhard Jüngel, 14 vols. (Leiden, Neth.: Brill, 2007–14), 5:24.

to salvation in Christ."[9] Who we are in essence is not who we have established ourselves to be through autonomous action. Who we are is determined in essence by our relationship, especially our relationship to the future prepared for us by God and present proleptically now in faith. "It is the power of faith that it places us outside ourselves, because in the act of trust our existence is built on the one to whom we entrust ourselves, to whom we quite literally leave ourselves. However, because such is the power of faith, the act of faith cannot adequately be understood as an action of the old subject, since that is to be left behind in the act."[10] What will be eschatologically new for us retroactively determines who we are now and who we were in the past. The soul is defined now by what it will be.

One's essential soul is determined by our relationship to God, and this relationship is defined by God's grace and the gift of justification. "Thus both things are true: that I am righteous here with an incipient righteousness, and that in this hope I am strengthened against sin and look for the consummation of perfect righteousness in heaven"[11] says Luther. Forell offers an interpretation. "Luther teaches us that justification by faith without this eschatological dimension is subjectivistic and individualistic self-hypnosis. . . . Luther insists on an objective event at the end of history."[12] We anticipate that objective eschatological event subjectively today, and this anticipation has a soul-forming impact.

My own *Doktorvater* at the University of Chicago, David Tracy, draws upon our anticipation of God's future kingdom of justice for our appropriation of justice in the present; and this gives shape to

9. Wolfhart Pannenberg, *Christian Spirituality* (Louisville: Westminster, 1983) 98.
10. Ibid., 99.
11. Luther, *Disputation concerning Justification, LW,* 34:22.
12. George W. Forell, "Martin Luther: Theologian of the Church," *Word and World* 2 (1994): 45.

our soul and to our very humanity. "As those empowered to become human beings by the gospel promise," Tracy writes, we

> face squarely the conflictual actuality of the present and commit ourselves, in that prophetic and apocalyptic hope which is faith's reality today, to the reality of God's reign by committing ourselves to the struggle for justice now. . . . The route to authentic selfhood for the Christian . . . remains the route of radical discipleship of an *imatio Christi.* The demands for real mutuality expressed in the Christian ideal and reexpressed in the *caritas* tradition, the radical self-sacrificial love disclosed in the cross of the Crucified One are themselves expressions of the gospel agapic gift and command to the self to live a radical equal regard for every human being, for the neighbor, not only the friend.[13]

Who we are as human beings is proleptically determined by our relationship to God's future. Our pursuit of justice today draws upon the divine promise for justice tomorrow.

Is Wright Right?

This is how justification-by-faith today fits with God's promise for tomorrow. God's future kingdom will be replete with justice imbued by love. The city of God will be a just society, and the key that unlocks the gate to this just society is mercy or forgiving love. The person of faith lives today in the presence of that future justice.

According to St. Paul, justification belongs together with resurrection into God's just society. Romans 4:25: "[Jesus Christ] was handed over to death for our trespasses and was raised for our justification." Our justification today is dependent upon God's promised just society—the kingdom of God, the New Jerusalem, the new creation, heaven—which will consummate natural and human

---

13. David Tracy, *The Analogical Imagination: Christian Theology and the Culture of Pluralism* (New York: Crossroad, 1981), 434–35.

history.[14] Today's church anticipates the coming of the just society. Our church's particular identity and mission only becomes clear after the resurrection of Jesus and our vision of God's promised future.[15] Just how do we fit together God's promised eschatological justice with living today in faith and trust that God's promise will be fulfilled?

New Testament scholar N. T. Wright objects to Lutherans who seem to forget the eschatological component to justification-by-faith. While Wright insists that the concept of justification is central and decisive for Christian theology, he adds that it is not the entire gospel. The Reformers should be faulted for taking a shortcut that makes this the doctrine on which the church stands or falls. According to St. Paul, there is much more to the story of Jesus and much more to the Christian life. "By using the word 'justification' *as though it described the entire process from grace to glory* it has given conscientious Pauline interpreters many sleepless nights trying to work out how what he actually says about justification can be made to cover this whole range without collapsing into nonsense or heresy or both."[16]

If justification-by-faith is too brief, what else is needed? Wright's answer is eschatology. Our present justification in faith is a prolepsis or anticipation of our final justification and eternal life with Christ. Our present justification is grounded in yesterday's resurrected Christ, to be sure, but this is decisive only because Christ's Easter resurrection opens the door to tomorrow's resurrection into God's

14. Marcus Barth draws the connection with new life: "Justification is resurrection: after the juridical condemnation and execution of all sinners, resurrection is the calling of all [persons] to new life." Marcus Barth, *Justification*, trans. A. M. Woodruff III (Grand Rapids, MI: Eerdmans, 1971), 57.

15. Cheryl Peterson draws the connection with the life of the church: "The *church's particular identity and mission* only becomes clear after the resurrection and with the coming of the Holy Spirit." Cheryl M. Peterson, "Who is the Church?," *Dialog* 51:1 (March 2012): 29, italics in original.

16. N. T. Wright, *Justification: God's Plan and Paul's Vision* (Downer's Grove, IL: IVP Academic, 2009), 102 (italics in the original).

transformed world. "The resurrection of the Messiah is, for Paul, the beginning of the entire new creation," Wright reminds us.[17]

Will there be a future judgment? Yes, there will be. The comforting message of the gospel is that our justification today will match the judgment of tomorrow. Wright returns to the courtroom metaphor, according to which our justification in faith acquits us and ascribes to us a status of innocence. We are at one with Jesus Christ himself, says Wright, "both in the *present* with the verdict issued on the basis of faith and faith alone, and also in the *future,* on the day when God raises from the dead all those who are already indwelt by the Spirit. The present verdict gives the *assurance that* the future verdict will match it; the Spirit gives the *power through which* that future verdict, when given, will be seen to be in accordance with the life that the believer has then lived."[18] Further, "The believer is righteous *in spe sed non in re*, in that there is an eschatological tension between the imputed status of righteousness (which is a proleptic anticipation of the final renewal of the sinner on the last day) and the present sinful nature of that same sinner."[19]

Is Wright right? In my judgment, he is. The salvation associated with justification is comprehensive, creation wide, history encompassing, final, and ultimate. Our individual justification can be what it is only as it takes part in the new creation, only as it participates in the advent of the eschatological consummation. God's consummate future takes up and fulfills the entire past—from the Big Bang to Abraham's promise to the fulfillment of Abraham's promise—into a single historical story. Within this comprehensive story all individual things find their meaning. There is but one God,

17. Ibid., 106.
18. Ibid., 251, italics in original.
19. Alister McGrath, "Justification," in *The Oxford Encyclopedia of the Reformation*, ed. Hans J. Hillerbrand, 4 vols. (Oxford: Oxford University Press, 1996), 4:363.

one history, and one future. This eschatological future retroactively defines our relationship to it today. This is what we mean by creation, and by redemption.

Eschatology: Temporal or Spatial?

Not every theologian is sanguine about a futuristic eschatology that unites all disparate stories into a single cosmic narrative, a single meaningful story that incorporates all of God's creation. Vitor Westhelle, for example, gives us pause. Westhelle is concerned about the diversity and specificity of little stories, such as community biographies that get overlooked when historians of dominant cultures leave them out of their metanarratives. Will God's retrieval of the inclusive story of creation look like another hegemonic metanarrative, snuffing out what is near and dear to us individually, as well as communally?

The kind of eschatology I am working with here relies upon universal history culminating in a single eschatological event that unifies previous disparate histories. The strength of this vision is that it looks forward to an eschatological consummation that confirms our faith in the God of Jesus Christ as the God of all reality. The weakness in my position, according to Westhelle, is that its universal vision risks imposing a hegemonic metanarrative that marginalizes humble spaces not yet on the radar screen of traditional theologians.[20] Contrary to Westhelle, it seems to me that what is entailed in this eschatological vision is the divine retrieval of the small and the humble and the local along with a divine celebration of each

---

20. Vitor Westhelle, *Eschatology and Space: The Lost Dimension of Theology Past and Present* (New York: Palgrave Macmillan, 2012). See also *Churrasco: A Theological Feast in Honor of Vitor Westhelle,* ed. Mary Philip, John Arthur Nunes, and Charles M. Collier (Eugene, OR: Pickwick, 2013).

particularity within the scope of its universal meaning. This is an eschatology that brings to fruition the infinite value of the human soul, and it does so for souls-in-context or souls-in-relationship.

In place of a temporal eschatology, Westhelle offers a spatial eschatology. The merit of his position is that it honors what is local, geographically or territorially discreet, separate, humble, and in need of respect and dignity. Westhelle's motive is to destabilize the metanarrative of linear eschatology. By taking time away and substituting space, linear eschatologists (if there is such a term) are left empty-handed. Westhelle has replaced their time with his space. Due to a change in the recipe, Westhelle's eschatological dessert will produce multiple tastes for multiple taste buds. More important than the conceptual change is the moral shift by which our attention is drawn to the *Other* who had previously been marginalized. No longer is eschatology a metaphysical or conceptual matter; it is now a moral matter.

Beatitudinal Eschatology

With this moral dimension in mind, I would like to describe the Christian vision in terms of a *beatitudinal eschatology.* On the one hand, beatitudinal eschatology begins with universal history and a single conusmmate fulfillment for all of creation. On the other hand, it treasures the purity of heart among the humble in their specific time and place. Like the widow's mite, it treasures the small while glorifying the magnificent. This is still a metaphysical or ontological treatment of reality, but it is tied inextricably with the moral dimension of human living.

Beatitudinal eschatology begins by recognizing that God has promised an apocalyptic scale transformation of the present creation into the new creation. Further, it recognizes that this transformation is cosmic in scope, embracing all creation of all time and all places. The eschatological event is not local only; it is universal, total, whole, and complete. Still further, the time of the consummate eschaton is not located on the calendar. It is almost, but not quite fully, present. It is imminent without being consummate. The totality of transformation is as close to us right now as the next moment is. In fact, it is the next moment emitting power and grace and transformation into the present moment.

The future is more real than the present. The future of God is the ground of all being, the support for all that exists. To exist is to have a future. It is the power of God's future that provides the present moment with its dependent reality. Without the power of God's future at work in the present, we would simply slip into non-being, into non-existence. The ground of our being is not the past or the present but rather the power of God to grant the present moment a future. The empty vortex around which our life swirls provides an ephemeral and vulnerable location for the human soul. Only God's promise of a future can rescue the soul from its dissipation and oblivion.

Still more importantly, the future that God grants us moment by moment is redemptive and transformative. Each moment God releases us from past bondages and opens up a freedom for unprecedented newness. The promised eschatological kingdom of God, or new creation, is the ground of all being, and God's promised future releases into the present moment a transformative reality that is, in fact, reality. God's future is more real than our present.

Jesus tried to communicate this in his Beatitudes. While they are certainly familiar, take a moment to look at some of them again. Matthew 5:3-9 reads:

> Blessed (*makarios*) are the poor in spirit, for theirs is the kingdom of heaven.

Blessed are those who mourn, for they will be comforted.

Blessed are the meek, for they will inherit the earth.

Blessed are those who hunger and thirst for righteousness (*dikaiosune*), for they will be filled.

Blessed are the merciful, for they will receive mercy.

Blessed are the pure in heart, for they will see God.

Blessed are the peacemakers, for they will be called children of God.

Note the proleptic structure. In most cases, Jesus begins with a present moment and then ties it to the future. Or perhaps the logic is reversed: the future determines the significance of the present moment. The future will be imbued with mercy, therefore, those who are merciful today belong to the future. The future will be imbued with righteousness—the term *dikaiosune* can be translated "justice" or "justification" as well as "righteousness"—therefore, those who thirst for justice today will find their thirst quenched in the kingdom of God. In other words, the future God has promised is present today, perhaps in a fragmented yet anticipatory way, when we find ourselves poor in spirit, mournful, meek, pure in heart, hungering and thirsting after justice, merciful, and striving to make peace. The future God has planned for all of creation is present right now in the robust lives of those who live, unknowingly, beatitudinally.[21]

The proleptic structure includes a strong dose of the reversal. The eschatological banquet that Jesus employs in so many of his parables reinforces what the Beatitudes say. The parable of the wedding feast provides an illustrative example (Matt. 22:1-14; Luke 14:16-24). A householder (a king in Matthew's version) plans a banquet for his

---

21. "All to whom the Beatitudes apply (Matt. 5:3ff; Luke 6:20ff.) will have a share in the coming salvation whether or not they ever heard of Jesus in this life." Pannenberg, *ST* 3:615.

son's wedding. Snobs are invited. but the snobs give excuses for not attending: one had just purchased new property that needed to be examined; another had just purchased five oxen that needed care; and a third had just gotten married and wanted to be attentive to his new wife. The wedding host rescinded the initial invitations and instead invited "the poor and maimed and blind and lame" along with those living along "the highways and hedges" (Luke 14:21, 23). The last replaced the first in the parable, portending a parallel reversal at the advent of God's eschatological kingdom. To put this beatitudinally—one's life on the margins today may be exchanged for life in the center of God's domain tomorrow.

This kind of proleptic structure, which reverses what is visible and what is invisible, elicits an initial tension in us. A beatitude frequently seems like an oxymoron. It sounds illogical and paradoxical at best. Just as we need to pause a moment to interpret Jesus' parables, we need to pause to reflect on the hidden meanings rising up from each beatitude. "Oxymorons hold immense tension," writes David Reid, "and their resolution releases miracle making power . . . for our salvation!"[22]

In this way, a beatitudinal epistemology hints at a theology of the cross, a *theologia crucis.* Those of whom Jesus speaks seem to press on with their beatitudinal living within an unacknowledged paradox: today's thirst for justice and heartache in the face of injustice is a thirst that is quenched by the imminent kingdom of God. What we experience every day is the heartache at the absence of justice, but this heartache marks the very presence of God's eschatological justice—whether or not the thirsty one is aware of it. In part, the pronouncement of a beatitude makes visible what has been invisibly

---

22. David P. Reed, SSCC, "A Strategy of Endurance: The Book of Revelation as Commentary on the Beatitudes, Blessed Are the Mourning and the Suffering," in *New Perspectives on the Beatitudes,* ed. Francis A. Eigo, OSA (Villanova, PA: Villanova University Press, 1995), 94.

the case all along. Jesus' word illuminates what we previously thought was visible, interpreting it with an ironic depth—a proleptic yet paradoxical mystery.

Living in Beatitude

The Beatitudes "send shudders up the spine, fill the heart with a sense of dread, mark the line between the sacred and the profane," warns my late Berkeley colleague Robert H. Smith.[23] "Jesus' Beatitudes are bolts of lightning splitting the skies. They crack open the heavens, astonish eye and ear, and carry with them the smell of burning ozone. They are ecstatic, inspired declarations trumpeted from the mouth of the revealer, and they are brimming with infinite grace."[24] Liberation theologian Gustavo Gutiérrez exhibits a similar exuberance: "The beatitudes of Matthew [are] the Magna Carta of the congregation . . . made up of the disciples of Jesus."[25] The Beatitudes adorn the life of the robust soul.

Before we turn to the individual beatitudes, let me remind you of a stunning exegetical fact. In the Gospel of Matthew, the word we translate *beatitude* is the same word Plato uses to name the Isle of the Blessed—the Isle of Justice—namely, *Makarios* (εἰς μακαρων νησους, the island of Makarios). No reader in the epoch within which

---

23. Robert H. Smith, *Matthew*, Augsburg Commentary on the New Testament (Minneapolis: Augsburg, 1989), 79–80.
24. Smith, *Matthew*, 80. "The concept 'blessed' (*makarios, beatus*) can be applied in a fragmentary way to those who are grasped by the divine Spirit. The word designates a state of mind in which Spiritual Presence produces a feeling of fulfillment which cannot be disturbed by negativities in other dimensions," writes Tillich. ST, 3:403. Tillich here trivializes blessing, I think, because he consigns it to a feeling thereby robbing it of its objective dimension. As we exegete some of Jesus' Beatitudes, we will see that one's state of blessing does not seem to rely upon our feeling of being blessed. Tillich goes on. "The Divine Life is the central conquest of the negative; this is its blessedness. . . . the Divine Life is blessedness through fight and victory." *SysT*, 3:405. That's more like it.
25. Gustavo Gutiérrez, *The God of Life* (Maryknoll, NY: Orbis Books, 1991), 118.

Matthew wrote would miss this connection. Anyone who could read Greek would know what Plato said in Greek. Matthew was calling Plato to the reader's mind so that the reader would ponder the connection between Plato and Jesus.

Let's ponder this ourselves. For Plato, entrance to Makarios is gained by dying with a just soul and being resurrected on the island of Makarios. According to Matthew, who is quoting Jesus, entrance to Makarios is a gift of God. God offers a declaration of justice, which is bequeathed to the human soul. In both cases, it is the just soul that rises into Makarios. The difference is that for Plato we create our own justness while for Jesus this justness is given to us as a gift of divine grace. This makes Jesus' aphorisms "be-attitudes," not "do-attitudes."[26]

Having offered this distinction, there remains something enigmatic about the Beatitudes. The structure and even the point of the Beatitudes is a bit puzzling. Jesus hints that the future Makarios is somehow present; it is not merely a future state that waits us beyond death. The future gift is given in the present, and we enjoy it in the present even if we are unaware of our enjoyment. This presence of the future expresses itself in our daily lives with certain characteristics, which Jesus describes in beatitudinal aphorisms.

Matthew 5:3: *Blessed are the poor in spirit, for theirs is the kingdom of heaven.* Those among us who are in poverty are unblessed, or at least

26. "I believe these blessings are literally be-attitudes or attitudes of being that disclose basic dispositions of Christian character formation." Susan Muto, "Blessed Are the Poor in Spirit and the Pure in Heart," in *New Perspectives on the Beatitudes,* ed. Francis A. Eigo, O.S.A. (Villanova PA: Villanova University Press, 1995) 130. Muto may be contradicting herself because she turns a be-attitude into a plan for character formation. Still, she is inspiring. "To live in freedom (and hence to live the beatitudes) means to assess the formative potentials in such seemingly negative experiences as suffering and death" (ibid., 131). Or, "In the Christian spiritual tradition, *kenosis* or self-emptying in imitation of Christ signifies that one is poor in spirit, humble, and open to the leading of God" (ibid., 129). It is too simplistic, in my judgment, to dub the Beatitudes as Jesus' teachings on ethics, as Harnack does. "The Beatitudes . . . contain his ethics and his religion, united at the root." Adolf Harnack, *What is Christianity?*, trans. Thomas Bailey Saunders (New York: Harper, 1957), 74.

seem unblessed. This beatitude seems obviously false, so why does Jesus say it? Can there be such a state as poor-yet-blessed?

Elsewhere I have enunciated a principle of proleptic ethics: "proffer the distinction between needs and wants."[27] To be human in any dignified form requires that certain basic needs be met: food, shelter, health, sleep, exercise, and protection from danger. Such needs are satiable. These basic needs take moral priority over our wants, over our desires to be unique or superior. Our wants are tragically insatiable. On a communal or even global scale, the *needs of all* take moral precedence over the *wants of some*. Among the sins of the rich is the self-imposed blindness that relabels wants as needs. After all, the central task of advertising is to make the buyer believe a want is a need. This is a lie, of course, but advertising cleverly cultivates our concupiscence; it fires the passions of "gotta have, gotta have, gotta have." In this way, we as consumers can always justify buying what we want by simply calling it a "need," which is also a lie. This combination of lies indirectly justifies economic structures that keep the poor in poverty while the affluent find themselves just barely able to make ends meet. The second use of God's law aims at exposing this lie, while the first use of the law aims at restorative justice on behalf of the needs of the poor among us.

If the justified sinner is to engage in loving living, the needs of the neighbor must come into his or her focus. When the need of the neighbor comes into focus, so does the language of this beatitude. Jesus is talking not about the fiscally poor but about the "poor in spirit." Does "poor in spirit" refer to someone who is discouraged? Perhaps. Or perhaps "poor in spirit" refers to one's own relationship to wants, possessions, wealth, and the economy. Perhaps "poor in spirit" indicates the soul's disposition of detachment in regard to

---

27. Ted Peters, *God—The World's Future: Systematic Theology for a Postmodern Era,* 2nd ed. (Minneapolis: Fortress Press, 2000), 389.

money. Perhaps the life of beatitude includes a level of satisfaction, contentment, serenity, and liberation from the greed that drives our ever-spiraling economic tornado.

Luther thought this way. "The Christian faith goes straight ahead. It looks at neither poverty nor riches, but only at the condition of the heart," comments Luther.[28] Five centuries ago this Reformer took a stand against the prosperity gospel, reminding us that a person who lives in financial poverty can very well enjoy a closer walk with God. In fact, Luther rightly worried that personal wealth could distract us from reliance upon God's grace and God's promise of everlasting life. He recommends that the spiritually poor-yet-blessed among us live with or without wealth in a detached manner. Even a wealthy person can be spiritually poor-yet-blessed if his or her heart is rightly ordered, rightly attuned to God's transcendent grace.

Daily checking the balance in one's retirement account or waiting breathlessly for the latest Dow Jones stock market report suggests an enslavement—to anxiety, concupiscence, covetousness, and perhaps even greed. To enjoy one's state of blessedness in light of God's promise is to enjoy liberation from this enslavement. "This is what it means: In our heart we should be able to leave house and home, wife and children. Even though we continue to live among them, eating with them and serving them out of love . . . a rich man may properly be called spiritually poor without discarding his possessions."[29] Oddly, Luther's allusion here is to a man who may remain detached. One wonders how his wife and dependent children might feel about this. Be that as it may, Luther is asking for a beatitudinal life that experiences freedom from the attachments that enslave, a freedom that enables the person of faith to give his or her possessions to help the poor and to do so with joy. Theologian and ethicist James

28. Luther, *Sermon on the Mount*, in *LW*, 21:14.
29. Ibid., 21:15.

Childs says that "for poverty of spirit, the struggle for justice is an anticipation of the promise in which we live as a people of hope. That is the key!"[30]

This reading of Jesus' beatitude seems to treat poverty of spirit as poverty in the literal sense of being penurious. Another more subtle or nuanced reading is possible: *poverty of spirit* refers to the broken soul, the soul for whom the moral universe seems to have evaporated. Theologians nickname this the "theodicy problem," but Jesus seems to be addressing the existential nihilism we personally feel rather than an abstract item on a theologian's agenda. Feeling poor in spirit is a feeling of angry helplessness. Poverty of spirit engulfs us when we are overwhelmed by injustice, atrocity, or meaningless suffering. When injustice crashes in upon us like a falling sky with nothing to hold it up, we raise our fists and rage against the crumbling heavens while, at the same time, doubting that there are any angels or divinities listening to our wailing.

Poverty of spirit comes frothing to expression in the Psalms.

O my God, I cry by day, but you do not answer;
and by night, but find no rest. (Ps. 22:2)

God doesn't answer. The supplicant is left with silence from heaven. A silent heaven produces anxious and angered emptiness in the soul. Not only is the soul denied protection from violence or the righting of injustice, it is also denied an explanation that makes sense. When heaven breaks, so does the soul.

Even Jesus could not escape his own moment with a breaking soul. Matthew 27:46: "And about three o'clock Jesus cried with a loud voice, 'Eli, Eli, lema sabachthani?' that is, 'My God, my God, why have you forsaken me?'"

---

30. James Childs, *Ethics in the Community of Promise: Faith, Formation, and Decision* (Minneapolis: Fortress Press, 2006), 57.

It is particularly important to observe that this painful human experience is reported in Scripture, even affirmed by Jesus in this beatitude.[31] Nobody asks for poverty of spirit. However, what we find in our poverty of spirit is the realization that we are not in charge, that the universe is not going to work according to our own direction. This new reality is difficult to discern because we had previously assumed that our own direction was actually the mechanism of justice behind the workings of the world. It now appears that the just universe is a fiction or a non-force. We cave in under the pressure of a nothing where we previously had trusted there to be a something. We grieve. We fret. We collapse.

But how can Jesus speak of poverty of spirit as a blessing? Curiously, our fretting and anger and demands are supported by an underlying trust in God. Despite the fact that we cannot see God's justice, we somehow presume it is still there and that God is responsible for seeing that justice gets administered. To feel desperate is painful, yet Jesus is trying to draw a connection between this pain and God's grace. I do not think Jesus is recommending that each of us seek poverty of spirit; rather, I believe Jesus is trying to offer comfort or consolation to those of us already poor in spirit, perhaps even to himself. The word of beatitude is offered as support to a broken soul.

Matthew 5:4: *Blessed are those who mourn, for they will be comforted.* If mourning is caused by grieving loss—such as grieving the death of a loved one—how could this possibly be considered a blessing? Grief hurts. Grief pierces the inner soul like a red hot iron hook; the mourner has nowhere to go relieve the suffering. Does Jesus actually

---

31. "Poverty of spirit is the foundation of any biblical discourse on God . . . The language of this God-mysticism is not first and foremost one of consoling answers for the suffering one is experiencing, but rather much more a language of passionate questions from the midst of suffering, questions turned toward God, full of highly charged expectation." Johann Baptist Metz, "Theology as Theodicy?," in *A Passion for God: The Mystical-Political Dimension of Christianity,* trans. J. M. Ashley (New York: Paulist), 66–67.

wish us to mourn? If mourning in the fragile soul is characterized by a generally depressed disposition that carries a gray cloud of discouragement into every group conversation, then most of us would rather do without this blessing. What might Jesus have in mind here?

Dietrich Bonhoeffer, like classical theologians before him, viewed conflict in the Christian life as a battle between the spirit and the world. The world tempts us away from God, even though we can find God only in, with, and under the physical and historical world in which we live. Still, Bonhoeffer reflects this struggle against the world as he wrestles with this beatitude's meaning. "By 'mourning' Jesus, of course, means doing without what the world calls peace and prosperity: He means refusing to be in tune with the world or to accommodate oneself to its standards."[32] Beatitudinal living includes a level of independence, a level of self-affirmation regardless of the world's image of us.

Childs draws out the implications of mourning by pointing out that mourning contributes to our compassion. "The heightened sense of one's own situation of sin, suffering, and utter dependence on God leads to compassion for others and a readiness, like that displayed by our Lord, to be with them in their trial."[33] Our own mourning sensitizes us to the mourning of our neighbor. This prompts us to offer comfort to those who, like ourselves, are mourning.

Luther thinks this beatitude has to do with our avoidance of life's aches and pains, our desire to slip through life immune to defeat, suffering, or sorrow. "The highest thing that [people] want [is] to have joy and happiness and to be without trouble. Now Christ turns the page and says exactly the opposite; he calls 'blessed' those who sorrow and mourn."[34] The Reformer speaks concretely.

---

32. Dietrich Bonhoeffer, *The Cost of Discipleship* (New York: Macmillan, 1959), 121.
33. Childs, *Ethics*, 63.

I said before that having riches is not sinful, nor is it forbidden. So also being joyful, eating and drinking well, is not sinful or damnable; nor is having honor and a good name. . . . A man is called 'spiritually poor,' not because he has no money or anything of his own, but because he does not covet it or set his comfort and trust upon it as though it were his kingdom of heaven. So also a man is said to 'mourn and be sorrowful'—not if his head is always drooping and his face is always sour and never smiling; but if he does not depend upon having a good time and living it up, the way the world does, which yearns for nothing but having sheer joy and fun here, revels in it, and neither thinks nor cares about the state of God or men.[35]

Perhaps our mourning over our own suffering is indirectly a blessing because we become blessings for others. The wounded healer lives beatitudinally. The wounded healer may not look outwardly like a robust soul; still, it's the divine truth expressing itself in, with, and under outward humility that exerts the power of transformation. Which brings us to the meek—that is, to the humble.

Matthew 5:5: *Blessed are the meek, for they will inherit the earth.* Frankly, a genuinely meek person would not want to inherit the earth. A meek person is in the habit of deferring. It's not difficult to imagine the meek saying, "Oh, don't give me the earth! Please give it to someone who really needs it."

The meek or humble among us are those who can live without retributive justice, without exacting revenge against those who have wronged us, without self-justification and scapegoating. For the meek, mercy trumps justice. "For Jesus justice's *lex talionis* [law of retributive justice] represents the entropy of an old moral dispensation; for his disciples at least, the old is superseded by a new dispensation of meekness and mercy, by a new vision of a righteous, benevolent community," writes James Gilman.[36] For the

---

34. Luther, *Sermon on the Mount*, in *LW*, 21:17.
35. Ibid., 21:18–19.

meek, mercy and peace trump self-justification and war and, hopefully, let loose in society a redemptive influence.

This is not a beatitude for leaders. Our leaders need to stand up before crowds and cameras, to speak before spoken to, to project visions of a better future and inspire confidence that we can incarnate those visions. Where the meek person would defer, the leader grabs the reigns and orders the horses to giddyup. Does this mean that our leaders are consigned to an unblessed life?

Wait a minute. Maybe this is, in fact, a beatitude for leaders. One characteristic of meekness, like humility, is that the cause the leader supports takes first place and his or her ego takes second place. If a leader exhibits a passion for justice and peace, then justice and peace take precedence over the leader's own position of influence or power. A meek leader does not need to stoop to self-justification or scapegoating. A meek leader becomes a servant to the good he or she is promoting.

This matter of a meek or humble person in leadership has arisen in one of the world's most successful companies, Google. Among the various technical abilities Google looks for when making a new hire, meekness or humility is high on the list of desirable qualities. New employees are not hired as leaders, but they are expected to become leaders when the situation calls for it. Google calls this "emergent leadership." Laszlo Bock, the senior vice-president of people operations, says, "What we care about is, when faced with a problem and you're a member of a team, do you, at the appropriate time, step in and lead? And just as critically, do you step back and stop leading, do you let someone else?" In Bock's mind, this quality is a combination of humility and ownership. "It's feeling the sense of responsibility, the sense of ownership, to step in to try to solve any

---

36. James E. Gilman, *Christian Faith, Justice and a Politics of Mercy: The Benevolent Community* (Lanham, MD: Lexington Books, 2014), 139.

problem—and the humility to step back and embrace the better ideas of others."[37]

Luther fails to see this subtlety, I think. As a result, he distinguishes between our professional and private lives. Leaders cannot afford to be meek, argues Luther. Therefore, this beatitude must apply only to our private or personal lives. In our unofficial or personal relations, "let everyone learn for himself to be meek toward everyone else, that is, not to deal with his neighbor unreasonably, hatefully, or vengefully."[38] I'm not exactly happy with Luther's interpretation here. Sure, it's good advice to deal with our neighbor reasonably and mercifully. But can't mercy apply to what we do in public life as well?

Given my earlier discussions of the self-justification and scapegoating that heads of state routinely practice, we can see how national pride, patriotism, nationalism, chauvinism, and jingoism lead to war and wreak havoc on the peoples of Earth. Self-justification and scapegoating are motivated by the opposite of meekness—namely, pride. One clear virtue of meekness is that it provides an alternative to war. But as Luther notes, perhaps it is difficult for a public leader to lead with meekness, even if meekness can be freely expressed at home or with friends. However, if we sequester meekness to the home, nothing will stand in the way of one war after another.

Matthew 5:6: *Blessed are those who hunger and thirst for righteousness, for they will be filled.* I call this the "justice beatitude."

Luke's version of this beatitude is confusing: *"Blessed are you who are hungry now, for you will be filled"* (Luke 6:21). For Luke, Jesus is addressing brute hunger—a food voucher for McDonalds would suffice to fill this hunger. For Matthew, hunger and thirst represent a

---

37. Cited by Thomas L. Friedman, "How to Get a Job at Google," *The New York Times*, February 22, 2014, http://www.nytimes.com/2014/02/23/opinion/sunday/friedman-how-to-get-a-job-at-google.html?partner=rssnyt&emc=rss.
38. Luther, *Sermon on the Mount*, in *LW*, 21:23.

passion for something other than food. In this case, it is an insatiable passion for justice or righteousness (*dikaiosune*). The hunger cannot be satisfied nor the thirst quenched until justice rolls down like waters and righteousness like an ever-flowing stream.

Luke's version draws attention toward the hungering, toward the passion that drives us. Alongside the other beatitudes, the justice beatitude indicates an essential element in the Christian vision of salvation, namely, the element of fulfillment. God's promises are more than promises of mere change. God promises that the healthy hungers and thirsts and needs and desires and expectations arising out of the human soul provide contact points between the present and the future. The seeds we plant will see a harvest. The race we run will lead to victory. God dreams our dreams and promises their fulfillment.

Whereas Luke's version of this beatitude focuses on the passion of hungering, Matthew's version focuses on the object of the passion—on justice or justification (*dikaiosune*). "Those who hunger and thirst for justice await it from God, but their waiting is not passivity," writes Gustavo Gutiérrez. "It implies a determination to bring about what they desire."[39]

When interpreting Matt. 5:6, Luther does not appeal to the concept of justice, except indirectly in our strivings for improving the "general welfare and the proper behavior of everyone."[40] Yet he encourages passion and dedication in the form of "a hunger and thirst for righteousness that can never be curbed or stopped or sated."[41]

As I discussed in earlier chapters of this book, our hunger and thirst for justice seems to be satisfied with the placebo of self-justification. Stopping short of universal or lasting justice, we pig out on pseudo

---

39. Gutiérrez, *God of Life*, 124.
40. Luther, *Sermon on the Mount*, in *LW*, 21:26.
41. Ibid., 21:27.

justice, gorging ourselves with self-ascribed justice and righteousness. We gourmandize by drawing delicate lines between good and evil and bellying up to what we have placed on the good side of the line. This is the lie we tell ourselves, and it deadens our appetite for the real thing: global justice and global peace. In short, every one of us hungers and thirsts for justice, but most of us short circuit the hard work of achieving global justice by living in self-justification and delusion.

It seems to me that Jesus is blessing something more than mere passion for justice or righteousness. It seems to me that he must have in mind those among us who temporarily forsake their own self-justification and dedicate themselves to real justice for the poor, the weak, the marginalized, the victims of discrimination, and the outcast. As Bonhoeffer puts it: "Not only do the followers of Jesus renounce their rights, they *renounce their own righteousness* too. They get no praise for their achievements or sacrifices. . . . They look forward to the future righteousness of God but they cannot establish it for themselves."[42] Genuine justice makes our own paltry self-justifications look like pebbles at the foot of Mount Kilimanjaro.

The passion for justice—genuine global justice—zigzags like a tornado through civilization; it razes repressive edifices, overturns class hierarchies, and dismantles scapegoating structures. At first, the passion for justice appears destructive as it disassembles socially constructed monstrosities that gobble up society's defenseless victims. The second use of God's law rips and tears and shreds the obstinate walls hiding repressive policies. However, the deconstruction is followed by construction, by an appeal to the first use of God's law on behalf of restorative justice. Signs of restorative justice may not quench the thirsty soul, but they certainly taste good.

---

42. Bonhoeffer, *Cost of Discipleship*, 123–24 (italics in the original).

Matthew 5:7: *Blessed are the merciful, for they will receive mercy.* Now this beatitude makes sense. It reiterates what we find in the Lord's Prayer, "forgive us our sins as we forgive others." Childs places mercy into the service of justice. "Mercy born of compassion not only signifies a readiness to forgive, but it is also the biblical way of responding to the needs of people. That is what it means to seek justice."[43] I call this the "mercy beatitude"; we need mercy if we are ever to have justice.

More than acts of mercy, I think that Jesus means a merciful heart. Luther suggests this when he excoriates the fragile soul safely protected by self-justifying duct tape. "His self-made holiness makes him so proud that he despises everyone else and cannot have a kind and merciful heart."[44] The self-justified Pharisee is unable to love the publican, or anybody else for that matter, with mercy.

Bonhoeffer follows Luther by describing those who actually live beatitudinally. "They have an irresistible love for the down-trodden, the sick, the wretched, the wronged, the outcast and all who are tortured with anxiety."[45] It is the merciful heart—the pure heart—that Jesus describes.

Matthew 5:8: *Blessed are the pure in heart, for they will see God.* A merciful heart is a pure heart. Robert Smith comments: "Jesus exalts purity of heart, which is a will and a mind neither divided nor confused in its affection, devotion, commitment."[46] I dub this the "purity beatitude."

What is purity? According to most of the world's religious traditions, purity is an achievement of the ladder-climbing soul. Purity is the product of denying the fleshly body, of overcoming

---

43. Childs, *Ethics*, 77.
44. Luther, *Sermon on the Mount*, in *LW*, 21:30.
45. Bonhoeffer, *Cost of Discipleship*, 124.
46. Smith, *Matthew*, 85.

the temptation to indulge in physical pleasures. The Hindu monk Śaṅkarāchārya, for example, contends that if a person "has any regard for this corpse-like body," then he "is impure, and suffers from his enemies as well as from birth, disease, and death; but when he thinks of himself as pure, as the essence of the Good, and the Immovable, he becomes free."[47] For this particular Hindu, purity consists of living a strictly disembodied or spiritual existence. Could this be what Jesus means by purity? I don't think so.

I get the sense that purity in this beatitude is not the product of a heroic spiritual achievement. Rather, it appears to be a naive yet authentic investment in single-mindedness. A pure heart is not divided or confused in its affection, devotion, or commitment. But can you or I make the kind of decisions that lead to a pure heart? Can the person of faith elect to live the life of purity? Kierkegaard, among others, answers yes.

This may be my favorite of the Beatitudes. As a young person, I was deeply moved by Søren Kierkegaard's book, *Purity of Heart.* The Great Dane's thesis is simple: the pure heart wills one thing. Not two things; one thing. Single-mindedness, not double-mindedness—that's the essence of a pure heart. The human willing of one thing corresponds to the transcendent oneness of the Good. "*In truth to will one thing, then, can only mean to will the Good,* because every other object is not a unity."[48] There is but one eternal Good—God—and by willing one thing only the pure heart orients itself toward God. "Commitment to the Good is a whole-souled decision," a decision that forms the self for eternal life.[49] While I

---

47. Cited by Joseph Campbell, *The Hero with a Thousand Faces,* 3rd ed., Bollinger Series (Novato, CA: Joseph Campbell Foundation, 2008), 102–3. According to James, "the saintly life must deepen its spiritual consistency and keep unspotted from the world." *The Varieties of Religious Experience,* Gifford Lectures Series 1901–2 (London: Longmans, Green, 1928), 274.

48. Søren Kierkegaard, *Purity of Heart,* tr. Douglas V. Steere (New York: Harper, 1938), 66, italics in original.

49. Ibid., 176.

have found power in Kierkegaard's admonition to will one thing, the Copenhagen eccentric might be out of step with other interpreters of Jesus.

Rather than think that a pure heart is the product of a decision, many among us would rather think of the pure heart as naive, trusting, and unaware of alternatives. To be pure is to be untarnished by temptation. When the conscience enters a person's awareness and tortures him or her with indecision, that person is torn between two things, two options, two manifestations of the ephemeral. According to Bonhoeffer, a person with a pure heart does not need a conscience. "The pure in heart have a child-like simplicity, like Adam before the fall, innocent alike of good and evil. Their hearts are not ruled by their conscience, but by the will of Jesus."[50] It appears here that the pure heart is innocent, unaware of temptation or the need to decide to will only one thing.

Luther uses the idea of the pure heart as an opportunity to admonish us to listen to the Word of God. "What is meant by a pure heart is this: one that is watching and pondering what God says and replacing its own ideas with the Word of God."[51] He then affirms and celebrates the meek and humble within society. "If a poor housemaid does her duty and is a Christian in addition, then before God in heaven she is a lovely and pure beauty, one that all the angels admire and love to look at."[52]

A person with a pure heart is inherently beautiful. We cannot help but admire such a person. It appears that God does as well, at least according to Matthew's Jesus.

Matthew 5:9: Blessed are the peacemakers, for they will be called children of God. I dub this the "peace beatitude."[53]

---

50. Bonhoeffer, *Cost of Discipleship*, 125.
51. Luther, *Sermon on the Mount*, in *LW*, 21:34.
52. Ibid.

If our world needs anything right now, it is an army of peacemakers. In the name of justice, current world leaders constantly rattle their sabers and cock their rifles. A brief look at human history and even prehistory shows that war has characterized the human race as far back in time as *Homo sapiens* can be traced. No other species on our planet wraps itself in wars and rumors of wars as does ours.

The peacemaker is an individual with a vision of a new and better order of existence. It is a godly vision. It is a wholesome vision. It is a vision lifted up by God's children, such as famed New York preacher Harry Emerson Fosdick.

> Cure your children's warring madness
> bend our pride to your control;
> shame our wanton, selfish gladness,
> rich in things and poor in soul.
> Grant us wisdom, grant us courage
> lest we miss your kingdom's goal,
> lest we miss your kingdom's goal.[54]

"The Lord honors those who do their best to try to make peace, not only in their own lives but also among other people, who try to settle ugly and involved issues, who endure squabbling and try to avoid and prevent war in the world."[55] These are Luther's words. "This also means that if you are the victim of injustice and violence, you have no right to take the advice of your own foolish head and immediately start getting even and hitting back; but you are to think it over, try to bear it and have peace."[56] Luther is saying no to vengeance and to retributive justice. Bonhoeffer adds that peacemakers "renounce all

---

53. "Real peacemaking takes courage," writes Roger Shinn. "Peace is a call to heroic activity." Roger L. Shinn, *The Sermon on the Mount* (Philadelphia: United Church Press, 1962), 19.

54. Harry Emerson Fosdick, "God of Grace and God of Glory," http://www.cyberhymnal.org/ htm/g/o/godgrace.htm .

55. Luther, *Sermon on the Mount*, in *LW*, 21:39.

56. Ibid., 21:40.

violence and tumult. In the cause of Christ, nothing is to be gained by such methods."[57]

The peace beatitude and the justice beatitude make a special pair. Peace without justice is tyranny; justice without peace is transient. "The spirit of peacemaking is in league with zeal for justice," contends Childs. When a national government deploys troops and commences battle, young men and women of the underclasses wear the uniforms and pull the triggers. "It is the poor who suffer. They are the ones who do most of the fighting in war."[58] A large nation with a large military finds it easy to turn a select class of its own citizens into invisible scapegoats. Peacemakers rescue scapegoats, among other valuable contributions they make.

Matthew 5:10: *Blessed are those who are persecuted for righteousness' sake, for theirs is the kingdom of heaven.* This beatitude, along with the next one, raise the fearsome specter of suffering at the hands of persecutors. In Matt. 5:10, persecution results from standing up for what is right, while in Matt. 5:11-12, it results from standing up for Jesus. In both cases, God offers blessing.

Blessing comes in the form of eternal life, of resurrection into God's promised new creation. When we are confronted with the prospect of persecution, we must decide whether to live as a coward or die as a hero. Luther challenges us: "You may take your choice. You have two ways before you—either to heaven and eternal life or to hell, either with Christ or with the world. But this you must know: if you live in order to have a good time here without persecution, then you will not get to heaven with Christ, and vice versa. . . . Briefly, anyone who wants to have Christ must put in jeopardy his body, life, goods, reputation, and popularity in the world. He

---

57. Bonhoeffer, *Cost of Discipleship,* 126.
58. Childs, *Ethics,* 82.

dare not let himself be scared off by contempt, ingratitude, or persecution."[59]

Choice may be inescapable. The blessed person makes a courageous choice and then willingly suffers the consequences.

Matthew 5:11-12: *Blessed are you when people revile you and persecute you and utter all kinds of evil against you falsely on my account. Rejoice and be glad, for your reward is great in heaven, for in the same way they persecuted the prophets who were before you.* In this beatitude, persecution is brought on by our witness to Jesus Christ. Even if we must face martyrdom, Jesus assures us that beyond the curtain of death we will find eternal life. Beyond the darkness of the grave, the light of eternity dawns. Confidence in eternal life fills us with courage, invincible courage.

The book of Revelation includes a number of beatitudes. A couple of them reiterate the one in Matt. 5:11-12: "Blessed (*makarios*) are the dead who from now on die in the Lord" (Rev. 14:13); and "Blessed (*makarios*) and holy are those who share in the first resurrection. Over these the second death has no power" (Rev. 20:6). With eternity as one's foundation, the ephemeral winds of this life will not threaten the beatitudinal heart.

"Who cares if a crazy prince or foolish emperor fumes in his rage and threatens me with sword, fire, or the gallows! Just as long as my Christ is talking dearly to my heart, comforting me with the promises that I am blessed, that I am right with God in heaven, and that all the heavenly host and creation call me blessed. Just let my heart and mind be ready to suffer for the sake of His Word and work."[60] That's Luther.

---

59. Luther, *Sermon on the Mount*, in *LW*, 21:45.
60. Ibid., 21:47.

Conclusion: The Attitude of Beatitude

The robust soul lives with the attitude of Beatitude, whether or not he or she is intentional about it. Again we ask: what kind of aphorisms are the Beatitudes? Their form is baffling. Each beatitude describes a present situation, and then it announces a blessing. In most cases, the blessing is a future blessing tied to the present circumstance. What is going on here?

Might the Beatitudes be substitutes for the Ten Commandments that were given to Moses? In Matthew's account, Jesus ascends a mountain just as Moses ascended Mount Sinai. Moses brought down the divine law, and Jesus presents God's new law, or at least a reiteration of Moses' ancient law. Symbolically, Jesus is the new Moses. Perhaps the Beatitudes are reiterations or extensions of the Law of Sinai.

The law God delivered to Moses on Sinai comes in the form of apodictic commands. In Exod. 20:3-17, for example, we find:

> You shall have no other gods before me . . . You shall not make wrongful use of the name of the Lord your God, for the Lord will not acquit anyone who misuses his name. Remember the Sabbath day, and keep it holy . . . Honor your father and your mother. . . . You shall not murder. You shall not commit adultery. You shall not steal. You shall not bear false witness against your neighbor. You shall not covet your neighbor's house; you shall not covet your neighbor's wife, or male or female slave, or ox, or donkey, or anything that belongs to your neighbor.

These commandments are rules for godly living.

But the Beatitudes do not look at all like commandments. One cannot ask a person to experience grief and mourn. It just happens. Nor can one ask a person to be persecuted. It just happens. As a result of happenstance, a person mourns or is persecuted. One cannot elect to mourn or be persecuted.

Simply put, the Beatitudes are not commandments. If you want some commandments, Jesus offers a good one in Matt. 5:43-44: "You have heard that it was said, 'You shall love your neighbor and hate your enemy.' But I say to you, Love your enemies and pray for those who persecute you." Jesus knows how to issue a commandment; but the Beatitudes do not look like commandments.

If the Beatitudes are not commandments, what are they? Might they be values we hold up to guide the moral life? This cannot be right either. We cannot honestly say that we value the victimization that comes from mourning or persecution. While we certainly place a high value on passion for justice and peacemaking, these are active ideals in contrast to the other beatitudes, which are passive states. Jesus must have something more in mind than lifting up moral ideals.

Perhaps the Beatitudes are character traits, virtues to be cultivated by the robust soul. Perhaps meekness and purity of heart and peacemaking are virtuous qualities that the climbing soul can pursue, master, and display. Perhaps these virtues might be the result of long years of self-discipline, like practicing to play the piano. Perhaps we should put the Beatitudes on our to-do list and tape this list to our bathroom mirror. Each morning we could read the list and commit ourselves to a full day of beatitudinal imitation.

Yet it seems to me that this interpretation doesn't fit Jesus' tone either. Jesus seems to be *describing* not *prescribing*. In a quite matter-of-fact way, Jesus is describing those persons who knowingly or even unknowingly are already participating in Makarios. Even though we might wish to put the task of purifying our hearts on our daily to-do list, Jesus seems to be lifting his eyes in the direction of those who, without strategizing, already live with pure hearts. Jesus seems to be encouraging those among us who already exhibit a passion for justice to proceed to express this passion, to actively pursue this passion because it belongs inherently to the kingdom of God. In the justice beatitude, Jesus is not asking us to adopt a passion for justice. Rather, the kingdom of God is celebrating the fact that some of us already possess a passion for justice.

Perhaps Jesus' demeanor is a clue here. Jesus displays his own attitude of beatitude. Perhaps Jesus, like God, is displaying compassion toward those among us who mourn or who suffer from poverty of spirit or who naively live out of a pure heart. Perhaps Jesus, like God, is displaying divine gratitude for the human spirit that presses passionately for justice and peace. Perhaps Jesus is providing us with one more example of God's heart, a divine heart ready to bless. Perhaps Jesus' attitude of beatitude is one more way in which we can discern the central message of the gospel—namely, that God is gracious.

If so, then how do you and I live the life of beatitude? Don't ask. Just do it.

Conclusion: Sin Boldly!

Be a sinner and sin boldly, but believe and rejoice in Christ even more boldly, for he is victorious over sin, death, and the world.
　　　　　　　　　　　　　　　　　　　　–Martin Luther[1]

I opened this book with an imperative: Sin boldly! This curious imperative arises out of faith in our gracious God who justifies us.

I began by asking whether faith understood as trust in God can make one's daily life better. My answer is yes, indeed! How? By relieving our anxiety over self-justification. When we discover that we don't need to justify ourselves because we have been justified by God, we experience both contentment and vitality. The key is found in Rom. 8:33b: "God is the one who justifies" (*theos ho dikaiosune*). What justification-by-faith points to is the presence of the crucified and living Christ in the human soul, placed there by our gracious God; this presence becomes transformative. More specifically, both the past Christ and the future Christ meet in your soul and my soul. The living power of both the Easter resurrection and the new creation (the kingdom of God) explode within us with joy and zeal.

1. Luther, Letter to Philip Melanchthon, August 1, 1521, *LW* 48:281–82.

This treatment of the classic Reformation theme has been subtitled, *Justifying Faith*. I have pointed out how this phrase could mean two things. First, it could mean that we are obligated to provide good reasons for what we believe. We need to justify why we choose to embrace the Christian faith in a secular world that seems to get along quite well without it. The aggressive atheists among us dub faith as something foolish, a residual from an outdated religious era that should be replaced with reason, science, and secularism. The spiritual but not religious (SBNR) among us replace old-fashioned faith with post-religious intuition, experience, and meditative practice. Therefore, we should be asking: Can faith be justified in this situation? My answer is yes. There are good reasons for believing in a God of grace and for living a life of faith, especially faith understood as trust in the gracious God.

The second meaning of *justifying faith* has occupied much of this book. It means that in the eyes of God we sinners are just. God treats me just as if I'd never sinned in spite of the injustice I may or may not perpetrate. This news may shock us enough to ask: But shouldn't we be living justly? Yes, of course. It's God's will that our daily lives be imbued from dawn until dusk with love, compassion, care, and the pursuit of justice in an unjust world. However, sometimes we miss the mark. To put it more subtly, the drive toward justice emits poison from the exhaust pipe, and victims suffer. Justice kills, just as injustice kills. Despite our best intentions, justice is a serial killer. The point is that justifying faith maintains our relationship with God despite the injustice that unavoidably attaches to the pursuit of justice.

The interaction between justice and injustice is torturously complex. It is not what it seems to be on the surface. Part of the very nature of injustice is the lie. Perpetrators of injustice cover over their deeds with the rhetoric of justice. The surface does not represent what is under the surface. We lie because we want to appear just, whether or not we actually are just. This desire to appear just leads to self-justification and, when necessary, the scapegoating of others to maintain our self-image as the just ones. It scandalizes us to hear the news that we are justified by an act of divine grace instead of by the works we perform or by the lies we tell. We want to own the justice we ascribe to ourselves.

The cauldron of self-justification and scapegoating is dark, sinister, and dangerous. I intended for this discussion of justifying faith to shine a light into the darkness. What does the light of justifying faith uncover? What does it reveal? It reveals how we lie. We deceive others, and we deceive ourselves. This deception does not take the form of a series of stories we tell others that we secretly know to be untrue. The stories we tell are largely true, at least at the level of consciousness at which the stories are told. What I have been illustrating is a pattern of misdirected self-understanding that operates at the hinge of the pre-conscious and the conscious. This deception turns on the articulation of what we believe to be true in light of who we think we are—or who we think we ought to be.

I refer to this pattern of self-deceit as *self-justification.* This term refers to justification apart from faith in the God who graciously justifies us. The second use of the law shines a light into the gloom of our fragile soul, revealing what has been hidden beneath our daily pattern of self-justification. Under the light of justifying faith, our self-examination uncovers depths and dimensions invisible on the surface level. We human beings are labyrinthine in our complexity. If we allow the dialectic between law and gospel to untangle the intricate web of self-deceits, we will come to see ourselves afresh as gifted by a gracious God and empowered to pursue genuine justice rather than the chimera of self-justification.

By countering *self-justification* with the term *justifying faith,* I have described the liberating and fulfilling and flowering life of the robust soul that results from trusting the God of grace. If we can avoid the temptation to justify ourselves, a cleanliness in our thinking takes over. This cleaner thinking liberates the inner self, making an un-self-protective, open, and vulnerable disposition toward loving oneself and others possible. Suddenly, the world looks more loveable. The psychic labor it takes for us to love the unlovable neighbor is drastically reduced; in turn, compassion and self-giving become as automatic as a smile or a chuckle. We sin boldly in the sense that with a pure heart we pursue justice and peace, recognizing that we cannot control the negative exhaust we emit in the process.

Atonement and Justification

In this book, I have stressed the objective work of God in Christ that we call *atonement*. As I said in an earlier chapter, it is important to distinguish between Jesus as scapegoat and Jesus as sacrifice. Despite the appearance in the New Testament of sacrificial images to convey the meaning of his death on the cross, I wish to emphasize that, ontologically, no sacrificial mechanism exists whereby human offering compels God to respond with a proportionate blessing. Nor does a mechanism exist whereby a cruel Father God can subject his divine son to unjust punishment and thereby provide a substitute sacrifice. Whether the death of Jesus on the cross was planned or accidental, it was a tragedy for God. The tragic death of Jesus is not a cause with forgiveness as its effect. Rather, the death of Jesus reveals just how we, as members of the human race, lie to ourselves and rely upon scapegoating to prop up our lies.

The power of atonement resides in God's raising Jesus from the dead on the first Easter, as Paul makes clear: Jesus "was handed over to death for our trespasses and was raised for our justification" (Rom. 4:25).

By raising Jesus from the dead on the first Easter, God achieved two things: first, God established the ground for our justification by grace; second, God changed the laws of nature so that in the future the dead could rise. The Easter Christ opened the mechanisms of natural law so as to admit a new phenomenon, namely, resurrection of the dead. Easter is the prolepsis of the new creation. I find 1 Cor. 15:20 to be crucial: "Christ has been raised from the dead, the first fruits of those who have died." As the Easter Christ was the first fruits, our resurrection will become the harvest at the advent of the eschatological new creation. What happened on Easter inaugurated the new reality—the eschatological kingdom of God—in the person of Jesus. We now await the coming of this new reality to the remainder of creation; we who are now justified will share in that future resurrection. What we here call *justifying faith* is justified by God's atoning work in Christ.

Atonement is objective. Faith is subjective. Atonement affects the world. Faith resides in the human subject. Atonement changes the universe. Faith transforms the person into a robust soul.

In this book, I have stressed the real presence of Christ in the faith that justifies. The theology of Christ's real presence can be summarized—albeit cryptically—in light of the Socrates Principle: Jesus died as a just person at the hands of unjust authorities. He is in himself just, so he needs no Glaucon-like self-justification. When the Holy Spirit places the just Jesus within our faith, Jesus' justice becomes our justice. He has justified us, so to speak. If in our faith we are justified by Christ, we have no need to self-justify and, hence, no need to scapegoat others. Our justification is a divine gift, not the product of our self-deception.

The Real Presence of the Living Christ in Faith

In addition, I have stressed that the Christ present in our faith is both the crucified one and the resurrected one. He is also the coming one. The suffering of the crucified one is present to us, even in our suffering. The eternity of the resurrected one is present within us—an eternity that transcends even our most sublime vision of the moral universe.

My hope is that two kinds of persons will especially benefit from this treatment of justifying faith: those with fragile souls and those with broken souls. Each of us knows what it means to live with a fragile soul, although some suffer more than others. Our souls become fragile when we're unable to handle the anxiety that wells up from the empty center within the self. Although we think of the soul as the essential self, we protect the self's existence by conforming it to the moral universe. Our moral universe provides the world of meaning within which we live, and to keep it from breaking, we codify it and legalize it and rigidify it and absolutize it. Most devastatingly, we engage in self-justification. That is, we tell ourselves the lie that our souls and our moral universe are in harmony.

For the fragile soul, justification-by-faith comes as both bad news and good news. The bad news first: before God, our lies don't work. Only truth does. The good news is found in what we call the *gospel*, namely, the announcement that by grace God offers the free gifts of forgiveness and relationship and promise. Because God justifies us, we don't have to justify ourselves. Our salvation is like a Christmas present; we only need to open it up and make it our own—then enjoy playing with it.

For the broken soul, the situation is quite different. The soul breaks when the moral universe breaks. Because the centered self is so dependent upon the moral universe that forms its identity, the shattering of the latter leads to the loss of the former. The moral universe evaporates in times of guilt-laden trauma, or worse, in times of moral injury. Violence and death accompanied by atrocity and betrayal can so overrun one's moral universe that it caves in like a trampled garden. Like a newly planted spring garden which gets uprooted and devoured by marauding wild boars, the soul gets uprooted and devoured by despair, by what Luther called *Anfechtung*. On its own, the soul cannot rescue itself; it cannot replant itself and blossom and blossom on its own. Nor will any amount of forensic justification dig the broken soul out of its hole. The despairing soul needs the grace of the gardener.

Only relational presence can heal the broken soul. The accepting presence of another allows the broken soul to mend, to re-form, to heal. The accepting presence must be gracious, understanding, loving, and transcendent to the now shattered moral universe. It must be the presence of ultimate reality. In this case, justification-by-faith suggests that the presence of the suffering and risen Christ in faith provides a spiritual accompaniment that coaxes a new robustness of soul to assert itself.

Beyond justification-by-faith lies the life of beatitude. God's promised future—symbolized by new creation (or the kingdom of God)—becomes present in faith, and faith expresses itself in beatitudinal living. Matthew 5:6: "Blessed are those who hunger and thirst for justice," says Jesus, "for they will be filled." To say it another way, God's future justice is already present in our thirst for it now.

For Further Reading

Barth, Marcus. *Justification*. Translated by A. M. Woodruff III. Grand Rapids, MI: Eerdmans, 1971.

Bayer, Oswald. *Living by Faith: Justification and Sanctification*. Translated by Geoffrey W. Bromily. Grand Rapids, MI: Eerdmans, 2003.

Bolz-Weber, Nadia. *Pastrix*. New York: Jericho Books, 2013.

Bonhoeffer, Dietrich. *Ethics*. Edited by Eberhard Bethge. Translated by Neville Horton Smith. The Fontana Library. London: Collins, 1949.

Braaten, Carl E., and Robert W. Jenson, eds. *Union with Christ: The New Finnish Interpretation of Luther*. Grand Rapids, MI: Eerdmans, 1998.

Brock, Rita Nakashima, and Gabriella Lettini. *Soul Repair: Recovering from Moral Injury after War*. Boston: Beacon, 2012.

Brondos, David A. *Redeeming the Gospel: The Christian Faith Reconsidered*. Minneapolis: Fortress Press, 2010.

Brondos, David A. "Criminal Justice: A View from South of the Border." *Dialog* 52, no. 4 (December 2013): 287–90.

Carder, Kenneth L. *Living Our Beliefs*. Rev. ed. Nashville: Discipleship Resources, 2009.

Chung, Paul S. *Postcolonial Imagination: Archaeological Hermeneutics and Comparative Religious Theology*. Hong Kong: Chinese University Press, 2015.

Dahill, Lisa E. *Reading from the Underside of Selfhood: Bonhoeffer and Spiritual Formation*. Eugene, OR: Pickwick, 2009.

Dalferth, Ingolf U. "Post-secular Society: Christianity and the Dialectics of the Secular." *Journal of the American Academy of Religion* 78:2 (June 2010): 317–45.

Falsani, Cathleen. *Sin Boldly: A Field Guide for Grace.* Grand Rapids, MI: Zondervan, 2008.

Forde, Gerhard O. *Justification by Faith—A Matter of Death and Life.* Minneapolis: Fortress Press, 1982.

Gilman, James E. *Christian Faith, Justice and a Politics of Mercy: The Benevolent Community.* Lanham, MD: Lexington Books, 2014.

Girard, René. *I See Satan Fall Like Lightening.* Translated by James G. Williams. Maryknoll, NY: Orbis Books, 2001.

Girard, René. *The One by Whom Scandal Comes.* East Lansing: Michigan State University Press, 2014.

Gregersen, Niels Henrik, Bo Holm, Ted Peters, and Peter Widman, eds. *The Gift of Grace: The Future of Lutheran Theology.* Minneapolis: Fortress Press, 2005.

Grossman, Lt. Col. Dave. *On Killing.* New York: Little, Brown, 2009.

Hopkins, Dwight N. *Being Human: Race, Culture, and Religion.* Minneapolis: Fortress Press, 2005.Johnson, Jay Emerson. *Peculiar Faith: Queer Theology for Christian Witness.* New York: Seabury Books, 2014.

Kwon, Jin-Kwan. "Justice and Subject in Christianity and Buddhism: An Ontological Study." *International Journal of Contextual Theology in East Asia* 19 (June 2013): 43–62.

Largen, Kristin Johnston. *Finding God among Our Neighbors: An Interfaith Systematic Theology.* Minneapolis: Fortress Press, 2013.

Lebacqz, Karen. *Six Theories of Justice: Perspectives from Philosophical and Theological Ethics.* Minneapolis: Augsburg, 1986.

Lo, Pilgrim W.K. "Luther between Theology and Cultural Studies." In *Lutherjahrbuch: Organon der Internationalen Lutherforschung,* edited by Christopher Spehr, 220–26. Göttingen: Vandenhoeck & Ruprecht, 2013.Mannermaa, Tuomo. *Christ Present in Faith: Luther's View of Justification.* Minneapolis: Fortress Press, 2005.

Mannermaa, Tuomo. *Justification.* Minneapolis: Fortress Press, 2005.

Marty, Martin E. *Lutheran Questions, Lutheran Answers*. Minneapolis: Augsburg, 2007.

Moe-Lobeda, Cynthia D. *Resisting Structural Evil: Love as Ecological-Economic Vocation*. Minneapolis: Fortress Press, 2013.

Nessan, Craig L. "Law, Righteousness, Reason, Will, and Works: Civil and Theological Uses." *Currents in Theology and Mission* 41, no.1 (February 2014): 51–56.

Niebuhr, Reinhold. *The Nature and Destiny of Man: A Christian Interpretation*. 2 vols. New York: Charles Scribner's Sons, 1941.

Niebuhr, Reinhold. *The Self and the Dramas of History*. New York: Charles Scribner's Sons, 1955.

Ouellette, Jennifer. *Me, Myself, and Why? Searching for the Science of Self*. New York: Penguin, 2014.

Pannenberg, Wolfhart. *Anthropology in Theological Perspective*. Translated by Matthew J. O'Connell. Louisville: Westminster John Knox, 1985.

Peters, Ted. *GOD—The World's Future: Systematic Theology for a Postmodern Era*. 3rd ed. Minneapolis: Fortress Press, 2015.

Peters, Ted. *Sin: Radical Evil in Soul and Society*. Grand Rapids, MI: Eerdmans, 1994.

Peterson, Cheryl M. *Who Is the Church? An Ecclesiology for the Twenty-First Century*. Minneapolis: Fortress Press, 2013.

Preus, Robert D. *The Theology of Post-Reformation Lutheranism*. 2 Vols. St. Louis: Concordia, 1970–72.

Rawls, John. *A Theory of Justice*. Cambridge, MA: Belknap Press of Harvard University Press, 1971.

Saarinen, Risto. *God and the Gift: An Ecumenical Theology of Giving*. Collegeville, MN: Liturgical, 2005.

Sen, Amartya. *The Idea of Justice*. Cambridge, MA: Harvard University Press, 2009.

Sites, Kevin. *The Things They Cannot Say: Stories Soldiers Won't Tell You about What They've Seen, Done or Failed to Do in War*. New York: Harper, 2013.

Stjerna, Kirsi, and Brooks Schramm. *Spirituality: Toward a 21st Century Lutheran Understanding*. Minneapolis: Lutheran University Press, 2004.

Streufert, Mary J., ed. *Transformative Lutheran Theologies: Feminist, Womanist, and Mujerista Perspectives*. Minneapolis: Fortress Press, 2010.

Tick, Edward. *War and the Soul: Healing Our Nation's Veterans from Post-traumatic Stress Disorder*. Wheaton: Quest Books, 2005.

Tillich, Paul. *Love, Power, and Justice*. Oxford: Oxford University Press, 1960.

Tillich, Paul. *Systematic Theology*. 3 vols. Chicago: University of Chicago Press, 1951–63.

Tracy, David. *Plurality and Ambiguity: Hermeneutics, Religion, Hope*. New York: Harper, 1987.

Trelstad, Marit A., ed. *Cross Examinations: Readings on the Meaning of the Cross Today*. Minneapolis: Augsburg, 2006.

Westhelle, Vitor. *The Church Event*. Minneapolis: Fortress Press, 2010.

Wright, N.T. *Justification: God's Plan and Paul's Vision*. Downer's Grove, IL: IVP Academic, 2009.

Index of Names

Index of Subjects